*Carluccio's*

COMPLETE ITALIAN FOOD

# Carluccio's
# COMPLETE
# ITALIAN
# FOOD

ANTONIO AND
PRISCILLA CARLUCCIO

PHOTOGRAPHY BY ANDRÉ MARTIN
ILLUSTRATIONS BY FABRICE MOIREAU

RIZZOLI
NEW YORK

## Dedication

We dedicate this book to all our Italian suppliers who still struggle to produce delicious and genuine food against the tide of mass production. A. & P. C.

First published in the United States of America in 1997 by
RIZZOLI INTERNATIONAL PUBLICATIONS, INC.
300 Park Avenue South, New York NY 10010

First published in Great Britain in 1997 by
Quadrille Publishing Limited,
Alhambra House,
27-31 Charing Cross Road,
London WC2H OLS

ISBN 0-8478-2037-8
LC 97-67797

Publishing Director: Anne Furniss
Editor & Project Manager: Lewis Esson
Design: Paul Welti
Photographic Art Direction: Priscilla Carluccio
Recipe Editor: Jane Middleton
Indexer: Hilary Bird
Typesetting: Peter Howard
Production Candida Lane
US Editor: Katherine Adzima

Color separations by Colour Scans, Singapore
Printed and bound in Italy by Arnoldo Mondadori Spa, Verona

ENDPAPERS: PAN DI SAN GIUSEPPE (PAGE 294)
HALF-TITLE PAGE: A VEGETABLE STALL AT TURIN MARKET
TITLE PAGE: THE ALTESINO VINES, MONTALCINO, IN LATE AUTUMN
RIGHT: GRAPES DRYING FOR VIN SANTO IN MONTALCINO

# CONTENTS

# INTRODUCTION

The twenty regions of Italy provide a gastronomic feast which is unsurpassed. Although the geography of these regions is immensely diverse, the basic principles of Italian cooking are the same —culinary simplicity and the use of the finest, freshest ingredients available. Italy can in many respects be seen as the perfect market garden, with sweet milk and meat from the mountains of the Alps in the North to the freshest fish, sun-ripened fruit, and vegetables of the South.

Geography apart, each region of Italy is also culturally different and each bears the distinctive marks of its past settlers and invaders: Barbarians, Arabs, Carthaginians, Etruscans, Phoenicians, Turks, Normans, Bourbons, Spaniards, and Austrians. Each civilization tried to reproduce its own home cooking, as we all do today when living in other countries. Among the earliest of these culinary invaders were the Islamic Saracens, who invaded Sicily, bringing with them exotic sweet-meats like marzipan and nougat, and giving birth to that island's famous tradition in these specialties.

In the days of the ancient Romans, sophisticated dishes and many fine wines were produced to please the emperors and their courts, and eating became a fashionable pursuit at that time. From this period up until the Middle Ages, it was the monasteries that preserved the culinary arts, and the spices that had once accompanied returning travelers disappeared, only to reappear with the rise of the great maritime republics in the eleventh to thirteenth centuries. The *Quattro Repubbliche Marinare*—Venice, Genoa, Pisa, and Amalfi—became the culinary centers of Italy, with the introduction of elegant tableware and customs.

Obviously some of the most important Italian food we know today was introduced from outside Italy. Olive oil was brought to Puglia and Sicily by the Ancient Greeks; and, in the North, *polenta* or corn came by boat from the New World to Venice, swiftly becoming the staple diet of northerners. Also from the New World came the now ubiquitous tomato. The cultivation of rice began in the fifteenth century in Lombardy, where the Po Valley's abundant water made it ideal for the crop. Germanic and Nordic influences are also very strong in the heavier dishes of the Alto Adige.

Within Italy itself, migration from the South to the North has been considerable in this century,

are growers as well. They have helped us to understand more about the local ingredients, the methods of cultivation, and the care with which the product is "manufactured." With the trend towards laboratory- and factory-prepared food, the skills these people inherited from their families are in danger of disappearing. This book is an attempt to recall these good traditions of the past and marry them with the culinary needs of a different age, in which people do much less physical labor and therefore have different dietary requirements.

Above all, however, this book is a personal view of real Italian food, where it comes from, and why it tastes the way it does. The simplicity of the recipes relies on one thing – genuine and excellent products! *Buon appetito!*

**PREVIOUS PAGES AND THIS PAGE: VARIOUS VIEWS OF THE WONDERFUL KITCHEN OF A FRIEND IN NAPLES**

**OPPOSITE: MAP SHOWING THE REGIONS OF ITALY AS DESCRIBED IN THIS BOOK**

and the traditions of Puglia, Campania, and Calabria have introduced a new culinary experience to be shared. *Pasta al pomodoro* is now eaten in Milan and Turin instead of their more traditional rice or *polenta* dishes.

If at the turn of the century the largest part of Italy was poor, it was not in its food and wine; these were then—and are now—treated as precious commodities as well as basic parts of Italian culture. It is the very strong desire to consume good food and drink that has given the farmers, winemakers, and fishermen the courage to cultivate and bring to market the best. Italians are motivated and inspired by the culture of their food and wine and will go to amazing lengths to source the best ingredients to achieve a perfect dish. The resourcefulness born of this desire has generated the produce that is so admired worldwide today.

In this journey through Italy we have investigated and sought out the products of traditional methods of agriculture, livestock husbandry, and fishing. Italian food is about flavor, something that has sadly disappeared from much of our mass-produced food in recent years. It is about ripe fruit picked off the tree and eaten while still warm from the sun, fish straight from the water, meat raised and butchered with skill, wine made with the genuine local grapes and matured in wooden barrels, organic vegetables just dug from richly manured fields with the earth still clinging to their roots. This is not a romantic vision, it is how our food should be!

Producing this book has been a fascinating experience. Traveling together, as we do, my wife and I have the rare privilege of sharing with our producers their inherited knowledge of food growing and processing – as most of our producers

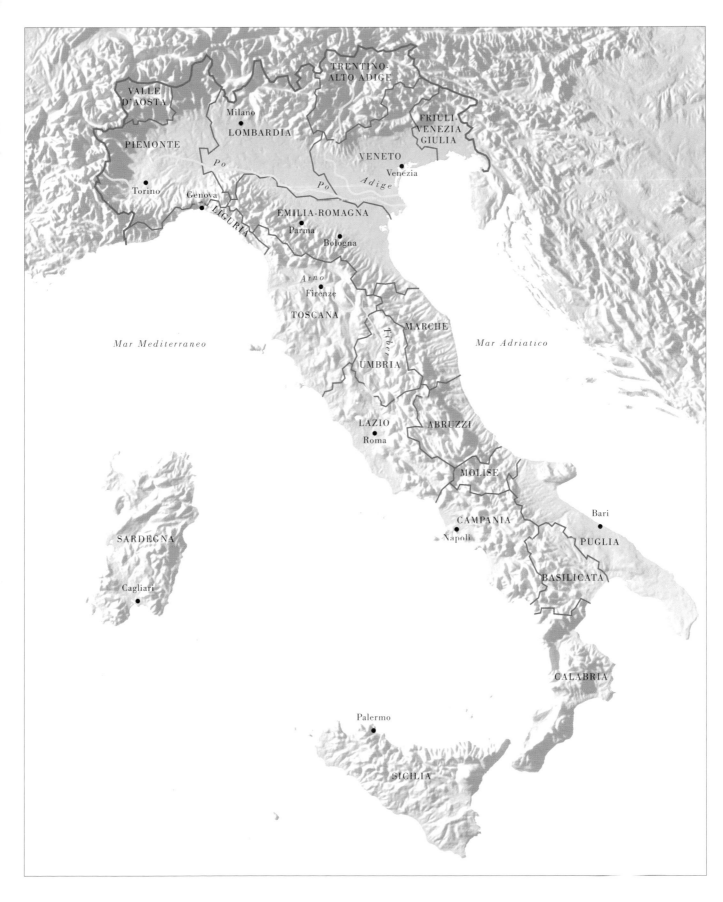

# FISH & SHELLFISH

## PESCI E FRUTTI DI MARE

Fish is becoming more and more popular worldwide and is replacing meat in many diets. Indeed one reason for its popularity is its greater health value compared to meat. In general, fish contain significantly less fat than meat, and the oil they do contain has been found to be beneficial in a normal diet.

With growing demand for fish however, there is greater pressure on the world's stock of fish, and this means that finding a supply of the best quality is becoming increasingly difficult. With the pollution of our seas and rivers, the fish stock is put under even greater pressure, so we are now in real danger of over-fishing to such an extent that we are likely to deny ourselves this splendid natural resource in the very near future. As fish wars break out between neighboring countries and everyone fishes to the limit of their allowance, fishing and eating the fruits of the sea has become a political issue. We will soon have to decide whether we can continue to gather and eat so vigorously, in the interest of having sufficient stock available to us in the future.

Italy is thankfully blessed with a particularly good supply of fish, and the coastal regions of Liguria, Tuscany, Lazio, Campania, Calabria, Basilicata, Apulia, Abruzzo e Molise, Marche, Emilia-Romagna, Veneto, Friuli-Venezia Giulia, Sicily, and Sardinia all have a part of the Mediterranean to themselves. This does not mean, however, that Piedmont, Lombardy, Trentino-Aldo Adige, and Umbria do not enjoy fish too, as they have their own supply of wonderful freshwater lakes providing a good number and variety of fish. Modern transportation methods also bring fresh sea fish to these regions within hours of being pulled from the sea.

Oddly enough, of all the regions, Sardinia has the shortest tradition of eating fish. The earlier inhabitants occupied more of the interior of the island, preferring to live on game rather than fish. However, the development of tourism in the past century has ensured that a variety of fish is available on the coast, and Sardinian fish has become highly prized.

Despite having a healthy supply of fresh and saltwater fish all over the country, Italian cuisine —like that of Spain and Portugal—also makes use of a great deal of *baccalà* and stockfish. Both are forms of preserved cod; *baccalà* is salted at sea and then dried in large

chunks when it is landed, and stockfish is whole, air-dried fish. One or the other is eaten in all the regions of Italy, partly for economic reasons and partly for religious ones. It used to be the fish of the poor, and was eaten on Fridays by fasting Catholics who did not have access to fresh fish. Now, though, it is valued for its distinctive flavor and versatility.

Other fish preserved in salt include anchovies and sardines, both of which have inspired many dishes. Preserved anchovies are particularly valued, and are used in a huge number of dishes—from the ancient Roman condiment *garum* to today's pizza. Fish are also pickled in vinegar, and this gives the flesh of freshwater fish like carp, *goregone*, eels, and trout, an almost Oriental sweet-and-sour tang.

Another traditional method of preserving fish is by smoke-curing it. In Italy, this method was used in the past only for meat such as ham, but in top restaurants it is now possible to order very thinly sliced smoked swordfish, tuna, and sturgeon, as well as air-dried and salted cod and mullet roe (known as *bottarga*), a very expensive specialty from Sardinia and Sicily. Salted and air-dried fillets of tuna, known as *mosciame*, are a delicacy that compares with the finest of foods. The smoked swordfish, tuna, and sturgeon are of a high enough quality to be exported to connoisseurs of fish in the Nordic countries, and consumed alongside their locally smoked salmon, mackerel, eel, and herring.

Today, however, the most common way of preserving many foods, including fish, is by freezing it, and a wide variety of frozen fish is offered conveniently prepared in supermarkets. This means fish can be eaten fresh all year round and all over the country, as it can be frozen and packaged at the coast immediately after it has been caught. In my opinion, however, this is no service to fishlovers as the taste and texture of any dish is compromised by using frozen fish. At least in Italy, if frozen fish is served in a restaurant it has to be declared as such on the menu, giving the consumer an opportunity to make an informed decision about what he or she eats.

Good fresh fish remains the highest prize, and it is therefore important to know what you are looking for when you buy it. It is crucial to have some knowledge of the flesh of the type of fish you are buying so you know the exact characteristics to look for, and then, of course, to know the best way to cook it to make the most of both the dish and the fish.

It is essential that a fish be at its absolute freshest when it is bought, so the first priority is to find a trustworthy supplier. Good indications of freshness for whole fish are clear, bright eyes and bright red gills. It is also important that it smell of the sea and that it does not smell of fish—this a is sure sign that it is old and will not taste fresh. Finally, the flesh of the fish should be firm to the touch, springing back to its former shape when pressed. Some fish like tuna and swordfish are, however, "hung" like game to develop the flavor and tenderness of the flesh.

When buying shellfish, the main points to look for are that the shells of molluscs, such as mussels, clams, and scallops, are tightly closed. If they are slightly open, tap them sharply on a hard surface—if the shells do not close, the contents are dead and should not be used. Crustaceans like crabs and lobster should be heavy and fresh-smelling. If they smell of fish it means they are not fresh, so reject them.

Above all, when buying seafood, trust your instincts and do not be afraid to reject anything that does not look, feel, or smell right. Good fish, when it is fresh and well cooked, is a wonderful experience. It is no surprise that it has been such a staple part of the Mediterranean diet for so long, and it is reassuring that its popularity is growing once again all over the world.

RIGHT: ON LAKE MAGGIORE, PAOLO PREPARES LAKE BREAM FOR DRYING ON THE BOAT OF THE BATTISTA FAMILY

TOP LEFT: LAKE BREAM AIR-DRYING FOR *MISSOLTIT* ON ISOLA DEI PESCATORI IN LAKE MAGGIORE

BELOW: THE CAMOGLI MADONNA AND CHILD CAST THEIR PROTECTIVE GAZE OVER THE SEA AND THE FISHERMEN

# A-Z of Fish & Shellfish

### Acciuga, Alice / Anchovy

Probably the best loved and most versatile of Italian fish, anchovies are small saltwater fish which live in deep waters and approach the shore only during the spring mating season. The fishing of this specialty is strictly controlled to avoid damaging the stock. A lovely blue-green color, anchovies are classified by Italians as among the *pesci azzurro*, or blue fish, along with sardines and mackerel.

Newly hatched anchovies, called *neonati*, *latterini*, or *bianchetti*, are caught with very fine nets and eaten, bones and all, with just a little lemon juice, or used for very delicate salads and fritters. The adult fish grow to a maximum of 8 inches in length and are either used fresh in a variety of regional dishes or are preserved in salt and olive oil. At their best, these preserved anchovies have all the flavor and aroma of freshly caught and filleted fish.

Anchovies are central to the cuisine of the southern coastal regions of Italy and so command a high price. The best fresh *acciughe* or *alici*, as they are sometimes called in the South, can be found in the Gulf of Naples—Salerno is particularly well known for producing high-quality preserved anchovies, and Sicily as well, where Cefalu is at the center of the anchovy industry.

Fresh anchovies should be used immediately, as the delicate and fragrant flesh deteriorates quickly. The fillets can be eaten raw with just a few drops of lemon juice sprinkled over them—or marinated in a mixture of lemon juice, parsley, and olive oil, then served with a green parsley sauce made with olive oil, chili, and garlic, and accompanied by plenty of crusty bread. When it comes to cooking fresh anchovies there are many different regional recipes to choose from, but my favorite calls for stuffing the boned fish with a mixture of bread crumbs, herbs, eggs, and Parmesan cheese, sprinkling them with olive oil, and baking them in the oven.

LEFT: *NEONATI*

## How Anchovies are Prepared for Bottling

Fresh anchovies are layered in coarse sea salt, weighted, and left for three months to mature. During this time the anchovies exude oil, which is skimmed off at regular intervals, and the brine is topped up. The anchovies are judged "ripe" when they develop a very pleasant smell and the flesh is a good pink color.

Then comes the rinsing process:

the first rinse takes place in brine at 175° F. The second is done in fresh brine at 105°F, and the last in cold water. By this stage most of the excess salt and oil will have been washed away.

The fish are then filleted by hand

and the fillets are wrapped in porous cloths and placed in a centrifugal spinner for 2 to 3 minutes to eliminate all the excess water. They are then carefully packed by hand into jars and covered with olive or vegetable oil.

ABOVE: *ACCIUGHE*

RIGHT: *ANGUILLA*

Anchovies to be preserved in oil are first cured in salt to make *acciughe sotto sale*, or salted anchovies. To do this the fish are layered with rock salt and left to mature for at least three months (see opposite). When they are ready, they are removed from the salt, any excess is brushed off, and their heads are removed and the backbone is cut away with a small knife. On no account should the salted fish be washed. In Alba, salted anchovies are layered with very thickly sliced white truffle before being steeped in oil. Anchovy fillets (*filetti di acciughe*) are also available in cans; those of a good size and packed in olive oil are the best.

Preserved anchovies have an infinite number of uses in Italian cuisine, one of the best known being *bagna caôda*, a specialty from Piedmont (see page 33). This famous sauce, used as a hot dip for crudités, is made from just anchovies, garlic, and oil. Anchovies are also used in the classic *salsa verde*, or green sauce, for *bollito misto*, as well as many other sauces, and of course are familiar to all the world on pizzas.

Another classic use of the fish is *burro di acciughe* (anchovy butter), which is made by mashing preserved anchovies to a paste and mixing this with butter. This preparation is excellent in sauces or delicious spread on bread or *crostini*. *Pasta d'acciuga* (anchovy paste) can also be bought in jars, cans, or tubes.

*Acciugata*, a Ligurian sauce made by dissolving fillets of anchovies in olive oil, is used to give a sharp, distinctive flavor to otherwise bland food such as boiled or steamed fish, and boiled eggs. It can also be used with tomatoes, oregano, and garlic as a sauce for either pasta or meat.

## ALBORELLA / FRESHWATER FISH

This is a very common freshwater fish, mostly found in Lake Como, which grows up to 8 inches in length and has a silvery skin. It is easily scaled and skinned and the flesh has a sweetish taste. The favored cooking method is to flour the whole fish or fillets and deep-fry them. The fish is sometimes marinated in vinegar and wine with bay leaves, then sautéed in oil with onions. The fish is often air-dried to make the specialty of Lake Maggiore, *missoltit* (see page 21).

## ALIOTIDE, PATELLA REALE / LIMPET

Limpets are single-shelled molluscs, looking like small pyramids, which are found attached to rocks. You need to have good eyes to spot them, and a knife with a pointed tip to detach them. As long as you know it has come from unpolluted waters, you can eat this shellfish raw with just a few drops of lemon juice. Limpets have a very nutty flavor and are delicious in fish soups. The best limpet dish I ever tasted was a truly memorable linguine with mussels and limpets at the Cambusa restaurant in Positano.

## ANGUILLA, BISATO / EEL

This remarkable creature is both a sea fish and a freshwater fish. But the most impressive thing about the eel is the fact that all eels begin their life in the Sargasso Sea off the North American coast, and within two hours of being hatched, are transported by the Gulf Stream thousands of miles to Europe, where they are caught and speedily consumed. In Italy, these, elvers (as they are called at this stage of their life) are known as *cieche* (meaning "blind"), not because they cannot see, but because they are so easy to catch that the fishermen say they are blind to the nets.

The fish that are not caught from the sea as elvers swim into fresh-water lakes and rivers to spend six or seven years maturing, before swimming back to their birthplace to breed and end their life. Eels from the Comacchio valleys at the mouth of the Po are especially good. There, the elvers are trapped in artificial lakes when they enter the Po Estuary south of Venice and are then effectively farmed until maturity.

Eels are traditionally eaten fried, broiled, baked, and stewed. In Sardinia, they are cooked with tomatoes. One of the most memorable eel dishes I have had was one in which it was simply baked with bay leaves and no other flavoring (see the recipe for *anguilla alla Luciana* on page 35).

The *capitone*, a large female eel which has reached its maximum weight, is perhaps worth a special mention. It is traditionally eaten at Christmas and is a delicacy in Rome and all over the South. The fish is cut into sections, cured with olive oil, garlic, mint, and vinegar, then grilled on charcoal.

### ARAGOSTA, ASTICE / SPINY OR ROCK LOBSTER, LOBSTER

Of many varieties of this crustacean in Italy, the spiny or rock lobster, *aragosta nostrana*, the one without claws, is the most common. The larger, darkish blue/green true lobster with claws is called *astice*, and is similar to the American Maine lobster.

The best way to cook lobster is to boil it in water, when the shell will turn bright red. There is considerable debate about what is the most humane way to cook a live lobster, and the current consensus seems to be that the swiftness of plunging it in rapidly boiling water is preferred. Once cooked, it can be halved and, while still warm, sprinkled with good olive oil (preferably the most delicate Ligurian) and a few drops of lemon juice. Don't forget to provide your guests with the appropriate tools so they can extract the juicy meat from the claws. I think the sweetish taste of lobster meat is particularly good when the meat is cooked with tomatoes to make a sauce for linguine (see page 155).

### ARINGA / HERRING

This North Atlantic fish is not caught in the Mediterranean but is widely used in Italy, generally in *antipasto*, once it has been salt-cured and smoked. One of the most remarkable recipes for it I have tasted comes from Sicily, where it is eaten in a salad with grapefruit and orange (see page 29).

### ARSELLA, SEE VONGOLA

### ARZILLA, SEE RAZZA

### ASTICE, SEE ARAGOSTA

### BACCALÀ, STOCCAFISSO / SALT COD, STOCKFISH

*Baccalà* and *stoccafisso* are respectively salted and air-dried cod. Like herring, this is another preserved northern fish which has successfully found its way into Italian cuisine. Some attribute its introduction to Christopher Columbus, who carried it in his ship's supplies on the way to America. For a long time, in fact, stockfish was the staple diet of navigators as it would last during long journeys. Both types of preserved cod come from the Lofoten Isles in Norway, where a whole industry and way of life has grown up around the fishing, salting, and drying of cod.

Two regions of Italy are famous for their *baccalà* recipes, Liguria and Veneto, whence it spread all over Italy. In the past it was the food of the poor and was especially useful because it could be eaten on religious fast-days in the landlocked valleys of the Italian Alps where access to fresh fish was difficult. Today, as with many other traditional peasant foods, it is enjoying a renaissance in Italian cuisine.

*Baccalà*, or salt cod, can only be used after having been soaked in frequent changes of fresh water for at least 24 hours to soften the flesh and remove the salt. Salt cod is usually sold dry in halves or sometimes quarters, but in some places you can buy it soaked and ready for use.

Stockfish, on the other hand, is air-dried and sold whole. Although it is unsalted, it requires lengthy soaking before cooking to rehydrate it, as well as vigorous beating with a mallet to tenderize it and break up the fibers. Strangely, it is called *baccalà* in Vicenza and Venice, although it is known as *stoccafisso* elsewhere in Italy. In fact, Vicenza is famous for its *baccalà alle vicentina*, which is usually eaten with white polenta.

Other regional specialties using stockfish and *baccalà* are *frittelle di baccalà* (fritters), *insalata di baccalà* (a salad of *baccalà* cooked with parsley, lemon juice, and chili flakes), and *stocco alla genovese* (a long-cooked stew, see page 40).

### BARBO / BARBEL

This freshwater fish, similar to the American catfish, can be found all over Italy, where it lingers in the muddy beds of many rivers and lakes. It is a very delicate fish, with few bones, and is best eaten fried or poached. It must, however, never be eaten raw, as the uncooked flesh is toxic.

LEFT: SOAKED *BACCALÀ* IN THE MARKET

BELOW: *STOCCAFISSO*

ABOVE: [LEFT]
*MOSCIAME* (SEE
*TONNO*, PAGE 26);
[RIGHT] BOTTARGA

FAR RIGHT: THE
INGREDIENTS
ASSEMBLED FOR
*CACCIUCCO*

**BIANCHETTI, SEE
ACCIUGA**

**BISATO, SEE
ANGUILLA**

## BOTTARGA,
BUTTARIGA /
ROE OF GREY
MULLET AND
TUNA

*Bottarga* is the
name given to
the roe of both
the grey mullet
(*bottarga di
muggine*) and
tuna (*bottarga
di tonno*). The
mullet roe is
much smaller than that of the tuna,
and is pressed, then cured in brine
before being hung up to dry. Sicily
and Sardinia are the main producers
and consumers of this specialty, and
there it is eaten in thin slices seasoned
with lemon juice and olive oil as an
appetizer, and on scrambled eggs.

The much bigger tuna roe can
weigh up to four pounds and is
traditionally pressed into an oblong
shape once cured. It is mostly used
grated over pasta and eggs, whose
bland, accommodating flavors are
the perfect foil for the strong flavor
of the salted fish. It commands very
high prices and can only be found in
the best delicatessens.

## BRANZINO, SPIGOLA /
SEA BASS

When Italians hear the words *spigola*
or *branzino* their culinary hearts start
to beat a little faster, for sea bass
is one of the best-loved fish
in Italy. It is widely
available, as it can be
caught off any coast
where the sea is fairly
rough. It can reach
up to three feet in
length and 22
pounds in weight.

Its popularity can
be attributed to its
delicate but firm flesh,
which is enormously
versatile and easy to cook.

Whether boiled, baked, or broiled,
sea bass always delivers its promise.
Because it is so well-liked, this fish
has to be farmed to meet the
demand. This means that the size
and weight of the fish can be
controlled for culinary use. Wild sea
bass are a wonderful silver color,
whereas their cultivated cousin is
darker and never quite matches up
in terms of flavor.

The fish is often baked whole in a
salt crust or in foil parcels with
parsley, garlic, lemon, and fennel.
The Sicilians cook it in sea water
(see *branzino all'acqua di mare*,
page 35).

**BURIDDA, SEE
CACCIUCCO**

## CACCIUCCO /
FISH SOUP

This classic Ligurian
fish soup, also called
*buridda*, is made using
a wide variety of fish,
but usually *murena*
and *scorfano*, with
wine, garlic, parsley,
olive oil, and tomatoes
(see page 29).

## CALAMARO / SQUID

There is quite a lot of
confusion about these
very popular
cephalopods related to
the octopus. They
come in many
varieties, which look
very similar and share
similar preparation
and cooking methods.
The differences
between the varieties have more to
do with size and shape than taste or
texture. The *totano seppia*, or flying
squid, is notable for its habit of
leaping from the water and gliding
for some distance. Found mostly off
the Ligurian coast, it is treated in
much the same way as other squid,
but has coarser flesh.

Squid have tube-like bodies with
two fins, and a head with ten short
tentacles attached. Two of these
tentacles are much longer than the

others and all are lined with small
suction cups. The skin of the
*calamaro* (squid) or *calamaretto*
(baby squid) is generally pinkish in
hue with flashes of white.

The squid carries ink in its body,
which it ejects to confuse enemies
that are in pursuit. Italians,
especially Venetians, have managed
to prepare wonderful dishes using the
black ink, *risotto nero* being perhaps
the best known.

To prepare squid for cooking, the
skin should be removed, and the
head cut from the tentacles and
discarded. Then the transparent quill

inside the tube and the hard beak in
the center of the tentacles are
removed and discarded. The black
ink sac behind the eyes should be
removed carefully and reserved if
you want to use it to color a dish.

Once cleaned, squid can be cooked
in a variety of ways. They are often
poached whole very briefly in sea
water and eaten in salads dressed with
olive oil and lemon. In Apulia, they
use very little water for the broth, and
then drink it as a tonic after cooking

the squid. Alternatively, whole small squid or large ones cut into rings are dusted with flour and deep-fried until crispy. They may also be grilled or stuffed whole—usually with the chopped tentacles, bread crumbs or rice, and flavorings like garlic and parsley or Pecorino and pine nuts— and baked in the oven, and they often join other seafood in soups.

### CANESTRELLO, SEE CAPASANTA

### CANNOCCHIA, PANNOCCHIA /
SQUILL FISH
This most Mediterranean of shellfish, which vaguely resembles a langoustine, is very much an Italian affair. Especially common in the Adriatic, it lives in the sand and mud of the seabed. It can reach 8 inches in length and has a sort of fortified shell on its back and tail that has two black marks on it which look like a pair of eyes. This crustacean has many different names and uses, depending on where it is fished. In Venice it is called *canoci*, in Puglia *caratiedde*, *spanocchio* in Naples, and *cicala* in Tuscany.

To get at the tender meat, it is best to cut a small strip down each side of the body with scissors so the meat can be extracted in one piece. It is mostly used in fish soups, but is also served freshly boiled and dressed with olive oil and lemon juice.

### CANNOLICCHIO, CAPPALUNGA /
RAZOR CLAM
This is a very peculiar mollusc that has two shells shaped like an old-fashioned straight razor. It lives on the bottom of sandy seabeds and is quite difficult to harvest because it sits in an upright position and the sharp shells can cut nets and hands. It is easiest to get when the tide is low and you can gently pull the shells out of the sand.

Razor clams can reach 1 foot in length, but the smaller ones are more tender. They can be broiled, added to fish soups, or used in seafood salads. They are usually sold in bundles—go for those that are heavy for their size. To get at the meat without cutting yourself on the shells, the *cannolicchi* must first be steamed open in a pan with a little olive oil and water.

### CAPASANTA, CONCHIGLIA DI S. GIACOMO, PETTINE /
SCALLOP
Many different names have been given by various Italian regions to this popular and distinctive shellfish. In Italy it is usually cooked without the pinkish coral, or roe.

One of the best varieties, the *canestrello*, or queen scallop, is particularly common in the Venice region, where it lives on the sandy seabeds

and is harvested by divers all year round. It is no surprise, then, that it is from Venice that some of the best recipes have evolved, including *risotto ai canestrelli*, an Italian version of Spanish *paella*, although the finest scallops are rightly reserved for a simple but exquisite seafood salad. The fine flavor of the scallop suits the simplest treatments—a little white wine, garlic, and parsley.

### CAPITONE, SEE ANGUILLA

### CAPONE, CAPPONE /
GURNARD
This is strange fish that looks like a red mullet, with a large head surrounded by bony scales and two very large fins just beneath the head. It lives in the sand on the seabed at various depths. There are several varieties ranging from small to quite large, and reaching up to $2^{1}/_{2}$ feet in length.

The flesh is very good, tender and not too firm. Cut in steaks, it can be broiled, but its best use is to flavor fish soups.

### CARPA / CARP
This freshwater fish loves quiet waters, where it usually sits in the mud on the river- or lake bed. There are many types of carp, the main differences between them being the number of scales on their body. They can reach up to 3 feet in length and attain quite significant weights.

As Italians are not fond of the muddy-tasting flesh of carp, there are not many recipes suggesting how to cook it. The best suggestion I could give is for carp in bread crumbs, a recipe from Venice, where the fish is popular. The fish is also boiled and stewed, often with celery, onion, and tomato.

CARPIONE, SEE PAGE 36

CAVIALE, SEE STORIONE

### CEFALO, MUGGINE / GREY MULLET
Because of its fine flavor, this is a very popular fish in Italy and is fished on every coast. Grey mullet is fond of estuaries, where it finds the best feeding grounds, so it sometimes tastes muddy and the best fish come from clearer waters. There are many varieties, but the most sought-after is the *volpino*, which in season has a rich roe used to make *bottarga* (see page 17). Careful cleaning of the fish helps to get rid of any muddy taste. Mullet is mostly eaten broiled, and only

LEFT: *CAPASANTA*

the best fish are baked in the oven, with only olive oil, lemon, and parsley.

### CERNIA / GROUPER

This solitary fish lives in warm seas and reaches huge sizes of up to 5 feet. Its tasty, firm white flesh is considered a delicacy in Italy. Due to its size, it is usually fished with harpoons, and when it comes to cooking it is usually cut in steaks and either broiled or braised, while other parts of the grouper are used to make a sauce to dress linguine. However, the most interesting way of cooking the fish comes from Sardinia, where the liver is used to an excellent sauce to accompany the roasted fish.

### CICALA, SEE CANNOCCHIA

### CIECHE, SEE ANGUILLA

### CODA DI ROSPO, RANA PESCATRICE, RÒSPO / ANGLER FISH OR MONKFISH

This ugly fish is becoming more and more sought-after by chefs all over the world. Its firm, tasty tail meat is almost completely boneless and, after cooking, it resembles lobster closely enough to be confused with it quite regularly.

With its large mouth, the monkfish is able to take quite large prey, and spends much of its life skimming the seabed in search of food. It is therefore fished with a flexible rod which is weighted to reach the seabed. Monkfish grow to quite a large size, but generally only the tail of the fish is used. The large, ugly head is usually discarded in Italy, although in some parts of the world it is used to make fish stock and gelatin, for which it is excellent. The tail is cooked in every way, from broiling and deep-frying to baking and stewing, with simple added flavorings like lemon, garlic, parsley, and olive oil.

### COLLA DI PESCE / FISH GELATIN

This is a flavorless setting agent obtained from the parts of fish that are normally discarded, and is less gluey than ordinary gelatin.

### CONCHIGLIA

*Conchiglia* is the Italian for shell. The term is often used to refer to the scallop as this is sometimes called *conchiglia di S. Giacomo*. See *capasanta.*

### COZZA, MUSCOLO, MITILE, MUSCIOLI / MUSSEL

One of the most common shellfish in the world, the mussel is used abundantly in Italian cuisine, especially in southern Italy and the Venetian lagoon, where the locally known *peoci* are prodigious.

In the clear waters near Chioggia in the Venetian lagoon there is farm after farm where mussels grow on long ropes hanging from wooden frames. The farms are carefully regulated to ensure high standards of hygiene because of the mussel's susceptibility to pollution.

When bought, mussels must be firmly closed and heavy, indicating that they are still alive and completely fresh. Before cooking, they should be well washed under cold running water; use a knife to scrape off barnacles and the beards. Mussels that come to the surface when submerged in water should be discarded, as should those that do not open after cooking.

At one time mussels were eaten raw like oysters, but today, with the risk of contamination from pollution, it is essential to cook them first. (See *cozze ripiene*, page 30.) They are most commonly cooked in a little wine with pepper, parsley, garlic, and sometimes chili, or they may be sprinkled with garlic and bread crumbs and baked.

### CROSTÀCEI / CRUSTACEANS

The general name for all limbed shellfish armored with a tough skin, such as lobsters, crabs, shrimp, and so on.

### DATTERO DI MARE / SEA DATE

This mollusc, related to the mussel, is so named because it looks like a date. It is oval shaped, usually reaches 2 to 4 inches in length, and is of a dark brown color. The sea date lives in rocks where, by using acids from its body, it is able to form a niche in the rock, which it enlarges as it grows.

The *dattero di mare* is highly sought-after and a real delicacy. In

Puglia and in the Gulf of Spezia, where it grows best, there are special laws to regulate the harvesting. To catch them, you literally have to break the rock to which they are attached, and the fishing boats need lifting tackle to heft the rocks on board. The practice is likely soon to be made illegal as it is ruining some stretches of coastline.

Provided you know where they come from, you can eat sea dates raw like oysters. Because of their unique habitat, unlike other mussels, they do not contain sand.

### DENTICE / SEA BREAM
This very popular Mediterranean fish can reach 3 feet in length. Its flesh is very delicate and can be cooked in any way, from broiling in fillets or baking whole to frying and steaming, with plenty of olive oil and parsley, tomato, and fennel as added flavorings.

In commercial terms, this fish is as important as the *cernia* or any of the other breams (see *orata* and *sarago*), all central players on the Italian culinary scene.

### DONZELLA
Related to the gurnard and weever, the *donzella* is one of the colorful Mediterranean fish often used in fish soups and stews.

### FRUTTI DI MARE / SEAFOOD
This is the generic term used for all seafood, but is most often used to refer to all shellfish, from oysters, mussels, sea dates, and sea urchins to crabs, shrimp, and lobsters. *Frutti di mare* can be eaten raw as long as they are extremely fresh, preferably alive, and come from unpolluted waters—which can be guaranteed by an excellent fishmonger.

### GAMBERO, GAMBERETTO, GAMBERONE, MAZZANCOLLA / SHRIMP, PRAWN
The many varieties of shrimp and prawn belong to the same family as the lobster. Indeed, one type of prawn, the *gambero di acqua dolce* (freshwater prawn or crayfish) is an exact miniature copy of the lobster, and is almost as popular on the culinary scene. Other types of shrimp do not have claws, although their armored body and head are very similar to those of their larger cousins. Also like the lobster, the many natural colors of raw shrimp, from pale orange and deep red to dark grayish-blue, all turn red when cooked. Shrimp and

prawns are well-loved and harvested all over the world, but Mediterranean shrimp have an unmatchable sweet taste and sea fragrance.

Today it is very difficult for most people to get fresh shrimp, although there is some farming to supplement the locally caught supply. Huge worldwide demand means that most shrimp are caught in large numbers and frozen on board enormous North Atlantic trawlers. The difference between fresh and frozen shrimp is great, but the world seems to have accepted the inferior product.

The smallest *gamberetti*, or gray shrimp, are usually eaten dusted in flour and deep-fried until crisp. They are so tender that often one can eat the entire thing without having to shell it. The larger *gamberoni* can be either boiled or broiled with the shells on, or sautéed in a pan with just the body shelled so all the delicious juices contained in their heads can be released.

The best recipes originate in the well-supplied coastal regions and include simple recipes such as freshly boiled shrimp dipped in dressings or eaten in salads. They are also fried, broiled and grilled, or baked with olive oil and lemon.

### GOREGONE / LAKE FISH
Almost every Italian lake harbors this well-known fish, also called *lavarello*. It usually reaches 1 foot in

TOP LEFT:
*DONZELLE*

LEFT: *DENTICI*

BELOW: *GAMBERI*

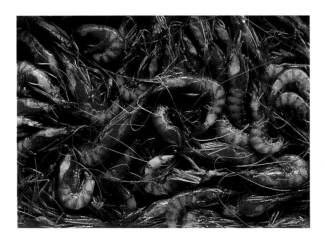

length and its meat is very delicate. It is especially popular in the northern regions of Italy, where it is used as an alternative to saltwater fish brought in from the coasts.

These very versatile fish can be cooked in many ways: it can be fried and marinated (in *carpione*, see page 36) to make an excellent appetizer, or cut into fillets, dusted with flour, dotted with butter and sprinkled with sage leaves, then baked in the oven. Fried, baked, or boiled they are equally good.

**RIGHT:**
*GRANCIPORRO*

## GRANCHIO, GRANCIPORRO, GRANSEOLA, GRANCEVOLA, GRANCEOLA / CRAB

The crab family includes a large variety of these extremely tasty crustaceans. In Italy, the smaller variety, such as the *granchio*, or sand or common crabs, are eaten in soups. The larger variety, called *granciporro*, is heavy and capable of yielding quite a lot of meat. For the best results these large crabs should be boiled while still alive, like lobsters. They need to be cooked for at least 20 minutes, then left to rest for 15 minutes in their cooking water. Spider crabs (*granseola*, *granceola*, or *grancevola*) are prepared in a similar way. The best crabs come from Venice, as do the best recipes.

After cooking, the crab is opened by exerting pressure between the eyes until the back shell lifts off like a lid from a box. After removing the "dead men's fingers," or gills, the meat from the body and claws is all collected along with the coral and mixed together and served dressed with salt, lemon juice, parsley, and a little olive oil. Larger spider crabs should be broiled or boiled whole, and the flesh added to a good tomato sauce for pasta.

There is a peculiar crab, called *moleca* in Venetian dialect, which is the equivalent of the American soft-shell crab. This is a male crab caught by expert fishermen during the spring and autumn when it discards its old shell and only has a new soft shell which has not hardened. Soft shell or "naked" crabs can be eaten whole, dusted in flour and deep-fried.

**GRONGO, SEE MURENA**

**LANGOSTA, SEE ARAGOSTA**

**LATTE DI PESCE, SEE UOVA DI PESCE**

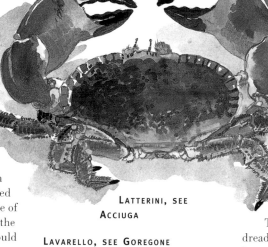

**LATTERINI, SEE ACCIUGA**

**LAVARELLO, SEE GOREGONE**

## LUCCIO / PIKE

This freshwater fish can reach a length of $4^{1}/_{2}$ feet and up to 9 to 11 pounds in weight. It is much sought after, especially in Piedmont, Lombardy, and Veneto, for its firm white flesh. It is traditionally cooked *in umido*, i.e. braised with tomatoes, or minced to produce pâtés or fish cakes.

**MARMORA, SEE ORATA**

**MAZZANCOLLE, SEE GAMBERO**

## MERLUZZO / COD

The mild-flavored cod is not often eaten as a fresh fish in Italy, only preserved. See *baccalà*.

## MISSOLTIT / PRESERVED FISH

This is a specialty of the northern Italian lakes Maggiore and Como. Fish from the lakes, like *alborella* and *agoni*, are hung to dry in the sun (see the picture on page 12). The dried fish is usually broiled until the skin swells, then this is removed and the fish is served with lemon juice or vinegar.

**MITILO, SEE COZZA**

**MOLECA, SEE GRANCHIO**

## MOLLUSCO / MOLLUSC

This is the general term for all the soft, invertebrate seafood, comprising univalves like limpets, and bivalves like clams, mussels, and oysters, as well as squid and cuttlefish.

**MORMORA, SEE ORATA**

**MOSCARDINO, SEE POLPO**

**MOSCIAME, SEE TONNO**

## MURENA, GRONGO / MORAY EEL, CONGER EEL

The *murena* or moray eel is the dread of every underwater diver because when it defends itself, it goes on the attack, and its bite is horrible as well as poisonous. It is a solitary fish that lives in holes in rocks and can reach 5 feet in length. The eel's meat was appreciated by the ancient Romans for its fragrance and was widely used in mixed fish soups like *cacciucco*.

The *grongo* or conger eel, unlike the moray, is neither venomous nor dangerous. However, great care needs to be taken when preparing it, as the raw blood is highly poisonous and it is only after it is cooked that the eel's flesh loses its toxicity. For this reason it is very important that any wound on the hands is covered when cleaning the eel.

Both the moray and conger eels are especially good when cut in slices and grilled or broiled, although great care must be taken to ensure that it is completely cooked before serving. See *anguilla* for more on cooking eel.

**MUSCOLO, MUSCIOLI, SEE COZZA**

### NASELLO / HAKE

Once prepared, this fish is often wrongly identified as cod, but raw hake does not look like cod at all, although it does belong to the same family. It reaches up to 3 feet in length, and large fish are sliced into cutlets before being cooked in any of a variety of ways. Its extremely fragile and delicate flesh is eaten all over Italy, cooked in many different ways according to regional variations. The fish may simply be brushed with oil and broiled, or fried in oil with tomatoes and garlic.

*Nasello al brodetto*, poached hake with bread, is a classic recipe in which the fish is briefly cooked in a court-bouillon made from garlic, parsley, a little salt and pepper, and chopped peeled tomatoes. The court-bouillon is simmered for 15 minutes so it is just cooked when the fish is added. The liquid must not completely cover the fish, which should also only be cooked for a few minutes in the sauce before being set aside for 10 minutes to rest. The hake should then be served on croutons made with good bread.

**NEONATO, SEE ACCIUGA**

### NERO DI SEPPIA, NERO DI CALAMARO / CUTTLEFISH INK, SQUID INK

Cuttlefish and squid ink come from a sac in the bodies of these cephalopods, and are mostly used in the making of sauces and *risotti*. They are also used in the making of pasta, in which the ink turns the dough black and gives it a distinctive, fishy flavor. The ink sac can be retrieved from any cuttlefish or squid bought fresh and whole from a fishmonger, or sometimes the ink can be bought separately in sachets.

### ORATA, MORMORA, MARMORA / BREAM

All Mediterranean bream are related, and, despite the differences in color, texture, taste, and general appearance, are very similar. Both the *mormora* or *marmora* (striped bream) and *pagello* or *pagro* (sea bream) are well-loved in Italy. Perhaps the best flavored is the *orata*, or gilthead, known to the French as the *daurade*, and baking is the favored way of cooking them. They are also often broiled after being brushed with *salmoriglio*, a mixture of lemon juice, olive oil, and chopped parsley and capers.

### OSTRICA / OYSTER

It is very curious that this Italian *frutto di mare*, so beloved of the Romans that they developed the first oyster farms, is now considered to be the French *fruit de mer* par excellence. In fact it was only after the French (and British) exhausted their own natural fishing grounds that they imported the farming know-how from Italy and made it such a primary industry that it is now France that dictates the rules of hygiene and other regulations for growing oysters.

In Italy the so-called belon, or round oyster, is still the best loved and is still farmed in the Adriatic Sea around Puglia, especially near the town of Taranto. Of the few varieties, Italians prefer the flat *Ostrica piatta* and the round belon, which is still eaten raw dressed with just a few

drops of lemon juice.

The oyster is easily digestible, and eating a dozen as an appetizer is quite normal. I remember once eating 126 small ones, but I certainly could not manage the remaining three courses or the dessert, and the effect one is said to experience after eating them was noticeable. Raw oysters should only be eaten when the shell is tightly closed, showing that the oyster is still alive. There are few Italian recipes for eating cooked oysters. One imported recipe prepares them *alla Rockerfella*, broiled in the American style.

**PAGELLO AND PAGRO, SEE MORMORA**

### PALOMBO / SHARK

This type of shark, found in the Adriatic, is seldom used in the kitchens of Italy any more due to the poor quality of its flesh. At one time, it was sliced and broiled like tuna and swordfish, or stewed in tomato sauce like tuna. It may still sometimes be sold in the Venice market as *vitello di mare*, or sea veal.

**PEOCI, SEE COZZA**

### PESCE AZZURRO / BLUE FISH

Although members of different families, anchovy, sardine, mackerel, herring, bonito, tuna, and swordfish are all categorized in Italy by the color of their skin. All are saltwater fish with oily flesh and are relatively easy to prepare and cook.

### PESCE PERSICO / PERCH

One of the most sought-after freshwater fish, the perch can reach 18 inches in length. It is very much at home in the northern rivers and lakes, and is usually sold filleted because it is difficult to prepare due to its very delicate flesh and many back fins and bones.

The favored cooking method is either to dust it with flour and fry it in butter, or to dip it in beaten egg, coat it in bread crumbs, and deep-fry in oil. Perch can also be preserved (see *carpione*, page 36) to be eaten as part of *antipasto* or as a snack.

### PESCE SAN PIETRO / JOHN DORY OR ST. PETER'S FISH

Legend tells how Saint Peter took

LEFT: *PESCE SAN PIETRO*

this fish from the water with his hands, leaving the imprint of his fingers on its skin. He was worried about the payment of a tax, but found exactly the right amount of money in the fish's mouth to pay the debt. This is how the fish got its name, and is supposed to explain the presence of two black spots on either side of the body.

John Dory has extremely delicate flesh, but it is expensive because only 30 to 35 percent of its total weight is in the fillets, which means that for four people you will need a fish weighing at least 4 pounds. The flesh is prized for its firmness and flavor, making it very popular with chefs the world over. The fillets are generally broiled, or they may be breaded and fried. John Dory is rarely available in the US, but porgy may be substituted.

## PESCE SCIABOLA /
### SABER FISH
The *pesce sciabola* really stands out when the fishermen bring their catches on board. Shaped like a large, flattened eel with a bright silver skin, it looks totally different from all other fish. Although quite common, because of its many small bones it is not often sought after for the kitchen. It is mostly used in fish stews and soups, in which it is cut into chunks to impart flavor. In parts of the South, it is also stewed with tomatoes, olive oil, and garlic in the same way as *baccalà*. Another common way of cooking it is to coat it in flour and fry it in oil, then marinate this in vinegar and red wine, with garlic and mint.

## PESCE SPADA /
### SWORDFISH
Swordfish reach up to 12 feet in length and 450 pounds in weight. The fish is readily identified by the long sword or spear on its snout. Many are harpooned by fishermen off the coasts of Calabria and Sicily. It is generally hung for at least one day before use. The flesh is very similar in texture, color, and taste to that of shark meat, and for this reason is cut and cooked in a similar way. It is mostly broiled, but more recently it has been served raw as *carpaccio*, and smoked. One of the most interesting ways to cook swordfish is in *involtini di pesce spada*, which is a specialty of Sicily (see page 32). Sicily has one of the highest consumptions of swordfish.

## POLPO, MOSCARDINO /
### OCTOPUS
There is a famous stand in the middle of the Vucceria market in Palermo, Sicily where you can eat locally caught, freshly cooked octopus from an old aluminum pot. Into the boiling water goes the fresh, creamy colored octopus, and after a few minutes out it comes, extremely tender and an appetizing pinkish-red. It is cut up on the stall so it can be eaten straight away. It does not need to be accompanied by any sauces or spices—nature has already provided all the essential ingredients.

Old fishermen's tales about this creature abound and most concentrate on the power of its eight tentacles, each of which is armed with two rows of suckers for grabbing hold of its prey. The entire length of the octopus can reach anywhere from 20 inches to 10 feet. Smaller octopuses, weighing up to 7 ounces, are very tender; anything over this size (and they can weigh as much as 55 pounds) needs to be tenderized either by beating it with a stick or repeatedly thrashing it against rocks to break up the fibers of the flesh.

The octopus can be found easily on all Italian coasts and is very highly prized. It has a strong beak in the center of its oval body, and this and the eyes have to be discarded when preparing it for cooking. It can be eaten in salads or freshly poached, *affogato*, as in Naples, or cooked in a covered pot with some oil, garlic, tomatoes, olives, chili, and parsley for about 30 minutes.

Similar to the *polpo* is the smaller *moscardino*, which has only one row of suckers on its tentacles and is less appreciated, although it is still very good. The same recipes can be used for both, as long as an adjustment is

made in the cooking time for the *moscardino's* smaller size.

### RANA PESCATRICE, SEE CODA DI ROSPO

### RAZZA, ARZILLA / SKATE
Skate is similar to monkfish and John Dory in that only a part of this fish is eaten, in this case the wings, or outer fins. The fish is completely flat and lives on the bottom of the seabed where it is perfectly camouflaged under the sand. Skate wings are sold skinned, and only the long structural cartilage is left in place. It can be enjoyed in a special fish stew or soup, boiled and eaten with butter or Hollandaise sauce, broiled, or deep-fried, coated with beaten egg and bread crumbs. Whichever way it is prepared, though, it is quite delicious and highly recommended, provided you do not mind navigating the cartilage, of course.

### RICCIO DI MARE / SEA URCHIN
Vactioners in the Mediterranean sometimes have the misfortune to tread on a sea urchin, whose fragile spines break at exactly the point where they enter the flesh, delivering a painful poison.
Sea urchins are common around the whole Italian coast, but mostly come from Puglia, Calabria, Sicily, and Sardinia, four areas where the water is particularly clean. As well as feeding the local population, these sea urchins are distributed to towns and cities all over Italy.

There are many varieties of sea urchin, and the roe of most is edible. The roe is the sea urchin's egg sac, which reaches maturity in the spring and early fall. Two varieties of sea urchin are particularly good—those with violet-to-dark-green spikes and those with shorter spikes of violet with a white spot at the end.

To prepare this most delicate of *frutti di mare*, cut off the bottom half where the mouth is located, using a scissors or a special tool, and clean the inside to remove the black impurities. Leave the star-shaped piles of roe intact and attached to the shell, then simply eat with a spoon or, as I prefer, simply lick them out with the tip of your tongue. The salty-sweet taste of the eggs is so delicious that no accompaniment is needed. A superb pasta dish with sea urchins comes from Puglia, (see *linguine con ricci di mare*, page 156).

### ROMBO / TURBOT AND BRILL
Belonging to the sole family, these flat fish live partly on the seabed, and are both highly sought-after for their extremely white and firm flesh with a very delicate flavor.

One of the two types available in Italy is the *rombo chiodato* (turbot), which can reach 3 feet in length and is recognizable by its dark gray skin covered with small bony humps. The other type, *rombo liscio* (brill), has a paler, smooth skin and a less elongated body.

Both fish are generally cooked and eaten as fillets, either poached and served dressed with olive oil and lemon juice, or stewed in a tomato sauce.

### ROSPO, SEE CODA DI ROSPO

### SALMONE / SALMON
Italians have discovered the appeal of freshwater salmon in the last few years, probably due to the fact that the farmed variety has only recently become affordable. Until now only a few Italians were familiar with salmon at all, and then only the smoked type. Although it is not native to Italy, everyone from restaurateurs to home cooks makes the most of this wonderful fish. It is usually broiled or poached, and often the flaked flesh is incorporated in creamy sauces for pasta.

### SARAGO, SARGO / WHITE BREAM
The Italians like to eat this much-loved Mediterranean fish all year round; either it is broiled with lemon juice and olive oil, or it is baked. The best variety is the *Diplodus sargus* which can reach 16 inches in length and a weight of $4\frac{1}{2}$ pounds. White bream prefers rocky seabeds with plenty of vegetation.

### SARDA, SARDINA, SARDELLA / SARDINE
The name of this fish, actually young pilchard, probably refers to the area where it was usually fished by the ancient Romans around the island of Sardinia. It is eaten in most of the Mediterranean countries and is almost a staple in all the coastal areas of Italy, where it is not only

TOP LEFT: FRESHLY BOILED *POLPO* IN PALERMO MARKET

BOTTOM LEFT: *RICCI DI MARE*

**ABOVE: CANNED SARDINES FROM SICILY**

**FAR RIGHT:** *SCORFANI*

**BOTTOM RIGHT: SARDINES IN PALERMO MARKET**

consumed fresh but also preserved in oil and in salt like the anchovy (see page 14). The flesh is relatively fatty, and the best way to eat sardines is brushed with a little lemon juice, olive oil, parsley, garlic, salt, and pepper and then broiled. They can also be boned and stuffed, or dipped in flour, egg, and bread crumbs and deep-fried.

The Sicilians honor the sardine in two special ways—first, as a sauce for *pasta con le sarde* (see page 166), and second, in *sardine alla beccafico*, which are fillets of sardines rolled and stuffed with bread crumbs, pine nuts, and raisins mixed in olive oil, and then baked in the oven and served with a sprinkling of orange juice (see page 33).

### SCAMPO / CRUSTACEAN

The *scampo* is similar to a small lobster, and is a very close relative of the Dublin Bay Prawn or langoustine, which is mostly fished on the Adriatic Sea on the eastern coast of Italy. Indeed, a great many scampi recipes come from the Venice area. It is a delightful crustacean with very sweet and tender meat, in my opinion superior to that of lobster.

They are delicious when extremely fresh and simply boiled, then dressed with good olive oil and lemon juice. Many of the scampi that come from the North Sea arrive frozen, and the taste is lost completely. Scampi are used for fish soups, and can be broiled and eaten cooked in salads. See also *gambero*.

### SCORFANO / SCORPION FISH OR RASCASSE

As their name suggests, scorpion fish have poisonous spines that can deliver a nasty sting. They live on rocky seabeds and come in a variety of colors, from reddish-brown to black. They look quite fearsome and are not very friendly if badly handled. However, this ugly fish has an excellent flavor and is highly sought-after for *cacciucco*, an excellent fish soup (see page 29). Smaller fish are best used in such soups, while the larger varieties (weighing 2 pounds or more) are wonderful steamed or poached and eaten with fresh mayonnaise.

### SEPPIA, SEPPIETTA / CUTTLEFISH

The cuttlefish has a shorter, rounder

body than the squid (see *calamaro*, page 17) but the same number of tentacles. It has a less chewy texture than the squid, but there is much debate about which has the better flavor.

The cuttlefish also carries ink in its body, which it ejects to confuse enemies that are in pursuit. The famous sepia or black ink was used by artists at the time of Leonardo da Vinci (see *nero di seppia*). *Seppiette in nero con polenta* is perhaps one of the most famous dishes made using the ink.

The striped skin is removed when the fish is prepared for cooking. The beak, eyes, and innards (including the "bone") are also removed, and the black ink sac in the center of the tentacles is carefully removed and reserved. The ink may also be bought separately in sachets.

Like the squid, cuttlefish are often stuffed and baked, or simply broiled or stewed in rich wine and/or tomato sauce.

### SGOMBRO / MACKEREL

One of the most common fish in the world, the mackerel is closely related to the tuna, and is one of the

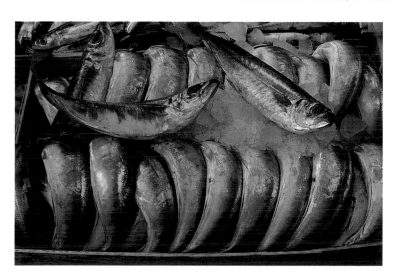

*pesce azzurro*, or blue fish, because of its unmistakably black-striped, bluish skin. The fatty flesh is very firm and rather delicate but, once caught, it deteriorates quickly, so freshness is paramount for the enjoyment of this fish.

Because the oils in its flesh are healthy and because it is cheap and widely available, it is among the most commonly eaten fish in Italy. There are many recipes for mackerel, but the best way to cook them is the simplest—grilled fresh from the sea over charcoal. They are also often stewed with a fresh tomato sauce.

## SOGLIOLA / SOLE
Italians coming into my restaurant in London are always impressed by the tastiness of the sole, mainly because they believe Italian sole are the best that can be eaten. I must admit that the Italian dish *fritto misto* (mixed deep-fried fish), when made with a few freshly caught shrimp and *sogliolette* (small sole), is one of life's greatest culinary pleasures.

Sole is available around the whole Italian coast, including the islands. They are many types of sole, which easily can be distinguished from other species of flat fish by the fact that both eyes are located on what would be the right side of the fish. The Dover sole lives on the sandy seabed and is so well camouflaged that it is almost impossible to see. It

is fished commercially and is so heavily exploited that the stock is in serious danger of depletion.

Whether it is served broiled, fried *à la meunière*, or cut into fillets and poached in court-bouillon, the sole is a delicious fish.

**SPANOCCHIA, SEE CANNOCCHIA**

**SPIGOLA, SEE BRANZINO**

**STOCCAFISSO, SEE BACCALÀ**

## STORIONE / STURGEON
This large fish, common to the Black and Caspian seas, used to live in the Po River in Italy. Now, because of pollution, they have died out there. The sturgeon is valued both for its eggs, which are eaten as caviar, and for its fatty but very delicate flesh. In Sicily, farmed sturgeon are delicately smoked. The largest sturgeon is known as beluga in Russia and can reach up to 33 feet in length and about one ton in weight. Imagine how much caviar it can produce. The flesh of the smaller sturgeon, about 6$\frac{1}{2}$ pounds, is eaten broiled, fried, stewed, baked, or steamed accompanied with various sauces.

## TARTUFO DI MARE /
SEA TRUFFLE
This mollusc is believed by gourmets to be the perfect *frutto di mare*. It is harvested with a comb, which drags up all the shells buried in the sandy seabed. Its shell is similar to that of the clam but, unlike that more common mollusc, it is both meaty and tender. It is usually eaten raw with lemon juice, although some connoisseurs prefer it without. It is also used in a sauce to accompany linguine, similar way to clam sauce, or

sautéed with other molluscs (see *sauté misto di vongole e datteri*, page 42).

## TINCA / TENCH
This small freshwater fish, related to the carp, lives in lakes, ponds, and rivers. Like many such fish, unless caught from clear water, it can have a distinctly muddy taste. Accordingly it is not one of the most popular fish for cooking. It is generally baked, fried, or cured in *carpione* (see page 36).

## TONNO / TUNA
'*Tonnara*' are the nets used by fishermen in Calabria and Sicily to catch tuna. These nets are placed in the sea in such a way as to channel shoals of tuna so they cannot escape, at which point they are harpooned. It is a messy way of catching fish, but one trip can produce tons and tons of tuna. Canned tuna fish probably first came into existence as a solution to these sudden gluts.

Canned tuna is eaten in dishes totally totally different from the fresh variety, often in sauces and *antipasti*. Fresh tuna, on the other hand, is eaten in a similar way to swordfish, usually broiled as a steak, or cooked with tomato sauce. Tuna can be eaten raw like *carpaccio* providing the meat is very fresh, and can also be eaten as *mosciame*—air-dried fillets. *Ventresca*, or the belly of the tuna, was often salted in barrels or canned as a particular delicacy. When tuna roe is salted and air-dried it is known as *bottarga di tonno* (see page 17).

**TOTANO SEPPIA, SEE CALAMARO**

### TRIGLIA / RED MULLET

This is probably one of my favorite fish, especially the rock mullet (*Mullus surmuletus*) when it is no more than 6 inches long and deep-fried after being dusted in flour. The freshness is the most important aspect of every fish, but for red mullet in particular it is essential. It is very delicate, easily perishable, and it offers one of the greatest treats if it is cooked within a day of being caught. It is impossible to freeze or preserve it in other ways. There are two types of red mullet; one has a more pronounced head and a pinkish-red skin, and the other is recognized by its sleek head and its red-and-yellow skin. The former tastes more muddy.

Red mullet is excellent baked, fried, or broiled, or used in fish soups to which it should be added at the last minute to avoid over-cooking. Larger fish are often filleted to remove the many bones. It can also be eaten in a pasta sauce, and the best I have ever tasted was *pasta con le triglie*, cooked by Pinuccia of the restaurant S. Giovanni at Casarza in Liguria.

### TROTA / TROUT

The trout is probably the best-known and most common freshwater fish in Italy, which with her many lakes and rivers offers it the most wonderful habitats. However, demand still exceeds supply, and farming is so common that it is almost impossible to buy wild trout. The two varieties favored by trout farmers are the *fario* and the rainbow. Both have wonderful firm flesh, made possible by the high quality of lifestyle reproduced in the farmed conditions.

Trout is as popular on the menus of Italian restaurants as it is in private kitchens. The people of the northern regions have an especially strong tradition in cooking this lovely fish. Smaller trout, called *trotelle*, are simply fried in butter, but all types of trout are broiled, baked *al cartoccio* (in a paper bag), and even marinated in *carpione* (see page 36) or, as they do exceptionally well in Umbria, served with truffles in *trota al tartufo*.

### UOVA DI PESCE, LATTE DI PESCE / FISH EGGS, FISH MILT

The eggs and milt of various fishes are delicacies in themselves. Eggs can be found in female fish and milt in male fish approaching sexual maturity, and thesy are sold by only the very finest fishmongers.

Especially sought-after is salted herring roe which is particularly popular in salads. Fresh herring roe has the same consistency as brains, and has to be soaked and thoroughly cleaned before being fried in bread crumbs.

Carp and mackerel roe is very tasty, but the most delicate is that of sea bass. Grey mullet and tuna roe are both salted and air-cured to make *bottarga*.

The most curious fish milt, that of cuttlefish, is consumed in Venice. It is called *latte di seppia* and is simply boiled and eaten with lemon juice and salt. The best place to eat this is, without doubt, the restaurant La Madonna, near the Rialto in Venice.

### VENTRESCA DI TONNO / TUNA BELLY

This is the juiciest part of the tuna and is usually canned as a preserve. The *ventresca* is particularly fine because of its fatty and gelatinous texture. It is usually more expensive than other parts of the tuna, partly because of its popularity as a preserve. Fresh, it is used like normal tuna for all sorts of dishes.

### VONGOLA / CLAM

Also known as *arsella* in Liguria and Tuscany, clams are small molluscs which are popularly used to make a sauce for spaghetti or linguine. They are very popular all over Italy, but especially in Naples and along the Amalfi and Adriatic coasts, where special machines are used to comb the sandy seabeds in search of them.

There are two different main types, the *gialla* and the larger

*vongola verace*, or carpet shell clam, the latter much sought-after for its better flavor, and occasionally eaten raw like oysters. The *tellina*, or wedge shell, is said to be the best for soup.

Clams are also very good eaten on their own. Put some good olive oil, garlic, parsley, and a little chili in a pan with a little water. Heat to a high temperature, then add the clams. Cover with a lid and steam for 5 or 6 minutes, or until all the shells have opened. I like to eat them straight from the shell with some good crusty bread to soak up the delicious juices.

# CACCIUCCO
LIGURIAN FISH STEW

**FOR 6**

1 POUND *SCORFANO*
(SEE PAGE 25)
1 POUND MONKFISH
8 OUNCES OCTOPUS
8 OUNCES SQUID
8 OUNCES CLAMS
OLIVE OIL FOR FRYING
6 TOMATOES, CHOPPED
SALT AND PEPPER

FOR THE STOCK:

1 LARGE ONION, CHOPPED
1 TO 2 CARROTS, CHOPPED
2 CELERY RIBS, CHOPPED
1 CHUNK WILD FENNEL, CHOPPED
2 TO 3 BAY LEAVES
12 BLACK PEPPERCORNS

*Every town on the coast of Italy claims a fish soup or stew. In Liguria it is called* cacciucco *and is made from local fish, which are available very fresh in the market as they have not had much traveling time.*

First clean and prepare the fish and shellfish. Set aside the good pieces. To make the stock, put the fish trimmings, such as heads and tails, in a large pan with the onion, carrots, celery, fennel, bay leaves, and peppercorns. Add enough water to cover and then simmer very gently for 20 minutes.

Meanwhile, heat a layer of olive oil in a large pan, add the pieces of white fish, octopus, and squid, and fry gently on each side for about a minute. Add the tomatoes. Strain the fish stock and pour it into the pan to cover the fish. Simmer for about 3 minutes, then add the clams and cook for a further 2 minutes, until the shells have opened. Season with salt and pepper and serve immediately.

# INSALATA DI ARINGHE, ARANCE E POMPELMI
SALAD OF SMOKED HERRING, ORANGE, AND GRAPEFRUIT

**FOR 4**

2 PINK GRAPEFRUIT
4 ORANGES
1 RED ONION, CUT INTO THIN RINGS
4 SMOKED HERRING FILLETS, THINLY
SLICED
4 TABLESPOONS EXTRA-VIRGIN OLIVE OIL
2 TEASPOONS WHITE-WINE VINEGAR
FRESHLY GROUND BLACK PEPPER
FENNEL FRONDS

*This typically refreshing Sicilian recipe probably came about as a way of using the abundant crops of citrus fruit and the smoked herrings that would have been brought to the island by visiting ships.*

Peel the grapefruit and oranges, removing all the white pith, then cut out the segments from between the membranes. Do this over a bowl to catch the juice, then squeeze out any juice from the membranes. Arrange the fruit segments on a plate and scatter over the onion rings, then arrange the herring slices on top.

To the juices, add the oil, vinegar, and some pepper to make a vinaigrette. Mix well and pour over the salad, then decorate with fennel fronds. Serve with good bread.

# ANTIPASTI DI MARE

*From Pinuccia, owner of the San Giovanni restaurant in Casarza, Liguria, comes this series of fish* antipasti. *They are all fun to prepare.*

## ACCIUGHE MARINATE

### MARINATED ANCHOVIES

*These are treated in a similar way as the lake fish or trout on page 37.*

Put the garlic in the lemon juice and leave for about an hour, then discard the garlic when the juice has taken on its aroma. Meanwhile, cut the heads off the anchovies, then slit them down the belly, gut them, and open them out flat. Lay them skin side down on a nonmetallic plate.

Whisk together the lemon juice, olive oil, parsley, and salt and pepper to taste. Pour this dressing over the anchovies and leave to marinate for at least a couple of hours before serving.

## INSALATA DI MOSCARDINI

### BABY OCTOPUS SALAD

Boil the *moscardini* in lightly salted water for 12 minutes (the larger they are, the more cooking time they require). Drain and dress with the olive oil, lemon juice, garlic, parsley, and salt and pepper to taste.

## COZZE RIPIENE

### STUFFED MUSSELS

Clean the mussels (see page 19) and place them in a large pan with the olive oil and garlic. Cook with a lid on for a few minutes, shaking the pan from time to time to allow the mussels to open. When they have all opened, season with black pepper and leave to cool.

Remove the mussels from their shells and enclose each one in a little of the sardine filling. Put back in the shell and then close the shell, leaving a little filling showing. Dip the mussels in the beaten egg and then in bread crumbs. Deep-fry in olive oil until golden.

## PESCE SPADA CARPACCIO

### SWORDFISH CARPACCIO

*Raw fish has not traditionally been eaten in Italy but it has recently become fashionable. This dish can easily be mistaken for smoked salmon.*

Lay the slices of fish on a nonmetallic plate. Mix together all the remaining ingredients, seasoning with plenty of pepper. Pour this mixture over the fish and leave to marinate for 30 minutes before serving.

---

**ALL DISHES SERVE 4**

1 GARLIC CLOVE, CUT IN HALF
JUICE OF 2 LEMONS
1 POUND EXTREMELY FRESH
     ANCHOVIES
1/3 CUP OLIVE OIL
1 TABLESPOON FINELY CHOPPED FLAT-LEAF
     PARSLEY
SALT AND PEPPER

1 POUND *MOSCARDINI* (SEE
     *POLPO*, PAGE 23)
4 TABLESPOONS OLIVE OIL
1 1/2 TABLESPOONS LEMON JUICE
1 GARLIC CLOVE, VERY FINELY CHOPPED
1 TABLESPOON CHOPPED FLAT-LEAF PARSLEY
SALT AND PEPPER

2 POUNDS LARGE BLACK MUSSELS
1 TABLESPOON OLIVE OIL
2 GARLIC CLOVES, FINELY CHOPPED
BLACK PEPPER
1 RECIPE FILLING FROM *SARDINE
     RIPIENE* (OPPOSITE)
1 EGG, BEATEN
BREAD CRUMBS FOR COATING
OLIVE OIL FOR DEEP-FRYING

8 VERY THIN SLICES FRESH SWORDFISH
     FILLET
3 TABLESPOONS OLIVE OIL
JUICE OF 1 LEMON
1 TABLESPOON VERY FINELY CHOPPED
     FLAT-LEAF PARSLEY
SALT AND PEPPER

## TOTANO RIPIENO

### STUFFED TOTANO SQUID

2 LARGE *TOTANO* SQUID, WEIGHING ABOUT
   1 POUND IN TOTAL

1¹/₂ TABLESPOONS BUTTER

BREAD CRUMBS FROM 2 BREAD ROLLS

MILK

1 GARLIC CLOVE, VERY FINELY CHOPPED

1¹/₂ TABLESPOONS PINE NUTS

1 TABLESPOON FINELY CHOPPED FLAT-LEAF
   PARSLEY

2 EGGS

SALT AND PEPPER

*The long body of the* totano *makes it ideal for stuffing. It is cut into slices and served cold. Ordinary squid will do—just cut them in half.*

Prepare the squid (see *calamaro*, page 17) and cut off the tentacles. Chop the tentacles and fry them in the butter for 6 to 8 minutes, then set aside.

Soak the bread crumbs in a little milk to cover, then squeeze out the excess liquid. Mix with the garlic, pine nuts, parsley, and salt and pepper to taste. Bind with the eggs and stir in the cooked tentacles. Stuff the squid cavities with this mixture and secure with a toothpick or sew up with a needle and kitchen string.

The squid are best steamed for about 30 minutes but you may also braise them in a pan with lard and a little butter for 20 minutes. When the squid are cooked, leave to cool and then slice.

## SARDINE RIPIENE

### STUFFED SARDINES

12 VERY FRESH LARGE SARDINES

1 EGG, BEATEN

BREAD CRUMBS FOR COATING

OLIVE OIL FOR DEEP-FRYING

FOR THE FILLING:

BREAD CRUMBS FROM 2 BREAD ROLLS

MILK

2 OUNCES EXTREMELY FRESH
   *MORTADELLA*, DICED

2 EGGS

1³/₄ OUNCES PARMESAN CHEESE, GRATED

1 GARLIC CLOVE, VERY FINELY CHOPPED

2 TABLESPOONS FINELY CHOPPED FLAT-
   LEAF PARSLEY

SALT AND PEPPER

Cut the heads off the sardines and bone them, leaving them attached down the back. Prepare the filling: soak the bread crumbs in a little milk to cover, then squeeze out the excess liquid. Mix the bread crumbs with all the remaining filling ingredients and season to taste with salt and pepper. Use to stuff the sardines, then close each sardine like a sandwich. Dip them in the beaten egg and then in bread crumbs. Deep-fry in olive oil until golden, then serve hot.

CENTER: SARDINE RIPIENE; CLOCKWISE FROM THE TOP: *TOTANO RIPIENO, COZZE RIPIENE, PESCE SPADA CARPACCIO, ACCIUGHE MARINATE, INSALATA DI MOSCARDINI*

# INVOLTINI DI PESCE SPADA
## STUFFED SWORDFISH ROLLS

8 SLICES SWORDFISH, 1/2 INCH THICK,
  MORE OR LESS THE SAME SHAPE

3 TABLESPOONS FRESH BREAD CRUMBS

8 BLACK OLIVES, PITTED AND FINELY
  CHOPPED

PINCH OF FRESH OR DRIED OREGANO

3 TABLESPOONS COARSELY CHOPPED FLAT-
  LEAF PARSLEY

SALT AND PEPPER

4 TABLESPOONS OLIVE OIL

2 1/4 CUPS TOMATO PULP (SEE PAGE 118)

*This recipe is typical of Sicily, where swordfish is regarded as a specialty. Almost every family uses their own filling but the results are always extremely tasty.*

Put the slices of swordfish on top of each other and cut off the pieces sticking out to obtain equal-shaped slices. Finely chop the trimmings.

Make the filling by mixing the bread crumbs with the olives, oregano, parsley, swordfish trimmings, and some salt and pepper. Place the mixture in the center of each swordfish slice, roll up, and secure with a toothpick. Heat the olive oil in a pan, add the swordfish rolls, and fry gently for 5 minutes on each side until cooked through. Remove the swordfish from the pan and set aside.

Put the tomatoes in the same pan and simmer for 5 minutes. Add salt to taste, return the fish to the pan, and warm through. Remove the toothpicks and serve.

# ACCIUGHE FARCITE AL FORNO
## STUFFED BAKED ANCHOVIES

6 TABLESPOONS OLIVE OIL

2 GARLIC CLOVES, VERY FINELY CHOPPED

4 TABLESPOONS FINELY CHOPPED FRESH
  PARSLEY

1 TABLESPOON FINELY CHOPPED FRESH
  BASIL LEAVES

5 SAGE LEAVES, FINELY CHOPPED

1 SMALL CHILI PEPPER, VERY FINELY
  CHOPPED

3 TABLESPOONS PINE NUTS

3 TABLESPOONS RAISINS

SALT AND PEPPER

JUICE OF 1 LEMON

24 VERY FRESH ANCHOVIES, BONED AND
  OPENED BUTTERFLY FASHION

4 TABLESPOONS DRY BREAD CRUMBS

*Nothing can surpass freshly caught anchovies, which are good eaten raw with just a few drops of lemon juice. This typical Sicilian recipe, with its raisins and pine nuts, has echoes of its Arabic origin.*

Preheat the oven to 425° F. and grease a baking sheet with some of the olive oil.

In a bowl, mix the garlic, herbs, chili, pine nuts, and raisins with salt and pepper to taste. Add 1 tablespoon of the olive oil and a few drops of lemon juice and mix well.

Lay 12 of the anchovies skin side down next to each other on the prepared baking sheet. Distribute the mixture on top of them, sprinkle with a few drops of lemon juice, and sandwich with the remaining anchovies skin side up. Sprinkle with the bread crumbs and drizzle with the remaining olive oil. Bake for 10 to 12 minutes, until just starting to brown.

Serve hot sprinkled with the remaining lemon juice, or cold arranged on lemon slices.

# SARDINE ALLA BECAFICO
## ROLLED BAKED SARDINES

2 TABLESPOONS EXTRA-VIRGIN OLIVE OIL

1 1/2 CUPS DRY BREAD CRUMBS

2 TABLESPOONS SOFT RAISINS (SOAKED IN ADVANCE IF NECESSARY)

2 TABLESPOONS PINE NUTS

JUICE OF 2 LARGE ORANGES

SALT AND PEPPER

16 VERY FRESH SARDINES, HEADS REMOVED, BUTTERFLIED, BACKBONE REMOVED

18 FRESH BAY LEAVES

*This celebrated Sicilian recipe is called* beccafico *because the rolled sardines resemble the little birds, "fig peckers," of which Italians have always been very fond.*

In a skillet, heat the olive oil and fry the bread crumbs gently, stirring with a wooden spoon, until toasted and brown. Allow to cool.

Preheat the oven to 400° F. Add the raisins, pine nuts, the juice of 1 of the oranges, salt, and abundant pepper to the fried bread crumbs. Mix well.

Wash the sardines and pat dry with a kitchen towel. Arrange them skin side down. Place a spoonful of the filling on each of the sardines and roll them up. Arrange tightly together on a baking tray, placing bay leaves between them, and bake for 20 minutes.

As soon as the sardines come out of the oven, sprinkle them with the juice of the remaining orange.

# BAGNA CAÔDA

FOR 6

1/2 CUP BUTTER

6 GARLIC CLOVES, CRUSHED

10 OUNCES ANCHOVY FILLETS (BEST IF TAKEN FROM SALTED ANCHOVIES)

3/4 CUP EXTRA-VIRGIN OLIVE OIL

MIXED RAW VEGETABLES, TO SERVE (SEE RIGHT)

*There are many versions of this hot Piedmontese dip, which is served with raw vegetables. Because of the amount of garlic, it is probably better to eat it over the weekend to avoid antisocial effects. It is usually enjoyed with friends, sharing a common terra-cotta pot, which is kept warm over a candle. Special pots for individual portions are also available.*

*The vegetables must be extremely fresh and tender, all cut into strips. Choose from cardoons (see* cardo, *page 105), Jerusalem artichokes (cleaned and cut into thin slices), red and yellow bell peppers, raw cauliflower florets, celery ribs, artichoke hearts, scallions, or whatever else is available. Abundant bread! Abundant wine!*

Put the butter and garlic in a terra-cotta pot over a very gentle flame and leave, stirring occasionally, until the garlic has dissolved in the hot, but not boiling, butter. Add the anchovy fillets and the oil and continue to cook extremely gently until the mixture becomes creamy. The *bagna caôda* is now ready to be enjoyed by dipping the vegetables in it.

LEFT [CLOCKWISE FROM THE TOP]: *ACCIUGHE IN SALSA VERDE* (PAGE 224), *SARDINE ALLA BECCAFICO, ACCIUGHE FARCITE AL FORNO*

# INSALATA DI NEONATO

## SALAD OF BABY ANCHOVIES

**FOR 4**

1¹/₄ POUNDS *NEONATI* (SEE
　*ACCIUGA*, PAGE 14)
3 TABLESPOONS EXTRA-VIRGIN OLIVE OIL
JUICE OF 1 LEMON
SALT AND PEPPER

*This very simple dish is a specialty of both Liguria and Sicily. The ingredients need only minimal cooking, thanks to their combination of quality and flavor. Baby elvers could be substituted for the anchovies.*

Wash the fish and cut away any impurities. Bring a large pan of water to a boil, add the fish and cook for 1¹/₂ to 2 minutes. Drain and dress with the olive oil, lemon juice, salt if desired and plenty of freshly ground black pepper. Delicious eaten as an *antipasto*.

# ANGUILLA ALLA LUCIANA

## EEL BAKED WITH BAY LEAVES

**FOR 6 TO 8**

1 LARGE EEL, WEIGHING ABOUT 2³/₄
   POUNDS, OR 2 WEIGHING 1³/₄ POUNDS
   EACH
FRESHLY PICKED LARGE BAY LEAVES
COARSE SALT

*Luciana Florio, a remarkable gentile donna I met in Naples, gave us an emormous amount of patient help and this wonderful recipe. The brilliant results belie the simplicity of the preparation. Needless to say, the eel has to be alive, or freshly killed by the fishmonger if you cannot do it yourself.*

Preheat the oven to 400° F. Kill and skin the eel if your fishmonger has not already done so. Gut the eel and rub with a cloth to remove some of the shine. Cut into 3-inch chunks and layer in a terra-cotta pot, adding some bay leaves and coarse salt between each layer. Bake, uncovered, for 30 to 40 minutes, depending on the size of the eel—test with a skewer to see if it is done.

# BRANZINO ALL'ACQUA DI MARE

## SEA BASS COOKED IN SEAWATER

**FOR 4**

2 SEA BASS, WEIGHING ABOUT 1 POUND
   EACH, CLEANED
EQUAL QUANTITIES SEAWATER, DRY
   WHITE WINE, AND EXTRA-VIRGIN OLIVE
   OIL (ENOUGH TO REACH THE BELLY OF
   THE FISH IN THE PAN)
JUICE OF 1 LEMON
1 TABLESPOON PARSLEY LEAVES
1 TABLESPOON OREGANO LEAVES
BLACK PEPPER

*This is a very curious recipe from Sicily, in which seawater functions as an ingredient; naturally it should be unpolluted if you manage to find it. Otherwise, use ordinary water and salt.*

Put the fish in a large pan with all the remaining ingredients. Cover the pan and bring to a boil. Remove the lid, reduce the heat, and simmer for 10 minutes. Turn the fish over and simmer for a further 12 minutes or until cooked through. Serve with boiled potatoes and a spoonful of the cooking liquid.

# SARDINE IN CARPIONE
## MARINATED SWEET-AND-SOUR SARDINES

**FOR 4**

12 LARGE FRESH SARDINES, CLEANED
FLOUR FOR DREDGING
OLIVE OIL FOR FRYING

FOR THE MARINADE:
1/3 CUP OLIVE OIL
1 LARGE RED ONION, THINLY SLICED
1 CARROT, CUT INTO VERY SMALL CUBES
2 BAY LEAVES
2 TABLESPOONS RAISINS
2 TABLESPOONS PINE NUTS
1 SMALL CHILI PEPPER
5 TABLESPOONS WHITE-WINE VINEGAR
1 SMALL GLASS DRY WHITE WINE
1 TEASPOON SUGAR

*This is a delightful summer dish which can be served as an* antipasto. *Perch, trout, and lake fish are all suitable alternatives for marinating in* carpione. *The most important thing is that the fish should be very fresh.*

Dredge the sardines in flour, then shallow-fry them in olive oil until crisp on both sides. Arrange them in a single layer in a shallow dish.

To make the marinade, heat the olive oil in a separate pan and fry the onion, carrot, bay leaves, raisins, pine nuts, and chili until the vegetables are soft. Add the vinegar, wine, and sugar, and mix well, then pour the marinade over the warm fish. Leave to marinate for a few hours before serving at room temeperature.

# CAPASANTE AL BURRO E LIMONE
## SCALLOPS WITH BUTTER AND LEMON

**FOR 4**

12 LARGE SCALLOPS, WITH THE CORALS
   ATTACHED
FLOUR FOR DREDGING
3 1/2 TABLESPOONS BUTTER
JUICE OF 1/2 LEMON
ABOUT 2 TABLESPOONS FISH STOCK
1 TABLESPOON FINELY CHOPPED FLAT-LEAF
   PARSLEY
SALT AND PEPPER

*Scallops are one of the most delicate of shellfish. They should be cooked briefly, either by frying or poaching.*

Dredge the scallops in flour. Melt the butter in a pan, add the scallops, and fry for 2 minutes on each side. Remove from the pan and set aside. Add the lemon juice and stock to the pan, stirring to scrape up the browned bits from the bottom. If necessary add a little more stock. Stir in the parsley and some salt and pepper. Return the scallops to the pan, heat through briefly, and serve.

# LAVARELLO E TROTA MARINATE

## MARINATED LAKE FISH OR TROUT

**FOR 4**

4 TABLESPOONS EXTRA-VIRGIN OLIVE OIL

JUICE OF 2 LEMONS

FINELY GRATED ZEST OF $\frac{1}{2}$ LEMON

1 TEASPOON SUGAR

1 TABLESPOON FINELY GRATED
   HORSERADISH

SALT AND PEPPER

$1\frac{1}{4}$ POUNDS LAKE BREAM OR TROUT
   FILLET CUT FROM A LARGE FISH,
   VERY THINLY SLICED

2 TABLESPOONS VERY FINELY CHOPPED
   FLAT-LEAF PARSLEY

*Only extremely fresh fish are suitable for this uncooked dish. The fillets are "cooked" by the acid of the lemon juice in the marinade. This modern way of serving fish in Italy is generally known as* carpaccio. *Tuna and swordfish can also be prepared like this, and, if you omit the horseradish, so can fresh, boned anchovies.*

To make the marinade, whisk together the oil, lemon juice and zest, sugar, horseradish, and salt and pepper to taste. Lay the slices of fish on a nonmetallic plate. Spread the marinade over the fish and leave for a couple of hours, then turn the fish over and cover with the marinade that has not been absorbed.

Sprinkle with the parsley and serve with bread or *grissini* as an *antipasto*.

# INSALATA DI MARE

SEAFOOD SALAD

**FOR 4**

2 GARLIC CLOVES, CUT IN HALF
JUICE OF 2 LEMONS
1¹/₄ POUNDS MIXED SEAFOOD
SUCH AS SHRIMP, MUSSELS, SMALL
OCTOPUS, SMALL SQUID (OR LARGE
ONES CUT INTO RINGS), CLAMS, OR
WHATEVER YOU FIND AT THE
FISHMONGER'S, CLEANED
¹/₃ CUP OLIVE OIL
2 TABLESPOONS FINELY CHOPPED FLAT-
LEAF PARSLEY
SALT AND PEPPER

*As with most Italian dishes, the taste of this salad depends on the freshness of the fish rather than on herbs and spices.*

Put the garlic in the lemon juice and leave for about an hour, then discard the garlic when the juice has taken on its aroma. Meanwhile, cook the shellfish in a little water in a covered pan for a few minutes until the shells open. Remove and discard all the shells. Simmer all the other fish in a large pan of water until just cooked and then drain.

Mix the lemon juice with the olive oil, parsley, and salt and pepper to taste. Toss this dressing with the fish, then leave to rest and cool to room temperature.

Mix again, then serve as an *antipasto* with bread or *grissini*.

# SPIEDINO DI GRANDI PESCI

SKEWERS OF FISH

**FOR 4**

2¹/₄ POUNDS MIXED FISH FILLETS
(SEE RIGHT), CUT INTO LARGE CUBES

FOR THE MARINADE:
JUICE OF 1 LEMON
1 SMALL GLASS WHITE WINE
1 TABLESPOON BALSAMIC VINEGAR
3 TABLESPOONS EXTRA-VIRGIN OLIVE OIL
1 TABLESPOON FINELY CHOPPED FLAT-LEAF
PARSLEY
1 TABLESPOON FINELY CHOPPED SAGE
1 TABLESPOON FINELY CHOPPED MINT
SALT AND PEPPER

*Cooking on a skewer works well if you choose chunks of large fish such as tuna, swordfish, large trout, salmon, turbot, halibut, or monkfish. A mixture of these is even better.*

Make the marinade by mixing all the ingredients together. Put the fish in a nonmetallic bowl and pour over the marinade. Leave for a few hours.

Thread chunks of alternate types of fish onto 4 long skewers and grill for 3 to 5 minutes on each side, depending on the size of the chunks, over a charcoal grill, on a ridged cast-iron pan, or under a domestic broiler. Baste with the marinade during cooking. Serve with an arugula salad.

# SEPPIE AL NERO
## CUTTLEFISH IN ITS OWN SAUCE

**FOR 4**

1¹/₂ TO 1³/₄ POUNDS FRESH
CUTTLEFISH

¹/₃ CUP OLIVE OIL

1 SMALL ONION, VERY FINELY CHOPPED

1 SMALL GARLIC CLOVE, VERY FINELY
CHOPPED

1 SMALL GLASS DRY WHITE WINE

SALT AND PEPPER

*You must use cuttlefish for this recipe to have enough black ink. Squid and octopus also contain ink, but in less quantity. Serve with boiled rice or with polenta and bread.*

Clean the cuttlefish very thoroughly (see *seppia*, page 25), detaching the small, silver-colored ink sac and setting it aside. Cut off the tentacles and wash them.

Heat the oil in a large pan, add the onion and garlic, and cook for a few minutes. Add the white wine and boil for a few minutes to evaporate the alcohol, then add the cuttlefish and tentacles, cover the pan, and cook gently for 20 minutes. Add the black ink and dilute with a little water. Season with salt and pepper and cook for another 10 minutes or until the cuttlefish is tender.

# STOCCO ALLA GENOVESE
## STOCKFISH STEW

**FOR 4**

2¹/₄ POUNDS STOCKFISH (SEE *BACCALÀ*,
PAGE 16)

¹/₃ CUP EXTRA-VIRGIN OLIVE OIL

1 LARGE ONION, FINELY CHOPPED

ABOUT 15 TASTY BLACK OLIVES, IDEALLY
*LIGURIAN TAGGIASCA*

2 GARLIC CLOVES, COARSELY CHOPPED

4 ANCHOVY FILLETS

2 TABLESPOONS COARSELY CHOPPED FLAT-
LEAF PARSLEY

BLACK PEPPER

*Of the many stockfish recipes from all over Italy, this one is the simplest but also the tastiest. In Liguria they use light local olive oil and the delicious Taggiasca olives, which impart a wonderful flavor to the dish.*

Soak the stockfish in cold water overnight, then drain, cover with fresh water, and bring to a boil. Reduce the heat and simmer for 2 to 2¹/₂ hours, until tender. Drain and remove the flesh from the bones.

Heat the olive oil in a pan and fry the onion in it until soft. Add the olives, garlic, and anchovies and cook for 5 minutes. Stir in the fish and parsley and cook for a further 5 minutes, then season to taste with black pepper. Serve with polenta (see page 173).

# TRIGLIE ALLE OLIVE
## RED MULLET WITH OLIVES

FOR 4

3 TABLESPOONS EXTRA-VIRGIN OLIVE OIL

8 WHOLE FRESH RED MULLET, EACH
  WEIGHING ABOUT 4¹/2 OUNCES, OR
  4 WEIGHING ABOUT 9 OUNCES,
  CLEANED AND SCALED

1 GARLIC CLOVE, FINELY CHOPPED

3 TABLESPOONS FINELY CHOPPED PARSLEY

ABOUT 20 SMALL TASTY BLACK OLIVES,
  IDEALLY LIGURIAN *Taggiasca*

4 ANCHOVY FILLETS, COARSLEY CHOPPED

4 TABLESPOONS TOMATO PASTE

1¹/2 CUPS PEELED, DESEEDED, AND CUBED
  TOMATOES

SALT AND PEPPER

*In Liguria it is still possible for those with a very good relationship with their fishmonger to obtain wonderful fresh red mullet. Combine this with the local olive oil, olives, and some herbs and you have a superb dish. For those who dislike the many bones in small fish, you can use fillets from larger fish.*

Heat the olive oil in a pan and fry the fish for 4 minutes on each side if small or 6 to 8 minutes if larger. Remove from the pan with a slotted spoon and set aside.

Add the garlic, parsley, and olives to the pan and cook gently for 2 to 3 minutes, then add the anchovies. Stir until the anchovies dissolve to a purée.

Add the tomato paste, followed by the tomatoes. Bring to a simmer and return the fish to the pan. Cook for 5 minutes on each side. Season to taste with salt and pepper and serve warm.

TOP: *SIUCCO ALLA GENOVESE*;
BOTTOM: *TRIGLIE ALLE OLIVE*

# Sauté Misto di Vongole e Datteri

MIXED SAUTÉ OF CLAMS AND SEA DATES

### For 4

**2 POUNDS CARPET SHELL CLAMS**
**1 POUND** *TELLINE* **(WEDGE SHELL) CLAMS**
**1 POUND SEA DATES OR SEA TRUFFLES (SEE** *DATTERO DI MARE*, **PAGE 19, AND** *TARTUFO DI MARE*, **PAGE 26)**
**4 TABLESPOONS EXTRA-VIRGIN OLIVE OIL**
**1 GARLIC CLOVE, FINELY CHOPPED**
**2 TABLESPOONS CHOPPED FLAT-LEAF PARSLEY**
**BLACK PEPPER**

*Everyone in the South likes to eat this specialty made with various types of clams and sea dates. We were very lucky to find sea dates—in my opinion one of the best shellfish—because fishing for them has now been restricted. You could use just one type of clam if that is all you can get, but the flavor won't be as interesting. It is customary to eat this dish with your fingers, sucking out the meat from the shells. Provide finger bowls!*

Thoroughly clean the shellfish under cold running water, discarding any that are open or that do not look very healthy.

Heat the olive oil in a large pan and briefly fry the garlic, taking care that it does not brown. Put all the shellfish in the pan and cook with the lid on. After a few minutes the shells will open up. Keeping the lid on, shake the pan so all the shells cook evenly. Check that all the shells have opened, then stir in the parsley and abundant freshly ground black pepper.

Serve on a plate with the sauce, which should be mopped up by very good bread.

# CALAMARETTI IN UMIDO

SMALL BRAISED SQUID

**FOR 4**

BREAD CRUMBS FROM 1 FRESH BREAD
    ROLL

MILK

1¼ POUNDS SMALL SQUID, CLEANED
    (SEE *CALAMARU*, PAGE 17)

1 GARLIC CLOVE, VERY FINELY CHOPPED

3 TABLESPOONS VERY FINELY CHOPPED
FLAT-LEAF
    PARSLEY

SALT AND PEPPER

4 TABLESPOONS EXTRA-VIRGIN OLIVE OIL

2 LARGE RIPE TOMATOES, PEELED,
    SEEDED, AND CHOPPED

*When I bought the fish for this recipe in Pozzuoli, I was given a handful of seaweed, which I dipped in an extremely light batter and then fried very briefly to serve with the squid.*

Soak the bread crumbs in a little milk to cover, then squeeze out the excess liquid. Cut off the tentacles from the squid. Chop the tentacles and mix them with the bread crumbs, garlic, parsley, and some salt and pepper. Stuff this mixture into the cavities of the squid, filling them about three-quarters full.

Heat the oil in a large pan and briefly fry the squid until they become slightly pink in color. Add the tomatoes and cook for about 15 minutes, until the sauce thickens.

# EGGS, POULTRY & GAME

## POLLAME E SELVAGGINA

During the past fifty years, the poultry business has undergone a kind of industrial revolution, and vast numbers of birds are now kept in huge sheds, often in terrible conditions. This means that free-range chickens are once again in demand, although both they and their eggs naturally cost more.

In many areas of Piedmont, Lombardy, Veneto, and Emilia-Romagna —and here and there all over the South— there are still, however, free-range farms producing the tastiest corn-fed chickens. The poor quality of mass-produced poultry also means that any Italian who can afford it still usually keeps domestic animals of their own. When I was growing up in Borgofranco D'Ivrea, this was quite common, and my family was able to keep a few chickens, some ducks, some rabbits, and a goat, so that we had milk every day, a couple of eggs, and, from time to time, the meat of one of the animals or fowl.

Ducks and geese are also favorites of Italians, although they are more popular in some regions than others. In Emilia-Romagna, geese are raised for their meat and for *fegato grasso*, the equivalent of the French delicacy *foie gras*, the enlarged livers of force-fed birds. In the province of Vercelli in Lomellina,

traditional *salame d'oca* or goose salami is made, although production is so small that there is only enough for local consumption and none is left for export.

Rabbit is also popular in Italy, and is often eaten in place of wild hare or used as an alternative to chicken because of its white meat. Rabbit is most frequently cooked in a sauce to make a *ragù*, as the meat, especially that of the farmed variety, does not have a highly developed flavor. One of the best ways to enjoy rabbit is cooked with mushrooms and accompanied by polenta to make *coniglio alla cacciatora*, rabbit the hunter's way.

It is well known that Italians particularly love to eat small, wild songbirds, and, while I have eaten *passeri* (sparrows) in Bergamo, where they prepare them best, I do not consider them a curiosity I could become passionate about because they simply do not have enough flesh on them. Something bigger is preferable, and wild quail, pigeon, and partridge remain my favorites. Tuscany, Piedmont, Liguria, Lombardy, Trentino, Veneto, and Calabria are the great game regions, and in these areas game is prepared in so many ways that recipes differ from village to village and sometimes from family to family.

In the past, hunting game was a natural way of putting meat on the table. Today the average Italian still eats game two or three times a year, which is very much part of a long culinary tradition. The whole range of game is eaten, from the smallest wild birds to the largest furred game such as deer. Nowadays, with growing concern for the preservation of wildlife, hunting is carefully controlled so people can satisfy their desires without compromising the balance of nature. A fine example of this is at the *Sagra del Tordo*, or festival of thrushes, in Montalcino, which still takes place each year, but uses farm-raised quails instead of wild ones.

Sardinia has an incredible tradition of hunting and cooking game, and the Sardinians cook most of their game on the spit, marinated and basted with unique natural ingredients and herbs that exist only on the island. Small *cinghiali*, or wild boar, are cooked in ovens made of hollows dug out of the earth. The prepared boar is cooked with *mirto*, a local wild bush like rosemary, and other herbs, all of which impart the most delicious flavors to the meat.

Larger game, like deer, chamois, and wild goat, inhabit the Aosta Valley and other Alpine valleys, and are used to make the unique recipes of the area, particularly *mucetta*, a kind of air-dried fillet of deer which is a great delicacy.

Tuscany is another region that has enjoyed a long history of hunting and cooking game. Of the many products and recipes from this region, the delicious wild boar sausages are particularly noteworthy. The locals also have a wonderful way of cooking wild fowl on skewers, with each bird separated by pieces of bread to absorb the cooking juices.

Eggs are no less valued than poultry or game in Italy, and when I was a child during the war, my grandmother used to make me suck the contents of a newly laid raw egg through a hole in the shell, presenting me with the first culinary challenge to my taste buds. I didn't much enjoy the experience, but I swallowed the thing down in the name of good health. Eggs have always been full of symbolism, evoking the very essence of the perpetuation of life. They are also probably one of the most popular and complete foods—the yolk alone contains many necessary vitamins, proteins, and trace elements.

It is possible to make a meal with a whole egg, especially if you shave some truffle on top, but the egg can also be used to thicken sauces, make pastries or mayonnaise, or it can beaten be with sugar to make a heavenly frothy dessert that can be flavored with Marsala wine or strong coffee. The whites, on the other hand, can be beaten to make a stiff foam that is used to lighten sauces and mousses, or cooked with sugar to make meringue. They are also mixed with flour to make egg pasta, which has a greater nutritional value and a special delicacy and flavor.

Eggs are particularly significant at Easter. In Italy a special pastry called *casatello* or *casatiello* is made for the festival. Whole raw eggs in their shells are embedded in the surface of the pastry and baked with it. Along with other Easter pastries, the *casatello* is given to friends and family to signify peace and prosperity, all represented by the quantity of eggs used to make it.

LEFT: A GAME BUTCHER PROUDLY DISPLAYS A RANGE OF WILD BOAR SPECIALTIES

RIGHT: TYPICAL UMBRIAN GAME COUNTRY

# A-Z OF POULTRY & GAME

### ALLODOLA / SKYLARK

This small bird can be found only in central and southern Italy, where it is in abundant supply during the months of October to November and March to April, when it is migrating. It could easily be mistaken for a sparrow, but unlike the sparrow, it builds its nest on the ground and mainly feeds on grains, giving it an exquisite flavor. It is just a pity that it yields such a small amount of meat. Hunting of the bird is now restricted and is soon to be made totally illegal.

Because of its size it is often cooked with other, larger birds, and is used to give flavor to *ragùs*. In Tuscany, skylarks are wrapped in *pancetta* and loaded on long skewers between chunks of bread and bay leaves, then spit-roasted or broiled and basted with virgin olive oil, salt and pepper.

### ANATRA, ANITRA / DUCK

Under these names are grouped all types of domestic and wild ducks. Whatever form it takes, however, duck is very much loved by Italians and it is much used in Italian cuisine, especially in the winter. Duck flesh is quite dark and gamy, and quite fatty. Always buy fresh duck, as the frozen variety lacks much of the quality of the meat.

The most popular variety of farmed duck is *anatra muta*, because of its free-range lifestyle (its wings are clipped so it can't fly away, but it is left free to forage for food in ponds and the like). The main farming areas for ducks in Italy are Piedmont, Lombardy, Emilia-Romagna, and Veneto. In Piedmont and Emilia-Romagna, ducks are force-fed to enlarge the liver to make *fegato grasso* (*foie gras*), more for export to other countries where this specialty is much more appreciated.

There is also an incredible variety of wild duck, *anitra selvatica*, which is usually hunted in the autumn. It is very different from farmed duck, not only in appearance and taste, but also in the tenderness of its meat. Italians do not hang wild birds for very long, and in some cases, as with pheasant, they tend to cook them straightaway, mostly by baking or broiling. Surprisingly for such a fatty bird, ducks for roasting are often barded with strips of Parma ham, and this does give an incomparable flavor.

### BECCACCIA / WOODCOCK

The woodcock is not native to Italy, but it does fly over when migrating in spring and autumn. It has a long flat beak and brownish plumage to camouflage it in its natural woodland habitat. Its flesh has a wonderful flavor and it is one of the best-loved wild birds. Because it cannot be farmed, it is in short supply and as a result has been over-hunted to the extent that in some parts of Italy the shooting or netting of this bird is forbidden.

Once caught, the woodcock should be hung for at least five days. It should only be plucked immediately before cooking. When plucking the feathers, great care needs to be taken not to tear the skin, and it is

also important not to wash the woodcock after plucking, to retain flavor. Instead, the bird should be singed over a flame to burn off any feather stubs. A small minority of purists prefer the woodcock undrawn for better flavor.

The bird is delicious oven-roasted for about 10 minutes only and served on a circle of toasted bread to collect its juices. Very young birds may also be broiled, basted with olive oil and the cooking juices; older birds are often casseroled with mushrooms. One bird is plenty for one person. The woodcock may also be stuffed with a thrush, as is done in Tuscany.

### BECCACCINO / SNIPE

Snipe enjoys a similar gastronomic reputation as the *beccaccia*, or woodcock. As with the woodcock, it cannot be raised commercially, which might in part contribute to its popularity. The snipe can be found in estuaries and lakes, where it rests while migrating in spring and autumn. It is particularly sought-after in the fall, when it is good and fat after a summer of feeding. The dimensions of this bird are similar to that of the woodcock and, as with its cousin, one bird provides a good meal for one person. It is prepared and cooked in a similar way to the woodcock.

### BECCAFICO / FIG PECKER OR BLACKCAP

Various small birds belong to this family, which takes its name from the birds' habit of eating figs, grapes, and other juicy berries. Their meat is especially flavorsome when they feed on figs, of which they are particularly fond. They are quite rare birds, and because of this their hunting is usually illegal. The majority of those sold in specialist stores come from abroad, so the consciences of the Italians who enjoy them are not troubled. The birds are prepared and cooked in the same way as sparrows. In Sicily, the name of this bird has been given to a recipe for sardines, *sardine alla beccafico* (see page 33), which probably indicates that the fish should be cooked in the same way as the bird.

### CAMOSCIO / CHAMOIS, WILD GOAT

This wild and very sprightly goat inhabits the northern Alps and Abruzzo. Its dark and very gamy flesh is treated very much as a

*LEFT: BECCACCIA*

delicacy in Italy and is particularly popular in the Aosta Valley and the Dolomites, where it lives above the tree line high up on the hills at altitudes of 5,000 to 10,000 feet.

In Italy, the hunting of chamois is limited because of its short supply, but frozen chamois can be bought from other countries. Although the frozen variety tends to be more tender, it does not, however, have the wonderful flavor of the fresh meat. Incidentally, chamois leather is a by-product of this animal.

*RIGHT: CERVO*

*Mucetta* is a special air-dried fillet of chamois, which is served thinly sliced as an *antipasto*. This traditional method of preserving meat was once necessary for inhabitants of the chamois' habitat as provision for the long winter months. Today, however, it is a delicacy sold at very high prices.

Another way of preparing chamois meat is to stew it with wine, carrots, onions, and celery, or in a spicy mix flavored with cinnamon and nutmeg, to be served with polenta.

## CAPPONE / CAPON

The production of capon (a castrated rooster) is almost exclusively limited to Christmas time, when this bird is the centerpiece of the celebrations. The main regions where capons are farmed are Veneto, Emilia-Romagna, Lombardy, and Piedmont.

Once castrated, it takes just six or seven months for the young rooster to grow to an impressive 6 to 11 pounds, with extremely tender and juicy flesh. It is prepared and cooked just like a normal chicken. Boiling is a particularly good method, common in various parts of Piedmont and Emilia-Romagna. This cooking method produces the most wonderful stock, which is used to cook *tortellini*. The bird itself gives a generous amount of meat that can be eaten as a part of *bollito misto* (see page 92), popular all over northern Italy with *cugna* (see *cotogna*, page 265) or with *mostarda di cremona* (see page 269).

## CAPRIOLO / ROE BUCK OR ROE DEER

The male of the deer family can be recognized easily by its antlers. It is a medium-sized deer with a red-brown coat that changes to gray-brown in winter. It lives in hilly woodland areas and thus cannot be found in Sicily or Sardinia, but is abundant in the rest of Italy, especially in the Alps and Apennines.

I once tried *capriolo carpaccio* made with the fillet of the roe deer, which was sublime—especially as it was garnished with a few slices of truffle. The meat can also be used to make a delicious *ragù di capriolo*, with rosemary, juniper berries, nutmeg, cinnamon, anchovy, and wine, which goes

wonderfully well with polenta and pasta in *pappardelle al sugo di capriolo*. It can also be cut into medallions and cooked with chanterelle mushrooms. These are, however, just a few suggestions for this highly-prized meat.

## CERVO / RED DEER

This most majestic of all deer is almost extinct in the wild in Italy. There are a few herds in national parks, such as Gran Paradiso in Piedmont, to remind people what Italian fauna used to be like. In addition to the attractions of its meat, known as venison, the deer's massive antlers have a multitude of uses and can be carved into many things, from knife handles to buttons.

Almost all the venison now eaten in Italy comes from Eastern Europe or from Scandinavia, where it is farmed. The deer can grow to a weight of 800 pounds and its meat is one of the best and healthiest, as it is low in fat and cholesterol. Because it tends to be dry, the meat is usually first marinated in wine and olive oil. It is excellent in stews, *ragùs*, and pot roasts, for which the saddle is especially good. The usual added flavorings include wine, garlic, and lemon. Finally, venison can also be roasted in the traditional manner.

CHIOCCIOLA, SEE LUMACA

## CIBREO / GIBLET STEW

There are various way of using the *rigaglie*, or giblets of chicken or other poultry, in Italian cuisine, but the two most popular recipes are *finanziera* from Piedmont and *cibreo* from Tuscany (see *cibreo di rigaglie*, page 58).

It is not certain who created the dish *cibreo*, but it must have been a gourmand of the Renaissance period who could not bear to throw anything away! Ingredients include the cockscomb and the testicles, the hen's unborn eggs, the liver, heart, and even the sliced gizzards—all in a simple butter sauce enriched with egg yolks and lemon juice.

Whichever bird is used, the result is stunning and extremely tasty, usually accompanied by rice or polenta. However, you should only eat this dish in places that are well known for using only the freshest ingredients.

### CINGHIALE / WILD BOAR

Given that Italians love pork of any description, either cooked or preserved, it is not surprising that the wild version excites them so much. Sometimes considered a pest, the boar lives in the hilly woods of Tuscany, Umbria, Abruzzo, and any other area where there is thick, inaccessible undergrowth in which it can hide and feed on juicy, tender shoots and berries.

Hunting wild boar can be dangerous because this animal, when threatened, will attack humans. Boar-hunting is, however, a major sport in the regions of Sardinia, Sicily, and Calabria, and a successful hunt is accompanied by enthusiastic celebrations.

In Tuscany, wild boar is used to produce many foods, including hams, salamis, and *salamini*. When fresh it is wonderful in stews and *ragùs*, such as *ciriole al ragù di cinghiale* (see page 61), and almost every Tuscan and Umbrian family keeps frozen wild boar to make a *ragù* to serve with the famous *pinci* pasta, hand-made giant spaghetti.

Due to high demand for wild boar, many half-wild boar are farmed in enclosed woody areas, leading a semi-wild life and producing a less gamy meat.

### CIVET, SEE SALMI

### COLOMBACCIO, SEE PALOMBACCIO

### COLOMBO, PICCIONE / PIGEON

This is the domestic version of *colombaccio* (wood pigeon) and is farmed almost everywhere because of the increasing demand for it. The common pigeon can be found everywhere, from San Marco in Venice to Piazza del Duomo in Milan, not to mention London's Trafalgar Square, and the bird has adapted itself to every situation. Obviously the city pigeon is not really suitable for human consumption, but it is a pity considering that they are magnificently fed with grains by the multitude of tourists trying to play Saint Francis of Assisi, and their meat must be particularly good.

Farmed pigeons are not only safe to eat, but tasty too, even if they are not as good as the wild variety—the advantage for some is that there is no need to disguise the gamy flavor and they don't require lengthy cooking like the wood pigeon.

Pigeons are sold cleaned and ready for cooking, and are used in famous dishes such as *piccione alle olive*, pigeon with olives, and in casseroles. You can tell the age of pigeon by the beak, which is more elastic in younger birds.

### CONIGLIO / RABBIT

After pork and chicken, rabbit is one of the most popular meats in Italy. Wild rabbit, *coniglio selvatico*, is rare, as the animal is almost totally extinct from the countryside. However, the *lepre* or hare is still likely

ABOVE: *CONIGLIO*

to be the happy trophy of the Italian hunter.

A small number of rabbits is kept in Italy by anyone who has the space and facilities, but most rabbit is farmed. *Coniglio alla cacciatora*, with mushrooms, is the best-known rabbit recipe, but rabbit *ragù*, made with tomatoes and served with polenta, is also a classic dish. In Liguria, the rabbit is also very much in demand (see *coniglio affogato alla ligure*, page 62).

### CRESTE DI GALLO, SEE POLLO

### DAINO / FALLOW DEER

The fallow deer reaches an adult weight of about 225 pounds, has a coat that varies from darker red-brown in the summer to pale brown in the winter, and the male can be identified by the flat horns on its head. Fallow deer lives in Sardinia and in some national parks in northern Italy.

The meat of fallow deer is similar to that of other venison and cooks in the same way, although it does need marinating for some time in red wine to tenderize it. I also add grapefruit juice to the marinade to take away the excessive gamy flavor. The best and most tender cuts are the saddle and the leg. See also *cervo*.

### DINDO, SEE TACCHINO

### FAGIANO / PHEASANT

The noble pheasant was introduced to Europe from Asia during the Middle Ages. It was particularly popular in Tuscany, where its

LEFT: A WILD BOAR IN UMBRIA, HUNTED BY CARLO MONTANI

feathers were used to decorate the tables and the serving dishes whenever it appeared on the menu. The male bird is famous for his beautiful and ornate feathers, while the female looks a little plain. The male is also larger in size than his female counterpart, a fact which is important when buying a brace, a pair of birds of which one is male and the other female.

Italians do not like wild pheasant to be hung for too long, and the farmed variety is not hung at all because it is so tender. Pheasant is popular in North and Central Italy, especially in Tuscany and Umbria, which have a culinary history in the preparation of these birds. Pheasant has a lovely gamy taste and fragrance, and the rather dark meat contains little fat. It is a fairly versatile bird and is often cooked in a casserole with wild berries to complement its flavor, or is simply roasted in the oven after it has been rubbed with olive oil, salt, and pepper, or occasionally flavored with truffles.

## FARAONA, GALLINA FARAONA /
GUINEA HEN
It is believed that this bird, well-known to the ancient

RIGHT: *FAGIANO*

Greeks and Romans, was introduced from the Gulf of Guinea into Europe by Portuguese sea adventurers around the fifteenth century.

In taste, the guinea hen has a flavor somewhere between that of the chicken and the pheasant. This bird lives wild in its country of origin, but in Italy and most of the rest of Europe it is mainly raised on farms. Its plumage is typically white, spotted with gray, making it one of the most elegant and beautiful birds. It is equally good roasted, casseroled, or braised, and its tender and delicate meat represents a welcome, tasty, and sophisticated alternative to chicken.

## FEGATINO DI POLLO /
CHICKEN LIVER
One of the most underrated parts of the chicken, the liver makes the hearts of variety-meat lovers beat faster. This is an extremely versatile ingredient, which can be transformed into many lovely dishes. It is particularly good for making pâtés, or as the foundation for various sauces for pasta and risotto. Chicken livers are also an ingredient in the famous dishes of *cibreo* (see page 58) and *finanziera*. See also *pollo* and *rigaglie*.

## FEGATO GRASSO, SEE ANATRA AND OCA

## FOLAGA / COOT
The coot is a bird that lives on and around river estuaries. Because of its fishy taste, it used to be eaten in Italy on Fridays as an acceptable alternative to fish. This distinguishing factor is exactly the reason that it is not often eaten in Italy today, and in this it has much in common with the rare yellow-and-red-beaked bird *gallinella d'acqua* or moorhen.

## FROLLATURA
This is the term for the hanging of game and other meat to allow the flesh to become more tender. *Frollare sotto pelle* means the animal is killed and drawn and left to hang with the skin or plumage on for anywhere up to seven days.

## GALLETTO, GALLINA, SEE POLLO

## GALLINELLA D'ACQUA, SEE FOLAGA

## GALLO, SEE POLLO

## GALLO CEDRONE / GROUSE
In my opinion this is the best of the game birds. Grouse is quite rare in Italy, and is a protected species, so I am especially grateful to live in Britain where I can get Scottish grouse, although it is increasingly scarce here too. In Scotland, grouse nest on open moorlands, while in Italy they prefer the habitat of pine forests. Its diet of berries and insects imparts an irresistible flavor to its very dark and fleshy breast. It needs to be hung, unplucked, for at least three or four days. When in season, it has a prime position on my restaurant menu, and I like to serve it lightly roasted, so it is still pink, with chanterelle mushrooms.

## LEPRE / HARE
The most coveted game of the Italian hunter is the hare. Belonging to the same family as the *coniglio*, or rabbit, the hare reaches a weight of up to 16 pounds. It differs from the wild rabbit, with which it is often confused, in that it has longer hind legs than forelegs and its meat is dark red. The astuteness and speed of the hare are legendary, and hunters who seek this prey without the help of a dog are rarely successful in catching it.

As the blood of the hare is a key ingredient for marinating and cooking the animal, it is especially important when buying hare that you check that it is very fresh and properly butchered. Frozen, farm-raised hare lack this vital ingredient, and as a result, dishes cooked with frozen hare cannot match the flavor of those using their freshly butchered, wild cousins. The hanging process, especially of heavier, older animals, takes place in

a marinade of blood, wine, and spices (see *lepre in salmi*, page 63) and can take at least two days.

Hare is usually stewed to produce a delicious *ragù* that can either be served with polenta or with pasta to form the famous *pappardelle al sugo di lepre*. It is often cooked with spices, such as nutmeg and cloves, and is even flavored with cocoa powder. Whichever way it is cooked, it should be on the menu of every serious restaurant in Italy.

## LUMACA DI TERRA, BOVOLO, MARRUZELLE / SNAIL

Snails are not easy to categorize as, although they are wild, they are totally different from any other game. Freshly collected snails need to be cleaned or deslimed by allowing them to feed on rusk, fresh nettle leaves, and salt for a couple of days. They can then be washed and cooked in salted water. When they are done, pull the snail out of its shell, discard the black tail, and wash the shell. The snails can then be prepared according to the recipe you are using. I cannot understand why anyone bothers with canned snails, which have been cooked then stuffed back into their shell, although frozen ones are acceptable.

You can cook snails at home, and one of the best ways is in *lumachine al sugo* (see page 63), although the larger snails are also good eaten briefly blanched then stuffed with plenty of butter, garlic, and parsley, and baked in a hot oven. The memory of eating *marruzzelle*, as they call them locally, on street corners in Naples is now dim, but I did see them recently being cooked and sold in a street market in Milan. In Naples, *marruzzelle al sugo* was made with snails harvested from plants growing near the sea and then cooked in a hot tomato sauce so they could be simply sucked out of their shells. They were delicious.

While freshly cooked snails are a true pleasure, the recent trend of eating snails' eggs or snail caviar is just a commercially generated fad. Although the eggs resemble fish caviar in appearance, unlike the sturgeon, snails produce very few eggs and those they do produce are extremely difficult to collect.

## MUCETTA, SEE CAMOSCIO

## OCA / GOOSE

There are two types of domesticated goose raised in Italy. The first, the smaller of the two, with gray plumage, is only kept for its meat

and comes mainly from Piedmont, Emilia-Romagna, and Padua. The second is the Toulouse type, which can reach a weight of 22 pounds and is especially raised for the production of *fegato grasso* (foie gras). In Italy, the goose used to have a similar status to the pig because, like the pig, the whole bird had a use, whether the meat and fat or the fattened liver and feathers.

In Lombardy and Piedmont, goose is made into a delicious triangular salami called *salame d'oca*. The meat and fat are ground, then stuffed into the skin of the long neck and sewn up tightly. The obvious benefit is that, because it does not include pork, the salami can be eaten by those whose religious belief precludes pork.

Geese are only raised for *fegato grasso* in Lomellina, a small area between Lombardy and Piedmont. This delicious liver of force-fed geese can be sliced and fried or made into delicate and expensive pâtés. The French are well-known for being particularly fond of their *foie gras*, but the ancient Romans also had a fond appreciation for it, and only now has it seen a revival in modern Italian cooking.

Goose is very similar in appearance and taste to duck, the only real culinary difference being that duck can be slightly undercooked, so that it is pink, and can be eaten cold. The fat content of goose means that it is probably only palatable when cooked all the way through and eaten warm. As with duck, goose benefits from being served or cooked with a slightly acidic sauce, to counter-balance this fattiness. Various fruits, such as cherries, blueberries, raspberries, and oranges, can be used, although balsamic vinegar will give the same contrasting tartness. A series of *asprettos*, vinegars made from fruit (see *aceto di frutta*, page 208) are now available to produce the most flavorsome sauces.

In Italy, goose is mainly eaten at Christmas, like turkey and capon. It is roasted or chopped into portions and cooked in a sort of casserole. If

TOP LEFT:
*LUMACHE DI TERRA*

BOTTOM LEFT:
*LUMACHINE*, SMALL
ROMAN SNAILS

ABOVE: *OCA*

you roast a goose, make sure you collect the fat from the roasting tray after it has been cooked because, it solidifies once cold, and is delicious served on toast or used to add flavor to other dishes, such as roast potatoes.

## PALOMBACCIO, COLOMBACCIO / WOOD PIGEON

Wood pigeon has a much higher reputation in Italy than the common pigeon. The flavor of the wood pigeon's very dark, gamy meat is loved by gourmets, who enjoy this bird with equal enthusiasm whether roasted or used in sauces for dressing pasta.

*Colombacci* sometimes mix with their city cousins when they migrate, but they generally prefer to live in the woods and countryside. Farmers in some parts of the country hang up terra-cotta pots on their outside walls where the birds can nest. Of course, this simply makes them easier prey for their landlords. The diet of the wood pigeon consists mostly of corn and this gives their meat a particularly fine wild taste.

Wood pigeons need to be hung for a few days, so they can ripen. After this they are sold unplucked, with their giblets still intact. They need to be plucked carefully and thoroughly cleaned. The liver is especially good, and thus it is worth saving when the bird is drawn. The wood pigeon is generally larger than the ordinary variety, and one bird

makes a fine meal for one person. They are cooked much like ordinary pigeons, as long as you bear in mind that the flesh is best slightly undercooked, to make the most of its juiciness. One curious way of preparing the bird is the Tuscan practice of puréeing the cooked flesh to a paste and spreading this on *crostini* (see *palombacci sui crostini*, see page 60).

## PERNICE / PARTRIDGE

There are three varieties of partridge in Italy. The most sought-after is the red-legged variety (*pernice rossa*), because it has the most delicate flesh and is the only variety that is still completely wild, and is available from specialist suppliers only. The gray-legged variety (*pernice grigia* or *starna*) is less flavorsome, and it is mostly raised on farms and sold commercially. The third type, the yellow-leg, can only be found in Sardinia, is similar to the red-legged variety, and is equally delicious.

Wild partridges should be hung, drawn but unplucked, for 2 to 3 days at least, to allow the meat to tenderize. The best way to cook partridge is to pan-fry the birds briefly to seal the juices, then roast them in a very hot oven for no more than 20 minutes. The heart and livers are also very tasty and are delicious when sautéed, reduced to a course paste, and smeared on toasted bread, with the roasted birds served on top.

### PICCIONE, SEE COLOMBO

## POLLO, POLLASTRELLO, POLLASTRINA / CHICKEN

The chicken is the most common source of meat in the world because it is extremely easy and economical to raise, as it is cheap to feed and quick to grow. The hen produces eggs as well as meat. The term *pollo*, like "chicken," is used for both the hen and cock birds, and *gallo* is the name for a fully grown male, or

cock. Try not to think the Italians barbaric because they eat the pride of a cock, his comb. These delicious *creste di gallo* are sought by quite a few gourmets.

A young, male cock is called *pollastrello*. *Cappone*, or capon, is a castrated rooster, which grows to maturity at between six and eight months, and is sought-after for its delicate meat (see page 49) *Galletto*, or poussin, is a very young rooster which has reached the lowest possible slaughter weight of 1 pound. Due to its tender age, it has very delicate flesh and is usually cooked spatchcocked, that is, opened out and weighted to keep it flat—also known in Italy as *al mattone* (with a brick). I personally do not think the *galletto* worth eating because of its lack of flavor. Older male birds are, however, best boiled because they are particularly tough.

The *gallina*, or hen, is the chicken that produces eggs. After a couple of years of egg-laying on a farm, the hen is destined to end up in a pot as the basis for a good stock. In Italy there is a saying that old chicken makes good broth (*gallina vecchia fa buon brodo*). Chicken stock, made with a 2- to 3-year-old egg-producing hen is widely used in Italian cooking, but the same type of bird boiled whole makes a wonderful *brodo di gallina*, a soup which can be eaten with *tagliolini* or *tortellini*. My memory of chicken will always be strongest in its liquid form as the *brodo* that my mother used to keep hot on the stove for when I returned home from long journeys. It was so soothing and invigorating that fatigue was instantly banished.

To prepare *brodo*, just put a well-blessed hen in a large pan and cover with cold water, add some carrots, celery, and onion, and then simmer over a gentle heat for 2 hours, taking care to skim off the scum as it cooks. Allow to cool, then store in the refrigerator or freeze for future use. The meat, although a little tough, can be eaten separately, and—if from a completely free-range bird—

will have plenty of flavor.

The best chickens are free-range and fed either with corn or other grains, imparting a full, wonderful flavor to the meat, which is not pale white but pinkish—with a yellow skin. In Italy there are special stores just dedicated to *pollame* (poultry). The butchers are very inventive, and in their refrigerated counters you may find oven-ready stuffed breast of chicken—lovely rolled breast filled with ham, garlic, rosemary, and parsley. Other parts are also skilfully prepared for cooking: *spezzatino di pollo*, cubed chicken meat ready to be cooked with tomatoes and peppers; *scaloppine* or *cotolette di pollo*, bread crumbed for frying, a favorite of Lombardy; or *galantina di pollo*, boned chicken stuffed with egg, bread crumbs, spices, and herbs; or *pollo alla cacciatora*, ready to be cooked with wine and mushrooms as in Tuscany. Above all there is usually *pollo arrosto*, chicken stuffed with lemon and rosemary ready for roasting, as they do on the Amalfi coast. See the recipe for *petti di pollo alla pizzaiola*, page 57.

## QUAGLIA / QUAIL
This small, well-camouflaged, beige-brown bird lives wild in fields and woods and is one of the most frequently cooked of the game birds hunted in Italy. As it is easy to raise quail on farms, however, Italians do not rely on wild quail, even if they are bigger and have a natural gamy flavor. The quail has a special place in Italian gastronomy and is much appreciated for its delicate meat and its eggs (see *uova*), which are also used to make delicious dishes.

Farm-raised quail are sold cleaned and fresh, without being hung, ready for cooking. If using such a bird, at least a couple are needed per person, and, unless it is boned and

stuffed, you can eat it with your fingers. Quail can be roasted, stewed, broiled, or even boiled.

## RANE / FROGS
Italians living in the regions of Piedmont, Lombardy, Veneto, and Emilia-Romagna are well acquainted with this animal, which is difficult to categorize as either game, meat, or fish. Frogs live in any area where water is abundant, and in Italy the rice fields of the Po Valley are the perfect place for them. Only the muscular back legs are eaten and these *coscette di rane* are sold pre-cleaned and ready for cooking.

Frogs' legs have a very delicate flavor and thus they are not well suited to a lot of herbs and spices. They are wonderful simply dipped in beaten egg and bread crumbs and then deep-fried or cooked *in umido*, casseroled in olive oil, with a little garlic, parsley, and tomatoes. In the rice region, they also make wonderful risottos.

## RIGAGLIE, FRATTAGLIE / GIBLETS
*Rigaglie di pollo* include the usual *fegatini* (liver), *cuore* (heart), *rognoni* (kidneys), *stomaco* (gizzards), as well as the *uovo* (unborn eggs of the hen) and *granelli* or *testicoli* (testicles) and the cocks' combs or crests. All these bits are particularly loved by Tuscans and Piedmontese, and used in the making of *cibreo di rigaglie* (see page 58) and *finanziera*. Chicken livers are also cooked with wine, herbs, and spices, then chopped and spread on *crostini*.

## SALMI, CIVÉ / COOKING METHOD
*Salmi* and *civé* both come from the French and describe ways of preparing game—especially hare, rabbit, and venison—either by marinating it in its own blood or by adding blood to thicken the sauce at the end of the cooking process. The terms are used confusingly differently from region to region. The principle is the same, however, and generally for *lepre in salmi* (see page 63), the hare is marinated for two days in the blood mixed with good red wine, garlic, thyme, rosemary, squashed juniper berries, crushed peppercorns, cinnamon, sage leaves, and bay leaves before being braised. The sauce is then strained, reduced, and served with the tender meat, usually accompanied by polenta.

### STARNA, SEE PERNICE

## TACCHINO, DINDO, PITO / TURKEY
The turkey is especially raised for the celebration of Christmas in Europe and Thanksgiving as well in America. This bird was introduced into Europe from the West Indies at the beginning of the sixteenth century, hence its other Italian name, *dindo*, meaning "from the Indies." Turkeys are huge and have an incredible breast, which can either be carved from the whole, cooked bird or removed and cooked separately like a veal roast.

Most turkeys are intensively farmed and can be obtained the entire year round, while the more flavorsome free-range variety can often only be enjoyed at the Thanksgiving and Christmas periods, when they are offered at a higher price. It takes about 2 months for a free-range turkey to grow to the ideal weight of 9 to 10 pounds for the female and 13 to 16 pounds for the male, when its meat is at its most tender and tasty.

In Italy, turkey breast is mostly eaten sliced and prepared like veal, i.e. as *scaloppine*, *involtini*, or simply *alla milanese* (bread-

LEFT: *QUAGLIA*

crumbed and fried). It is only in Lombardy that the whole bird is boned, then stuffed with fruit, ground pork, ground giblets, and chestnuts for roasting.

## TORDO /
### THRUSH
There has been a loud outcry abroad about Italians eating this wonderful migrating bird. In a time when everyone is concerned about the preservation of wildlife, Italy has now joined in banning the hunting of these birds. In Montalcino, where a festival celebrating the birds used to take place, the thrushes are now replaced with quails, although it is still called the *Sagra del Tordo*.

## UOVA / EGGS
Eggs are very versatile in the kitchen as they can be boiled, baked, scrambled, fried, and poached, prepared in omelets (see *frittata di carciofi*, page 128) and used in cakes, pasta, custards, ice cream, and mayonnaise, scrambled in soups, or used to thicken sauces. Perhaps the most remarkable dish in which eggs are used is *zabaglione* (see page 65), for which the yolks are beaten in a bain-marie with sugar and marsala, sherry, or Moscato to make one of the most desirable desserts. Italians use eggs a lot but, curiously, seldom at breakfast. At Easter-time, eggs feature prominently as symbols of new life.

*Uova di anatra*, ducks' eggs, with their distinctive pale blue color, can be distinguished easily from other eggs. They have a very rich, pale yellow yolk with an intense flavor.

Ducks' eggs can be used in place of hens' eggs, but the stronger taste gives a more powerful result.

*Uova di gabbiano*, gulls' eggs, are only available seasonally, as they are from wild birds. They were very highly esteemed by the ancient Romans for their purifying qualities and because, unlike other seabird eggs, they do not taste of fish. Gulls' eggs are used in a similar way to quails' eggs. They also have a speckled shell, although they are larger. Their flavor is very delicate and they are used in making *antipasti* or simply eaten hard-boiled with salt.

*Uova d'oca*, goose eggs, are among the most sought-after by gourmets, who appreciate the large size and the intense, almost oily, taste. The color of the shell is

dirty white and the eggs are quite large, almost three times the size of the average hens' egg. The culinary use of the goose egg is a little limited because of its intense flavor, and they do have to be used when still very fresh.

*Uova di quaglia*, quails' eggs, are the only other type of bird's egg to be commercially produced. The tiny egg is appreciated both for its flavor and its decorative qualities. When boiled, it cooks solid in about $2^1/_2$ minutes, and I particularly like to use it with recipes that include truffles (see page 65).

*Uova di tacchino*, turkeys' eggs, are similar in size to ducks' eggs, but have white shells finely speckled with brown. They are mostly used like hens' eggs, but are difficult to find unless you know a friendly farmer who can supply them.

Eggs have to be fresh to be good, and those laid by free-range chickens, fed on corn, are the best. The way to judge the freshness of an egg is to place it in 2 cups of water with a scant $^1/_2$ cup of salt dissolved in it. If the egg sinks to the bottom of the bowl it is very fresh, probably only a day or two old. If it sinks a little way below the surface it means it is five or six days old, and if it floats on the surface it could be ten or more days old. If its bigger end floats to the surface first, it is very old indeed and I would not use it.

As the shells of eggs are porous, eggs can absorb strong scents and flavors, including that of the truffle. If you store the two together, the egg will have the delicate flavor of the truffle, a great delicacy.

# QUAGLIE ALLO SPIEDO

QUAILS ON A SKEWER

## FOR 4

8 MEATY QUAILS

10 PIECES *PANE DI CAMPAGNA*
(COUNTRY-STYLE WHITE BREAD),
ABOUT 1¹/₂ INCH SQUARE AND
1¹/₂ INCH THICK

10 THIN SLICES *PANCETTA*, THE SAME
SHAPE AS THE BREAD SQUARES

FOR THE BASTING LIQUID:

4 TABLESPOONS OLIVE OIL

JUICE OF 1 LEMON

1 TABLESPOON FINELY CHOPPED FLAT-LEAF
PARSLEY

2 TABLESPOONS DRY MARSALA

1 TEASPOON HONEY

1 GARLIC CLOVE, MINCED

SALT AND PEPPER

*This Tuscan dish used to be made with a variety of birds. Nowadays the hunting of many birds is restricted but good-quality, farm-raised quail make a fine substitute.*

Preheat the oven to 475° F. Clean the quails and remove and discard the livers if necessary. Roast the birds on a rack in a pan for 15 minutes. Remove from the oven and thread the birds onto 2 long skewers, alternating them with the bread and pancetta.

Mix all the ingredients for the basting liquid, adding plenty of salt and pepper. Cook the quails over a wood-fired or charcoal grill for 10 to 15 minutes, basting their breasts regularly with the liquid and turning the skewers often to prevent burning. When they are golden brown, serve with the bread *croûtes*, which will have collected some of the juices from the birds, and with polenta (see page 173).

# ANATRA ARROSTO AL PROSCIUTTO

ROAST DUCK WITH PARMA HAM

**FOR 4**

1 MEATY FREE-RANGE DUCK, WEIGHING
  ABOUT 4½ POUNDS
4 SLICES PARMA HAM, WITH PLENTY
  OF FAT
1 GARLIC CLOVE, CHOPPED
SMALL SPRIG ROSEMARY
PINCH FRESHLY GRATED NUTMEG
SALT AND PEPPER
OLIVE OIL

*This is a specialty of Emilia-Romagna, where both ducks and Parma ham are local produce.*

Preheat the oven to 400° F. Singe the duck over an open flame to remove the down, if necessary. Grind together the ham, garlic, and rosemary to make a paste, then season with the nutmeg and plenty of freshly ground black pepper. Rub the duck with a little oil and sprinkle with salt. Spread the paste over the breast and put the duck in a roasting pan. Cover with foil and roast for 1 hour, then remove the foil and cook for another 30 minutes, until the skin is crisp and golden.

When carving, distribute a little of the crunchy crust on each plate.

# PETTI DI POLLO ALLA PIZZAIOLA

CHICKEN BREAST IN PIZZAIOLA SAUCE

**FOR 4**

4 SKINLESS BONELESS CHICKEN BREAST
  HALVES (2 WHOLE BREASTS)
4 TABLESPOONS EXTRA-VIRGIN OLIVE OIL
2 GARLIC CLOVES, FINELY CHOPPED
1 TABLESPOON SALTED CAPERS, SOAKED
  IN WATER FOR 10 MINUTES, THEN
  DRAINED
1 TEASPOON CHOPPED FLAT-LEAF PARSLEY
2 ANCHOVY FILLETS, CHOPPED
2 CUPS TOMATO PULP (SEE
  PAGE 118)
1 TABLESPOON OREGANO LEAVES
SALT AND PEPPER

*Pizzaiola sauce originally came from Naples and contains more or less the same ingredients as pizza topping, hence the name.*

Fry the chicken breasts in the olive oil for 8 to 10 minutes on each side, until brown and cooked through. Add the garlic, capers, parsley, and anchovies to the pan and fry briefly, then stir in the tomatoes, oregano, and salt and pepper. Simmer for 5 minutes and then serve.

# CIBREO DI RIGAGLIE

GIBLET STEW

**FOR 4**

4 LARGE COCKS' COMBS (SEE *RIGAGLIE*,
    PAGE 54)

GIBLETS OF 6 CHICKENS—LIVERS,
    HEARTS, GIZZARDS, AND, IF AVAILABLE,
    *GRANELLI* (TESTICLES)

4 TABLESPOONS BUTTER

ABOUT 1 CUP CHICKEN STOCK

2 EGG YOLKS

1 TABLESPOON FLOUR

JUICE OF 1 LEMON

SALT AND PEPPER

*This very delicate dish uses the variety meats of chicken and something that is rather difficult to come by now—the cock's comb. You may be lucky enough to find some in Chinese food stores, as Chinese cooks commonly use every part of the chicken. A similar dish is made in Piedmont, called* finanziera di pollo.

Clean the cocks' combs and put them in a saucepan of cold water. Bring to a boil, then drain the combs and peel them, discarding the tough coarse skin. Cut them into chunks. Remove all the impurities from the livers, hearts, and gizzards and cut them into smaller chunks.

Heat the butter in a pan and cook the combs and the hearts until tender, adding some stock from time to time to prevent the mixture from becoming too dry. Check with a point of a small knife to see if the meat is done, then add the livers, gizzards, and *granelli*, if using, and cook for another 10 minutes.

Mix the egg yolks with the flour, lemon juice, and some salt and pepper. Stir in a little of the stock from the pan, then pour this mixture onto the *rigaglie*. Mix well and serve immediately.

# FEGATO GRASSO AL BALSAMICO

*FOIE GRAS* WITH BALSAMIC SAUCE

**FOR 4**

2 CUPS STRONG RED WINE

1 TABLESPOON SUGAR

1 TABLESPOON BALSAMIC VINEGAR (NOT
    TOO OLD)

8 FRESH *FOIE GRAS* SLICES WITHOUT THE
    SKIN, WEIGHING 1³/₄ OUNCES EACH

1¹/₂ TABLESPOONS BUTTER

SALT AND PEPPER

FLOUR FOR DREDGING

*From the Lomellina, between Lombardy and Piedmont, comes this recipe made with local fresh* foie gras. *Although* foie gras *is highly valued by the French, it plays only a minor part in Italian gastronomy. However, gourmets adore this dish, which I modified and adapted a little after seeing the enthusiasm with which the customers in my restaurant ate it.*

Boil the wine with the sugar until it has reduced to a third of its original volume and is beginning to thicken. Add the balsamic vinegar and some salt and pepper and mix well; the sauce should be thick and dark.

Dredge the slices of *foie gras* in flour and fry briefly in the butter until brown on each side. Place the *foie gras* on serving plates and pour the sauce next to it.

# FAGIANO AL TARTUFO DI NORCIA

PHEASANT WITH TRUFFLE, NORCIA-STYLE

FOR 4

2 PHEASANTS
3¹/₂ TABLESPOONS BUTTER
1 SMALL GLASS DRY WHITE WINE
SALT AND PEPPER
ABOUT 3 OUNCES BLACK SUMMER
    TRUFFLE

*A noble treatment for a noble bird, this remarkably simple combination of ingredients makes a superior dish that is hard to beat.*

Preheat the oven to 350° F. Roast the pheasants for 30 minutes; they should not be completely cooked. Cut off the breasts and thighs and set aside. (The rest of the pheasant can be used to make stock.)

Melt the butter in a large pan, then add the wine and some salt and pepper. Put the pheasant breasts and thighs in the pan and heat through for 1 or 2 minutes, just to finish the cooking. Grate the truffle over the meat and serve immediately.

# PALOMBACCI SUI CROSTINI

WOOD PIGEON ON TOAST

*Now famous throughout the world,* crostini *are a type of canapé consisting of slices of toasted bread which serve as a base for all sorts of spreads. They are very popular topped with liver, but here is a special Tuscan version made with wood pigeon.*

**MAKES 12** *CROSTINI*

**3** WOOD PIGEON, CLEANED, WITH LIVERS
**12** SLICES *PANE DI CAMPAGNA*
    (COUNTRY-STYLE WHITE BREAD)
**12** CAPERS

**FOR THE MARINADE:**
**2** GLASSES RED WINE
**4** TABLESPOONS OLIVE OIL
A FEW SAGE LEAVES
**1** TABLESPOON SALTED CAPERS, SOAKED IN WATER
    FOR **10** MINUTES, THEN DRAINED
**1** GARLIC CLOVE
**3** ANCHOVY FILLETS
SALT AND PEPPER

Blend all the ingredients for the marinade in a blender and pour into a nonmetallic bowl. Add the pigeons and leave to marinate for a few hours.

Preheat the oven to 425° F. Remove the birds from the marinade and roast for 30 minutes. Leave to cool and then remove all the flesh and the livers from the birds and discard the bones. Put the marinade in a saucepan over medium heat, add the meat and livers, and cook for 10 minutes, stirring from time to time. Transfer to a blender and blend to a paste, then leave to cool.

Toast the bread, spread with the paste, and decorate each piece with a caper.

# CIRIOLE AL RAGÙ DI CINGHIALE

## *CIRIOLE* PASTA WITH WILD BOAR SAUCE

**FOR 4**

3 TABLESPOONS VIRGIN OLIVE OIL
1 ONION, CHOPPED
1 GARLIC CLOVE, CRUSHED
10 JUNIPER BERRIES
PINCH FRESHLY GRATED NUTMEG
PINCH GROUND CINNAMON
4 BAY LEAVES
2 TABLESPOONS TOMATO PASTE
1¹/₂ POUNDS GROUND WILD BOAR
1 CUP RED WINE
²/₃ CUP CHICKEN STOCK
SALT AND PEPPER
1 POUND *CIRIOLE* PASTA (SEE
    *BIGOLI*, PAGE 144)
FRESHLY GRATED PECORINO CHEESE
    (OPTIONAL)

*This wonderful dish is from Umbria, where wild boar are at home (until the hunters find them). It is a really delightful combination of strongly flavored ragù and robust pasta. Wild boar sounds exotic, but it is now available from specialist butchers and some supermarkets.*

Heat the oil in a large pan, add the onion, garlic, spices, and bay leaves, and fry gently until the onion is softened. Add the tomato paste, meat, wine, and stock and simmer gently for about 1¹/₂ hours. Season to taste with salt and pepper. Cook the pasta in boiling salted water until *al dente*, then drain. Add to the sauce, mix well, and serve sprinkled with some Pecorino cheese if desired.

# CONIGLIO AFFOGATO ALLA LIGURE

RABBIT STEW, LIGURIAN STYLE

### FOR 4

1 RABBIT, WEIGHING ABOUT 3$^1$/$_4$ POUNDS,
   CUT INTO CHUNKS

FLOUR FOR DREDGING

$^1$/$_2$ CUP LIGURIAN EXTRA-
   VIRGIN OLIVE OIL

1 LARGE ONION, THINLY SLICED

1 GARLIC CLOVE, COARSELY CHOPPED

SPRIG ROSEMARY

A FEW SAGE LEAVES

SMALL SPRIG THYME

ABOUT 24 TASTY BLACK OLIVES,
   PREFERABLY TAGGIASCA

2 GLASSES DRY WHITE WINE

8 TABLESPOONS TOMATO PULP (SEE
   PAGE 118)

SALT AND PEPPER

A LITTLE STOCK IF NECESSARY

*Rabbit is very much loved all over Italy and, as usual, each region has its own recipes. The Ligurian version uses local herbs and, naturally, plenty of olive oil.*

Wash and pat dry the chunks of rabbit, them dredge them in flour. Heat the oil in a large casserole and brown the rabbit on all sides. Add the onion, garlic, herbs, and olives, reduce the heat, and cook until softened. Stir in the wine and bring to a boil to allow some of the alcohol to evaporate. Add the tomato pulp and salt and pepper to taste, and cook over medium heat for 1$^1$/$_2$ hours, until the rabbit is tender. Add a little stock if the mixture becomes too dry. Adjust the seasoning to taste and then serve. Delicious accompanied with polenta (see page 173).

# LEPRE IN SALMI

JUGGED HARE

**FOR 6**

1 LARGE HARE, WEIGHING ABOUT
6¹/₂ POUNDS, BLOOD RESERVED
SCANT ¹/₂ CUP ALL-PURPOSE FLOUR
SCANT ¹/₂ CUP BUTTER
1 ONION, VERY FINELY CHOPPED
3¹/₂ OUNCES *PANCETTA*, DICED
7 OUNCES CALVES' LIVER, CUT INTO
SMALL STRIPS
3 TABLESPOONS BRANDY
1³/₄ OUNCES UNSWEETENED CHOCOLATE
SALT AND PEPPER

**FOR THE MARINADE:**

1 (750 ML) BOTTLE STRONG RED WINE,
SUCH AS BAROLO
1 CARROT, FINELY DICED
1 ONION, FINELY CHOPPED
4 CELERY RIBS, FINELY DICED
1 GARLIC CLOVE, SMASHED
A FEW SPRIGS THYME
A FEW SPRIGS MARJORAM
A FEW SAGE LEAVES
A FEW BAY LEAVES
10 JUNIPER BERRIES
1 TEASPOON BLACK PEPPERCORNS,
LIGHTLY CRUSHED

*A classic of northern cuisine, this is usually served with polenta, while the sauce is served separately with* pappardelle.

Mix together all the ingredients for the marinade. Cut the hare into large chunks, add to the marinade, then cover and leave in the refrigerator for 24 hours.

Remove the chunks of hare from the marinade and pat dry, then dredge them in some of the flour. Heat the butter in a large cast-iron skillet and fry the pieces of meat, a few at a time, until browned all over. Remove from the pan and set aside. Reduce the heat, add the onion and *pancetta* to the pan, and fry until the onion begins to color. Return the meat to the pan together with the blood, calves' liver, and the marinade. Cover and cook gently for 2 hours or until the meat is tender.

Remove the pieces of hare and liver from the pan. Strain the sauce through a fine sieve and discard the solids. Mix together the brandy and just enough of the remaining flour to make a paste. Put the meat and the strained liquid back in the pan and bring to a boil. Whisk in the flour and brandy paste a little at a time to thicken. Let it boil for a minute or two, then add the chocolate, allow it to dissolve, and season with salt and pepper to taste.

Serve the hare with polenta (see page 173) and the sauce with pappardelle. Hare cooked like this can be kept for a couple of days.

# LUMACHINE AL SUGO

SNAILS IN TOMATO SAUCE

**FOR 4**

2¹/₄ POUNDS SMALL SNAILS,
POSSIBLY STILL DORMANT OR CLOSED
4 TABLESPOONS OLIVE OIL
1 GARLIC CLOVE, FINELY CHOPPED
1 CHILI PEPPER, FINELY CHOPPED
1 TABLESPOON COARSELY CHOPPED FLAT-
LEAF PARSLEY
1³/₄ CUPS TOMATO PULP (SEE PAGE 118)
2 BASIL LEAVES
SALT AND PEPPER

*The small snails collected in southern Italy in autumn are best for this dish. They are a real gastronomical amusement. If you manage to get small snails, they will not need purging and cleaning.*

Wash the snails thoroughly. Heat the oil in a pan, add the garlic, chili, and parsley and fry for a few minutes. Add the tomatoes, basil leaves, and snails, then cover and cook gently for 40 minutes. Season with salt and pepper to taste and serve with pins to remove the snails from their shells.

# FILETTO DI CAPRIOLO AL BAROLO

VENISON TENDERLOIN IN BAROLO WINE

FOR 6

1³/₄ POUNDS VENISON TENDERLOIN FROM
    A LARGE DEER
FLOUR FOR DREDGING
3¹/₂ TABLESPOONS BUTTER
A FEW SLICES WHITE TRUFFLE (OPTIONAL)

FOR THE MARINADE:

1 (750 ML) BOTTLE GOOD BAROLO WINE
4 TABLESPOONS EXTRA-VIRGIN OLIVE OIL
A FEW JUNIPER BERRIES
A FEW BAY LEAVES
SMALL SPRIG ROSEMARY
1 ONION, THINLY SLICED
3 OR 4 CLOVES
PINCH FRESHLY GRATED NUTMEG
SALT AND PEPPER

*This is a typical recipe from northern Italy, where it is possible to find venison in specialist stores.*

Mix together all the ingredients for the marinade. Trim the meat of gristle and skin, then add it to the marinade, cover, and leave to marinate for at least 12 hours.

Remove the meat and pat dry, then cut it into medallions ³/₄ inch thick. Put the marinade in a pan and bring to a boil, then lower the heat and boil until reduced to a third of its original volume. Pass through a fine sieve and keep warm.

Dredge the medallions in flour and fry in the butter for 3 minutes on each side; they should be rare and tender. Serve very hot with the sauce, together with polenta (see page 173), sprinkled with a few slices of white truffle if desired.

# RANE ALLA GHIOTTONA

FROGS' LEGS IN TARRAGON CREAM SAUCE

FOR 4

2¹/₄ POUNDS FROGS' LEGS, CLEANED
FLOUR FOR DREDGING
SCANT ¹/₂ CUP BUTTER
JUICE OF 1 LEMON
¹/₃ CUP DRY WHITE WINE
1 TEASPOON TOMATO PASTE
SALT AND PEPPER
4 TABLESPOONS HEAVY CREAM
1 TABLESPOON VERY FINELY CHOPPED
    TARRAGON

*Frogs are served with risotto, with pasta, and in soup, mostly in one area of Italy where these animals are abundant: Vercelli, Novara, Pavia, Milan, Padua, and all the other cities lined up along the Pianura Padana, the Po flat where the rice fields are.*

Dredge the frogs' legs in flour. Heat the butter in a large pan and fry the frogs' legs for 10 minutes, until brown on each side. Add the lemon juice, white wine, tomato paste, and some salt and pepper and bring to a boil, stirring to loosen the browned bits on the bottom of the pan. Stir in the heavy cream and tarragon and cook for a further 4 minutes, then serve with rice.

# UOVA AL TARTUFO

TRUFFLED EGGS

**FOR 4**

BUTTER FOR GREASING

8 EGGS

8 TABLESPOONS HEAVY CREAM

SALT

ABOUT 1½ OUNCES WHITE TRUFFLE (OR MORE)

*This is one of the most elegant and refined of Piedmontese dishes, and can be served as a first course at the most elegant of dinner parties, but, because of its simplicity, is equally suitable for a lesser occasion.*

Preheat the oven to 350° F. Grease 4 large ramekins with butter. Break 2 eggs into each one and pour over the heavy cream. Season with salt and then place in the oven. Start checking after 5 minutes to see if the whites have set. Cut the white truffle into slivers and scatter over the eggs. Serve immediately, with bread.

# ZABAGLIONE GELATO

ZABAGLIONE ICE CREAM

**FOR 6 TO 8**

16 TO 18 FREE-RANGE EGG YOLKS

HEAPING 1¼ CUPS SUPERFINE SUGAR

¾ CUP *MOSCATO PASSITO DI PANTELLERIA* OR MARSALA (SEE PAGES 312–13)

2 CUPS WHIPPING CREAM

*Eggs are a complete food, and this recipe in their honor is always a success.*

Put the egg yolks and sugar in a large bowl and whisk with a hand-held electric beater or a whisk until foamy and doubled in volume. Put the bowl over a saucepan of gently simmering water, making sure the water does not touch the base of the bowl. Continue to whisk until the mixture is very thick and has a homogeneous, creamy, but not crumbly texture. It is crucial not to let it overheat or you will end up with scrambled eggs.

Leave to cool, then fold in the Moscato or Marsala. Whip the cream until it forms soft peaks and then fold it into the mixture. Place in an ice-cream maker and freeze. If you do not have an ice-cream maker, transfer the mixture to a shallow bowl and place in the freezer for about 1 hour, until it is beginning to solidify around the edges. Whisk it well with a fork, then remove from the freezer. Repeat this process 3 times and then freeze until firm.

# FRESH & CURED MEATS

## CARNI E SALUMI

Italians eat 160 pounds of meat per person per annum, and more than a third of that is eaten in the form of pork. This is, of course, balanced by a large quantity of fresh vegetables and fruit. As is to be expected from the heartland of the Mediterranean, the average Italian meal, divided into anything from three to five courses, rarely includes large pieces of meat. A notable exception is the famous *bistecca alla fiorentina*, a huge T-bone steak that weighs at least 1 pound per portion. The beef used for this dish comes from special beef cattle raised in a valley near Florence, the Val di Chiana. The steak is so tender that it is usually broiled and eaten rare, an exception for Italians who prefer their meat to be slightly more thoroughly cooked.

In Piedmont, cattle are raised to make other local specialties like *bollito misto* (mixed boiled meats), *brasato al barolo* (topside braised in red wine), *insalata di carne cruda* (a special salad of raw beef), and *carne all'Albese*, (a raw meat salad served with white truffle from Alba). The cattle used to provide meat for these dishes are known as *sanato* or *vitellone*, which, although more mature and developed than veal calves, are still fairly young, with very tender flesh.

The farming practices for some animals, especially that of veal calves, cause much controversy. I must say that, while I agree that humans have to be fed, I think it is possible to be more scrupulous about the manner in which the farming is done. Veal has always been popular with chefs for its short cooking time and its blandness, qualities that allow the meat to act as a backdrop to the flavors cooked with it. Personally, I prefer a firmer meat with a more pronounced taste.

In Italy there is no indication that veal calves, which produce an appreciably pale meat while still milk-fed, are kept in narrow crates to avoid exercise. Veal calves are still kept with the mothers in the majority of cases. The "industrialization" of meat production is avoided, if possible, because Italians like good meat—even if it is a little more expensive. The best beef animals are fed with hay or with a mixture of grains and corn-based fodder in winter, and fresh grass in summer.

Pigs are a different matter as, unfortunately, they are raised in barns to fatten them up. They are, however, fed on a mixture of whey (a by-product of Parmesan cheese) and a mixture of grains. In Emilia-Romagna, some of the best pigs are fed on acorns to achieve the particularly flavored meat that distinguishes Parma ham from others.

Many Italians still keep animals if they can, and the pig is the most popular, both for its taste and because the whole animal can be used—either for fresh meat and sausages, for salamis, or for lard. When I was a boy, during the War, my family was given two suckling pigs. We housed the piglets in an especially made hut at the end of a disused railroad line, and when they were fully grown and fattened my father called in the local *norcino*, or pork butcher. One of the pigs had to be offered to everyone in the village, a rule made by all the villagers when war broke out. With the remaining pig, my mother made salamis, lard, and hams.

From Bolzano in Alto Adige, where speck is produced in the Austrian tradition, to Sicily, where a dessert is made with pork blood, every region has its customs and recipes for pork. Pigs are usually slaughtered in winter, with much local celebrating.

One region that has made pork famous is Emilia-Romagna, where Parma ham and many other preserved meats are made, including salamis, mortadella, and *culatello di zibello*. These products, especially *mortadella di Bologna*, *pancetta*, and *zampone* (stuffed pigs' trotters), are enjoyed all over Italy. Calabria also has some specialties, including

TOP LEFT: HARVESTING HAY TO FEED THE CATTLE AT PRATOROTONDO

BOTTOM LEFT: CATTLEMAN NOE BOVO IN THE AOSTA VALLEY

**ABOVE: A HERD OF PEZZATANERA CATTLE GRAZING THE SPRING GRASS IN THE AOSTA VALLEY**

*salsiccie piccanti* (spicy sausages), while Piedmont has *salam d'la duja*, salami preserved covered in lard in a terra-cotta pot. Another specialty is *porchetta* (stuffed piglet), a dish much loved by the Romans—ancient and modern.

As well as pork, beef, and veal, Italians also eat lamb, goat, and sometimes horse and donkey meat. Lamb and goat are most popular in southern Italy, where it easy to raise them. Some people believe that horse meat is particularly healthy and that the best *mortadella* is made with donkey meat. Only a few specialist stores now sell equine

meat and these are very strictly controlled.

Choosing fresh meat, is a special skill, but one that should be developed by anyone who wants to eat just a little of the very best meat. I remember being sent to buy meat when I was a child. I returned home with it proudly, only to be sent straight back to the butcher as it was not a good enough cut. I learned an important lesson then — not only to be sure of what I was being given, but also to know what constitutes a good cut. It is worth finding a good butcher to help you. Pay more and eat less, that is my recommendation.

# A-Z of Fresh & Cured Meats

**ABBACCHIO, SEE AGNELLO**

**AFFETTATO / SLICED MEATS**
This term covers all preserved meats, but is mostly used for pork products like prosciutto and salami. However, items as varied as *bresaola*, *mucetta*, and wild boar may be included in the *antipasto* of *affettato misto* so beloved of many Italians.

**AGNELLO, AGNELLONE, ABBACCHIO / LAMB, MUTTON**
Lamb is a typically Italian meat, and has been eaten in Italy through the ages. The tradition of raising lamb has been kept alive in the central and southern regions and the islands, where the pastures give the meat a particularly good flavor. Because of the hard work involved, however, the farming of sheep for their meat has declined in the last generation.

*Agnello da latte* (called *abbacchio* by the Romans) are milk-fed lambs slaughtered at 3 or 4 weeks old, when their meat is very pale and tender. *Agnello* are slightly older lambs,

between 9 and 12 weeks old, weighing up to 30 pounds. They are both milk-fed and reared on pasture, and their flesh is tender and flavorsome. Lambs of this size are often cooked whole on a spit. *Agnellone* are killed at about 6 months old and have very tasty meat which is mostly used in stews and *ragùs*.

*Castrato* or *montone*, the meat of a castrated ewe, is more popular in southern Italy where they love a stronger taste of lamb. The meat is of an intense red color and not so lean. It is ideal for stews but is also roasted if the animal is not too old, or even broiled with rosemary and basted with olive oil and lemon juice. *Pecora*, meat from the adult ewe, is used in the same way, but will be a little tougher. Mutton has a good flavor, but is only eaten in the South where many recipes were developed for its use in stews.

*Abbacchio* is also the name given to a dish traditional in Rome at Easter. The lamb is cut into pieces and cooked in a sort of egg-and-lemon sauce, probably based on the Greek recipe *avgolemono*. One of my favorite lamb recipes, *agnello ripieno* (stuffed breast of lamb, see page 93), comes from Campania. The most popular flavorings with lamb in Italy are garlic, of course, thyme, rosemary, and mint.

Little baby lamb cutlets, called *bistecchine* or *costolette*, are often broiled, when they are called *scottadito* ("finger burn") because they are usually eaten with the hands.

**ANIMELLE / SWEETBREADS**
Sweetbreads are the thymus glands, and only those of young calves and lambs are normally eaten. They are used all over Italy, either sautéed, deep-fried in a bread-crumb coating, or incorporated in *ragùs*, such as Bolognese. They are also popular as

stuffings for various items, including ravioli, and as part of *fritto misto*. The mild taste of sweetbreads is usually paired with lemon juice, and sometimes sage leaves.

To prepare sweetbreads, they must first be soaked in cold, acidulated water for several hours, changing the water fairly often to eliminate any blood and impurities. They are then blanched for a few minutes in boiling water so that the nerves and veins can be trimmed easily and discarded.

**ARISTA / PORK LOIN**
This Tuscan pork specialty consists of an oven-roasted loin on the bone, which has been larded with rosemary, fennel seeds, and garlic. It has become popular all over Italy. There is a version of the joint without the bone, for slicing by machine in good delicatessens.

**ASINO, SEE CAVALLO**

**BATTUTO / MEAT SAUCE BASE**
*Battuto*, meaning beaten, consists of lard, *pancetta*, or ham mixed with flavorings like rosemary, garlic, onion, and chili until it resembles a fine creamy paste. It is used as a base for soup, stews, or sauces, or can be smeared on top of roasts to give extra flavor.

**BISTECCA, BISTECCHINE / BEEF STEAKS AND CUTLETS**
A *bistecca* is a slice of tender meat—with or without bones, depending on where you are in Italy—suitable either for frying or broiling. The most famous and succulent of all Italian steaks is the *bistecca alla fiorentina* (Florentine-style steak), a T-bone cut from the Chiana cow, raised in the Val di Chiana near Florence. This steak is much larger than the sirloin and tenderloin, weighing at least 2 pounds and about $1^1/_2$ to 2 inches thick. Brushed with olive oil and sprinkled with salt, it is grilled over charcoal for only a few minutes on each side to allow the flavor and tenderness of the meat to come through. *Bistecchine* are cutlets from young calves and other smaller animals such as lambs, goats, and pigs.

**BOCCONCINO / VEAL PIECES**
From the diminutive of *boccone*,

LEFT: A PIEDMONTESE ANTIPASTO CONSISTING OF *COPPA*, *PROSCIUTTO*, AND *MORTADELLA*, WITH SWEET-AND-SOUR ONIONS, PRESERVED WILD MUSHROOMS, AND ARTICHOKE HEARTS

literally "mouthful," *bocconcini* can be made of many things. *Bocconcini di vitello*, for instance, are small escalopes of veal containing various fillings like cheese, prosciutto, eggs, and herbs and braised in a sauce (see *involtini*). *Bocconcini* are also tiny mozzarella cheeses (see page 238).

## BOLLITO MISTO / MIXED BOILED MEATS

This is one of the grandest dishes of northern Italian gastronomy, native to the regions that traditionally raise beef, veal, chicken, and pork. Piedmont, Lombardy, Emilia-Romagna, and Veneto are all famous for this dish, and in some regions is sometimes called simply *bollito* or *lesso* (from *lessare*, to boil). The mixture should contain at least four different types of meat, including some sausages that are cooked separately (see recipe, page 92).

Typical meats for this dish include brisket of beef, veal cheek and breast, capon or chicken, tongue, pork belly, and stuffed or plain pigs' trotters. When everything is cooked, the meats are sliced and served with some of the flavoring vegetables and some sauces. In Piedmont, *salsa verde*, or green sauce (page 224), is served with the *bollito*, while in Lombardy and Emilia-Romagna a *salsa rossa*, or red sauce, based on onions, tomato, and chili, as well as some *mostarda di Cremona* (page 269), accompany the dish.

The town of Carrú in Piedmont is famous for the celebration of *Bue Grasso* every December. As the climax of a festival to find the finest beef animals, the prize awarded is a big pot of *bollito*, and this is said to be the best in the region.

## BOVINO / COW

Pezzata Nera (Black Dappled), the Italian Frisona and the Bruna Alpina are the main cattle varieties used for Italian beef, although such herds are also raised for their milk. The Piemontese, Chiana, Marchigiana, and Romagnola are, however, raised exclusively for their meat.

*Vitelli* are young calves fed on

milk, and as a result they have very pale meat. *Vitellone* is the meat of an animal 1 to 2 years old, that has not borne its first calf. *Manzo* is a 3-year-old castrated bullock or a heifer that has not borne its first calf. Once it is aged over 4 years the *manzo* is called *bue*, equivalent to ox. *Toro* and *vacca* are the terms for the adult bull and cow.

All of these types of meat are used in different ways in the kitchen. Regionally, there are also huge differences, not only in the types of meat but also in the cuts. There are national guidelines to beef cuts, which nobody observes because they are very happy to name the cuts in their own dialect, and the same piece of meat is often known by quite different names in different parts of the country.

## BRACIOLE, BRACIOLINE, BRACIOLETTE

This name describes a different cut or dish depending on which part of Italy you are in. In the northern regions *braciole* is used to describe a cut of meat similar to the cutlet, which can be grilled over charcoal or stewed. In the South, the same term is used to describe slices of meat, such as beef or pork, rolled around fillings and then usually braised in a tomato sauce. See *involtino* and *bocconcino*.

## BRASATO, BRACIATO / BRAISED BEEF

These terms are used to describe casseroles of beef slowly braised in wine with carrots, onions, celery, and spices. *Brasato*, typical of northern Italy (especially Piedmont and Lombardy), is usually made with *manzo* (mature beef), and takes

about 2 hours to cook. It is normally eaten in slices, accompanied by vegetables.

## BRESAOLA / AIR-DRIED BEEF

The Valtellina Valley in Lombardy has a long tradition of curing and air-drying beef, which is then thinly cut and sprinkled with lemon juice and oil at the last minute for serving as an *antipasto*. Round in shape and only lightly salted, *bresaola* is similar to the Swiss *Bündner-fleisch*. It may have been invented to provide a source of protein when fresh meat was scarce.

## BRODO DI CARNE / BEEF CONSOMMÉ

To make beef consommé, the beef has to be boiled until the liquid is greatly reduced, and it is this that gives it its name—*consommé*, French for consumed or reduced. *Brodo* is a very popular Italian soup, but it can also be used as stock in any type of cooking. To make it, mince some beef to make it easier to extract all the juices and flavors from it. Place the minced beef in cold water with a bay leaf, some celery leaves, finely chopped carrots and onions, and some whole peppercorns. Bring to a boil and simmer for 2 to 3 hours until the *brodo* has reduced. The broth is then strained, and can be clarified.

For clarification, it is first passed through a fine sieve, then it is brought to a boil again and some beaten egg white is added. The solidifying egg white collects all the impurities, leaving a very clear liquid once stained. Season as necessary.

## BUDELLO / INTESTINE

Intestines are mostly used as skins and containers for salami. The gut of of cows, lamb, and pigs are those most frequently used by butchers, but the intestines of very young lambs are also popular because, as the animals have only been fed on milk, their guts are relatively clean. A part of veal intestines produces tripe, one of the best-loved offals in Italy, for which there are many recipes (see *trippa*, page 85).

In Sicily, a special dish called *stigghiole* is prepared with the intestines of milk-fed lambs. They are flavored with spices, then threaded on wooden skewers and grilled over charcoal. I bought some from a roadside vendor in Sicily, and my wife Priscilla, usually a little reserved about such foods, agreed that it was delicious. Similar specialties can also be found in Puglia, Calabria, and Sardinia.

**BUE, SEE BOVINO**

**BÜSECCA, SEE TRIPPA**

## CACCIATORI, CACCIATORINI / SALAMI

Every Italian loves freshly cut *salami* and *cacciatore*, weighing about 7 ounces, or the smaller *cacciatorini*, about 3 ounces, are the ideal *salami* for picnics. Traditionally these come from Piedmont and Lombardy, and are made from coarsely ground pure pork and cured for at least 3 months. Their name means "hunter," as the *salami* were a traditional and handy breakfast for those in the field.

## CAPICOLLO, CAPOCOLLO, OSSOCOLLO / PRESERVED NECK OF PORK

This is neck of pork, cured so that, after about a year, it can be thinly cut and eaten as a part of an *antipasto*, or alone with bread. It is a specialty of the South, where it is made using different spices and cured in different ways according to the region. In some regions it is even smoked. When made from the meat of free-range pigs, *capicollo* is especially delicious. In the North, *coppa*, a similar cut, is air-cured, but

it is not as exciting as its southern counterpart.

## CAPPELLO DEL PRETE / SALAMI

Two wonderful charcuterie products come from the area near Busseto, where Giuseppe Verdi lived: the first is the ham, *culatello*, and the other is *cappello del prete*, a *salame* made from the leftover ingredients used to make *culatello*. The name means "priest's hat," because of its triangular shape. The meat is ground and stuffed in the skin from the haunch of the pig. When sewn together, it takes on its characteristic shape. It needs to be boiled for at least 2 hours, and is traditionally served with lentils, cabbage, and potatoes.

## CAPRA, CAPRETTO / GOAT, KID

I myself was a shepherd when I was 13 or 14 years old. Just after the war, my father decided to buy a goat and keep it in a railroad shed near the station. I was in charge of feeding the animal, which each day gave a couple of liters of milk—enough for the whole family. I certainly never wanted to eat Sisina (as she was called) and she was eventually sold when we couldn't keep her any more. Although it was not the custom to keep goats in the North, my family always had them because my parents originally came from the South, where it was quite common.

Some goats are only good for milk, but *capretto* (kid) can also be eaten. The meat is different from that of lamb, with more of a wild taste. We usually had kid for Easter, and I had to assist with the preparation of the meat, a process which—despite my tendencies as a gourmet even then—I was always reluctant to witness. The butcher cut the kid's head into halves and I had to help with the salting and

oiling of it before it was baked in the oven.

## CARBONATA / BEEF STEW

In the Aosta Valley, where this recipe is mostly found in Italy, this dish is known as *carbonnade* because the local dialect is more French than Italian. It is, in fact, a beef stew cooked for at least 2 or 3 hours in a butter, onion, and red wine sauce. It is usually served with boiled potatoes or polenta.

## CARPACCIO / SLICED RAW BEEF TENDERLOIN

This dish of very thin slices of raw beef, dressed with a sauce based on mustard, ketchup, and other spices, was made for the first time in the legendary Harry's Bar in Venice. The term *carpaccio* is now used all over the culinary world to indicate very thinly cut food—meat, fish, or even vegetables—dressed with a marinating sauce, usually based on lemon juice or vinegar, oil and spices. See also *fesa* and *carne all'albese* (page 86).

**CASTRATO, SEE AGNELLO**

## CAVALLO / HORSE

Meat from both horses and donkeys (*asini*) was eaten during the war, when meat was scarce and prices were high. Some Italians still have a taste for them, partly because they believe the deep red color of the meat indicates that it is very good for you. Few butchers still sell horse or donkey, with no more than one or two places in the major Italian cities supplying the demand of those nostalgic gourmets.

In Puglia, however, horse meat is very much in demand during the summer, especially because it is thought to keep better than that of pigs or sheep. In Puglia there exist many stores, called *equina*, where one can only get horse meat. In Alberobello in Puglia I also discovered a dish made of escalopes of donkey meat formed into rolls and then stewed for several hours in a tenderizing sauce. It was a piece of *bravado* that did not really meet with my approval.

In Turin, the famous *insalata di carne cruda* (raw beef salad) is still sometimes made with horse. The very lean meat is ground and dressed with olive oil, lemon juice, garlic, and parsley, and left to cure for several hours. It has a rather rich flavor. Salami and sausages are also still made with horse meat.

### CERVELLA / BRAINS

Brains are believed to be particularly nutritious, which is why they are often served to people who need extra nourishment. In fact, brains contain a very high level of cholesterol and have less protein than the rest of the animal. It is only calves' and lambs' brains that are generally used in the kitchen.

It is easiest to ask your butcher to prepare the brains for you, but if this is not possible, begin by washing them in very cold water, then remove all the veins and blood vessels on the surface with a small sharp knife. Next, soak the brains in water acidulated with a little lemon juice for a couple of hours, changing the water frequently. Remove the remaining membrane and any more veins before blanching the brains in boiling water for a few minutes. Allow the brains to cool before cooking as desired.

Brains are a must for *fritto misto alla piemontese* (see page 89), but are also dipped in flour, beaten eggs, and bread crumbs, then fried in butter until golden, and served with

lemon juice. Another popular dish, leaning to the French, is brains with black butter: the brains are sliced and fried in very hot butter with the addition of chopped capers. The butter is then further heated until it goes a nut-brown in color, and is poured over the brains with more whole capers and chopped parsley scattered over the top.

### CICCIOLI, CICOLI, SFRIZOLI / PORK SCRAPS

When pork or goose fat is melted to make lard, the cubes of fat still contain some meat which, when pressed after cooking to extract all the lard, can be salted and kept to be eaten with bread. This is an interesting and very tasty *amuse-gueule* that is quite different from Anglo-Saxon pork crackling.

My mother used to make lard, and we would eat the *ciccioli* with some bread while they were still hot and juicy. My mother took special care not to squeeze the cubes of meat and lard too hard, and the result, compared to *ciccioli* made by local butchers, was like the difference between day and night. In some parts of Italy they include the *ciccioli* in the dough when making bread, producing a very appetizing loaf called *pane con i cicoli*.

### CODA ALLA VACCINARA / VACCINARA-STYLE OXTAIL

Probably one of the best-known recipes of Roman cuisine, the lengthy preparation required for this dish—about 4 or 5 hours—makes it difficult to cook, but it is a real treat! The oxtail and part of the cheek of the ox are first soaked in fresh water for 4 hours, then cut into chunks and browned in lard with onion, carrots, celery, and parsley. This is then braised over a low heat until the herbs and

vegetables are soft. White wine is then added, and slowly cooked off. The braise is then covered with tomato *polpa* and allowed to finish cooking gently for 3 to 4 hours, replenishing the liquid from time to time with some stock as needed. Finally, golden raisins, pine nuts, and bitter cocoa powder are added, and the dish is cooked until the sauce becomes thick and succulent.

### COPPA / NECK END OF PORK

Fresh neck of pork is very juicy if braised or slowly roasted. The neck of pork is, however, often cured in salt brine, stuffed in a gut casing, bound, and set to air-dry for at least six months to make the cured meat known as *coppa*. Due to its composition of large pieces of fat and lean meat, *coppa* looks much like a very fatty sausage. However, it is in fact only 40 percent fat, less than other meat preserves. It is eaten thinly sliced as an *antipasto*. See also *capicollo*.

### CORATA, CORATELLA / LAMB PLUCK

If everyone tasted the *coratella* produced in Umbria and Lazio just

RIGHT: *COPPA AND PANCETTA AIR-DRYING IN EMILIA-ROMAGNA*

once, the demand for and price of this lamb and kid pluck would leap. In most parts of Italy, the variety meat of young lambs, including the liver, lungs, and heart, are discarded or given to animals. In Umbria and Lazio, however, there is a revival of their use in traditional dishes, usually soupy stews flavored with sage, rosemary, garlic, chili, and thyme. These are so excellent that I have put my version on the menu of my restaurant in London, and it has already found many fans. A similar specialty called *soffritto di maiale* is prepared in Campania using the pluck of pork, and it is equally delicious.

## COSTA, COSTATA, COSTOLA / CUTLET, STEAK, CHOP

A great deal of confusion is caused in Italy by the different names given to the same cuts of meat. The confusion exists at the highest level, and detailed discussions take place between chefs from different regions before they understand each other. Cutlets are usually taken from the rib and neck. The *costola* (rib) is very tasty and popular because the meat, when attached to bone, has a great deal of flavor and is ideal for cutlets. *Costa* is a term that is only used for beef cuts. It refers to the rib to which the sirloin and the tenderloin are both attached and, because of its shape, is called the T-bone steak. The most famous of the T-bone steaks is *costata alla fiorentina* (see also *bistecca*).

## COSTOLETTA / VEAL CHOP

This term is generally used to indicate a beaten-out veal escalope cooked *alla milanese*, that is, dipped in egg and bread crumbs and then shallow-fried.

## COTECHINO / PORK SAUSAGE

This sausage is made from *cotica*, or pork rind, mixed with lean pork meat, fat, and spices, and some parts, like ears, which when properly boiled for a long time give it incomparable juiciness. The pork rind turns gelatinous and is essential to the taste of the sausage. *Cotechino* is usually served with lentils, cabbage, and sauerkraut. It is an essential ingredient in a good *bollito misto* (see page 92). It can also be eaten in the same way as *zampone*, stuffed pigs trotters. In Puglia they make a type of *cotechino* that is cooked and eaten cold instead of hot — the difference being an incredible amount of *peperoncino* (chili) added to it to guarantee that it is washed down with plenty of wine!

**COTICA, SEE COTENNA**

## COTOLETTA ALLA MILANESE / VEAL CUTLET

The name of this dish derives from *costoletta*. In Milan, the cutlet with the bone in it is cooked in exactly the same way. With or without the bone, the dish is very popular throughout Italy (see also *costletta*).

## COTENNA, COTICA / PORK SKIN OR RIND

Slightly fatty pork skin is very gelatinous and strong and is usually used for making the skins of certain types of sausage. It is also ground and used to make *zampone* or *cotechino*. In some parts of Italy, such as Piedmont, most of the fat is removed from the skin and it is then richly spiced with pepper, salt, nutmeg, and parsley, rolled up, bound with string, and boiled for a couple of hours until it is soft. It is usually eaten with stewed beans and a little mustard. The gelatinous taste is delicious. In Piedmont, they use it in the famous specialty called *tofeja* (see page 95). Today, the *cotenna* is sold already prepared by butchers.

Ham rind is also used to impart flavor to any bean or vegetable soup. Once it has been used, however, it is usually so hard that it has to be discarded.

## CRESPONE / PURE PORK SALAMI

This fairly large salami is made only with pork. It is mostly available in the North of Italy and takes its name from the skin of the intestine of the pig. It is usually eaten sliced as part of an *antipasto*. See *salame*.

LEFT: *COTECHINI*

## CULATELLO / HAM

Zibello, a town near Modena, is the center for the manufacture of this famous Emilia-Romagna ham. *Culatello* is the heart of the ham, the most tender part, cut in a round, cured in brine, and enclosed in a gut-like skin before being left to air-dry for a long time. It tastes very sweet and, if correctly prepared, melts in the mouth. To further enhance the taste of this delicacy, the air-dried ham can be stripped of its skin, then soaked in red wine to moisten it and add flavor. Soaked or unsoaked, this very special ham is usually served thinly sliced as part of an *antipasto* or by itself.

## CUORE / HEART

You can find devotees of heart all over Italy, although they are concentrated in the South, where variety meats are generally more popular. The largest heart eaten in Italy is that of the ox, although it is only used in stews because it is quite tough, while the smaller and more tender veal heart is popular cut in slices, then fried or broiled. It is, however, probably the heart of the pig that is most often used

BELOW: *CULATELLO DI ZIBELO*

in the Italian kitchen, especially in the South, where it is prepared with other variety meats and used in *ragùs*. Lamb's heart, especially that of very young animals, is usually eaten as part of *coratella* (see previous page), but it can also be fried or stewed in wine with the addition of rosemary, garlic, and sage.

## EQUINO, SEE CAVALLO

## FARSUMAGRU /
BEEF OR VEAL DISH
Probably the most celebrated meat dish from Sicily, the reason this is called *farsumagru*, meaning "false lean," is because a huge slice of beef or veal, 1½ inches thick, is stuffed with all sorts of goodies, then rolled and tied with string and braised or baked in a tomato sauce. The filling generally consists of *prosciutto*, *Caciocavallo* cheese, sausage meat, eggs, *mortadella*, garlic, onion, ground veal, and even fresh peas. These ingredients are cut into square batons and placed lengthwise in the middle of the roll so that, when cooked and cut in slices, a nice multicolored section is revealed.

RIGHT:
FINOCCHIONA

## FEGATO / LIVER
Liver is the best-known and most popular variety meat in all of Italy. It contains the important vitamins A and D and some of the B vitamins, as well as quite a lot of iron. The liver of all domesticated animals is sought-after and in some cases are quite expensive. Naturally, like most variety meat, liver must be very fresh. Whichever liver you use, you must remove and discard the fat and membrane surrounding it before cooking, as these make the liver bitter and inedible.

Ox liver is large, dark, and tough. It is usually sliced and braised in wine. Calves' liver is the most frequently used in Italy and is popular for its tenderness and fine flavor. It is smaller than ox liver, although it still weighs about 4½ to 6½ pounds. As well as being simply fried or broiled, calves' liver is also the foundation of many recipes, including *fegato alla veneziana*, in which it is stewed with onions, and as the basis for pâtés. Pigs' liver is also popular in Italian cooking: like ox liver it is very dark in color, but is much smaller and has an excellent flavor. It can be cooked in various ways, including in *fritto misto* (see page 89) or in *fegatelli*, little bundles of chopped liver enveloped in caul fat and baked or fried in lard. My mother used to pin the caul around the liver using pieces of a bay tree branch to give it even more flavor.

Many regions, including Puglia, Calabria, and Sicily, have recipes for specialties using liver. Popular flavorings include wine, sage, parsley, garlic, and balsamic vinegar. *Coratella* (see previous page) from Puglia uses both lambs' and goats' liver, while recipes from other regions involve tying the liver in bundles with pieces of lung and other meat and then broiling it (see the *involtini* recipe, on page 92).

## FESA / RUMP OF VEAL
This veal cut from the back leg is extremely tender and is usually broiled or fried. Sliced extremely thin and drizzled with olive oil and lemon juice, and perhaps dotted with a few shavings of truffle, it becomes *carne all'albese* (see page 86). It is also the best cut for *carpaccio*.

## FETTINE / VEAL ESCALOPES
*Fettine* are little veal escalopes, which, as they are among the easiest cuts of meat to cook, have been adopted by many busy cooks. They can be fried in bread crumbs or simply sautéed in butter with Marsala, lemon juice, or vinegar added to flavor the rather bland meat. *Fettine* are used to make the well-known *piccata milanese* (see page 87).

## FILONE, SEE MIDOLLO

## FINOCCHIONA / FENNEL
SAUSAGE
This sausage is mostly found in a typical Tuscan *antipasto*. It takes its name from *finocchio*, or wild fennel, the seeds of which were traditionally used to spice the finely ground pork fat. This savory salami is huge, reaching 10 inches in diameter. The meat is aged in pigs' intestines for up to one year. Salted Tuscan bread is the ideal foil for balancing the spiciness of this salami. Fennel is also used to spice various other types of salami and sausages, especially those from Campania, Calabria, Puglia, and Sicily.

## GALANTINA DI CARNE /
MEAT GALANTINE
Although the best-known galantines are made with chicken, there is also a version made with a mixture of meats, including large pieces of pork, veal, and chicken. The meat is first boiled, then mixed with pistachio nuts, truffle, and vegetables, put into a mold, and covered with aspic. Cut in slices and served with a little oil and vinegar, the finished galantine may be included in an *antipasto* and makes a lovely snack.

## GIAMBONE, SEE PROSCIUTTO COTTO

## GIRELLO / TOP ROUND OR EYE
This round cut of beef is distinctly Italian. Taken from a rather coarse-grained muscle, it is therefore not suitable for broiling or frying, although the meat looks as good as tenderloin. It is usually ground to break down the fiber in the meat, and is used for raw beef salads or

steak tartare. After boiling, it can also be eaten in thin slices with tuna sauce (see *vitello tonnato*, page 87).

## GRANELLI / TESTICLES

I was once asked to test some unusual foreign foods for a London daily paper, and one of the things I tried were rams' testicles, a specialty of Iceland. I was reassured that it was not only the Italians who love to eat these private parts. Although not exactly a common food, the testicles of veal, lamb, mutton, and bulls are eaten everywhere in Italy, but are mostly enjoyed in the North. In the South, however, they eat lambs' testicles as part of an *involtino*. Otherwise they are usually thinly sliced and either broiled or fried. You need to ask the butcher to prepare them for you.

## GRASSO / FAT

In the plural, *grassi* refers to all cooking fats, animal or vegetable. The fats used in different regions of Italy are dictated by the availability of local products. The northern custom is to cook with butter or lard. With modern nutritional awareness, however, today olive oil from the South has been widely adopted. Animal fats, like lard, are still used in the North, not only for reasons of economy, but also for their flavor. Certain recipes do not work with oil and need the original butter or lard to create the right texture or flavor. (See *lardo*.)

## GRIGLIATA MISTA / MIXED GRILL

This much-loved specialty is enjoyed all over Italy. Different cuts from of a variety of meats are brush-ed with olive oil and lemon juice, salted, then grilled over charcoal. Many restaurants have this dish on their menu, but nothing can beat a *grigliata* eaten *al fresco* in the company of good friends. A decent mixed grill should contain slices of liver, heart, testicles, sausages, tender lamb and kid chops, and pieces of chicken or turkey. Naturally, if there are also some wild birds, like thrushes or sparrows, then all the better. Italians do not serve sauces with barbecued meat, just lemon juice.

## GUANCIALE / PORK CHEEKS

This specialty of Lazio consists of pork cheeks cured in salt then air-dried for a few months. *Guanciale* is the main ingredient for genuine *carbonara* and *amatriciana* sauces. *Pancetta* is a good substitute, but it is not as tasty.

## INSACCATO, SEE SALAME

## INTESTINO, SEE BUDELLO

## INTINGOLO / MEAT SAUCE

This term basically describes what would be scraped and deglazed from a pan after frying or roasting meat. The resulting sauce either can be served with bread or used as a gravy, or even to dress pasta dishes. Today, *intingolo* is synonymous with a thick meat *ragù*.

## INVOLTINI / MEAT PARCELS

*Involtini* consist of thin slices of meat wrapped around fillings of various ingredients, such as *prosciutto*, Parmesan cheese, *mortadella*, olives, parsley, garlic, golden raisins, etc. They are then braised in a tomato sauce or baked. Beef is usually used because it has stronger texture, allowing it to cook slowly without breaking and leaking the filling. When very small, the rolls are also called *bocconcini*.

*Involtini*, in regions such as Puglia or Calabria, are mostly of lamb variety meats, including the heart, liver, lung, and even testicles,

LEFT: GNEMERIDDE ON SKEWERS FOR GRILLING IN PALERMO.

are tied together with a piece of gut, salted and spiced with pepper, chili, and parsley, and then grilled over charcoal or baked in the oven. In Puglia these parcels are called *gnemeridde*; in Calabria, *ghunerieddi* or *ghunerielli*; and in Sicily, *stigghiole*. For Neapolitans, *involtini di carne* are a festive must, usually for Sundays, and they cook them for a long time in a tomato sauce to be eaten with pasta, usually *penne* or *rigatoni* (see recipe, page 92).

## LARDELLARE OR LARDARE / LARDING

This terms denotes the practice of using a special needle to thread strips of lard or other fatty ingredients into lean meats, like veal, to give flavor and moisture while roasting.

## LARDO / LARD

Fresh lard is taken from the fatty sides of the pig when the meat is butchered. It is then soaked in brine and hung for a few months and used for cooking. The lard is cut as required during the year and used as the base for sauces (see *battuto*, page 70).

*Lardo di Arnad*, famous for its preserving qualities, is produced in a small town in the Aosta Valley.

LEFT: PIGS' HEADS

This lard comes from particularly fat pigs, in which the thickness of the fat can reach 4 inches. It is cured with salt, pepper, and rosemary, and then left to dry. In Piedmont and the Langhe area (Alba and Bra Cuneo), lard is thinly cut and eaten sprinkled with freshly ground black pepper. It has plenty of flavor and gives a wonderful sensation in the mouth as it melts.

In an effort to preserve as much of the pig as possible for the following year, the fat may be cut into cubes and melted in a saucepan with bay leaves. This is cooked until the meat and bay leaves end up swimming in the liquid fat. Two precious products are made from this: *sugna*, or pork fat, which is used for frying, and *ciccioli*. A Piedmontese specialty with *sugna* is to use it while still liquid and warm to cover freshly made pure pork sausages in terra-cotta pots. When the fat solidifies it keeps the sausages perfectly preserved so that they are fresh and tender up to a year later. This is called *salam d'la duja*.

### LESSO, SEE BOLLITO MISTO

### LINGUA / TONGUE

Tongue is popular all over Italy. Veal tongue is the most tender and is usually boiled and served sliced with an acidic sauce, tuna sauce, or *salsa verde* (see page 224). Tongue is an important ingredient in a classic *bollito misto* (see page 92). To achieve the vivid red color characteristic of the meat, it needs to be pickled in a salt solution for several hours and then boiled until tender. When buying tongue, make sure it is already pickled.

### LOMBO, LOMBATA, LOMBATINA, LONZA / LOIN

These are the terms used to describe loin of beef, the tender and succulent cut of meat taken from the area around the lower part of the rib cage. Pork sirloin is called *lombo di maiale*, while in central Italy *lombatina* is the name describing *costoletta*, or veal sirloin. One of the best ways of cooking loin is to broil it, or bind it with string and roast it for a short time in the oven, like beef (allow 12 to 15 minutes per pound). *Lonza*, in certain parts of southern Italy, is called *capocollo* or *coppa*.

### LUGANIGA, LUGANEGA, LUGANECA, LUCANICA / FRESH PORK SAUSAGES

These long, thin, fresh pork sausages are probably the ancestors of the hot dog. They are made with relatively coarsely ground pork and have a 40 percent fat content. The ground meat is stuffed into a single piece of gut and sold by the meter, divided into long sausage segments. Such sausages are very common in Italy, especially in the northern and central regions where, in winter, they are eaten cooked in a tomato sauce, and accompanied with polenta. They can also be broiled, fried, or braised. The meat can also be extracted from the gut, crumbled, and fried as part of the base for a pasta sauce or a risotto. I particularly like them fried with peppers, or as in *polenta concia con salsiccia*, (see page 96).

### MACELLERIA / BUTCHER'S SHOP

In the old days, the shopkeeper used to butcher the animals himself on the premises. The *macelleria* of today is more likely to be just a retail store selling meat, but sometimes also selling meat products, such as salami, etc.

### MAIALE, MAIALINO, PORCO, PORCELLO, PORCELLINO, PORCEDDU, SUINO / PIG, PORK, PIGLET

Italians have always loved pork, not only because it is so easy to raise, but because every scrap of the animal can be used. When I was a boy, almost anyone who could kept a pig, feeding it on leftovers and scraps. Today their feed is more rationalized, mixing polenta with other high-energy grains. The industry, however, feeds pigs on other, less-valuable grains, obtaining larger production, but of a less flavorsome meat. Better-quality pork is, however, still sometimes obtained from herds partly fed on the whey by-products of cheese-making, and pigs lucky enough to graze in the wild and consume foods like acorns are said to give much of the flavor to better *prosciutto*.

As well as for their meat, pigs were also needed for their fat. Of the 400-plus pound yield from the average pig, at least a quarter was fat, and this was turned into solid and liquid lard. Today, with more information about the dangers of eating too much saturated animal fat, the pig is raised mainly for its meat, and the commercially farmed pig—now available all year round—reaches an average weight of 320 pounds.

When a pig was raised individually, it would be slaughtered in December or January so that its meat could be processed during cool weather to be preserved for use all year round. After the butcher slaughtered the pig, hams and sausages were made with the fresh meat, while the perishable variety meats and other parts that could not be preserved were cooked for especially invited friends to celebrate the occasion. Nothing was wasted. Even the bones, once stripped of their meat to make salami, were boiled with cabbage, potatoes, and beans to make a tasty soup. The blood, which was drained from the pig to keep its meat pale, either would have been cooked with onion, or mixed with pork fat to

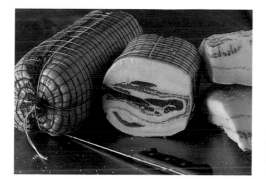

RIGHT: *LARDO*

make blood sausage or *marzapane*, or even used to make a dessert, *sanguinaccio*, with milk, raisins, sugar, and spices. Some people still keep pigs today, but the products so loved by Italians are now usually made commercially, not from the pig in the back yard.

Italians are very fond of eating suckling pigs (*maialino, porcello,* or *porcellino*), which are slaughtered at anywhere from 8 to 12 weeks of age, and sometimes younger. The meat is regarded as a delicacy. In Sardinia, suckling pig is called *porceddu*, and is traditionally roasted on a spit made of *corbezzolo*, the branches of a strawberry tree (see page 264), for at least 2 hours and brushed with lard from time to time. The wood fire is made of the branches of aromatic trees such as olive, juniper, and myrtle to give extra flavor to the meat. Suckling pigs are also baked whole in a wood-fired oven. Moreover, *porchetto* or *porcetto*, stuffed roast whole adult pig, is also prepared for local festivals or weddings.

Pork is eaten with equal avidity all over Italy, though perhaps the North makes better use of it, because it is eaten during all the seasons. The South, for reasons of climate, tends to consume it only in winter. A great deal of pork is eaten in preserved

form by all Italians either as ham, *salami*, or sausages of any type. The northern style of cooking these is boiled and accompanied by beans or *crauti* (sauerkraut); from central to southern Italy they are preferred roasted, broiled, or stewed.

### MANZO / BEEF
*Manzo* is the general Italian term for mature beef (see *bovino*).

### MARZAPANE / PIGS' BLOOD SPECIALTY
Not to be confused with the almond paste, *marzipan, marzapane* is pigs' blood mixed with pepper, nutmeg, salt, cubes of lard, bread crumbs, and garlic, and marinated in red wine. The mixture is either roasted or cooked in a bain-marie. When it is solid, it is cut into slices and then either fried with onions or, as in Novara, dipped in beaten egg then fried.

### MEDAGLIONE / MEDALLIONS
*Medaglioni* are pieces of beef, veal, lamb, or pork tenderloin cut at least $^3/_4$-inch thick and 2 to 4 inches in diameter to resemble large medals. Because the meat is usually very tender, *medaglioni* are either briefly pan-fried or broiled, and then served with a suitable sauce.

### MIDOLLO, SCHIENALE / MARROW, BONE MARROW
One of the attractions of *ossobuco alla milanese*, or shin of beef cooked in a tomato sauce, is the marrow. It is pure fat, and tastes heavenly. Bone marrow is also used to flavor *risotto alla milanese*. When my mother cooked beef stock she used shin of beef, and I would amuse myself

by extracting the marrow from the cooked bone, putting it on toast, and seasoning it with salt and pepper for a real treat. The round marrow that fills the length of the spinal cord is known as *midollo spinale, schienale*, or *filone*, and is considered quite a delicacy. It is cut into short sections and fried as part of *fritto misto* (see page 89).

### MILZA / SPLEEN
The spleen is one variety meat that is seldom used, as it does not have a very high culinary value. The only place I have seen it cooked and eaten was in Sicily, in the extremely interesting market of Vucceria, in the center of Palermo. At around midday, a few stands were preparing the typically Palermitan snack of *guastedde*. Pork spleen is grilled over charcoal, sliced very thinly, and then fried in olive oil with chili, salt, and pepper, and served between two pieces of bread like a hot dog. Judging by the long queues, it must have been very good.

### MONTONE, SEE AGNELLO

### MORTADELLA / SAUSAGE
Probably the best-known Italian sausage, *mortadella* is made of pork, but sometimes includes some beef, veal, or even horse and donkey meat. Traditional in Bologna (hence its nickname, "baloney"), this is the largest of the Italian sausages, weighing between 11 and $32^1/_2$ pounds. Giant *mortadellas* made for exhibitions can reach up to 325 pounds in weight.

*Mortadella* is 60 percent pork meat and 40 percent fat. The pork is finely minced, and the fat takes the form of long, square-cut strips of lard. The mixture is seasoned with spices, and sometimes contains pistachio nuts and coriander seeds. Today, the sausage meat is forced into a synthetic gut, but in the past, pig's bowel was used. The sausage is then steamed or poached in a special oven.

ABOVE: *MORTADELLA*

BOTTOM LEFT: PIGS BEING READIED FOR MARKET IN EMILIA-ROMAGNA

ABOVE: VARIETY
MEATS ON SALE
FROM A
NEAPOLITAN
STREET VENDOR

RIGHT: A *NORCINO*
OF NORCIA

The best *mortadella* is made of pure pork and is called *puro suino*, with the letter "S" stamped on the skin so that it can be identified. The branding "SB" means *suino/bovino*, to indicate that it is made with beef and pork or lamb and pork. A less well-known *mortadella* from Lago d'Orta, called *mortadella di fegato*, is made with pigs' liver.

*Mortadella* must be sliced very thin to bring out the flavor and can therefore only be cut by a machine. It is mostly eaten with bread, especially *focaccia*, but it is also used as part of a meat stuffing. In wartime, when meat was hard to come by, my mother would bring home very thickly sliced *mortadella* which she dipped in beaten eggs and bread crumbs, and then fried like a cutlet. Served with salad, it made a perfect lunch.

## MUSETTO / SAUSAGE

This sausage, made with flesh from the pig's snout (*muso*), is a specialty of Friuli and the area of Trentino Alto Adige, in the northeast of Italy. The pork meat is very finely ground with some fat and put in a gut with part of the snout and sometimes the pig's skin. It is served and cooked like *cotechino*, but in the North is accompanied by either sauerkraut or red cabbage stewed with vinegar and wine.

## NERVETTI / TENDONS AND GRISTLE

*Nervetti* is veal and pork cartilage, mainly from the foot, boiled until tender, then sliced very thin and seasoned with olive oil, vinegar, and raw onions. In Venice, *nervetti* thinly cut and spiced with oil,

vinegar, salt, and pepper are eaten as snacks or with an aperitif. In Naples it is sold extensively from colorful little roadside stands that also sell cooked veal heads ('*o musso*) and tripe dressed with lemon juice and olive oil.

## NODINO / CUTLET

*Nodino di vitello* is a veal cutlet with the bone in it, and not too thickly cut. *Nodini* are mostly fried slowly with butter and sage or rosemary (see *nodino di vitello al rosmarino*, page 88).

## NORCINERIA / PORK BUTCHERS

In the town of Norcia in Umbria, the local specialty is based on pork and wild boar. The local butchers, called *norcini*, are very famous for their skill, and have given their name to the art of pork and boar butchering. Their stores are called *norcineria*, the equivalent of *macelleria*.

## OMENTO, SEE RETE DI MAIALE

## ORECCHIO / PORK EARS

Only the ears of pigs and veal calves are generally eaten. They are cooked for about 2 hours and then thickly sliced and served in a similar way to *nervetti*. Pork ears are also ground and added to *cotechino* or *zampone* (see recipe, page 97).

## OSSOBUCO / VEAL SHANKS

*Osso*, meaning bone, and *buco*, meaning hole, this is taken from the part of the leg where the muscle is particularly thick, giving a cut of meat about 3$\frac{1}{2}$ inches across, cut into 1-inch-thick sections with the bone and marrow in place. The dish *ossobuco alla milanese* (see page 95), in which the shank pieces are stewed in a tomato sauce, has been made popular all over the world by Italian restaurants. It is usually served with a *gremolada* and accompanied by saffron risotto (see page 178).

## OSSOCOLLO, SEE CAPICOLLO

## PAGLIATA / VARIETY MEAT DISH

This Roman variety meat dish is best sampled in restaurants because of the very particular principal ingredient—which needs to be very fresh—and the elaborate and lengthy preparation required. The variety meat used is part of the intestines, normally of milk-fed calves, complete with their creamy contents. It is normally lightly flavored with parsley and then broiled. Although veal variety meat is most often used, *pagliata* can be made from beef, lamb, or even goat. The tripe taste is very intense.

## PANCETTA / FAT BACON

A very important ingredient in the preparation of many Italian dishes, *pancetta* is bacon cured from belly of pork, or *pancia*. *Pancetta* is usually fried as a base for sauces, the best known of which is *carbonara*, a sauce for pasta based on small cubes of fried *pancetta*—or *guanciale* as the purist requires—with the addition of raw egg at the end. Fresh *pancetta* can be used to make *minestrone* and other soups. *Pancetta curata*, salt-cured, air-dried, or even *arrotolata*, rolled *pancetta*, is used thinly sliced as part of an *antipasto*. Today you can also find *pancetta affumicata*, smoked *pancetta*, which is used in many

northern Italian dishes that are influenced by the cuisine of neighboring Austria. Tuscany also produces *rigatino pancetta*, "streaky bacon," a very thin bacon that has the same uses as other *pancettas*.

### PECORA, SEE AGNELLO

### PETTO / BREAST

This cut is also called *punta* and can be veal (*punta di vitello*) or other meats. In the North of Italy, breast is a cheap way of making a little meat go a long

way. A large pocket is cut into the breast between the layers of meat and fat; this is stuffed and sewn up, and the breast is then roasted. The best-known version is *cima alla genovese*, a very long-cooked, boned, and rolled breast of veal.

The southern version, made in Campania and all the regions to the South, is made with lamb breast. The filling is made of bread crumbs, eggs, Parmesan, parsley, and garlic. After the pocket has been sewn up, it is cooked for a long time in a *ragù*. The sauce is used to dress a first course of pasta, and the meat is sliced and eaten accompanied by spinach.

### PICCATA, SEE SCALOPPINA

### PIEDINO, SEE ZAMPI

### POLMONE / LUNG

Only pork and lamb lung is used in Italian cuisine and this use is mainly concentrated in the South. Lung is part of the pluck, and is used finely chopped in Umbrian *coratella*, a mixture of finely cut variety meats which is fried in olive oil with onions, chili, and wine (see page 73) and *soffritto alla napoletana*, in which finely chopped pork variety meats is cooked in lard with chili,

bay leaves, tomato paste, onions, and wine. *Soffritto* and *coratella* are both winter dishes, generally eaten a little at a time, diluted with stock and reheated, then put on slices of toasted bread like soup.

### POLPETTE, POLPETTINE, RISSOLE / MEATBALLS

*Polpette* and *rissole*, made from ground meat (*polpa*), are cooked all over Italy and are considered to be the most economical and tasty way of using ground meat. Different meats can be ground to vary the flavor. The classic recipe for *polpette* is ground beef or veal mixed with beaten egg, crushed garlic, grated Parmesan cheese, chopped parsley, salt, and pepper. The ingredients are thoroughly mixed together, the mixture is shaped into *rissoles* or balls, which are deep-fried until crispy. They can be eaten either as they are, or cooked and served in sauces to dress pasta, as they do in southern Italy, especially in Puglia. *Polpettine* are tiny meatballs crisply fried and used as fillings for pasta timbales (see *timbalo di ziti*, page 161).

### POLPETTONE / MEATLOAF

Meatloaf used to be eaten by the poor as a substitute for a large cut of meat. Made from either ground beef or pork, it was traditionally braised for several hours in a rich tomato sauce. The sauce would be used to dress a first course of pasta and the meat was eaten as part of the main course. Today, however, *polpettone* is extremely popular all over Italy, particularly with the Neapolitans.

The recipe for meatloaf is similar to that for meatballs. Mix the ground meat with fresh bread crumbs, parsley, coarsely chopped onion, beaten eggs, Parmesan cheese, nutmeg, salt, and pepper.

Form this into a single meatloaf and, in a large pan, carefully brown it on each side in olive oil. Take care, when turning the meatloaf, not to break it. Add more chopped onions to the pan when the *polpettone* has been browned almost all over. When the onion is translucent, add the tomato sauce and cook slowly for a couple of hours. The sauce will be flavored with the juices from the meatloaf and can be used to dress pasta. You can also roast meatloaf, without any sauce, like any other piece of roast meat. In this case the mixture is kept juicier by reducing the amount of bread crumbs.

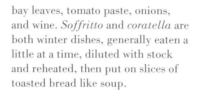

LEFT: *PANCETTA*

### PORCELLINO, PORCEDDU, PORCELLO SEE MAIALE

### PORCHETTA

*Porchetta*, which originated in Umbria but is now more strongly associated with Lazio and more especially Rome, is one of the most spectacular of the Italian pork specialties. This rather special dish consists of a whole, boned pig, weighing 65 to 90 pounds, which is stuffed with its own variety meats, such as the liver, heart, and lungs, which have been sliced and sautéed in oil and seasoned with garlic and herbs like bay and rosemary. The pig is then roasted on a spit over a wood fire or baked in a wood-fired oven for 4 to 5 hours, or until the skin is a red-brown and is wonderfully crispy. It often forms the centerpiece of local festivities, and slices of it are sold from little roadside stands.

### PORCO, SEE MAIALE

### PROSCIUTTO / CURED HAM

In the past, meat had to be preserved so that it kept for a long time without the benefit of refrigeration. This need gave birth to a vast industry given over to the production of hams enjoyed as specialties in their own right rather than simply as preserved meat. *Prosciutto*, probably from the Latin *perexuctus* meaning dried, is among the most renowned and is probably

## HOW PROSCIUTTO IS PREPARED

*Prosciutto* is made from the cured hind leg of the pig. It is cut so that one end is rounded. To preserve it, the meat is massaged with salt daily for a whole month until the salt has penetrated right through to the center of the flesh. The

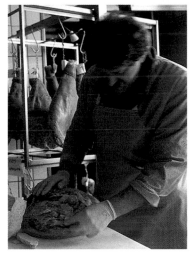

hams are then hung In special well-ventilated rooms to mature. This takes from 12 to 16 months, and during this time the ham loses at least 30 percent of its weight. The curing process gives the meat and fat the wonderful, concentrated taste that is characteristic of Italian hams. To avoid the loss of water-weight that

occurs naturally during the curing process, some unscrupulous producers release their hams after only nine months. Although such hams look fully cured, they still taste of raw flesh after only this short curing time.

one of the best-loved foods from Italy worldwide. *Prosciutto crudo* is the essential ingredient in an Italian *antipasto*. It is eaten accompanied by either melon or figs, and with *grissini* or good bread. It can also form part of a main course, served, for example, with buttered asparagus and boiled potatoes.

*Prosciutto di Parma*, just one of the types of *prosciutto* produced in Italy, is so well known that any Italian ham is almost exclusively associated with it, although many other regions produce their own local hams. Parma ham is made from pigs raised in Emilia-Romagna or Lombardy, where the raw weight of the ham has to be at least 22 to 24 pounds. The production of Parma ham is controlled by the local producers' association, which guarantees that the ham is locally cured and dried in the traditional way. It is also a guarantee that the

pigs from which the hams are made are raised traditionally, and fed on the whey used to make Parmigiano-Reggiano cheese, corn, and other natural food, so that the meat is tender and full of flavor. Other good local hams include the slightly smaller but very sweet-flavored San Daniele from Friuli.

Other regions that produce good hams are Tuscany, Veneto, Campania, in the towns of Langhirano and San Leo (where, it is said, the pigs are partly fed on acorns). The best hams are cured for anywhere from 16 to 18 and up to 24 months. They are cured on the bone and cut as thin as possible by hand.

To make hams suitable for slicing by machine, the bone is removed from an aged ham with a special tool by an especially trained *norcino*. The ham is then pressed in a mold to reshape it, and vacuum-packed in heavy plastic wrap once it is turned

out. However, the best ham is sold freshly sliced from the bone, as those sold molded and packed have little resemblance to the real thing.

According to the Association of Parma Ham Producers, during the curing process, much of the saturated fat in the ham turns into unsaturated, so *prosciutto* is actually a much healthier food than it might at first seem, with perfect balance of proteins, fats, low cholesterol, and an abundance of vitamins and trace elements.

### PROSCIUTTO COTTO /
COOKED HAM

This is a variation on *prosciutto crudo*, using the same cut of meat. The seasoned meat is pickled and pressed in a square-shaped mold before being steam-baked in a special oven. Like cured ham, *prosciutto cotto* is eaten as part of an *antipasto*, as well as used for flavoring sauces and cooked vegetables, or for stuffings. A cheaper version is made from shoulder of pork. In some parts of northern Italy, *prosciutto cotto* is known as *giambone*.

**PUNTA DI VITELLO, SEE PETTO**

**RENE, SEE ROGNONE**

**RETE DI MAIALE, OMENTO** / CAUL FAT
Caul fat is a lacy membrane of fat lining the stomach of (normally) the pig, used to bard tender pieces of meat or variety meats before roasting or baking, and imparting a wonderful flavor to any meat. After the caul fat is taken from the stomach of the pig, it forms a solid ball. Soaked in lukewarm water, this separates into a kind of veiled net; it is then cut into squares for ease of use. Just season a piece of pig's liver, wrap it in caul fat, then fry for a minute or two on each side.

**ROGNONE, ROGNONCINI, RENE / KIDNEY**
After liver, kidney is the simplest and most commonly used variety meat in Italian cuisine. The kidneys of veal calves, lamb, and sometimes pigs are used in all Italian kitchens. Tender, small kidneys from very young animals, called *rognoncini*, are a particular specialty. To get rid of any residual unpleasant tastes or smells, kidneys should be cut into slices and doused in salt or soaked in milk for an hour to draw out the impurities. They must then be thoroughly washed before being cooked.

Veal kidneys are characterized by a series of lobes connected by fatty strands, which need to be cut out and discarded before cooking. Kidneys are embedded in a large lump of suet, which is sometimes melted and used for cooking. However, it is also possible to bake the entire kidney, still embedded in that lump of fat, for a long time.

Lambs' kidneys, shaped like large kidney beans, are much smaller than veal and pigs' kidneys. They should be prepared in a similar way to veal kidneys, and first need to be cut open with a knife in order to discard the fatty core inside.

The classic dish for kidneys all over Italy is *trifolati*. Gently fry a chopped garlic clove in butter. Slice the kidneys thinly and toss them in flour. When the garlic is slightly browned, add the kidneys to the pan and fry for 1 to 2 minutes. Pour in a little dry white wine or Marsala, then add some chopped parsley and fry for another 3 to 4 minutes, but no longer or the kidneys will be tough. Season with salt and pepper before serving.

**ROSTIDA, RUSTIDA, ROSTICIADA, ROSTICIANA / MEAT DISH**
This is a *ragù* made of a mixture of meat cuts, mainly pork, which is cooked in wine until tender. In a separate pan, a large amount of chopped onion is sautéed in olive oil. When both are ready, they are mixed together with some chili and tomato *polpa*. This dish, a specialty from Lombardy, and the region's equivalent of *soffritto di maiale*, or Umbrian *coratella*, is then eaten with polenta.

**RUMINE, SEE TRIPPA**

**SALAMA, SALAMA DA SUGO, SALAMINA / CURED SAUSAGE**
This is an ancient specialty of the city of Ferrara. Both its contents and the way it is cooked contribute to its special status and make it impossible to reproduce on a commercial basis. You can only buy it locally or find it on the menu of local restaurants.

It is traditionally made using the bladder of the pig as a container, and it weighs between 1¹/₄ and 2¹/₄ pounds. This classic *salame* is made entirely of pork tongue and liver, and is spiced with salt, pepper,

cloves, and cinnamon, with perhaps Marsala, brandy, or even rum added for more flavor. Every kitchen in the town has its own particular recipe and spice mixture, which the cooks guard jealously. This mixture forms the center of the *salama*, which and is then wrapped in ground pork taken from the neck and the head. Once the bladder casing has been completely stuffed, it is bound and hung to dry for at least six months, much like Scottish haggis.

Before eating the *salama*, it is very carefully cooked for about 5 hours, with the bladder tied to a stick so it does not touch the bottom of the pot of simmering water. The cooked *salama* is cut open and eaten with a traditional accompaniment of potato purée. It smells and tastes absolutely delicious.

**SALAME / CURED SAUSAGE**
Like many preserved meats, *salame* is known as *insaccato*, or "bagged goods." Over many years, various methods have been developed for preserving meat, including air- or sun-drying, or using salt, sugar, honey, vinegar, or alcohol. Preserving meat, especially that of the annually butchered pig, has given rise to specialties like ham and sausages as well as a variety of other commodities which Italians have incorporated into their diet. As well as having an exquisite flavor, compared to a slice of plain, cooked meat, good *salame* is highly nutritious and has the benefit of being ready to eat at any time. It is therefore not surprising that Italians have dedicated so many of their natural resources to the creation of this unique food, and today many *salami* are made using the traditional methods.

After proper cleaning, the intestines of various animals can be preserved over a long

LEFT: A PRESS FOR COOKED HAMS.

BELOW: *SALAME DI TESTA DI MAIALE* (PIG'S HEAD SALAMI) AND *COPPA*

RIGHT: *SALAME VARZI*

period, as the ground meat contains certain agents, which, along with preservatives, allow the meat to age without deteriorating. The meat for *salame* is usually seasoned with spices, which also help to preserve the meat, and it is then forced into skins and carefully cured.

*Salame* is made up of about 40 percent fat in the form of lard or hard fat cut into cubes of different sizes, as softer fat has a tendency to turn rancid. This fat starts out highly saturated, but during the curing process much of this turns into unsaturated fat.

The meat used for *salame* is predominantly pork, although some *salami* contain a mixture of pork and beef—or sometimes even horse meat—and the label always indicates whether it contains pure pork (*puro suino*) or pork and beef (*suino e bovino*), etc. The meat is ground to different textures and fineness depending on the type of *salame* being made. Additional flavorings of garlic, salt, peppercorns, chili, fennel seed, wine, Marsala, and even brandy are added to the mixture. After it has been forced into the gut and molded to the traditional shape, it is tied with string and hung in especially constructed curing rooms, where the sausages are left for at least 2 to 4 months to cure at carefully controlled air-flow and temperature. When the *salumi* are sold, they are fully matured, and will have lost at least 35 percent of their initial weight in drying.

In every town, in every region, there is a *salami* specialist and each one has its own local variation. Some of these *salami* are now made on a large scale and sold throughout the world. The following are just a few of the many that can be found in Italy. The first group use finely ground meat, and are sometimes referred to generically as "*milano*" or "*ungherese*."

*Salame milano*, also called *crespone*, is made with very finely ground pork spiced with salt, saltpeter, coarsely milled black pepper, and in some cases, crushed garlic marinated in red wine. The ground meat is forced into a natural gut to make a sausage with a diameter of about $3^{1}/_{4}$ inches. Once bound, it is aged for at least three months, during which time it loses 30 percent of its initial $4^{1}/_{2}$-pound weight. It is served very thinly cut.

*Salame ungherese*, or Hungarian salami, has been adopted by Italians who enjoy its smoky flavor. The finely ground meat is made up of equal parts pork, beef, and pork fat. It is aged for at least three months and weighs around $3^{1}/_{4}$ pounds when cured. It has a diameter of $2^{1}/_{2}$ to $2^{3}/_{4}$ inches and is served very thinly sliced.

*Cacciatori*, or hunter's salami, is small, weighing only about $3^{1}/_{2}$ ounces, and only needs to be aged for a short period. It gets its name from its size, which made it convenient for hunters to carry with them. Today it makes an ideal addition to any picnic basket.

The meat of the following *salami* is of a medium coarseness, and little chunks of meat and fat can be clearly distinguished. These *salami* are called *nostrani*.

*Salame varzi*, from the area of Pavia in Lombardy, is an excellent pure pork *salame* with 30 percent fat. Only salt, saltpeter, whole black peppercorns, and wine are added. It is about $2^{1}/_{2}$ to $2^{3}/_{4}$ inches in diameter and is aged for 3 to 4 months. Only about 25 percent of its weight is lost during the curing process.

*Salame di Felino* comes from a little town near Parma and is probably one of the best Italian *salame*. It is traditionally very sweet, and the meat includes trimmings from the leg of pork used in making Parma ham, as well as some shoulder meat. The added spices are salt, whole black peppercorns, saltpeter, and perhaps some garlic and wine. Because of the type of gut used as a casing, it has a long and irregular shape, with a smaller diameter at the top than at the bottom. It takes at least three months to cure.

*Salame fabriano*, *salame genovese*, and *salame veronese* are all very similar to the *salame di felino*, containing only a few different spices and a slightly different ratio of meat to fat.

*Salame toscano* or *finocchiona* or *sbriciolona*, unlike the previous *salami*, contains equal amounts of pork and fat. It is also much larger than the others, with a diameter of about 6 inches, and tends to crumble when cut, which is why it is called *sbriciolona* (meaning crumbly). The name *finocchiona* was given because, in addition to the usual flavorings, fennel is also added.

*Salame napoli* is a very popular *salame* made up of equal parts pork, pork fat, and beef. It also contains garlic, pepper, wine, salt, saltpeter, paprika, and chopped chili, making it ideal for those who prefer a stronger, spicier flavor. Similar *salami* include the *campagnolo*, *salame all'aglio*, *salame abruzzese*, *ascolano bellunese*, *cadorino*, and *ventricina*.

Other spicy or hot *salami* include the excellent *salsiccie* made in Calabria (*salsiccia calabrese* and *napoletana*). Both are made in the same way, with the meat pressed into a small round gut and tied into a circle. They are easily distinguished from other *salsiccie* by their hot spices, including chili, paprika, and whole peppercorns.

The *soppressata* is a sort of pressed *salame* available all over Italy. The Venetian type, called *soppressa*, is made with pork and has a fat content of 30 percent. It is cured for 10 to 15 months. The Calabrian *soppressata* is probably the most sought-after and is made up of three-quarters pork and one-quarter pork fat. The meat and fat are cut quite coarsely with a knife and mixed with garlic, pepper, blood, paprika, wine, salt, pepper, and chili. It is forced into a short gut and then placed under a wooden board and weighted down to create the traditional flat shape. It is then smoked and cured for 3 to 4 months.

### Salame Cotto / Cooked Salami

This is mostly eaten in the North of Italy, where the temperatures allow unpreserved sausage to be kept for longer periods of time. It is made in the same way as *cotechino*, but is boiled in water and sold cooked and ready to eat as part of a *bollito misto* (see page 92) or ground to make meat stuffings or fillings for *ravioli*.

### Salam d'La Duja, see Lardo

### Salsiccia, Salsicciotto, Salsiccine, see Luganica

### Saltimbocca / Veal Dish

Literally translated as "jump in the mouth," this Roman specialty is based on small *scaloppine* of veal covered with sage leaves, topped with slices of *prosciutto*, and fried in a pan. These morsels are now made of other ingredients, such as in *saltimbocca d'animelle*, in which the veal is replaced by sweetbreads.

### Salumeria / Pork Shop

*Salumi* is the generic term for preserved meat products, mostly

pork, and a *salumeria* is a store specializing in such fare. There are two basic types of preserved meats, the whole cured hams and other meats like *prosciutto*, and the sausages made of ground meat and fat, like *salami*.

### Sangue / Blood

The only blood that is used in the Italian kitchen is pigs' blood. It has to be stored very carefully and beaten so that it does not coagulate. It is used to make black pudding, or a very tasty tart called *sanguinaccio* (see *maiale*, page 78).

### Scaloppina, Piccata / Veal Pieces

Sirloin of veal is a tender cut, and small thin slices of it are known as *scaloppine*. They are usually dusted with flour and fried in hot butter for one minute on each side. With the addition of some stock, white wine, Marsala, or lemon juice and a little garlic and parsley, the *scaloppine* are then ready in a few minutes. See also *fettine*.

### Schienale, see Midollo

### Sfrizoli, see Ciccioli

### Speck / Smoked Ham Shoulder

This Austrian specialty was introduced into Italy fairly recently, and was previously known only to those who lived on the Austro-Italian border. *Speck* is a smoked, salt-cured, air-dried ham. It is extremely delicious on its own, but is widely used in sauces, *ragùs*, and stews, and to add a distinguished flavor to vegetables. It is similar to, but much cheaper than, Parma ham, and many people eat it as an alternative as part of their *antipasti*. To me they seem so different that it is impossible to compare them.

### Spezzatino / Beef Stew

Anyone who was in the military service in Italy will remember *spezzatino* for the rest of his life. It is a very economical meat dish, as any cut of beef can be used to make it. Other ingredients include tomatoes, onion, and puréed olives. The sauce was used to dress pasta and the meat was eaten with vegetables.

### Stinco / Veal Shank

A typical Lombardian dish, *stinco di vitello* is whole veal shank cooked slowly in stock, wine, and perhaps a little lemon juice for at least 2 hours, or until tender. Once cooked, the meat is served off the bone. Similarly, pork shank can be roasted with herbs such as rosemary and sage, as well as a little wine.

### Stracotto / Braised Beef

This term, from the word for overcooked, describes a beef stew cooked for at least 3 hours in a slow oven until the meat is very tender. The other ingredients include red wine, celery, carrots, onion, and a few tomatoes (see page 88).

### Stufato / Stew

From *stufa*, meaning stove, *stufati* are meat stews cooked slowly in the oven, sometimes for up to 12 hours.

### Suino, see Maiale

### Sugna, see Lardo

### Testa, Testina / Head

*Testa* is the head of pork and *testina* is the head of veal. Pork head is used mainly in the South to make *cotechino* or *salame cotto*, while veal head is mainly used in the North of Italy as part of *bollito misto*. *Testina* also refers to the head of a sheep or goat, which is popular in central and southern Italy, where it is baked in the oven. The head is usually sold cut in half so that it can be spiced and eaten more easily.

## TESTICOLI, SEE GRANELLI

## TRIPPA, TRIPE, BÜSECCA / TRIPE

Tripe is part of the stomach of ruminants, such as calves. If properly prepared, it is a delicious dish. Today, it is a national dish in Italy, and people in every region and every town, whether poor or rich, eat tripe prepared in many different ways according to their own regional traditions.

Only perfect, fresh tripe is worth eating, so it is important to start with the right cut of a high quality. Tripe is made from the four parts of the ruminant's stomach. The *ricciolino* or *riccia* is the first section and looks like a curly gut full of glands, and has a rich flavor. The second part is the *rumine*, or blanket, and the third is the *reticolo*, or honeycomb. The fourth is for me the best of all, and is the *millefoglie*, so, called because of its many membranes, which look like leaves or the pages of a book.

Tripe should be bought cleaned but uncooked. It is, however, quite difficult to get it like this unless you know a butcher who will sell it in this state. I find that, outside Italy, the only place in which tripe is sold uncooked is in Chinese shops.

For all the various regional recipes, at least one per region, there is a basic preparation which calls for blanching the uncooked tripe for 30 minutes. After it is cool, the pieces are rubbed together like clothes being washed, and then rinsed to get rid of impurities. It is then cut into bite-sized pieces, ready to be cooked for up to 3 or 4 hours, depending on its initial tenderness.

Usually onion, celery, carrots, pepper, and bay leaves are the basic flavorings for tripe. Or, the tripe can be eaten with oil, lemon juice, and parsley as they do in Naples. However, ingredients like rosemary, *pancetta*, cinnamon, tomatoes, chili, and sage are among the favorite flavorings in other regions. Fried in lard, butter, and oil, and then topped with stock, tripe is also made into a moist stew, which in some cases is topped with grated Parmesan cheese before serving.

## VIOLINO DI CHIAVENNA / CHIAVENNA HAM

This curious ham takes its name from the town of Chiavenna in Veltellina. It is made from the leg of a lamb or goat seasoned with garlic, spiced with juniper berries, and washed in red wine, then air-dried for a few months. It is called *violino* because, in order to cut it, the ham must rest on the shoulder, like a violin.

## VITELLO / VEAL

After pork, the veal from milk-fed calves is the most important meat in Italian cooking. All the cuts are used to produce the most varied dishes: cubed in stews with a little white sauce veal becomes a *spezzatino*, similar to the French *blanquette de veau*. The most popular cut is the *paillard*, a large thin slice of veal, which is seared on the griddle for a minute on each side or dipped in beaten egg and bread crumbs and then fried as *cotoletta alla milanese*. *Saltimbocca* is a specialty of Rome, with the veal slices covered with just a slice of ham and some sage leaves, and fried. Rolled and stuffed with *pancetta*, the slices become *uccelli scappati* ("flown-away birds"), a specialty of Reggio nell'Emilia. Of course, we must not forget *scaloppine al limone*, with Marsala and lemon juice, and *ossobuco alla milanese* (see page 95), just to mention a few of the regional dishes made with

veal. See also *bovino*, *fettine*, and *scaloppina*.

## ZAMPI, ZAMPETTI, ZAMPONE, PIEDINO / PIGS' FEET

Only veal and pork feet are used in Italian cooking. The foreleg feet are favored because they have more meat than the back. Veal feet develop a wonderfully tender gelatinous quality after they have been cooked for a long time, and they make a perfect thickener for stock. Otherwise veal feet can be eaten sliced and dressed with olive oil and lemon juice or vinegar, either warm or cold.

As pigs' feet they need to be thoroughly cleaned, I suggest that you let your butcher take care of the preparation. Once they reach the kitchen, however, they need to be boiled for at least an hour. They can then be tossed in bread crumbs and shallow-fried in butter. When the skin is crispy and the flesh is very soft, they can be served with lemon juice. Alternatively, once they have been blanched, they can also be slowly braised in tomato sauce for a couple of hours. Another popular recipe is to stuff the skin around the shin with a mixture of ground pork, the meat on the shin itself, and the ears, to make *zampone*.

RIGHT: *ZAMPI* AND *TRIPPA* IN THE FLORENCE MARKET

# CARNE ALL'ALBESE

ALBA-STYLE RAW BEEF WITH PARMESAN CHEESE AND WHITE TRUFFLE

### FOR 4

**14** OUNCES BEEF TENDERLOIN, CUT INTO
    VERY THIN SLICES

SALT AND PEPPER

**4** TABLESPOONS EXTRA-VIRGIN OLIVE OIL

JUICE OF **1** LEMON

**4** CELERY RIBS, THINLY SLICED

**12** FRESH ASPARAGUS TIPS, COOKED
    UNTIL JUST *AL DENTE*

**3** OUNCES PARMESAN CHEESE, THINLY
    SLICED

**1¹/₂** OUNCES WHITE TRUFFLE, CUT INTO
    THIN SHAVINGS

*The attraction of this sophisticated dish from Piedmont lies in its simplicity and, naturally, in the unbeatable combination of the meat with truffles. Locally in Alba, not only wealthy people enjoy this dish—the truffle-hunters themselves are very fond of it.*

Put the slices of beef between 2 sheets of heavy-duty plastic wrap and beat gently with a meat pounder or the end of a rolling pin until very thin. It should be about ¹/₁₆ inch thick. Spread the meat over 4 large serving plates without letting the slices overlap. Season with salt and pepper, then brush with the olive oil and lemon juice. Distribute the slices of celery, asparagus tips, Parmesan, and white truffle over the meat. Serve with *grissini*.

# VITELLO TONNATO
VEAL IN TUNA SAUCE

**FOR 6**

4$^1/_2$ CUPS DRY WHITE WINE

2 CELERY RIBS, CHOPPED

1 CARROT, CHOPPED

1 ONION, CHOPPED

1 GARLIC CLOVE, CHOPPED

A FEW BAY LEAVES

2$^1/_4$ POUNDS VEAL TOP ROUND OR EYE
OF SIRLOIN, TIED WITH KITCHEN
STRING TO MAKE A LARGE, LONG
SAUSAGE

SALT AND PEPPER

PARSLEY LEAVES AND CAPERS

**FOR THE SAUCE:**

1$^1/_2$ CUPS MAYONNAISE

1$^1/_2$ TABLESPOONS SALTED CAPERS,
SOAKED IN WATER FOR 10 MINUTES,
THEN DRAINED AND VERY FINELY
CHOPPED

2 TABLESPOONS VERY FINELY CHOPPED
PICKLED GHERKINS

9 OUNCES TUNA IN OIL, DRAINED

2 TABLESPOONS FINELY CHOPPED FLAT-
LEAF PARSLEY

*Fish and meat are very seldom combined, but in this famous recipe they make a perfect and delicate* antipasto.

Put the wine, celery, carrot, onion, garlic, and bay leaves in a large pan with the meat and add enough water to cover. Season with salt and pepper, bring to a boil, then reduce the heat and simmer for 1$^1/_2$ hours, until the meat is tender.

Meanwhile, mix together all the ingredients for the sauce and purée in a blender or food processor. Season to taste with salt and pepper if necessary.

Remove the meat from the pan, take off the string, and cut the meat into very thin slices. Spread them over a large serving plate and cover with the sauce. Decorate with parsley leaves and capers.

# PICCATA MILANESE
MILANESE-STYLE VEAL WITH PARMA HAM

**FOR 4**

4 THIN SLICES VEAL, WEIGHING ABOUT
4$^1/_2$ OUNCES EACH

7 TABLESPOONS BUTTER

1$^3/_4$ OUNCES SPECK (SEE PAGE 84) OR
PARMA HAM, CUT INTO SMALL STRIPS

SALT AND PEPPER

FLOUR FOR DREDGING

4 TABLESPOONS STOCK

1 TABLESPOON FINELY CHOPPED FLAT-LEAF
PARSLEY

JUICE OF 1 LEMON

*You can use chicken or turkey breast here instead of veal if you prefer. What these meats have in common is that they cook very quickly and absorb the flavoring, which can also be wine (see* scaloppina, *page 84).*

Trim the slices of veal to a uniform shape. Heat 3 tablespoons of the butter in a large pan and fry the speck or Parma ham for a few minutes. Season the veal with salt and pepper and dredge in flour, then fry in the same pan until golden on each side. Remove from the pan and keep warm.

Add the rest of the butter to the pan, then stir in the stock to loosen the bits on the bottom of the pan. Add the parsley and lemon juice, bring to a boil, then pour over the meat and serve immediately.

# NODINO DI VITELLO AL ROSMARINO

## VEAL CUTLETS WITH ROSEMARY

### FOR 4

4 TENDERLOIN VEAL CHOPS, WEIGHING
ABOUT 9 OUNCES EACH

FLOUR FOR DREDGING

6 TABLESPOONS BUTTER

4 SMALL SPRIGS ROSEMARY

1 GLASS DRY WHITE WINE

3/4 TABLESPOON SALTED CAPERS, SOAKED
IN WATER FOR 10 MINUTES, THEN
DRAINED AND FINELY CHOPPED

ZEST OF 1 LEMON

1 TABLESPOON FINELY CHOPPED FLAT-LEAF
PARSLEY

SALT AND PEPPER

*Nodino is a cutlet taken from the ribs. This is one of many ways of cooking it, typical of the North where this kind of meat is most frequently consumed.*

Dredge the chops with flour on both sides. Heat the butter in a skillet and gently fry the chops, 2 at a time if necessary, for 15 minutes on each side, until well browned. Remove from the pan, add the leaves from the rosemary sprigs, and pour in the wine. Bring to a boil, stirring to scrape up the browned bits from the bottom of the pan, then add the capers, lemon zest, and parsley. Reduce the heat and mix well. Return the chops to the pan and cook gently for 10 minutes. Season with salt and pepper to taste, then serve.

# STRACOTTO

## BRAISED BEEF

### FOR 6

4 TABLESPOONS OLIVE OIL

A NICE PIECE OF BEEF SUCH AS RUMP OR
BRISKET, WITH A LITTLE FAT, WEIGHING
ABOUT 3 1/4 POUNDS

2 CARROTS, CUT INTO VERY SMALL CUBES

1 LARGE ONION, FINELY CHOPPED

3 CELERY RIBS, CUT INTO SMALL CUBES

10 JUNIPER BERRIES

20 PEPPERCORNS

A FEW BAY LEAVES

3 1/2 OUNCES FATTY PARMA HAM, CUT
INTO THIN STRIPS

4 1/2 CUPS DRY WHITE WINE

4 1/2 CUPS BEEF STOCK

SALT

3 TABLESPOONS BUTTER

*Literally translated, stracatto means "overcooked," which reflects the way this dish is cooked very slowly for a long time.*

Heat the olive oil in a large, preferably cast-iron casserole; add the beef and brown on each side, then remove from the pan and set aside. Add the carrots, onion, celery, juniper berries, peppercorns, bay leaves, and Parma ham and fry until the vegetables are soft. Return the meat to the pan and add the wine, stock, and a little salt. Bring to a boil, then reduce the heat, cover and cook slowly until the meat is very tender, about 2 hours. Pierce the meat with a skewer to check if it is well cooked; if necessary, cook for a little longer. By the end of the cooking time most of the liquid should have evaporated.

Remove the meat from the pan, whisk in the butter, and add a little more stock or wine—enough to bring it to a velvety consistency. Pass the sauce through a fine conical sieve. Serve the meat thinly sliced, accompanied by the sauce.

# STINCO DI VITELLO
### SLOW-ROASTED VEAL SHANK

**FOR 8 TO 10**

1 WHOLE VEAL SHANK, WEIGHING
    4½ TO 6½ POUNDS
2 TABLESPOONS OLIVE OIL
SALT AND PEPPER
½ CUP WHITE WINE
ABOUT 4½ CUPS VEAL OR BEEF STOCK
SMALL BUNCH EACH SAGE, ROSEMARY,
    AND THYME
JUICE OF 3 LEMONS
3½ TABLESPOONS BUTTER, ROLLED IN A
    LITTLE FLOUR

*This dish originated in both the Veneto and Lombardy and has now spread all over northern Italy. Veal shank has to be cooked whole, and can serve quite a few people.*

Preheat the oven to 325° F. Wash and pat dry the veal shank, then place it in a large roasting pan and rub with the olive oil and some salt and pepper. Pour the wine into the pan, with enough of the stock to make a layer ½ inch deep. Add the herbs and cover with foil.

Cook in the oven for 1½ hours, checking from time to time that it has not dried out and adding more stock if necessary.

Remove the foil, increase the oven temperature to 400° F. and cook for another 30 to 40 minutes, basting the meat regularly with the liquid. Remove the meat from the pan and leave to rest for 10 minutes before serving. Meanwhile, put the roasting pan on the stovetop and add enough stock to the meat juices to make a sauce consistency. Bring to a boil, stirring to scrape up the bits from the bottom of the pan, then whisk in the butter rolled in flour. Strain through a fine sieve. Thinly slice the veal lengthwise and serve with the sauce.

# FRITTO MISTO ALLA PIEMONTESE
### PIEDMONTESE MIXED FRIED SURPRISE

**FOR 6**

6 LAMB CUTLETS
7 OUNCES CALVES' LIVER, THINLY
    SLICED
7 OUNCES CHICKEN BREAST IN THIN
    ESCALOPES, SLICED
7 OUNCES BEEF TENDERLOIN IN THIN
    ESCALOPES, SLICED
2 ARTICHOKE HEARTS, (SEE *CARCIOFO*,
    PAGE 105), THINLY SLICED
1 EGGPLANT, THINLY SLICED
1 CARDOON (SEE *CARDO*, PAGE 105),
    PEELED, LIGHTLY BLANCHED AND
    THINLY SLICED (OPTIONAL)
2 CRISP EATING APPLES, PEELED, CORED,
    AND THICKLY SLICED
12 *AMARETTI* COOKIES
4 EGGS, BEATEN
SEASONED FLOUR FOR DREDGING
OLIVE OIL FOR FRYING
LEMON WEDGES

*It is said that this very typical Piedmontese dish should consist of at least 13 different ingredients, but its true afficionados prefer at least 17 or 18 meats of all types, vegetables, even cookies and fruit.*

Leave the lamb cutlets on the bone but pound out the meat until thin. Dredge the meat and vegetables, the apples, and amaretti biscuits with flour and then coat them in the beaten egg. Heat a good layer of olive oil in a large skillet and shallow-fry everything until golden brown, starting with the vegetables, then the apples and cookies and finally the meat. Serve imediatcly, with lemon wedges.

# ARROSTO DI VITELLO AL LATTE

## MILK-ROASTED VEAL

**FOR 6 TO 8**

3¹/₂ TABLESPOONS BUTTER

3¹/₄ POUNDS LEAN SIRLOIN OR
    TOP ROUND OF VEAL

3¹/₂ OUNCES PARMA HAM, CUT INTO
    SMALL STRIPS

PINCH FRESHLY GRATED NUTMEG

SALT AND PEPPER

2¹/₄ QUARTS CUPS MILK

*This is a very delicate dish, which should be served in thin slices with green beans, Swiss chard, or spinach.*

Melt the butter in a large casserole into which the veal will just fit snugly. Add the meat and brown on all sides. Add the Parma ham strips and the nutmeg and season with salt and pepper. Pour in just enough of the milk to cover the meat by two-thirds. Cover and simmer gently for 2 to 2¹/₂ hours, until tender, topping up with more milk from time to time to prevent the meat becoming dry.

# TRIPPA ALLA MILANESE
MILANESE-STYLE TRIPE

**FOR 6**

2 CUPS LARGE WHITE BEANS

2³/₄ POUNDS MIXED TRIPE,
 CLEANED AND BLANCHED (SEE *TRIPPA*,
 PAGE **85**)

1 ONION, FINELY CHOPPED

1 LARGE CARROT, THINLY SLICED

2 OR 3 CELERY RIBS, THINLY SLICED

1³/₄ OUNCES *PANCETTA*, CHOPPED

4 TABLESPOONS BUTTER

2 TABLESPOONS OLIVE OIL

1 POUND TOMATOES, SKINNED, SEEDED,
 AND CHOPPED

A FEW BAY LEAVES

A FEW SAGE LEAVES

SALT AND PEPPER

A LITTLE STOCK IF NECESSARY

3¹/₂ OUNCES PARMESAN CHEESE,
 GRATED

*Of the many ways of preparing tripe, the* busecca, *as they call it in Milan, is the one that seems to pleases most palates.*

Soak the beans in a large quantity of cold water overnight and then drain.

Cut the prepared tripe into strips. Fry the onion, carrot, celery, and pancetta in the butter and oil until soft. Add the tripe and cook until the moisture has evaporated, stirring often to prevent sticking. Add the tomatoes, bay leaves, sage leaves, salt, and plenty of black pepper, then cover and cook gently for 2 hours. If the mixture becomes too dry, add a little stock.

Put the beans in a separate pan, cover with water and bring to a boil. Cook for an hour or so, until tender, then drain and add to the tripe. Cook for a further 15 to 20 minutes or until everything is tender. Add more stock if necessary. The result should be neither soupy nor dry.

Serve sprinkled with the Parmesan cheese and a few sage leaves.

# GRAN RAGÙ NAPOLETANO
MEAT STEWED IN NEAPOLITAN RAGÙ

**FOR 6**

¹/₃ CUP OLIVE OIL

1 LARGE ONION, FINELY CHOPPED

2¹/₄ POUNDS BEEF BRISKET

1 POUND PORK SHOULDER ON
 THE BONE

1 POUND LAMB SPARERIBS

1 GLASS DRY RED WINE

2¹/₄ POUNDS VERY RIPE TOMATOES,
 SKINNED, SEEDED, AND CHOPPED

2 TABLESPOONS *ESTRATTO DI POMODORO*
 (SEE PAGE **118**) OR 6 TABLESPOONS
 TOMATO PASTE

1¹/₄ POUNDS *RIGATONI*

3 OUNCES PARMESAN CHEESE,
 GRATED

SALT AND PEPPER

*Not a Sunday goes by for most Neapolitans without a piece of meat cooked in a tomato sauce. The sauce is used to dress large pasta and the sliced meat is then served separately with some vegetables. The little lamb spareribs in this recipe, known in dialect as* spullicarielli, *give a meaty flavor to the sauce and, when cooked, have a little meat left on them, which you can have some fun eating with your fingers. Sometimes the various cuts of meat are replaced by* polpettone *(see page 80), a meatloaf large enough to feed many people.*

Heat the olive oil in a large pan or casserole and fry the onion and pieces of meat until the meat is browned on all sides and the onion is soft. Add the wine and allow to evaporate a little, then stir in the tomatoes and tomato paste, cover and simmer on a low heat for 1¹/₂ to 2 hours, adding salt and pepper about half way through the cooking time.

Cook the pasta in boiling salted water until *al dente*, then drain. Dress with the sauce and serve sprinkled with the Parmesan cheese. The meat is then eaten with some vegetables as a main course.

# BOLLITO MISTO

**FOR 10 TO 12**

4 CELERY RIBS, CUT INTO CHUNKS

3 CARROTS, CUT INTO CHUNKS

1 LARGE ONION, PEELED AND SPIKED WITH 4 TO 5 CLOVES

A FEW PEPPERCORNS

SALT

3¼ POUNDS BEEF BRISKET

1 VEAL TONGUE, WEIGHING 1 TO 1¾ POUNDS

1 BOILING CHICKEN, WEIGHING 4½ POUNDS

2¼ POUNDS VEAL BRISKET

PIECE OF VEAL CHEEK, WEIGHING 1 POUND

2 *COTECHINO* SAUSAGES (SEE PAGE 74), WEIGHING ABOUT 10½ OUNCES EACH

*SALSA VERDE* (SEE PAGE 224) AND *MOSTARDA DI CREMONA* (SEE PAGE 269), TO SERVE

*Piedmont and Lombardy both claim to be the birthplace of this gargantuan dish. Boiled meats have always been eaten everywhere in Italy after being used to make soup. For bollito misto the different types of meat are cooked specifically to produce something really succulent. Don't be put off by the enormous piece of meat in the picture. The butcher was a little too enthusiastic, and after the picture was taken a local restaurant sold that piece to literally hundreds of customers. However, this dish is still only worth doing for large numbers on special occasions.*

Put the vegetables and peppercorns in a very large pot of lightly salted water and bring to a boil. Add the beef and cook gently for 30 minutes. Then add the tongue, chicken, veal brisket, and cheek and simmer for 2 hours, skimming regularly to remove any scum from the surface. (If you don't have a large enough pot for all the meat, divide the vegetables and meat between 2 pans.) Top up with boiling water if necessary to make sure the meat is always covered.

Prick the skin of the *cotechino* sausages with a needle, put them in a separate pan and cover with cold water. Bring to a boil and cook gently for 1 to 1½ hours.

When all the meats are cooked and tender, remove them from the water. Peel and trim the tongue. Slice the meats and arrange them on a large serving plate. Serve hot, accompanied by the sauces, vegetables, and a little stock.

# INVOLTINI DI AGNELLO E MAIALE

## BUNDLES OF PORK AND LAMB

**FOR 4**

7 OUNCES VERY FRESH LAMBS' LIVER

7 OUNCES PIGS' LIVER

7 OUNCES PIGS' HEART

SALT AND PEPPER

CAYENNE PEPPER

3 TABLESPOONS EXTRA-VIRGIN OLIVE OIL

JUICE OF 1 LEMON

1 PIECE CAUL FAT (SEE *RETE DI MAIALE*, PAGE 82)

2 LAMBS' TESTICLES (SEE *GRANELLI*, PAGE 76), CUT INTO QUARTERS

*This is an Apulian specialty. I ate it in Alberobello and it was exquisite. It may be difficult to find all the ingredients, but if you know a good butcher he or she should be able to obtain them for you.*

Cut the liver and heart into longish strips the size of a finger. Sprinkle with salt and pepper, cayenne pepper, and the olive oil and lemon juice. Soften the caul fat in lukewarm water to obtain a type of lacy net. Cut it into 8 long strips and wrap the mixed meats in them, including the testicles. Place on a very hot charcoal grill and cook for 5 to 6 minutes on each side. They should be crisp on the outside and succulent inside.

# PUNTA DI PETTO D'AGNELLO RIPIENO

STUFFED BREAST OF LAMB

**FOR 4 TO 6**

- 1 PIECE *PUNTA DI PETTO* OF LAMB (SEE RIGHT), WEIGHING 2$^1$/$_4$ POUNDS
- 3 EGGS, BEATEN
- 8 TABLESPOONS SOFT FRESH BREAD CRUMBS
- 1 TABLESPOON RAISINS
- 1 GARLIC CLOVE, FINELY CHOPPED
- 1 TABLESPOON PINE NUTS
- 2 OUNCES PARMESAN CHEESE, FINELY CHOPPED
- 1 TABLESPOON FINELY CHOPPED PARSLEY
- SALT AND PEPPER
- OLIVE OIL

*This specific cut, more often used for veal, is the extremely soft part of the breast of lamb, underneath the cutlets. The various layers of meat and fat are ideal for making a pocket, which is filled, sewn together, and cooked. Naturally, the younger the animal, the more tender will be the final dish, which resembles a small pillow.*

Preheat the oven to 350° F. Slit open the breast of lamb along one side and made a pocket among the layers. Mix together the eggs, bread crumbs, raisins, garlic, pine nuts, Parmesan, parsley, and some salt and pepper. Stuff the pocket with this mixture and then sew it up with a needle and kitchen string. Brush with a little olive oil and roast in the oven for 1$^1$/$_4$ hours.

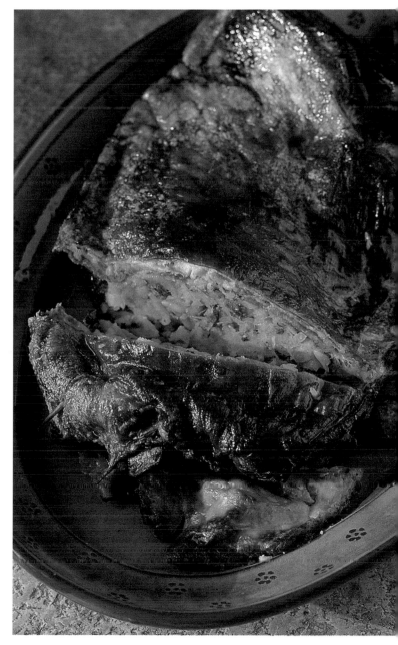

*TOFEJA DEL CANAVESE*

# TOFEJA DEL CANAVESE
## PORK AND BEANS

**FOR 8 TO 10**

2¼ CUPS DRIED *BORLOTTI* BEANS

2¼ POUNDS PIGS' FEET, TAIL,
    EARS, SPARERIBS, AND SMALL
    *COTECHINOS*

1 POUND FRESH PORK SKIN
    (SEE *COTENNA*, PAGE 74)

SALT AND PEPPER

SMALL SPRIG ROSEMARY, FINELY
    CHOPPED

2 GARLIC CLOVES, FINELY CHOPPED

A FEW SAGE LEAVES

2 CELERY RIBS, FINELY CHOPPED

1 CARROT, FINELY CHOPPED

1 ONION, FINELY CHOPPED

5 TABLESPOONS OLIVE OIL

1 CHILI PEPPER, FINELY CHOPPED

PINCH FRESHLY GRATED NUTMEG

A FEW BAY LEAVES

*Tofeja is the name of the lidded terra-cotta pot specifically designed for cooking this very rich, but exceptionally succulent peasant dish. Canavese is the northern part of Piedmont bordering the Aosta Valley where I grew up. We used to eat this dish at* carnevale *(carnival time). All the gelatinous parts of the pig are included.*

Soak the borlotti beans in plenty of cold water overnight and then drain.

    Preheat the oven to 325° F. Singe the tail and ears to remove any hairs; they should be immaculately clean. Cut the pork skin into rectangles about 3 x 5 inches, and season with salt and pepper. Mix together the rosemary and 1 chopped garlic clove and place a pinch of this mixture and a whole sage leaf in the middle of each piece of pork skin. Roll up and tie with kitchen string.

    Put the drained borlotti beans in a large casserole. Lay the vegetables on top, then sprinkle with the oil, chili, nutmeg, and some salt and pepper. Top this with all the meats and the pork skin rolls and cover with cold water. Scatter the bay leaves and the remaining chopped garlic clove over. Put the lid on and cook in the oven without touching or stirring for 3 to 3½ hours, then serve.

# OSSOBUCO ALLA MILANESE

**FOR 4**

2¾ POUNDS VEAL SHANKS, CUT
    INTO 1½-INCH LENGTHS, WITH
    THE MARROW BONE IN THE CENTER

SEASONED FLOUR FOR DREDGING

ABOUT 4 TABLESPOONS OLIVE OIL

1 ONION, DICED

2 CELERY RIBS, DICED

1 CARROT, DICED

2 GLASSES DRY WHITE WINE

ABOUT 1¼ CUPS VEAL STOCK

SALT AND PEPPER

Dredge the veal in the seasoned flour. Heat the olive oil in a large casserole, add the meat, and fry until browned on all sides. Remove from the pan and set aside. Add more oil if necessary, then gently fry the onion, celery, and carrot in the same pan until lightly browned.

    Return the meat to the pan, pour in the wine and stock, and bring to a slow boil. Cover and cook for about 1½ hours, until the meat is tender, removing the lid toward the end of cooking. Check from time to time and add a little more stock if the mixture is getting too dry.

    Adjust the seasoning and serve with *risotto allo zafferano* (see page 178) and *gremolada*, a mixture of finely chopped lemon peel, garlic, and parsley.

# FEGATO ALLA VENEZIANA
SAUTÉED LIVER WITH ONIONS

FOR 4

3 TABLESPOONS BUTTER
1 LARGE ONION, THINLY SLICED
1 POUND CALVES' LIVER,
    VERY THINLY SLICED
SALT AND PEPPER
FINELY CHOPPED FLAT-LEAF PARSLEY
    (OPTIONAL)

*This is another classic of Italian cuisine, this time representing the Veneto; it differs a little from Venice's version, which contains a shot of vinegar.*

Heat the butter in a large skillet, add the onion, and cook until it begins to color. Add the slices of liver and cook until browned but still moist and pink in the center—about 3 to 4 minutes on each side. If you prefer it well done, cook a little longer. Add salt and pepper to taste and serve immediately. Some people add parsley or even a few drops of lemon juice. It is up to you.

# POLENTA CONCIA CON SALSICCIA
DRESSED POLENTA WITH SAUSAGE

FOR 6 TO 8 (OR EVEN MORE)

3/4 OUNCE DRIED PORCINI
    MUSHROOMS
14 OUNCES *LUGANIGA* SAUSAGE (SEE
    PAGE 77), CUT INTO 4-INCH CHUNKS
4 TABLESPOONS OLIVE OIL
2 GARLIC CLOVES, COARSELY CHOPPED
1 SMALL ONION, THINLY SLICED
SPRIG ROSEMARY
1 SMALL CHILI PEPPER, FINELY CHOPPED
3 TABLESPOONS DRY RED WINE
2 1/4 CUPS TOMATO PULP (SEE
    PAGE 118)
SALT

FOR THE *POLENTA CONCIA*:
1 1/4 CUPS WATER
3/4 OUNCE SALT
1 POUND COARSE POLENTA
SCANT 1/2 CUP UNSALTED BUTTER
3 1/2 OUNCES PARMESAN CHEESE,
    GRATED
5 OUNCES FONTINA CHEESE,
    PREFERABLY FROM THE AOSTA VALLEY,
    CUT INTO SMALL CUBES

*One of the most warming dishes you can get high up in the mountains, especially of the Aosta Valley, is* polenta concia *(see page 174), which sustains even the hardest worker. It is usually accompanied by a stew of chicken or venison. With pork sausages, however, it blends to a perfect marriage.*

*I like to use traditional polenta but if you use quick-cook polenta instead, the cooking time is only 5 minutes. The Bramata polenta is by far the tastiest.*

Soak the porcini mushrooms in lukewarm water for about 30 minutes. Put the *luganiga* in a large pan with the oil and fry until brown on all sides. Add the garlic, onion, rosemary, and chili and fry for 5 minutes. Drain the porcini and squeeze out the excess water, then cut them up roughly and add to the pan. Pour in the wine and boil to evaporate, then add the tomato pulp and some salt and simmer for 20 minutes. Keep warm while you prepare the polenta.

To make the polenta, bring the water to a boil with the salt. Gradually add the polenta, stirring constantly with a long wooden spoon until all the flour has been incorporated into the water and is lump-free. At this stage you must be careful that you do not splash hot polenta onto your hands. Stir the polenta constantly over medium heat for about 30 minutes, by which time it should be pulling away from the side of the pan. Add the butter, Parmesan, and Fontina and stir well until everything has amalgamated.

There are two ways of serving this: either by the spoonful on a plate or, as the local cooks traditionally do, by pouring the polenta onto large wooden board and leaving it to cool a little, then slicing it with a steel wire and putting it on the plate with the sausage stew.

# ZAMPONE E LENTICCHIE

ZAMPONE AND LENTILS

**FOR 4 TO 6**

1 COOKED *ZAMPONE*, WEIGHING AT
   LEAST 2¼ POUNDS, OR 2
   SMALLER ONES
1¾ CUPS *CASTELLUCCIO* LENTILS
   (SEE *LENTICCHIA*, PAGE 113)
4 OR 5 SAGE LEAVES
SMALL SPRIG ROSEMARY
A FEW CELERY LEAVES
2 GARLIC CLOVES, PEELED
2 SUN-DRIED TOMATOES, HALVED
A LITTLE *PEPERONCINO* (CHILI)
3 TABLESPOONS EXTRA-VIRGIN OLIVE OIL
SALT AND PEPPER

*A truly Emilian dish where, thanks to the abundance of local Parma ham, zampone, or stuffed pigs' feet, are freshly available. The skin of the feet, including the toes, is filled with a mixture of gelatinous parts of the pig, plus meat and spices. It takes a long time to cook (3 or 4 hours' simmering) and tastes deliciously porky. The alternative to fresh zampone is to buy cooked ones packed tightly in foil, which just require simmering for 20 minutes. It is best to use castelluccio lentils for this recipe; they do not need soaking and are ready in 20 minutes.*

Put the *zampone* in a pan of cold water and bring to a boil, then reduce the heat and simmer for 20 minutes, or according to the instructions on the package.

Meanwhile, put the lentils in a pan of cold water with the herbs, garlic cloves, sun-dried tomatoes, and chili. Bring to a boil and simmer for 20 minutes or until tender.

Discard the herbs and the whole garlic cloves, then add the olive oil and salt and pepper to taste. Slice the *zampone* and serve with the lentils.

*POLENTA CONCIA CON SALSICCIA* [TOP LEFT AND RIGHT];
*ZAMPONE E LENTICCHIE* [BOTTOM]

# VEGETABLES & LEGUMES

## VERDURE E LEGUMI

One of the things that makes me very proud of Italian cuisine is the way we prepare and cook vegetables, which are generally served in place of meat rather than as side dishes with it. Especially in the summer, we eat and enjoy vegetables without even thinking of missing meat. This may be due to the fact that Italy's geography and climate are suited much more to the growing of produce than the rearing of animals.

Every Italian region has locally grown vegetables, which, when they are in season, are the very best available for the preparation of the excellent regional, traditional dishes that have grown up around them. Due to the Mediterranean climate and their mild winters, Sicily, Calabria, Campania, and Puglia are the primary regions for the cultivation of vegetables of all types. The extremely fertile soil is also a factor, not to mention the intelligent and hard-working farmers of the regions. All combine to produce beautiful, tasty vegetables.

Italians very much look forward to the seasons of certain produce, such as asparagus, tomatoes, and artichokes, so they can enjoy those particular tastes that are only available in vegetables that are cultivated organically in the open fields. Favorite vegetables of the Italians include asparagus, eggplants, tomatoes, and artichokes, and the best recipes combine these with pasta, polenta, rice, or just bread, to make simple but delicious meals. This way of eating vegetables has been passed down through the centuries by farmers and peasants, and is still one of the healthiest ways to eat. *La cucina povera* or "poor food" used to consist of the less-romantic, cheaper vegetables like potatoes, beans, and cabbage. Today, though, many specialties are produced with these ingredients, and often by top chefs who charge a great deal of money for them.

It is really a fantastic sight to see Italian markets, where all the vegetables are exhibited in such an inviting way that it is impossible not to be tempted to buy a lot more than you need. The piles of fresh-cut fennel bulbs sprinkled with droplets of water, or the display of ten different types of field herbs, already clean and just waiting to be used, is an irresistible invitation.

I still vividly remember the market in Venice, near the Rialto Bridge, where the market stall-holders sell ready-peeled onions and ready-cleaned artichoke hearts to save such chores at home. This super-service obviously costs a little more, but it is highly valued by the customers. Food handled in this way, with such care and knowledge, produces excellent dishes. The way in which the produce is exhibited in the markets shows that the vendor cares for his merchandise, as well as wishing to attract and keep his customers. Quite often you will hear a conversation between the customer and the shopkeeper or stall-holder about the best way to cook or prepare certain special vegetables—a common enough occurrence in most shops in Italy.

When I was a child, my family had a small garden where we grew vegetables. I often walked with my father through row after row of tomatoes, and when I brushed against one of those magnificent plants, the intense scent of the tomato was released—even the leaves of the plant emanated very distinctive smells, which I still remember today. This scent—and the strong flavor

of all Italian vegetables—probably comes from the abundant sunlight imparting a very special taste.

Italians do not believe in having all fruit and vegetables all year round—the produce has to be seasonal and, if possible, field-grown. Only then can proper ripeness and maturity, the right taste, and the vitamin content be guaranteed. It is quite rare to find a domestic freezer in Italy used to stock pre-cooked or convenience foods. I only keep large quantities of porcini mushrooms in mine. On the other hand, there is a long tradition of preserving all sorts of vegetables in many different ways— from drying to preserving in vinegar, salt, or oil— and for many different purposes.

For instance, no family in Italy would be without a jar of at least one type of vegetable pickle for their *antipasto*—the vinegar's acidity is essential to stimulate the gastric juices and balance the fattiness of the meats. More recently, preserves have begun to be valued as foods in their own right, and the number of dishes prepared with them seems infinite.

A good example is the traditional sun-dried tomatoes of Italy, which have, in recent years, become one of the fashionable innovations in international cuisine. This is an extraordinary phenomenon to Italians, since tomatoes have been dried in southern Italy for many centuries. The discovery of the unique taste of concentrated tomatoes has spawned a great array of similar specialties, like dried peppers, eggplant, and even zucchini.

Legumes have a longer history of being dried, although they are also eaten fresh with equal enthusiasm. They are also almost as nutritious when dried. Any well-balanced diet should include legumes, whether fresh or dried, for their vitamins, proteins, and trace minerals. Prepared in many ways, each reflecting regional habits, legumes still have an image as peasant food, which has recently

LEFT: CORN
GROWING IN
EMILIA-ROMAGNA

BOTTOM LEFT:
CASTELLUCCIO, IN
THE WONDERFUL
UMBRIAN VALLEY
OF MONTE
SIBILLINI, HOME
OF THE FABLED
LENTILS

BELOW: ADELVIO
AND BEDULLIA, AN
UMBRIAN COUPLE,
HARVESTING THEIR
VEGETABLES

become very fashionable. They have a wonderful flavor, most famously exploited in *pasta e fagioli*, a complete meal containing a perfect balance of carbohydrate, protein, and fiber. Other legume recipes include *insalata di fagioli*, a Tuscan salad of boiled cannellini beans dressed with a little virgin olive oil, salt, and pepper, which is a simple but healthy delicacy. Legumes also make excellent soups that are so thick and tasty that they are meals in themselves. The best bean soups are based on dried fava beans, chickpeas, and lentils, all of which are available in every region and in every possible guise.

Castelluccio lentils from Umbria are famous not only for their high iron content and for being extremely easy to cook, but also because they are not prone to disease and parasites. Above all, though, it is their unique flavor that distinguishes them from other lentils. On the way from Umbria to the Marche, one has to drive through the plateau of Castelluccio, and as one drives along, one often sees farmers with their tractors parked on the roadside near the village, selling their lentils directly to customers who stop on their journey. The lentils are always in high demand because they are only grown organically, which makes them expensive. Anyone who is familiar with the flavor, though, always seems prepared to pay three or four times the price of ordinary lentils to get them.

# A-Z OF VEGETABLES & LEGUMES

## ACETOSA / SORREL

This sharp-tasting plant, also known as *erba brusca* or "sour grass," is not as often used by the Italians as it is by the French, which is why it is not widely cultivated in Italy, although it can be found growing wild in May and June. It is used in soups and salads for its pungent flavor and I find it irresistible as a base for risotto.

## AGLIO, AGLIETTO / GARLIC

Garlic has been cultivated in Italy for many centuries, and 70 percent of its entire production is now exported. The major areas of cultivation are Campania, Emilia-Romagna, Veneto, Puglia, and Sicily, and it is an important ingredient in the cuisine of all these areas.

There are many varieties of garlic, including the white *Bianco Napoletano* and *Bianco Piacentino*, and the pink *Rosso Napoletano*, *Rosso di Sulmona*, and *Rosso di Agrigento*. Sometimes during the spring you can find *aglio selvatico*, or wild garlic, but instead of eating the bulb, eat only the dark-green heavily scented leaves (see right).

I was once given an elephantine garlic, ten times bigger than the normal variety, but it lacked flavor and aroma: so remember, when it comes to choosing garlic, small is beautiful. To spot a good-quality garlic bulb, look for one with a diameter of at least 1¹/₂ inches, with compact, firm cloves. Avoid any with green shoots sprouting from the top, as these are past their best and will be very strong, producing an antisocial aftertaste.

If carefully trimmed and kept whole, garlic will keep for up to a year, although in Italy it is so abundant and cheap that no one needs to store it unless they have grown their own. To peel it, press on each clove with the palm of your hand until the skin breaks and comes away easily. If you want to get rid of the smell of garlic on your hands, rub them with salt before washing with soap as usual.

Garlic is used in many Italian recipes as a flavoring to enhance the recipe rather than dominate it. There are, however, a few notable exceptions, including the famous recipes for *bagna caôda* (see page 33) and *pesto* (see page 228), in which garlic is the predominant flavor. Another less well-known garlic recipe is *agliata*, a pungent Ligurian sauce served with boiled meat, made with garlic crushed in a mortar with bread crumbs that have been soaked in vinegar then squeezed dry, with olive oil added at the end. My wife likes to cook garlic with roast chicken, roasting whole, unpeeled cloves in the same pan as the chicken toward the end of the cooking time, so that they are wonderfully creamy and sweet. Garlic is also delicious in salads and soups. In Piedmont, they make *aja* or *agliata*, a paste made of garlic pounded in a mortar along with walnuts and olive oil, which is absolutely delicious spread on bread. Garlic is also used on *bruschetta*, for which a raw clove is rubbed over the surface of toasted bread. It may be antisocial, but it tastes wonderful.

To reduce the strength of flavor of garlic, soak it in cold milk for a few hours before use. This is what they do in Piedmont when making a less powerful version of *bagna caôda*; the garlic is even cooked in milk to control its powerful aroma. If you want only a hint of garlic in your dish, try rubbing a cut clove over the surface of the pan you are going to cook in, or around the bowl in which you are going to make a salad. Try coarsely chopping a little garlic, adding it to a bottle of vinegar or oil and leaving it to infuse for a day or two. The strained oil or vinegar can then be used to dress salads and other dishes in which only a hint of garlic is required. *Aglietto*, a younger and less powerful garlic, is also ideal for more delicate dishes and salads.

As well as its culinary value, garlic also has many healing properties, and was often used as an antiseptic before the discovery of antibiotics. During the war, it used to be placed on wounds to disinfect them and to keep bacteria at bay. Today, it is valued as a means of reducing blood cholesterol levels, as well as warding off vampires, of course!

LEFT: *AGLIO*

## AGLIO SELVATICO / WILD GARLIC

The best part of wild garlic (*Allium ursinum*) is the tender leaves, which are delicious in salads, soups, or as an ingredient in wild garlic butter. Wild garlic is plentiful in the spring, when you can literally smell it in the air on country walks. The bulbs of wild garlic are tough, so leave them behind to grow.

## ASPARAGO / ASPARAGUS

A vegetable much loved by Italians, asparagus is generally only eaten in season so that its natural wild flavor can be enjoyed. Asparagus is a shoot which, if allowed to grow to maturity, blooms into a wonderful, delicate lace-like head that can be used in floral arrangements. When the tip of the shoot emerges from

BELOW: ASPARAGUS IN TURIN MARKET

the earth, it is cut below ground at its base with a special long knife, leaving about 6 inches of tender, edible shoot attached.

The regions in which most asparagus is cultivated are Emilia-Romagna, Veneto, and Piedmont, but there are some smaller areas around Vesuvio in Campania. There are three main types of asparagus grown and enjoyed in Italy—the white, the purple, and the green. The white variety, *Bianco di Bassano*, is derived from German varieties and grows in the Veneto. Every year the restaurants in the pretty town of Bassano del Grappa on the Piave River compete to present the most original recipe using white asparagus, with the public as the jury. Purple asparagus is called *argenteuil*, and is cultivated in Campania, from which it also takes its Italian name of Napoletano, while the green variety is grown in Piedmont and Emilia-Romagna. This is especially tasty and tender, and has a dark green tip fading to white at the base.

Asparagus needs to be prepared and cooked with special care and, to my mind, the best way to cook it is by steaming, so that the delicate tip stays intact after cooking and retains its flavor. To be at its best, asparagus should be very fresh, the finest stalks being those with firm heads with tightly closed tips. To prepare them, peel away the tough, stringy skin at the base. If you boil the asparagus, stand it in a tall, narrow pan, keeping the tender tips out of the water so that they do not overcook. Do not cover the pan with a lid or the heat of the steam will cook the tips faster than the stems.

In Italy, the most popular way of serving asparagus is boiled and served with melted butter and a sprinkling of Parmesan cheese, or perhaps as they do it in Milan, with a fried egg on top. It is good *pasticciati*, chopped and mixed with onion and scrambled eggs. In springtime, asparagus is delicious with freshly boiled new potatoes,

dressed with a little melted butter and accompanied with a few slices of thinly cut Parma ham. Asparagus risotto is a must, and young, tender asparagus spears can even be eaten raw with *bagna caôda* (see page 33).

There are only small quantities of wild asparagus (*Asparagus selvatico*), which is slightly bitter but has a very intense scent. Once when I was in Sardinia in wild asparagus season, it was possible to find it on sale at the roadside, freshly cut by the locals. The spears were thin, did not need peeling, and were delicious in an omelet (*frittata con asparagi*).

## BARBABIETOLA / BEETROOT

This root is from the same family as sugar beet, and is much-loved as a cooked (or sometimes raw) root for salads. It is also the principal ingredient of soups like the traditional Russian *borscht*. The leaves of fresh beetroot can also be eaten.

To cook beetroot, first cut off the top leaves without damaging the skin, and boil the roots for about two hours, depending on the size. They can also be baked in a moderate oven, covered with their own leaves and with water around

them, for about 1 to 1½ hours. Once cool, cooked beetroot may be peeled and cut in slices to add to mixed salads. However, I prefer them in a salad of their own, with just fresh cilantro, scallions, salt, virgin olive oil, and some good wine vinegar.

## BARBA DI BECCO, BARBA DI FRATE, BARBA DI CAPPUCCINO / SALAD GREEN

This salad plant is similar to chives and, like the herb, has long, narrow green leaves with a slightly sour taste. It is seldom cultivated commercially, but grows wild all over Italy and, in the springtime, can be picked to make a welcome contribution to salads.

## BORLOTTO / BORLOTTI BEAN

One of the best-known and most popular beans in central and northern Italy, whether in its fresh or dried form, the borlotti bean distinguishes itself from others by the startling patterns of its skin. The pod (*baccello*) of the fresh bean is yellowish in color, with bright red-and-green speckles, while the bean itself is white with red speckles. There are many varieties of borlotti bean, including the British-developed 'Taylor's Horticultural' which is much-used in Italy.

The borlotti is harvested when the pods are completely dry and the beans have taken on a darker color. It is mostly used in its dry form and, like the fresh bean, is used in soups—especially *minestrone*—or served simply boiled for about 30 minutes and dressed with extra-virgin olive oil, oregano or rosemary, and a little vinegar. Salt is only added at the end of the cooking time, otherwise the skin of the beans becomes tough and hard.

Borlotti beans are widely used in the famous northern Italian soup,

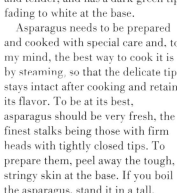

*pasta e fagioli* (see page 157), which has become very popular all over Italy. In the North, however, it is prepared differently, in that half the beans are mashed to give a creamy and velvety texture to the soup. Borlotti beans are also good married with rice in the thick soup *panissa* (see page 178). The Piedmontese town of Saluggia is also renowned for its borlotti dishes, which consist of borlotti bean soups cooked with *cotenna* (pork skin).

## BORRAGINE, BORRANA /
### BORAGE
This robust flowering herb always makes me think of Liguria, where it is widely used in *preboggion*, a mixture of wild herbs (see page 167), and it is also used in Campania to make a delicious soup. With its large hair-covered leaves, borage is best as a fresh vegetable cooked and dressed with a little virgin olive oil and a squeeze of lemon juice. It also makes a wonderful filling for ravioli (see *pansôti*, page 149). The extremely pretty pale-blue flowers are edible and can be used as a decoration for salads or for making little fritters to go with drinks.

## BROCCOLO, BROCCOLETTO /
### BROCCOLI
Broccoli belongs to the same family as cabbage and cauliflower and comes in many different varieties. It is formed by the thousands of buds of the flower at the top of the plant. If the buds flower, the broccoli becomes yellow, and that is why the freshness of broccoli is measured by the tightness and the intensity of the deep green-blue color of the buds.

*Broccolo* is mostly known as *calabrese*, because it grows best in Calabria, in Sicily (where, incidentally, *broccolo* means cauliflower). The most common variety, *Piccolo di Verona*, is pale green and ready to eat in the early spring, while *Grosso Romano* or *Violetto di Sicilia*, as it is also known in Italy, has very pretty conical florets and a distinctive purple color that turns green during cooking.

Italians eat a great deal of broccoli, and there are many recipes for cooking it. These include a purée that is eaten as an accompaniment to veal or chicken, or as a sauce for Pugliese pastas such as *orecchiette*. Blanched broccoli is also good dipped in egg and deep-fried.

*Broccoletti* are little branches, or florets, of broccoli. Like Brussels sprouts, they grow on the main stem after the head (main flower) has been cut. They can be cooked for about 5 minutes until just tender or for 8 to 9 minutes, until slightly softer, then stir-fried for a few seconds in olive oil with a few slices of garlic and half a chili. Another popular way of serving lightly boiled broccoli is just to drizzle it with a little extra-virgin olive oil and a few drops of lemon juice.

## BROCCOLO DI RAPA /
### BROCCOLI RABE
These shoots related to the turnip and the cabbage look like little spears with flower heads that turn yellow when they open. The shoots should only be used, however, while they are still green. *Broccolo di rapa* is very popular in the South, where the shoots are called *friarielli*. They can be blanched before any further cooking to moderate their very strong flavor. The most popular way of cooking broccoli rabe is braising it in a tightly covered pan with olive oil, garlic, and chili until tender. It is wonderful served with polenta cake.

## BRUSCANDOLI, BRUSCANSI /
### HOP SHOOT
The hop is a climbing plant with small thorns on its stems, and only the tops of the tender young shoots are used in cooking. This plant grows wild all over Italy, but is a specialty of the Veneto, where it is cooked in risottos. In springtime, little bunches of hop shoots can be found in the vegetable market of the Rialto. In the South, they are used in omelets or simply boiled, then sautéed with garlic. I eat them like asparagus, boiled with a little melted butter or, even better, with some hollandaise sauce.

## CANNELLINO / CANNELLINI
### BEAN
Cannellini beans have spread from the kitchens of Tuscany to become a favorite of all Italians, especially in central Italy. The popularity of the bean is due to its flavor, its perfect creamy-white color, and its ease of use in the kitchen. It is the most canned and jarred bean in Italian gastronomy.

The beans are difficult to harvest when ripe, and are thus harvested in autumn, when the pod is completely dry. As a result, the beans are rarely eaten fresh. To prepare the dry beans, soak them overnight. To cook them, place them in a pan, cover them with unsalted water, and bring to a boil. Reduce the heat, then simmer gently for 2 hours without stirring.

Cannellini are used in *minestrone* and in the famous *pasta e fagioli* (see page 157), especially in Campania, where the bean is heavily cultivated. There is a curious recipe in Tuscany, called *fagioli al fiasco*, which involves cooking the beans in a Chianti flask with water, oil, garlic, and sage. The flask is placed in the embers of a fire to cook the beans very slowly until they have swelled to the point where they can only just slip down the very narrow neck of the bottle. Cannellini are also

RIGHT: CLEANED
ARTICHOKE HEARTS

wonderful simply-cooked and seasoned with extra-virgin olive oil, salt, pepper, garlic, and rosemary, and eaten with bread.

CAPONATA, SEE SEDANO, AND RECIPE PAGE 135

### CARCIOFO / GLOBE ARTICHOKE

Artichokes belong to the thistle family. The edible parts of the plant are the tender parts of the flower bud and the adjacent stalk. In fact, if you put the stem of an artichoke in water, it may flower, with the choke turning a wonderful purple color. Artichokes grow best in the Mediterranean region, where the climate and the well-drained soil are perfect. The major areas of production in Italy are Campania, Sicily, Puglia, and Lazio, but they are grown in most regions for local use. About 98 percent of the Italian crop is exported, but Italians adore them too, so a huge crop is grown; in fact, Italy is the world's biggest producer of this vegetable.

BELOW:
ARTICHOKES ON
SALE IN PALERMO

Artichokes come in a wide variety of colors and shapes, from purple to green, both with and without thorns. There are basically three sizes of artichoke; the biggest and first to appear is *La Mamma*, which is usually boiled and eaten leaf by leaf down to the fleshy heart, discarding the hairy choke. Smaller, secondary plants called *figli* (children) grow later just below the main head, and are wonderfully tender. Finally, even smaller artichokes called *nipoti*

(nephews) grow further down the plant, and these are usually preserved in vinegar and oil as pickles for *antipasto*.

The main variety is the *Romanesco*, a large purple globe artichoke without thorns. A smaller artichoke, the *Violetto Toscano*, is also purple and, as its name implies, is cultivated in Tuscany. It is very tender and used mainly in *pinzimonio* (see recipe, page 223), a traditional Tuscan version of crudités. Finally, there is a violet artichoke from Sicily, called *Spinoso di Palermo*, which has a prickly flower that needs to be handled with great care. It has a fantastic flavor and is particularly delicious in *frittella*, a dish of fresh fava beans, artichokes, and onion as prepared in Palermo (see page 133). Finally, there are two Venetian artichokes, the first and largest, called *Precoce di Chioggia*, is harvested around October or November and is grown with the much smaller *Castraure della Laguna*.

To prepare artichokes, first cut off the top third of each vegetable and pluck the tough outer leaves. As only a small part of the stem of very young and tender artichokes is edible, it will need to be peeled, and the hairy white choke at the center of the leaves should be discarded. This is done by cutting the artichoke in half and scraping the choke away with a knife, leaving the tender heart. Alternatively, especially if you want to stuff them, the artichokes may be left whole and the chokes scooped out with a sharp spoon. Once prepared, artichokes should be kept in acidulated water to prevent discoloration.

Artichokes are full of protein, vitamins, and fiber, and contain phosphorus, calcium, potassium, sodium, iron, copper, and zinc. In Italy, they are eaten raw in salads or in *pinzimonio* and *bagna caôda* (see page 33), but they may also be blanched, quartered, dipped in flour and beaten egg, and then deep-fried. They are also cooked *in umido* with tomatoes and olive oil. I like them slowly braised in plenty of extra-virgin olive oil, with onions, capers, and parsley.

One of the most delicious ways of cooking artichokes is as they do in Sicily. The leaves are loosened from the top by hand and coarse sea salt is scattered over the center. Extra-virgin olive oil is then sprinkled on top and the artichoke is placed on a bed of charcoal embers and cooked slowly until the outer leaves are charred, but the heart is deliciously tender, with a smoky flavor.

### CAROTA, PASTINACA, PASTANACHE / CARROT

This root vegetable is available all year round and grows mostly in temperate climates, with Sicily and Abruzzo as the main areas of production in Italy. The carrot ranges in color from pale yellow to deep purple and has a strong aroma and taste. It can be boiled then sautéed in butter with garlic, or reduced to a purée and served as a side dish. Finely chopped and added to *minestrone*, meat stews, and *ragùs*, it gives a particularly sweet flavor. Raw carrots are eaten in southern Italy, where they are very tender and sweet, and are called *pastinaca* or *pastanache* in the local dialect. I enjoy raw carrots coarsely grated and dressed with fresh mint, cilantro, and a little olive oil, lemon juice, salt, and pepper. Carrots are also an important ingredient in *giardiniera* (see page 112).

### CARDO / CARDOON

The cardoon is related to the thistle and—like its other close relative, the artichoke—it has long leaves. Unlike the artichoke, however, it is the

stem of the cardoon, not the flower, that is eaten. To make it tender enough to eat, the cardoon is specially cultivated, as in Piedmont, where around September or October the long stems and leaves are bent over (each region bends the stem in a different way) and mounded with earth to protect them from the harsh winter weather. Over the following months they become perfectly white and extremely tender. Because of this peculiar way of blanching them, they take on a permanently curved shape and are commonly called *gobbi* (hunchbacks).

Cardoons can be eaten raw in the famous dish *bagna caôda* (see page 33) or *alla parmigiana*. To prepare cardoons, simply discard the stringy outer fibers by peeling them off with a knife, like a celery stalk, then cut the stalk into $^1/_2$-inch chunks. Place these in water acidulated with lemon juice so they do not turn black, simmer them until tender, then drain and place in a buttered ovenproof dish, dot with more butter, and bake in a fairly hot oven for 20 minutes.

### CATALOGNA, SEE CICORIA

### CAVOLINO DI BRUXELLES / BRUSSELS SPROUT
This sprout, which looks like a kind of mini cabbage, has only recently been adopted in Italy,

despite the fact that the ancient Romans are said to have taken them to Belgium in the first place. The sprouts grow on the long stems of this plant of the cabbage family, which grows up to 3 feet in height. They are harvested in late autumn to winter and make an interesting alternative to other types of cabbage.

To cook Brussels sprouts, first discard any damaged exterior leaves, trim the short stalk and make an incision in its base to ensure even cooking. Blanch in boiling salted water for 7 to 8 minutes before using in other recipes, or cook for 10 to 15 minutes, until just tender, to be eaten as a side dish. In Italy, Brussels sprouts are mostly blanched and baked in the oven covered with a bechamel sauce or, as in Parma, boiled and served dotted with butter and Parmesan cheese.

### CAVOLFIORE / CAULIFLOWER
There are many varieties of *palla di neve* (snowball), the name given to this king of the cabbage family. In principle, it is the same as broccoli, except that the immaculate white florets that make up the head are extremely compact and heavy and are surrounded by a few leaves

whose freshness indicate the quality of the cauliflower. The most tender of the pale green leaves are also edible.

Cauliflower is grown all over Italy, with major growing regions in Campania, the Marche, Puglia, and Sicily. There are also many varieties, including *Precoce Toscano*, *Gigante di Napoli*, and *Tardivo di Fano*. The cauliflower has a very long growing season and is available from October until the end of May.

Italian cuisine makes good use of the cauliflower in a range of dishes from *minestrone* to the famous regional dish of *pasta e cavolfiore* from Campania. It is also wonderful puréed with butter and Parmesan cheese, served in a cheese sauce, *au gratin* (or *gratinato*, as the Italians say), cut in thin slices and dressed with oil and vinegar, or dipped into mayonnaise, and freshly boiled and dressed with extra-virgin olive oil, garlic, and lemon juice. Cauliflower is also a major component of *giardiniera*, the Italian pickle of garden vegetables, and *insalata di rinforzo* (see page 136).

One of my favorite ways of cooking cauliflower is as fritters, for which parboiled florets are coated in a batter of beaten egg, bread crumbs, and a little Parmesan cheese, then deep-fried. They can also be dipped in a batter of beaten eggs with a few tablespoons of plain flour and a pinch of salt, then shallow-fried in olive oil until golden. Both versions make wonderful party snacks.

### CAVOLO / CABBAGE
An old Italian saying *"come il cavolo a merenda"* translates "like cabbage for tea," meaning something completely out of place or without sense. I would be very offended if I were a cabbage, because this underrated vegetable is one of the foundations of modern Italian cuisine, and is as popular in the South as the North.

My childhood memories

LEFT: *CARDO*

LEFT: GREEN, WHITE, AND PURPLE CAULIFLOWER

take me back to Borgofranco during the war, when—at the age of fifteen—my friends and I were constantly hungry. I would often create improvised afternoon teas at around five o'clock. We used to pass a field of cabbages on our way home from school, and when they were ready for eating we "allowed ourselves" to take one from the fields. Each of us brought the other ingredients from home—olive oil, salt, pepper, vinegar, bread, and a big bowl. With a large knife and a chopping board, we made a cabbage salad in the open countryside. We thinly sliced the white and crunchy internal leaves, then placed them in the bowl and seasoned them with the rest of the ingredients. Sometimes we crushed a little garlic and marinated it in vinegar before adding it. Sitting around the bowl, we then proceeded to eat this intermediary meal, which would carry us through to dinner. It was a mad but wonderfully innocent time.

**RIGHT:** *CAVOLO NERO*

The cabbage helped us to get through the war, and I remember eating it disguised in many ways by my mother, who was keen to give us satisfying and nutritious food. She used various types of cabbage, allowing us to appreciate her unforgettable cooking, which has been such a great inspiration in my professional life.

There are four basic types of cabbage cultivated in Italy, with the precious summer variety grown in the North, and the autumn and winter varieties grown in the warmer climes of the South.

*Cavolo cappuccio* (flat cabbage): This flat, compact, football-sized cabbage has greeny-blue leaves on the outside and very white leaves on the inside. These internal leaves are very tender and are used to make *crauti*, the Italian equivalent of sauerkraut (see page 110). This type of cabbage is also used to make soups, like *minestrone* and bean soups, and in rice dishes such as *riso e cavoli*.

*Cavolo verza* (Savoy cabbage): Piedmont, Lombardy, and the Veneto make particular use of this type of cabbage. It is distinguished from the other varieties by its wrinkled and curly leaves. The deep green, almost blue, outer leaves are often wrapped around a meat stuffing, tied into a parcel and braised (see *caponnet*, page 130). The paler internal leaves are very tender and make a wonderful salad if their thick ribs are removed. The leaves are then finely shredded and dressed with a vinaigrette of olive oil, vinegar, a few puréed anchovy fillets, and a little mild mustard.

Another wonderful way of using Savoy cabbage is in a recipe created by my old friend Nina from the Aosta Valley (see page 234). She boils the shredded cabbage until tender, layers it in a pot with chunks of stale bread, cubes of Fontina cheese, and Parmesan cheese, covers all this with chicken stock, and finishes with a generous layer of melted butter. She lets this rest to allow the bread to absorb all the flavors, and then mixes everything together. This is called *zuppa valpellinense*, and reminds me of a similar, if more caloric, dish my mother used to prepare.

*Cavolo nero* (black cabbage): This is an unusual variety of cabbage, not just because the leaves are dark green, almost black, but because they are also quite long and curled. It is mostly cultivated in the South and in Tuscany, where it forms an essential part of the famous *ribollita* soup, in which it is teamed with beans. The soup is always made a day or two in advance and then re-boiled, hence its name. In the South this cabbage is mostly braised until soft with garlic, a little lard, some *peperoncino*, and water. My wife cooks it in a similar way with a few slices of smoked bacon, which imparts an interesting flavor to the dish.

*Cavolo cappuccio rosso* (red cabbage): This very compact cabbage is a deep red in color, with leaves that grow so tightly together that each cabbage can weigh around 3 pounds. It is often used in northeast Italy in recipes similar to those of the Austrians. I usually cut it very fine and place it in a pan with lard or, if possible, goose fat, with a finely chopped onion, a few peppercorns, some juniper berries, 2 to 3 peeled and thinly sliced Newton pippin apples, plenty of apple juice, and 1 or 2 chicken stock cubes. Bring this to a boil, then braise the cabbage for about 2 hours until it forms a soft, jam-like consistency with the apples. This is wonderful with pork or game of any description.

## CAVOLO RAPA / KOHLRABI

Although this vegetable belongs to the cabbage family, it is the root, not the leaves, that is eaten. The root can grow as large as a grapefruit, and its spindly stalks and leaves emerge from the top in a rather haphazard manner. It has a pale green skin and an even paler flesh. When young it is extremely tender, with only a hint of cabbage flavor. To prepare it, peel and discard the tough, woody skin. Cut the peeled head into quarters and boil them in salted water for about 15 minutes, or until soft, then drain and dress with butter or *mascarpone* and season with salt and pepper. In Puglia the boiled root is cut in slices and dressed with olive oil and vinegar as a salad.

**CAZZIMPERIO, SEE CRUDITA**

## CECE / CHICKPEA

This legume, popular all around the Mediterranean, has been adopted in every Italian region. For climatic reasons, the chickpea, with its unmistakable round shape and cream color, is cultivated only in the warmer South. It is probably the only legume that maintains a similar quality whether fresh or dry, which is why large quantities are sold commercially canned and bottled, ready for use. Dried chickpeas need to be soaked in water for 8 to 24 hours, depending on their age. They can then be boiled for at least 3 hours (or half that time in a pressure cooker). It is worth remembering that chickpeas double in volume and weight during cooking.

*Pasta e ceci* is a dish of chickpeas and pasta enjoyed in Puglia, Piedmont, and Lombardy. Chickpeas can also be reduced to a purée and dressed with crisply fried slivers of *speck*. Dried chickpeas can also be ground to a flour, which, in Italy, is mainly used in Liguria to make *farinata* or *faina*, a sort of flat bread.

## CETRIOLO, CETRIOLINI / CUCUMBER, GHERKINS

The *cetriolo*, or cucumber, epitomizes summer for me—a salad without cucumber just isn't a salad. It is a pity that its year-round availability has caused it to become so underrated. The Italian cucumber is shorter than its foreign counterpart, as Italians prefer varieties like *Marketer* or *Carosello*, which are not cylindrical, but rounder, like their squash relatives. Great care has to be taken when choosing cucumbers—they should not be too big, and should be quite firm to the touch. Peeling off the skin makes cucumbers more digestible, as does removing the seeds of larger varieties.

Italians are also very fond of *cetriolini*, gherkins or immature cucumbers, which are specially grown for pickling in vinegar to be eaten as a part of an *antipasto*. I have developed a salad that includes peeled and very finely sliced fresh gherkins with salt, olive oil, a few tablespoons of milk, a few drops of lemon juice, and plenty of finely chopped dill.

## CICERCHIA / LEGUME

This type of dried bean, closely resembling the chickpea in both appearance and flavor, is widely used throughout Italy. It is most often incorporated in soups, like the Apulian *ciceria e tria*, in which it is cooked with short-cut *tagliatelle*, or with potatoes in *minestra di cicerchie e patate*.

## CICORIA, CICORIETTA, CATALOGNA / CHICORY

A great variety of salad and

vegetable plants is included under this name. They have a common characteristic in that they are all bitter, because they descend from the wild plant *Cicoria selvatica*, a close relation of the *dente di leone* (dandelion).

*Catalogna* is a cultivated relative of wild chicory, and is similar in shape to the dandelion, but is much larger, growing up to 20 inches high. Its dense leaves grow from a root which, along with the tender white part of the stems, can be braised in a similar way to the wild dandelion. It can also be simply boiled and dressed with extra-virgin olive oil and lemon juice, or mixed with ricotta, cheese, eggs, and spices and used to fill vegetable tarts. *Catalogna puntarelle* (little tips) is a bushy variety of the same plant, with 20 to 30 tender, juicy little shoots attached to the root. It can be eaten cooked and dressed with extra-virgin olive oil and lemon juice.

*Cicoria di Bruxelles* (Belgian endive) was discovered by a Belgian horticulturist in the middle of the nineteenth century and has since been successfully cultivated all over the world. One of the main appeals of Belgian endive is its tightly packed, 6-inch-long, creamy white leaves which, as well as being delicious braised and broiled, add wonderful variety to salads. My own favorite salad is made up of $^3/_4$-inch chunks of Belgian endive dressed with a mixture of extra-virgin olive oil, a few drops of truffle oil, some lemon juice, salt, and pepper. It is then scattered with slices of fresh black truffle. An older and simpler way of preparing it is to cut the endive head in half, lay it in a pan with garlic, olive oil, capers, and salt, cover with a lid, and braise it.

Radicchio is a salad leaf belonging to the

**ABOVE: FLAT**
**PIATTA DI**
**BASSANO ONIONS**

**RIGHT: TROPEA**
**RED ONIONS**

chicory family that is widely used for its slightly bitter taste and its deep red-mauve color. There are two principal varieties of radicchio. The first, *Rossa di Verona*, is a round and tightly formed ball of leaves, similar to a small red cabbage. It is mostly cultivated in Veneto, especially around Chioggia. The second is the famous *Radicchio di Treviso*, so-called because it is mainly cultivated in that province. While *Rossa di Verona* is available all year round, the Treviso variety only makes its appearance in winter, when it ripens from a reddish-green color to a wonderful deep red. The leaves are long and pointed, and it is usually sold with the edible, fleshy root attached.

*Radicchio di Treviso* undergoes quite lengthy preparation before it is sold or eaten. After it is pulled from the earth, in order to tenderize it and remove the bitterness, it is bundled with willow branches for 2 or 3 days with its roots sitting in running rainwater. It is then cleaned, leaving only the immaculate leaves in the center. In Treviso, the traditional way of cooking radicchio is to broil the entire head. As well as in salads, it is used in risottos or pasta sauces with *speck*. There is even a recipe for making grappa from radicchio.

*Ceriolo verde* and *ceriolo rosso* are two pretty salad leaves from the chicory family. They are both formed like a rose, one with green leaves and the other with red. Both have the typically bitter chicory taste. *Cicorietta da taglio* is another, quite tiny salad leaf, which grows quickly. The little plants are tightly sown so that they form a delicate green carpet, and are cut at the base so that only the small, tender leaves are used. The plant grows back after being cut.

*Scarola* (Batavia) grows in the form of a bushy head of deep green with robust outer leaves, but only the pale cream and yellow center of this plant is used in salads because the outer leaves are a little tough. It has the slightly bitter taste characteristic of the family. The entire head can be cooked like a vegetable, usually braised with olive oil, garlic, tomatoes, and capers.

*Indivia* (curly endive or frisée) is a curious salad leaf which is from the same branch of the family as *scarola* and is quite similar to it, having tough outer leaves and a very tender center, which is the part of the head used in salads.

### CIME DI RAPA / TURNIP GREENS

*Cime di rapa*, also called *broccoletti di rapa*, is the leafy top of the turnip. The leaves are used in much the same way as broccoli, usually boiled then sautéed in olive oil with garlic and chili. The taste is definitely stronger than broccoli and slightly bitter, and is very much loved by the Romans and Neapolitans, who call them *friarielli*. See also *brocollo di rapa*, page 104.

### CIPOLLA, CIPOLLOTTO, CIPOLLINE / ONION

The onion has been used for thousands of years in Italy. Introduced by the Egyptians, then taken up by the Romans, it has been put to use in all sorts of ways, including being fermented to make an alcoholic drink. In the Italian kitchen it is widely used in *ragùs*, soups, and risottos. The main areas of cultivation are Sicily, Puglia, Campania, and Emilia-Romagna.

The onion has been cultivated through the centuries to produce thousands of varieties, with all manner of shapes, colors, and strengths. Most are named after cities, such as *Ramata di Milano* and *Rossa Piatta di Bassano*, but there are far too many to list here.

The pink- and golden-colored onions have the most intense flavor, while the white and red are usually milder. The best red onions are those from Tropea in Calabria, which are celebrated for their sweetness.

There is a basic difference between onions for cooking and onion used for pickling or eating raw in salads, and that is size. Cooking onions are larger, and the very large ones are as likely to be eaten stuffed and baked as chopped for use as an aromatic flavoring. Some of the traditional Italian dishes that make the best use of onion are *fegato alla Veneziana* (liver Venice-style) and *zuppa di cipolla* (onion soup). Onions are also good in omelets, or deep-fried in rings in a coating of beaten eggs and bread crumbs.

Smaller onions are used raw in dishes such as *tonno e fagioli* (bean and tuna salad). My father used to scoop this salad up with a leaf of a salad onion, which he would eat along with the salad itself. The *cipollotto* (salad onion) is a special variety of onion that is harvested in the spring when it is still small and tender. It is especially important in *pinzimonio* (see page 223) and in salads. The *cipollina* (scallion) is another small white onion that can be round or flat. The round variety is usually pickled to be eaten as part of *antipasti*, while the flat one is used to make *cipolline in agro dolce*. The peeled onions are blanched, then fried in olive oil with vinegar and sugar until tender.

I have two tips to help overcome the worst effects of onions when preparing them: first, to stop them from making you cry, soak them in water for 30 minutes before handling them and breathe through

## CHAR-GRILLING VEGETABLES

Char-grilling is most effective when done over real charcoal, because of the woody, smoky flavor it gives to the food. It is a very healthy way of cooking vegetables and also gives them a more interesting flavor than just boiling them. Although radicchio was one of the first vegetables to be grilled, vegetables such as zucchini, eggplants, peppers, onions, and artichokes are also good for the grill. Just after they have been removed from the grill, the skin of certain vegetables, like peppers and tomatoes, can be peeled off with ease. Harder vegetables like fennel and celery root need to be blanched first, then cut in slices before being put on the grill.

To keep the vegetables from getting too charred and to give them even more flavor, brush them with a marinade of olive oil, lemon, crushed garlic, salt,

and pepper. Char-grilled vegetables can be eaten on their own as a starter, or served as a side dish with grilled meat or fish.

LEFT: CHAR-GRILLED
EGGPLANTS

your mouth rather than your nose when you cut them; second, to get rid of the smell of onions on your fingers, rub your fingers with salt.

**COCOZZA, SEE ZUCCA**

**CONCENTRATO DI POMODORO, SEE POMODORO**

### CONTORNO / VEGETABLE SIDE DISH

An important part of any meal is the *contorno*, or vegetable side dish, to accompany the main course. The term is most often applied to the vegetable most suited to the main dish. A *contorno* can consist of potatoes and one other vegetable.

### COSTE / SWISS CHARD

Similar in flavor to spinach, chard is called *erbette* in Emilia-Romagna—which is the word used to refer to parsley in Rome. Chard leaves are the basis of an Emilian flan called *erbazzone*, which is basically an omelet made with Swiss chard leaves gently cooked and then puréed, before being mixed with bread crumbs, a little flour, a couple of

beaten eggs, a handful of grated Parmesan cheese, salt, pepper, and some nutmeg, then fried in lard or butter as one would an omelet.

In addition to cooking the leaves of chard in the same way as spinach, the white ribs of the long leaves can be cut in chunks and braised until tender to make a good accompaniment to meat dishes.

### CRAUTI / SAUERKRAUT

This piece of Germanic culinary culture has infiltrated the northern border regions of Alto Adige, Friuli, and the Veneto, and has been adopted because it perfectly suits the local pork dishes, which are also in all likelihood echoes of Austrian invasions. A platter of boiled mixed pork delicacies like smoked loin, belly, sausages, and *cotechino*, accompanied by *crauti* makes a wonderful peasant dish.

There are a few good brands of ready-made *crauti* in jars, but if you like making it yourself, as many families do, this is how. Trim a flat white cabbage of the tougher outer leaves, then shred the rest very finely. Layer the shredded cabbage

with salt in a wooden or ceramic container and put a large weight directly on the cabbage. After a few days, the cabbage will start to ferment, a process which will take about 4 weeks, after which the *crauti* is ready to use. Before use, rinse the *crauti* with fresh water and cook with the addition of some juniper berries, caraway seeds, a little white wine, and some lard. After an hour or so, the *crauti* is ready.

### CRUDITA / CRUDITÉ

Crudités are simply raw vegetables eaten with dips or in salads. There are two important specialty *crudite*, one from Piedmont and the other from Tuscany. The first is the famous *bagna caôda*, meaning "hot dip" in Piedmontese, which is based on a sauce of anchovies, garlic, and butter, all dissolved together and kept warm in special terra-cotta containers heated by candles. Into this aromatic mixture, one dips selected tender autumn or winter vegetables, all accompanied by bread and washed down with plenty of Barbera wine. The classic vegetables for *bagna caôda* are Jerusalem artichoke, cardoon, celery, peppers, artichoke, and carrot, but any tender raw vegetable will do. Because of the amount of garlic used it can be a rather antisocial meal, but if the garlic is soaked in milk first, it is far less pungent. (See recipe, page 33.)

The other well-known crudité is the Tuscan *pinzimonio* (see page 223), which is known as *cazzimperio* in other parts of southern Italy. This is nothing more than seasoned extra-virgin olive oil in a little bowl, into which one dips spring vegetables like asparagus, artichokes, carrots, cucumbers, fennel, scallions, celery, artichokes, and any other tender, tasty vegetable available. It is usually served in Tuscan trattorias as a starter.

BELOW:
*CATALOGNA
PUNTARELLE
(LITTLE TIPS)
CHICORY, AND
DANDELION LEAVES*

### DENTE DI LEONE /
#### DANDELION

Also known as *pissialetto* because of
their diuretic quality, wild
dandelion leaves can be used in
salad in spring, when new growth
makes them very tender. Toss the
leaves with hard-boiled eggs,
anchovy fillets, and a vinaigrette of
extra-virgin olive oil and wine
vinegar. Larger leaves are wonderful
braised slowly until tender with
garlic, olive oil, chili pepper, and a
little stock.

### ERBA BRUSCA, SEE ACETOSA

### ESTRATTO DI POMODORO, SEE POMODORO

### FAGIOLINO / GREEN BEAN

Italians use *fagiolini* frequently,
especially in summer when, as well
as making a delicious summer
vegetable, they are ideal as an
ingredient in salads. This much-
appreciated vegetable comes in a
broad number of varieties. Most
green beans are collected when they
are still young and not quite mature,
so that they are tender and full of
flavor. The smallest and most
slender bean is 'Contender,'
although the slightly larger *Bobis*
(Italian for Bobby) has a little more
substance and, when fresh and
picked very young, in my opinion
tastes much better. *Re dei bleu*
(King of the Blues) is much longer
than either of these, at about 6
inches, and has a good flavor.

Two other varieties of *fagiolini*
are a creamy white rather than green.
One is *Burro di Roquencourt*, which
possibly originated in France and is
the same size as the *Bobis* bean. The
other is *Meraviglia di Venezia* or
'Venice Wonder,' a fairly large but
very tender bean if picked young,
resembling the snow pea in size. An
exceptionally long bean is the
*Stringa* (string bean), which can
reach up to 20 inches in length and
is a green to greeny-red color.

Almost all beans, and especially
the older ones, need to be topped
and tailed so that the tough ends of
the bean are removed, along with
any stringy fibers. One of the most
evocative sights in Italy is women
gathered at the back of a country
trattoria preparing beans. This is a
fine indicator of the freshness of the
produce, most of which is locally
grown without chemicals and is
wonderfully fresh, tender, and very
tasty. Only the youngest and
freshest beans do not need to be
topped and tailed. To check the
freshness of a bean, break it in half.
If it snaps easily and is moist on the
inside, it is fresh.

The traditional method of cooking

beans is to boil them in salted water
for 7 to 12 minutes, depending on
the size and freshness of the bean.
Another method is to blanch them
in a large pan of salted boiling water
for 2 to 3 minutes or until *al dente*,
then finish the cooking by sautéing
them in butter or dressing them
with vinaigrette. My own special way
of serving them is dressed while still
warm with slices of garlic, extra-
virgin olive oil, wine vinegar, salt,
and abundant fresh mint leaves.
They are also extremely delicious
cold in *fagiolini in umido*, which is
made by braising uncooked beans in
a pan with olive oil, garlic, and
tomatoes. A few minutes before the
end of the cooking time, salt and
basil are added for flavoring. My
mother used to add new potatoes to
the dish to make a main course,
which we would eat with bread.

### FAGIOLO / BEAN

Known since antiquity, beans have
been eaten by peasants through the
ages because they are easy to
cultivate and preserve. Today, dried
beans have become an increasingly
important part of our diet, and they
are valued for their high protein,
their vitamin and mineral content,
and for their fiber. Every region in
Italy can claim at least one bean or
legume dish. See also *borlotto*,
*cannellino*.

### FAVA / FAVA BEAN

These beans have only one thing in
common with green beans, and that
is the color of the pod. Unlike their
cousins, however, they need to be
podded before being eaten. This is a
very pleasant exercise because, as
the finger enters the pod, it touches
the soft, velvety, almost woolly
padding inside, in which the beans
are embedded.

Fava bean plants grow up to 3 feet
high, first producing a wonderful
white flower, and then the fruit—
the pod with the beans inside. Fava
beans are a very old food indeed,
adopted by the Romans after being
introduced by the Egyptians. For a
long time they were the only beans
eaten in Italy, and then mostly by
peasants. Now the fava bean is eaten
and cultivated with great enthusiasm
all over Italy, although the main area
of growth is in the warmer South.

Fava beans are only eaten raw in
springtime, when they are young
and tender. One of the best ways to
enjoy them is Tuscan-style with
fresh Pecorino cheese. Otherwise
both fresh and dry beans can be
cooked. The fresh variety, if tender,
takes only 10 minutes to cook, and
less if you discard the tough outer
skin. If you use dry beans, they have
to be soaked in water for 18 to 24
hours before being cooked in boiling
water for at least 2 hours, but test
them during the cooking time to
make sure they do not get too soft.

When buying fresh fava beans,
check that the pod is shiny and firm
and that the beans inside are firm
and tightly packed. One important
tip for buying fava beans is to allow

for the fact that three-quarters of the weight will be discarded with the pods, so if you need 1 pound of shelled beans, you will need to buy 4 pounds.

I like fava beans cooked with onions and *speck* or Parma ham cut in little cubes. They are also good reduced to a purée and eaten with pork. They can also be used as part of a larger dish, as in the case of the Sicilian specialty *frittella* (see recipe, page 133).

## FINOCCHIO / BULB FENNEL
Fennel has such a sweet taste and pleasant aroma that it often used to be served at the end of a meal as a dessert in Italy. It is delicious in every form, raw or cooked, and is an indispensable ingredient in *pinzimonio* (see page 223), in which the curved blades can be used as a spoon to scoop up the olive oil. Fennel grows from spring through October, depending on the area in which it is grown, and which of the many varieties is cultivated.

It is used all over Italy, thinly sliced in salads, baked in the oven with butter and Parmesan cheese, and blanched, quartered, dipped in an egg batter, and deep-fried. One of the main signs of summer for me is a

fennel salad in which the bulb is thinly sliced, then dressed with extra-virgin olive oil, salt, pepper, and a few drops of lemon juice.

**FIORE DI ZUCCA/ZUCCHINA, SEE ZUCCA/ZUCCHINA**

**FRIARIELLI, SEE BROCCOLI DI RAPA**

**FRITTELLA, SEE CARCIOFO AND PAGE 133**

## GIARDINIERA / MIXED VEGETABLE PICKLE
An *antipasto* is not complete without a *giardiniera*, or *vegetali alla giardiniera*, meaning "garden vegetables." This wonderfully crunchy and very appetizing pickle is made up of a mixture of vegetables, such as carrots, beans, onions, cucumbers, zucchini, cauliflower, kohlrabi, and anything else that is in season, cut in small pieces and cooked in wine vinegar until tender (see page 134). When the pickle is eaten with slices of salami or *prosciutto* as part of an *antipasto*, the acidity of the vinegar helps stimulate the appetite.

*Giardiniera* is usually made at home in the summer, when the ingredients are fresh and abundant, and it can then be stored in jars for the winter. Over time, its commercial production has grown into a huge industry because it is such an intrinsic part of *antipasto*.

**INDIVIA, SEE CICORIA**

## INSALATA / SALAD
The word *insalata* comes from the old Italian verb *insalare* meaning "to add salt" and is now the general term used for vegetables, green salad leaves, and all manner of other ingredients combined and dressed with olive oil, vinegar or lemon juice, salt, and pepper. Italians eat salad with the main course as an accompaniment to meat, especially when the meat is broiled or grilled.

*Insalata* used to refer only to a collection of edible green leaves with

lettuce as its foundation, but today there are literally hundreds of varieties of salad leaves, including Belgian endive, radicchio, corn salad, etc. A salad made up of green leaves and herbs like arugula, mint, or dandelion is called *insalata verde* (green salad), whereas a salad made of a mixture of ingredients including tomatoes and cucumber is called *insalata mista* (mixed salad). Salads can also be made with raw, shredded root vegetables, such as fennel, celery root, carrots, Jerusalem artichokes, and radishes, or with diced, cooked vegetables like green beans, carrots, fennel, zucchini, and cauliflower. Salads are so flexible that almost any combination of ingredients, or even a single ingredient, can be called a salad, for example pasta salad or *insalata di carciofi* (artichoke salad).

## LAMPASCIONE, LAMPAGIONE, LAMPASCIUOLO / MUSCARI
This bulb of the *muscari*, or wild hyacinth plant, is much-used in Puglia and southern Italy, and is now cultivated as a vegetable to meet growing demand. Similar in appeasrance to a shallot, it is slightly bitter and is usually eaten in the summer when ripe. *Lampascione* can be pickled, like onions, without losing its bitter taste. It is also good boiled, then dressed with olive oil and vinegar.

## LATTUGA / LETTUCE
The Italians are very fond of lettuce. A salad almost invariably contains one or two of the very different varieties grown in all seasons all over Italy. *Romana*, or romaine, is the most universally popular for its crispness and flavor. There is also *lattuga d'inverno* or winter lettuce, which is more resistant to cold weather, and *insalata primaverile* (springtime lettuce), with its pale but very tender leaves. *Lattuga da taglio* are those lettuce plants that produce small bunches of very tender leaves which may be cut at the base every time lettuce is needed and the lettuce will grow back again.

LEFT: *FINOCCHIO*

## LEGUMI / LEGUMES

This is the general term for peas, beans, and lentils. See also *borlotto, cannellino, cece, fagiolino, fagiolo, fava, lenticchia, pisello.*

### LENTICCHIA / LENTIL

Probably the world's most-used legume, the lentil comes from a small climbing plant that never grows more than 20 inches high. Its pods are rectangular and usually contain four lentils each. The plant originated in southern Asia, but lentils arrived in the Mediterranean region a long time ago, and the ancient Romans immediately adopted them as a means of feeding their troops as well as solving the problem of feeding the poor. The name lentil comes from the Latin *lens*, and, incidentally, gave the name to the optical lens due to its similar shape.

There are numerous varieties of lentils, all bearing the name of the area where they are produced. The best-known are the *lenticchie di Castelluccio* from Umbria, which are organically grown and are tasty, full of iron and many vitamins, and cook in just 20 to 30 minutes without being presoaked. Naturally, demand for these lentils is very high and so is their price! Another famous variety are the lentils of Alta Mura in Puglia.

After being cooked until tender, lentils can be prepared in salads, dressed in olive oil, vinegar, salt and pepper, and a pinch of oregano. Lentils are deemed lucky in Rome, where they are consumed in large quantities during New Year's celebrations. I prefer them served with *zampone* or *cotechino* (see recipe, page 97).

### MELANZANA / EGGPLANT

This vegetable is common throughout the Mediterranean region, and is used in an infinite number of recipes. In Italy, it is mainly eaten in the South and is grown in Campania, Puglia, Calabria, Sicily, and Sardinia. Eggplants may be long and oval in shape, or round like a huge egg. When fresh, they should be quite firm to the touch. They usually have rather tough skins, ranging in color from dark purple to pale violet, and even white (hence their name, eggplant). The pulp is white or slightly green, with a lot of little soft seeds. The eggplant has a slightly bitter taste, especially in the thinner varieties, so prior to cooking, these are often sliced and sprinkled with salt, then left to rest while the bitter juices are drawn out.

Eggplant can be used in many ways, including *melanzane al funghetto*, in which it is peeled,

cubed, and fried in olive oil with garlic, parsley, and salt. To keep the eggplant from absorbing too much oil, blanch it prior to cooking. *Parmigiana di melanzane*, often thought to be an Emilia-Romagnan recipe, actually originated in Sicily. In this recipe the eggplant is cut lengthwise and sprinkled with salt to remove any bitterness and excess moisture. It is then dipped in flour, and then in beaten egg, and fried until golden brown. The eggplant slices are then layered in an ovenproof dish with tomato sauce and Parmesan and mozzarella or fontina cheese, then baked for 30 minutes in a hot oven. It is eaten hot or cold as a main course.

Another way of preparing eggplants is to slice them lengthwise and fry the slices, then place a mixture of bread crumbs, anchovies, capers, oil, salt, and pepper in the center and roll up the stuffed slices, secure them with a toothpick, and broil them. A wonderful Sicilian recipe calls for peeled, cubed, and blanched eggplants squeezed of excess water and mixed with bread crumbs, anchovy paste, beaten egg, crushed garlic, a few capers, plenty of chopped parsley, salt, pepper, and a little cinnamon powder to make a paste. Teaspoons of the mixture are then gently fried in hot oil until golden.

Perhaps the best-known recipe for eggplant in Italy is an eggplant preserve, *melanzane sott'olio*, in which the eggplant is cut lengthwise into ribbons, then cooked in vinegar and salt before being thoroughly drained, mixed with dried oregano, very finely chopped garlic, and pieces of chili put into a jar and covered with good olive oil. Another popular dish is the Sicilian recipe *melanzane alla norma*, in which fried eggplant is mixed to a paste with salted ricotta, then dressed with garlic, basil, and tomato sauce.

Finally, from the Amalfi coast comes an eggplant recipe that is eaten as a dessert! Two slices of eggplant are fried in oil, then nuts and various candied peels are placed in the middle of one slice, and the slices are sandwiched together. The "sandwich" is then dusted with flour, dipped in beaten egg, and deep-fried until golden. While still warm, the eggplant sandwich is then dusted with cocoa powder and sugar and left to cool. When cool it is given a final dip in melted chocolate.

## MISTICANZA, MESTICANZA / WILD SALAD

This is a Roman expression for a mixture of wild salad leaves, including wild mint, wild arugula, dandelion, wild garlic, wild fennel, and wild sorrel, usually mixed with traditional greens like endive or lettuce. It is traditionally dressed with extra-virgin olive oil, wine vinegar, salt, and pepper. The same word in Umbria refers to a mixture of dried beans used to make soup.

## ORTICA / NETTLE

One of the most annoying of weeds, nettles are nevertheless edible and enjoyable. There are various types, but the edible one is the common stinging nettle with a white flower. It is essential that you wear gloves when you pick the tender spring tips. To stop them from stinging, put them in the refrigerator for a while, then boil them in lightly salted water for 5 minutes or until tender. You can then use them in soup, or dress them with olive oil and lemon juice to serve as a vegetable. They may also be used in risotto, or mixed with ricotta, Parmesan cheese, and egg, and used instead of spinach as a filling for ravioli.

## PANISCIA / BEAN SOUP

From the middle of the rice-producing area of Novara comes this bean soup, which is similar to a soft risotto. Cook fresh borlotti beans slowly together with Savoy cabbage, celery, tomato, onion, and a piece of *cotenna* (pork shin) for a couple of hours. In another pan put some butter, lard, a fresh sausage, and a finely chopped onion. Cook briefly, then add the rice as if making a risotto. Add a glass of Barolo wine, and then slowly, ladleful by ladleful, the vegetables and the broth. After 18 to 20 minutes the *paniscia* is ready. There is a similar version of this specialty called *panissa*, from neighboring Vercelli.

## PANNOCCHIA / CORN ON THE COB

Broiled, tender young corn cobs are called *pannocchia di granoturco arrostita* and boiled corn on the cob is *pannocchia lessa*. In season, these are sold at little stands by the roadside, especially in the South.

## PAPPA AL POMODORO, SEE POMODORO

## PASTINACA, PASTANACHE, SEE CAROTA

## PATATA / POTATO

Although it plays the same role in northern Europe as bread does in southern Europe, the potato has never been part of the staple diet in Italy. Indeed it was only in the middle of the nineteenth century that the potato started to be widely used as a vegetable in Italy. Originally from South America, the potato is mostly cultivated in the Veneto, Puglia, Campania, and Calabria, where the soil is particularly well-suited to them.

Early potatoes, usually known as *patate novelle* (new potatoes), are small, firm, and waxy, and are ideal in potato salads in which the cooked potatoes are dressed with olive oil, vinegar, scallions, salt, and pepper. Of the many varieties available, the most important are the floury winter potatoes such as *Tonda di Napoli* and *Bianca di Como*, the white flesh of which is used to make purées, gnocchi, croquettes, and toppings for savory pies. They can also be baked whole with their skins on, cut in cubes, or sliced with onions. They make a useful thickener for soups such as *minestrone*, and a tasty accompaniment to pasta in *pasta e patate*. Potatoes are probably most popular fried in matchsticks or thin slices called *patatine*. Those with a firmer, more waxy yellow flesh, such as *Primura* and *Sirtema*, are ideal for making French fries or sautéed potatoes. There is a potato called the Bintje, which has been developed in Holland and can be used for every type of dish.

Potatoes can also be reduced to a flour called *fecola di patate*, which is used to make cakes or to thicken sauces and soups. The importance I place on the potato shows in my recipe for *insalata di due tuberi* (see page 200).

## PEPERONE / SWEET PEPPER

Along with the eggplant, the bell pepper is perhaps the vegetable most closely associated with Mediterranean countries. Native to South America, the pepper was introduced to Italy toward the end of the eighteenth century, and it became a popular ingredient in Italian cooking. The cultivation of the pepper, which takes its name from the spicy flavor similar to that of a peppercorn, is widespread throughout Italy.

LEFT: *MISTICANZA*

RIGHT: *LUNGO MARCONI* PEPPERS

The squarish *Quadrato di Asti* is grown all over Italy, but most notably near Carmagnola in Piedmont, where it is used in the local dish, *bagna caôda* (see page 33). There is also the *Carnoso di Cuneo*, a large, meaty pepper that is yellow or red and sometimes green. Another variety looks like a tomato, as it is bright red in color and square-looking, almost squashed. My mother used to pickle this type in vinegar for the winter, when she would cook it with chunks of pork. Peppers may also be long and conical in shape like the *Lungo Marconi*. I think the best peppers are the yellow and red, but the very small green ones are good cooked whole, although it is worth tasting one first to check the flavor. These are called *puparuoli* in Naples.

RIGHT: *POMODORO*

Although the pepper (*peperone*) should not to be confused with its close relative the *peperoncino*, or chili pepper (see page 219), it can still have a spiciness mingled with its sweet flavor. When cleaning it, discard the internal seeds and membranes and take care to wash your hands after handling them.

As well as being fried and preserved, peppers can also be broiled or grilled, skinned, cut in ribbons and dressed with olive oil, salt, and garlic, before being served either hot or cold with all sorts of meat. They can also be cut in quarters and baked with a little olive oil to form a natural container for a *bagna caôda* sauce to be eaten as an antipasto. Peppers are also an important part of *peperonata*, a sort of ratatouille made with onions, celery, and tomatoes, to be eaten with polenta.

My mother used to make *peperoni fritti* for me whenever I returned home after a journey. She would cut the peppers into small ribbons, then fry them in good olive oil until soft and slightly burned at the edges before adding some garlic and finally a few spoonfuls of wine vinegar for flavor. I still remember the sublime flavor.

Finally, peppers can also be cut in half and stuffed with a variety of mixtures, including one of fresh bread crumbs moistened with olive oil, tomato juice, garlic, capers, anchovies, and parsley, then baked in the oven until the pepper is soft and the filling is crispy on top (see recipe, page 126).

Peppers are now sun-dried and stored like tomatoes; the best of these are the yellow and red varieties. They can be reconstituted at any time with a little vinegar and water and their concentrated, intense flavor makes a powerful addition to salads and sauces.

PINZIMONIO, SEE CRUDITA, AND PAGE 223

## PISELLO / PEA

Peas are grown in almost every region in Italy, since the plant can grow in most climates. The best-known varieties are *Senatore*, *Superbo di Luxton*, *Piccolo Provenzale*, and *Meraviglia d'Italia*. When buying peas, the pod should be as freshly green as the pea itself. If it is yellow or a pale green it means that the peas are old and will be hard. Try to insist on being allowed to open and sample at least one pod.

Eaten as a vegetable, usually as an accompaniment to meat, peas can find wonderful expression on their own. My mother used to use them for *pasta e piselli*—the *piselli* were very sweet, and as I always helped to pod them, more than the odd one disappeared into my mouth. For this dish, the pasta my mother made was eggless, made with just flour and water. For the sauce, a little *prosciutto* was fried with onion in a pan, and then the peas were added with a little water to cook gently. The dish was finished with a sprinkling of olive oil and black pepper on top. The sweetness of the fresh peas still lingers on my taste buds.

Dried peas can also be used to make excellent soups, with potatoes, *salamini* or spare ribs, or smoked ham. They are also puréed to accompany *zamponi* and various other cooked meats.

Also a member of the pea family is the *taccola* or *pisello mangiatutto* (snow pea), a kind of pea for which the pod and the barely developed pea inside are eaten as one. They should be cooked only briefly to maintain their color and crunchiness.

## POMODORO / TOMATO

This fruit is one of the most versatile and important of foods, and forms the backbone of much of Italian cooking. It can be used for salads, sauces, and pickles, it can be preserved, dried, reduced to a pulp or paste, and even used as a drink, or to make jam.

Originally from Mexico, the tomato was brought to Europe by explorers, where it made its first appearance in the second half of the sixteenth century.

## SUN-DRIED TOMATOES

The principle of the sun-dried tomato is similar to that of *estratto*. A tomato—usually the *San Marzano*—is cut in two, sprinkled with salt and placed in the sun to dry. The dehydration and concentration of salt in the dried tomato ensure that it can be kept for a long time. Because it is fairly inedibly salty in this form, however, its use is limited to stews, to which you certainly would not add any salt, or it can be soaked in water for a couple of hours to let it swell and lose some of the salt—then eaten as an *antipasto*. Alternatively, sun-dried tomatoes are first soaked in a solution of 2 parts wine vinegar and 1 part

water for 4 to 5 hours, then completely drained and dried and immersed in olive oil—possibly with the addition of flavorings like chili, small pieces of garlic, basil, or oregano. In this way, they keep for a long time and can be eaten as a snack with some good bread. My favorite way of cooking sun-dried tomatoes is to make them into fritters, which are excellent with aperitifs: simply dip the rehydrated tomatoes into a batter of water, salt, fresh yeast, finely chopped garlic, and parsley, and then deep-fry them until golden brown.

For a long time it was considered a curiosity and used as an ornament rather than in the kitchen. In Italy, the first appearance of the tomato in cooking was recorded in 1765 in a book by Vincenzo Corrado, *Cuoco Galante* (The Gallant Cook), in which he used tomatoes in sauces, for stuffing, and for frying. From that moment on, it seems, the tomato was taken to the Italian heart.

Once it was discovered which regions had the best climate and soil, the tomato became—alongside pasta—one of the first industrialized

food products to be used all year round. All Italians who had access to a little land cultivated tomatoes for themselves, which they either consumed raw or preserved in bottles. *Estratto*, or concentrated tomato paste, and sun-dried tomatoes were created to extend the use of the tomato, giving every family, even those that bought tomatoes for preserving, the pleasure of capturing the taste of summer.

Emilia-Romagna and Campania became the leading regions for the cultivation and preserving of

tomatoes. A new technology was soon invented to improve an expanding industry. In the Parma area, small engineering companies developed specialist machinery, and in Parma are still found the leading producers of state-of-the-art methods of canning and bottling various tomato derivatives. The Italians consume approximately 110 pounds of tomatoes per head per year, most of this in the form of sauces and purées.

Among the most famous varieties of tomatoes for eating raw in salads are *Cuore di Bue* (Ox's heart) and

ABOVE: SUN-DRYING TOMATOES AT THE PLANT OF FIORDELISI, CERIGNOLA IN PUGLIA IN JULY

FAR LEFT: GRADING AND WASHING TOMATOES BEFORE DRYING

NEAR LEFT: SALTING THE TOMATOES WITH SEA SALT AS A PRESERVATIVE

mostly used for canning or bottling. These are the bright-red, plum-shaped tomatoes that are found in cans worldwide, and do not require the addition of sugar to make sauces.

The *pomodorino* (cherry tomato or vine tomato) is small and grows in bunches. This type of tomato is mostly found in the South, Puglia, Sicily, and Calabria, and is generally used fresh. It has a tough skin, does not grow bigger than a cherry, and can be kept in bunches for the entire winter. It is consumed raw in salads, but is mainly used in the preparation of quick pasta sauces. Of the varieties grown, the *pomodorino di Cerignola* is the most sought-after.

One of the best ways to use tomatoes is in *fresella*, a peasant dish in which slices of Pugliese bread are baked twice until dry and biscuitlike, then they are quickly passed under cold running water, allowing excess to drip off, and are arranged on a plate. The moistened toasts are then covered with freshly chopped ripe tomatoes, drizzled with a little extra-virgin olive oil, sprinkled with salt, and topped with freshly chopped basil.

My mother used to produce a sort of *pappa al pomodoro*, which was made of pieces of celery (leaves included), onion, very ripe tomatoes (collecting all the juices), a little fresh oregano, good olive oil, and

FAR RIGHT: TOMATOES ON THE VINE

BOTTOM RIGHT: *CUORE* DI BUE TOMATOES

*Palla di Fuoco* (fireball). In southern Italy they prefer to eat tomatoes very ripe and they also generally eat a variety of tomato that is usually used in preserving, the *San Marzano*. In the North, they prefer tomatoes almost green, with a lot of acidity. They use these in salads, without any vinegar for dressing, just virgin olive oil,

salt, and pepper.

The *San Marzano*, *Roma*, *Napoli*, and *Marena* are all types of tomatoes that prefer a rich potash soil—like the wonderful terrain around the Vesuvius area, where material from the volcano has made the soil extremely fertile. These varieties are

sometimes a little garlic. All these ingredients were finely chopped and mixed together with some slightly moistened stale bread and left to stand for a couple of hours. It may have looked like chicken food, but it was delicious. In the northern Italian tradition, she also used to make a sweet jam from green tomatoes, finely chopped and slowly cooked with sugar, cinnamon, and vanilla.

Various types of *concentrato di pomodoro*, or tomato paste, are used in sauces and stews, and to enhance the flavor of many dishes. Only in Sicily do they produce the *estratto di pomodoro*, which is a super-concentrate of tomato (in fact, six times more concentrated than the usual paste). It is tomato pulp from which most of the moisture has been removed by drying, producing a thick paste with a very dark red color. It is slightly salted, so it will keep for a long time. The typical use of this is in the Sicilian *pasta all'anciova*, in which a sauce for *bucatini* pasta is made out of olive oil in which some fillets of anchovies have been dissolved. The *estratto* (or *strattu*, as it is called in Sicily) is dissolved in water and brought to a sauce-like consistency, then the parts are combined, with pine nuts and toasted bread crumbs sprinkled on top instead of Parmesan cheese. I like to eat *estratto* thinly spread like jam on a piece of toast sprinkled with a little virgin olive oil.

The tomato industry is also developing products such as *passata di pomodoro*, a very finely strained tomato sauce. While it is very convenient and useful, I think it is no more than a thick tomato juice or a thin tomato purée, rather than a product with an intrinsic culinary worth. I prefer *polpa di pomodoro*, which includes chunks of tomato. Using this can save you the work of chopping up peeled tomatoes for fine sauces such as *salsa di pomodoro*, a simple sauce based on olive oil, garlic, onion, tomatoes, and basil. This sauce is used as the foundation for all Italian tomato sauces, which are usually indicated with the word *napoletana*.

However it is used and in whatever form, the tomato deserves its Italian name of *pomodoro*, or "golden apple" (the first tomatoes, used for decoration, were yellow), because no other vegetable is more versatile—and it is, without doubt, the most important item in Italian cooking!

## PORRO / LEEK

This vegetable is like a cross between garlic and onion, and belongs to the same family. It is cultivated all over Italy, but mainly in Liguria, Marche, Abruzzo, and Puglia. The varieties have such names as *Gigante d'Inverno*, *Mostruoso di Carentan*, *Elefante*, and *Porro d'Italia*. The Romans took this vegetable with them all over Europe—indeed, the leek is now the symbol of Wales.

In Italy, it is eaten in soups, and for that purpose both the white and green parts are used. Leeks cultivated in the summer are more tender, and they are usually eaten raw in *pinzimonio* (see page 223).

Leeks are also eaten with béchamel sauce. I prefer them freshly boiled and eaten as an *antipasto*, dressed with a little olive oil and vinegar.

## PORTULACA / PURSLANE

This wild, leafy, summer plant grows almost anywhere and is characterized by its reddish branches, which spread over the ground. It has small, thick leaves which, when young, add a special juiciness to salads.

### RADICCHIO, SEE CICORIA

## RAPA / TURNIP

Part of the cabbage family, the turnip is one of the most widely used winter vegetables. It has a delicate flavor akin to that of kohlrabi, and is particularly good as an accompaniment to meat or fish. I like turnips freshly boiled and sautéed in butter with a little garlic and parsley. They need to be thoroughly cleaned, with as little of the skin as possible removed. Very young turnips can be eaten raw, shredded in salads. Turnip greens are also eaten.

## RAVANELLO / RADISH

This wonderful vegetable is mainly eaten raw. The little roots come in varying shapes, from round or conical to straight. They are very hot in flavor, but refreshing, and their red-and-white coloring can enliven many salads and *antipasto* plates.

LEFT: *ESTRATTO DI POMODORO*, MADE BY SUN-DRYING PURÉED TOMATOES

BELOW: THE FRUIT AND VEGETABLE MARKET IN FLORENCE

RIBOLLITA, SEE CAVOLO

## RUCOLA, RUCHETTA / ARUGULA

The longish but small, irregularly shaped leaves of *ruchetta* have a sharp taste, which is exceptionally good when mixed with other salad leaves, as in *misticanza*. Arugula is often used as a tasty garnish for *carpaccio*, in a salad with tomatoes and mozzarella, and as a flavoring for pasta sauces and sometimes risottos. *Rucola*, the cultivated version of *ruchetta*, has much larger and rounder leaves.

RIGHT: *SPINACI*

## SCALOGNO / SHALLOT

The shallot, which looks like a small onion, is divided into two sections inside. Its flavor falls somewhere between that of onion and garlic, but its use is limited to salads, in which it is raw and finely chopped, or flavoring special sauces cooked with butter. Shallots keep better than onions, and so can be stored for a long time. With the rise in interest in Mediterranean food, they have recently become fashionable again, but in the past they were very much peasant food in the Italian South.

### SCAROLA, SEE CICORIA

## SCORZONERA / BLACK SALSIFY

This is a very long, straight root vegetable that belongs to the lettuce family. It is harvested in autumn and winter and is enjoyed for its delicate but bitter flavor. The root can grow up to 1 foot in length and must be thoroughly scraped with a knife until the white pulp is visible. If it is old, cut it in two and discard the woody center. If it is very young, though, it can be boiled whole and eaten with melted butter like asparagus. In Italy nowadays there are few enthusiasts of the vegetable, but it makes an interesting change to the usual fare.

## SEDANO, SEDANO RAPA / CELERY, CELERY ROOT

Celery is very versatile plant that is valuable both as an herb and as a vegetable. There are two basic varieties, one of which is a plant with a long stem of green on the outside and creamy white on the inside. The other variety is *sedano rapa* (turnip-rooted celery or celery root) because it grows mainly underground in a round root. The leaves of this root are usually sold as an herb for salads and soups. The root has a strong scent and its skin is quite tough but full of flavor.

Celery is grown almost everywhere in Italy, but most notably in Puglia, Calabria, and Campania, while Sicily cultivates a small amount of stick celery that has small stems and larger leaves than flat parsley. It is mostly used in the local specialty called *caponata* which is made with eggplant, celery, onion, capers, and pitted green olives, all stewed with the best extra-virgin olive oil, a little sugar, and vinegar (see recipe, page 135).

Celery root can be peeled, boiled, cut in slices and baked in the oven with butter, nutmeg, and pepper and a touch of heavy cream, and it is also good both braised and deep-fried. Finely shredded young celery root is good raw in salads.

White celery is shaded from the sun so that it is blanched of its green coloring. It is used cut in small pieces in salads. Green celery can be used in soups, cut in 4-inch chunks and boiled as a vegetable, or served *gratinato*, dotted with butter and Parmesan cheese. Naturally, the most tender parts of both varieties of stalk celery can be eaten raw (see *pinzimonio* and *bagna caôda*).

## SOTTACETI / PICKLES

Generic name for all vegetables pickled in vinegar and used in *antipasto* or for aperitifs (see *giardiniera*).

## SPINACI / SPINACH

The Arabs introduced this popular vegetable to Italy around the year A.D. 1,000 and it is now grown in northern and central Italy, where the climate is mild but not hot. It grows close to the ground and has substantial deep green leaves. Modern cultivation techniques mean that spinach is available all year round rather than just in the fall and winter as in the past. Spinach contains large amounts of vitamins A and C, but is best known for being rich in iron.

It is served in a multitude of ways, including *alla fiorentina*, with a thick white sauce flavored with Parmesan cheese, and it is also good raw in salads as long as the leaves are young and tender. Spinach requires careful cleaning, especially if it has been grown organically.

My favorite way of preparing spinach is cooking it briefly in a very small amount of water, draining it, and dressing it with extra-virgin olive oil and lemon juice while it is still warm. It is particularly good mixed with ricotta and Parmesan cheese and used to fill *crespelle* (small pancakes), ravioli, or large pasta shells. My own recipe for *uovo in raviolo* is based on a mixture of spinach and ricotta, which is formed in a ring on a large

FAR LEFT:
CARDOON AND
PUMPKIN

NEAR LEFT:
PUMPKIN FLESH

square of pasta. An egg yolk is placed in the center of the spinach mixture, and another large square of pasta is pressed on top. The whole thing is cooked in boiling water and served with melted butter and a few slivers of truffle.

Fresh or frozen spinach can also be liquified and added to pasta dough to color it green (see page 142) and it also makes a wonderful soup if cooked in a good stock with a couple of beaten egg yolks quickly stirred in, and served sprinkled with Parmesan cheese.

### TACCOLA, SEE PISELLO

### VALERIANELLA / CORN SALAD, MÂCHE

One of the most delicate wild salad leaves, this plant is now widely cultivated. It is used largely in modern cuisine to decorate various dishes and is usually eaten raw on its own or as part of a green salad. The little bushy leaves are extremely tender and delicate. I prefer to eat it dressed with extra-virgin olive oil and a little lemon juice. As with all their salads, Italians like to dress *valerianella* at the table, first pouring on the oil to avoid damaging the delicate leaves with the acidity of the lemon or vinegar.

### ZUCCA / SQUASH, PUMPKIN

One of the most widely used families of vegetables in Italy, all types of squash, pumpkins, and the smaller zucchini are loved for their flavor, varying shapes, and wide range of uses in the kitchen. Only the marrow is not much eaten in Italy, as it is considered to be no more than an overgrown zucchini without the flavor. The family of plants originates in South America, where they were cultivated for decoration, some varieties reaching gigantic proportions. The largest today are the *Mammouth* or the *Melone Gigante*, which can reach more than 250 pounds in weight.

Pumpkins and other types of thick-skinned winter squashes will keep for up to a month as long as the skin is not broken. Once cut, however, they will only last for a day or two. For the best flavor, squash and pumpkins should only be picked when fully ripe.

All varieties of squash, including zucchini, grow close to the earth,

spreading long tentacles over the ground, then producing the fruit from the flower.

Today, pumpkin is popular in Piedmont, where the whole thing is baked in the oven and the cooked flesh is spooned out, in the Veneto where they serve it with pickled vegetables, and in Lombardy, where they use it to make risotto. In Campania it is called *cocozza*, and is sliced and lightly boiled, then fried. It is also known as *salmone di campagna*, or country salmon, because of its orange-red color. In Emilia-Romagna it is used to make *tortelli di zucca* (see page 160), which calls for cooked pumpkin mixed with *mostarda*. Dried pumpkin seeds can also be eaten, and are particularly tasty when toasted and scattered over gratins or salads. They are mostly sold and eaten in southern Italy.

One unusual variety of squash is the spaghetti squash, whose cooked flesh forms strings, like spaghetti. It is delicious eaten simply with butter and Parmesan cheese. Another curiosity is the *Piena di Napoli*, also knows as the *Piena di Chioggia* or *Piena di Albenga*. It grows up to 3 feet in length and has to be suspended from a pergola so it has room to grow to full size. It can also be picked before it is completely ripe, when it is just 2 to $2^1/_2$ inches in diameter and can be cooked in the same ways as zucchini. In Sicily this type of squash is also cut in long strips and candied for the making of *cassata Siciliana*, a ricotta and marzipan dessert.

Squash and pumpkin flowers are also used in the same way as zucchini flowers. Generally slightly smaller than those of the zucchini, they do, however, have a more intense flavor.

LEFT: *VALERIANELLA*

## ZUCCHINO / ZUCCHINI

Like the other larger *zucca*, *zucchini* also grow over the ground, but are more bushy than other plants in the family. When buying them, try to get them organically grown, and try to buy them in season, when their flavor is at its best. Zucchini are delicious when freshly picked, blanched and served dressed with a little melted butter and salt, or extra-virgin olive oil and lemon juice.

Zucchini come in a huge range of shapes, colors, and sizes, from the round, dark green *Tonda di Nizza* to the long, straight, dark green *Verde di Milano*, and from the common *Striata di Italia* or *di Napoli* to the pale green *Bianca Sarda*. What they all have in common, though, is their flavor, which is almost exactly the same

regardless of their outer appearance. To get the best zucchini, look for those that are firm to the touch with a shiny skin. Inside they should be white with small edible seeds. They are grown all over Italy and they adapt themselves quite readily to many soil types. They are

universally popular for their culinary versatility and their nutritional value.

Like other plants in the family, zucchini have exquisite, edible flowers. Only the non-fruit-bearing male flower, with its characteristic long, thin stem, is usually sold in huge bunches at markets all around Italy. Zucchini flowers are at their best when open, and are ideal for stuffing with mixtures of spinach, ricotta, and Parmesan cheese before being dipped in beaten egg and deep-fried. They are also good simply dipped in a batter of flour, water, and salt, then deep- or shallow-fried in good olive oil (see recipe, page 123).

Recently, due to demand for the flowers, zucchini plants have been bred expressly for the flowers, and only tiny zucchini are produced as a result. These baby zucchini are extremely tender but, like all plants that are not allowed to reach maturity, they lack flavor in comparison with the fully grown vegetable.

Zucchini can be served in a huge variety of ways. Tender young zucchini are delicious simply eaten raw, grated in salads or, as in my own recipe *marmellata di zucchini*, as a zucchini marmalade — finely shredded with garlic and extra-virgin olive oil, and a final few drops of lemon juice added after the mixture has gently simmered for about 20 minutes.

Zucchini can also be served as a vegetable accompaniment or as a snack with drinks, cut in batons then dipped in a batter of egg and

flour and shallow-fried. They are also delicious in the Neapolitan dish *alla scapece*, in which they are cut in thin slices and fried until lightly browned and served dressed with extra-virgin olive oil, vinegar, garlic, and mint (see recipe, page 124). Alternatively, they can be sliced then broiled and served dressed with extra-virgin olive oil and vinegar. They are also delicious cooked *al funghetto*, fried in cubes with garlic, extra-virgin olive oil, and parsley. They may also be sliced lengthwise, shallow-fried, and used in place of eggplant to make *parmigiana* (see *melanzana*) or stuffed with a meat or bread-and-egg filling and baked, or chopped and added to a *minestrone* soup.

Finally, *tenerume*, or tender zucchini plant tops, can be used at the end of the season to make a *zuppa* with potatoes, tomatoes, garlic, and extra-virgin olive oil (see recipe, page 123).

*ZUPPA DI VERDURE* (TOP), *FIORI DI ZUCCHINI FRITTI* (BELOW).

# ZUPPA DI VERDURE
VEGETABLE SOUP

**FOR 4**

2 TABLESPOONS OLIVE OIL

1 ONION, SLICED

2 GARLIC CLOVES, CHOPPED

3 TOMATOES, FINELY CHOPPED

4¹/₂ CUPS CHICKEN OR
    VEGETABLE STOCK

5 OUNCES NEW POTATOES, PEELED
    AND CUT INTO ¹/₄-INCH SLICES

2¹/₄ POUNDS *TENERUME* (SEE
    *ZUCCHINO*, PAGE 121) OR 2 TO 3
    ZUCCHINI, CHOPPED

SALT AND PEPPER

*This soup uses* tenerume, *the tender shoots at the top of the zucchini plant, including the young flower and zucchini still attached.*

Heat the oil in a large pan, add the onion and garlic, and fry briefly until softened. Add the tomatoes, stir well together, then pour in the stock and bring to a simmer. Add the potatoes and *tenerume* or zucchini and cook for about 20 minutes or until the potatoes are tender.

Season to taste and serve immediately with some good bread.

# FIORI DI ZUCCHINI FRITTI
DEEP-FRIED ZUCCHINI FLOWERS

**FOR 4**

2 EGGS

SALT AND PEPPER

1¹/₄ CUPS ALL-PURPOSE FLOUR

4 TABLESPOONS BEER

20 ZUCCHINI FLOWERS, ORANGE-
    COLORED BUT STILL CLOSED

OLIVE OIL FOR DEEP-FRYING

*There are two ways of cooking this curious dish—with the flowers either stuffed (see overleaf) or simply dipped in batter and fried. Both ways are wonderful.*

Beat the eggs together with some salt and pepper and then add the flour and beer and mix well to obtain a light batter. If the flowers are already open, check for insects inside.

Dip the flowers in the batter one by one and deep-fry in hot oil a few at a time until golden. Use a fairly small pan for frying so the oil level is higher and you will need less.

# FINOCCHIO FRITTO
FRIED FENNEL

**FOR 4**

3 LARGE BULBS FENNEL

SALT AND PEPPER

2 EGGS, BEATEN

4 TABLESPOONS BUTTER

FLOUR FOR DREDGING

*This is a very simple way to prepare fennel, versatile enough to accompany all sorts of delicate meat and fish dishes.*

Cook the fennel bulbs in boiling salted water until tender; check by inserting the tip of a knife. Drain and leave to cool, then cut into quarters.

Beat the eggs together with some salt and pepper. Dredge the fennel segments in the flour, then dip them in the beaten egg to coat them completely. Melt the butter in a pan over a gentle heat and fry the fennel on each side until golden.

# FIORI DI ZUCCHINI RIPIENI
STUFFED ZUCCHINI FLOWERS

**FOR 4**

3 EGGS
SCANT 1/2 CUP ALL-PURPOSE FLOUR
4 TABLESPOONS COLD WATER
12 ZUCCHINI FLOWERS
10 OUNCES RICOTTA CHEESE
PINCH FRESHLY GRATED NUTMEG
1 BUNCH CHIVES, CHOPPED
4 TABLESPOONS FRESHLY GRATED
  PARMESAN CHEESE
SALT AND PEPPER
4 TABLESPOONS OLIVE OIL

*The Italians pay special attention to the flowers of the zucchini and squash. They are sold in bunches at the street market and in good stores, when they are in season.*

Beat 2 of the eggs lightly in a bowl, then stir in the flour. Gradually add the water to make a smooth consistency; set aside.

Clean the zucchini flowers carefully. Gently wash and dry the outside and make sure there are no insects inside. Prepare the filling by mixing together the ricotta, nutmeg, chives, the remaining egg, grated Parmesan, and salt and pepper to taste. Fill the flowers with spoonfuls of this mixture.

Heat the oil in a large frying pan. Dip the flowers in the batter and fry them, a few at a time, in the hot oil until golden brown, turning from time to time. Drain on paper towels before serving.

# ZUCCHINI ALLA SCAPECE
MARINATED ZUCCHINI

**FOR 4 TO 6**

1 3/4 POUNDS YOUNG ZUCCHINI, CUT
  INTO SLICES 1/2 INCH THICK
2 TABLESPOONS MINT LEAVES
1 GARLIC CLOVE, PEELED AND CUT IN HALF
SALT
ABOUT 2 TABLESPOONS WHITE WINE
VINEGAR
OLIVE OIL FOR FRYING

*Scapece probably comes from the Portuguese word* escabeche, *which means marinated. This is a delightful little accompaniment for broiled lamb or pork, or to eat as part of an* antipasto.

Fry the zucchini slices in abundant hot oil until browned on both sides (not too dark). The zucchini have to float freely in the oil; if necessary, fry them in batches. Drain in a sieve to get rid of excess oil and then put them in a porcelain dish.

When all the zucchini have been fried, add the mint leaves and the garlic (which is only to flavor the zucchini and should be discarded before eating). Season with salt to taste and stir in at least 2 tablespoons of vinegar, more if desired. Leave to marinate for at least 2 hours.

# MELANZANE FRITTE
FRIED EGGPLANT

**FOR 4**

2 LARGE EGGPLANTS, CUT INTO FINGER-
  SIZED STRIPS
SALT
1/2 CUP OLIVE OIL

*In this very simple way of eating eggplant the flavor is provided by good olive oil and the eggplants themselves.*

Leave the eggplants in lightly salted cold water for 1 hour, then drain and squeeze out the excess water. Heat the oil in a large pan, add the eggplants, and fry until brown on each side. Season with salt to taste. They can be served hot or cold.

# PEPERONI E OLIVE
## PEPPERS AND OLIVES

**FOR 4**

1/2 CUP OLIVE OIL

2 EACH YELLOW AND RED PEPPERS,
SEEDED AND CUT INTO LARGE STRIPS

2 TABLESPOONS FINELY CHOPPED BLACK
OLIVES

2 GARLIC CLOVES, FINELY CHOPPED

2 TABLESPOONS WHITE WINE VINEGAR

1 TEASPOON SUGAR

SALT

*This is a very welcome southern addition to an* antipasto.

Heat the oil in a pan, add the peppers and fry, stirring from time to time, for about 20 minutes, until they are tender. Add the olives and garlic and fry for another couple of minutes. Add the vinegar and stir until it has evaporated, then add the sugar and salt to taste. Serve hot or cold.

CLOCKWISE FROM TOP LEFT: *ZUCCHINI ALLA SCAPECE, PEPERONI FRITTI, PEPERONI E OLIVE, MELANZANE FRITTE*

# PEPERONI RIPIENI
## STUFFED PEPPERS

**FOR 6**

**3** LARGE YELLOW OR RED PEPPERS, OR A
   MIXTURE OF BOTH

**10** OUNCES FRESH BREAD CRUMBS

**1** TABLESPOON SALTED CAPERS, SOAKED
   IN WATER FOR **10** MINUTES THEN
   DRAINED

**1** TABLESPOON FINELY CHOPPED BLACK
   OLIVES

**3** LARGE TOMATOES, PEELED, SEEDED,
   AND FINELY DICED

**1** GARLIC CLOVE, VERY FINELY CHOPPED

**2** TABLESPOONS COARSELY CHOPPED
   FLAT-LEAF PARSLEY

**4** ANCHOVY FILLETS, FINELY CHOPPED

**1/2** CUP OLIVE OIL

SALT AND PEPPER

*This way of preparing peppers, and also eggplant and zucchini, is typical of the South. With a few variations, this is how they are cooked in Naples.*

Preheat the oven to 350° F. Cut the peppers in half and discard the seeds.

Soak the bread crumbs in enough water to cover and then squeeze out the excess liquid. Mix with the capers, olives, tomatoes, garlic, parsley, anchovies, half the olive oil, and salt and pepper to taste. Fill the peppers with this mixture and put them on a baking sheet. Drizzle with the remaining olive oil and bake for 30 minutes, until the peppers are tender and starting to char a little at the edges.

They are excellent hot or cold.

# PEPERONI AL POMODORO
## PEPPERS AND TOMATOES

**FOR 4**

¹/₃ CUP OLIVE OIL

1¹/₄ POUNDS *PEPERONCINI DOLCI* (SEE *PEPERONE*, PAGE 114), STEMS TRIMMED

1 GARLIC CLOVE, FINELY CHOPPED

14 OUNCES RIPE TOMATOES, PEELED, SEEDED, AND CHOPPED (OR THE EQUIVALENT AMOUNT OF TOMATO PULP – SEE PAGE 118)

6 BASIL LEAVES

SALT

*In some parts of the South these small bell peppers are also called* friarielli— *confusingly, since* cime di rapa *(see page 109) is given the same name. This is a common way of eating the very small peppers that look like chilies but taste sweet. When buying them you have to be sure to get the real thing. My mother used to add some new potatoes and serve these as a first course accompanied by bread.*

Heat the oil in a pan and fry the whole peppers (the little seeds inside are edible) for 10 minutes, stirring constantly. Add the garlic and fry for 1 minute, then stir in the tomatoes, basil, and salt. Cover and cook for about 15 to 20 minutes, until the peppers are soft.

# PEPERONI FRITTI
## FRIED PEPPERS

**FOR 4**

6 TABLESPOONS OLIVE OIL

1¹/₄ POUNDS WHOLE BABY SWEET PEPPERS

2 GARLIC CLOVES

¹/₂ SMALL CHILI PEPPER, SEEDED AND CHOPPED

SALT

Heat the oil in a heavy-bottomed pan and, when hot, put in the peppers. Fry the peppers for 5 minutes, stirring from time to time so that they cook on all sides. Their skins will begin to blister, and at that point add the garlic and almost immediately afterwards the chili and salt to taste. Cook for a further 5 minutes.

Serve hot or cold as part of an *antipasto* or as a side dish.

# CICORIA BELGA AL TARTUFO NERO
## BELGIAN ENDIVE WITH BLACK TRUFFLE

**FOR 4**

5 LARGE HEADS BELGIAN ENDIVE

1 TABLESPOON TRUFFLE OIL

2 TABLESPOONS EXTRA-VIRGIN OLIVE OIL

1 TABLESPOON BALSAMIC VINEGAR

1 SUMMER TRUFFLE (SEE PAGE 195), WEIGHING ABOUT 1³/₄ OUNCES, THINLY SLICED

SALT AND PEPPER

*This is one of the favorite appetizers in my restaurant. The simple combination produces a wonderful result*

Cut the endive into strips ¹/₂ inch wide, removing the tough core, which is slightly bitter. Put the endive in a bowl and add the oils, vinegar, and salt and pepper to taste. Mix well and serve topped with thin slices of summer truffle.

# CARCIOFI RIPIENI

STUFFED ARTICHOKES

FOR 4

2¹/₂ POUNDS VERY FRESH YOUNG
   ARTICHOKES
10 OUNCES FRESH BREAD CRUMBS
SMALL SPRIG MINT, ROUGHLY CHOPPED
ZEST OF ¹/₂ LEMON
3 ANCHOVY FILLETS, FINELY CHOPPED
1 SMALL GARLIC CLOVE, VERY FINELY
   CHOPPED
2 TABLESPOONS CHOPPED FLAT-LEAF
   PARSLEY
1¹/₂ TABLESPOONS SALTED CAPERS,
   SOAKED IN WATER FOR 10 MINUTES,
   THEN DRAINED AND ROUGHLY CHOPPED
3 TABLESPOONS EXTRA-VIRGIN OLIVE OIL
SALT AND PEPPER
OLIVE OIL

*It is essential to use very fresh and tender artichokes for this recipe.*

Discard the tough outer leaves of the artichokes until you reach the tender leaves, then slice off the top. Cut off the stems so they will stand upright. Remove the choke from the center with a melon baller, leaving a cavity (see page 105).

Soak the bread crumbs in a little water to cover, then squeeze out the excess moisture. Mix the bread crumbs with the mint, lemon zest, anchovies, garlic, parsley, and capers. Stir in the extra-virgin olive oil, then add a little salt and plenty of pepper.

Fill the cavities of the artichokes with this mixture and put the artichokes in a large pan, making sure they stay upright. Add enough water to come halfway up the artichokes and then pour in enough olive oil to increase the level of the liquid by about ¹/₂ inch. Bring to a simmer, cover with the lid, and braise over a very gentle heat for 30 minutes.

# FRITTATA DI CARCIOFI

ARTICHOKE OMELET

FOR 4

8 FRESH YOUNG MEDIUM ARTICHOKES
4 TABLESPOONS OLIVE OIL
1 LARGE ONION, THINLY SLICED
6 FREE-RANGE EGGS
2 TABLESPOONS COARSELY CHOPPED
   FLAT-LEAF PARSLEY
1¹/₂ OUNCES PARMESAN CHEESE,
   GRATED
SALT AND PEPPER

*Artichokes combine extremely well with eggs. This frittata is not turned during cooking; it is cooked on one side only, until the eggs are set.*

Discard the tough outer leaves of the artichokes until you reach the tender leaves, then slice off the top. If the artichokes are young and tender, simply trim the stems, leaving about 2 inches still attached, then peel them. Cut them into quarters and remove the chokes with a knife. Put the artichokes in a frying pan with the olive oil, onion, and about 6 tablespoons water. Cover and cook gently until they are tender and all the liquid has evaporated.

Beat the eggs together with the parsley, Parmesan cheese, and some salt and pepper. Pour the egg mixture over the artichokes and cook over a medium heat without stirring. When the eggs have set the *frittata* is ready. Serve cut into wedges.

# CARCIOFI IN AGRODOLCE
SWEET-AND-SOUR ARTICHOKES

**FOR 4**

12 FRESH YOUNG MEDIUM ARTICHOKES

SALT

3 TABLESPOONS WHITE WINE VINEGAR

1 TABLESPOON SUPERFINE SUGAR

3 TABLESPOONS COARSELY CHOPPED
    FLAT-LEAF PARSLEY

3 TABLESPOONS EXTRA-VIRGIN OLIVE OIL

*This is a very appetizing and unusual way to prepare artichokes, and it can be eaten as an* antipasto.

Discard the tough outer leaves of the artichokes until you reach the tender leaves, then slice off the top. Trim the stems, leaving about 2 inches still attached; if you peel the stem it will be very edible and tender. Cut the artichokes into quarters and remove the chokes with a knife. Boil the artichokes in lightly salted water for about 15 minutes or until tender; check by piercing with the tip of a knife. Drain and set aside.

Heat the vinegar and sugar in a small pan until the sugar has dissolved. Leave to cool, then mix with the parsley, olive oil, and a pinch of salt. Pour over the artichoke quarters and leave to absorb the flavors for an hour or so before serving.

CLOCKWISE FROM TOP LEFT:
*FRITTATA DI CARCIOFI, CARCIOFI IN AGRODOLCE, CARCIOFI RIPIENI*

# CAPONNET

## SAVOY CABBAGE PARCELS

**FOR 4**

8 **S**AVOY CABBAGE LEAVES (SEE RIGHT)

3¹/₂ OUNCES *LUGANIGA* SAUSAGE (SEE
   PAGE 77)

7 OUNCES LEFTOVER ROAST BEEF OR PORK

2 EGGS, BEATEN

2 TABLESPOONS DRIED BREAD CRUMBS

1 GARLIC CLOVE, VERY FINELY CHOPPED

PINCH FRESHLY GRATED NUTMEG

1³/₄ OUNCES **P**ARMESAN CHEESE,
   GRATED

SALT AND PEPPER

1¹/₂ TABLESPOONS BUTTER

*In Canavese, and especially in Ivrea, this dish is a must at winter parties and celebrations. It is served as part of a very varied antipasto. The leaves for making the parcels must be from a Savoy cabbage. Choose the second layer of leaves because the outer layer will be too tough. Finely ground leftover roast meat and some sausage meat are used in the stuffing but if you don't have any leftover roast meat, use ground beef that has been briefly browned.*

Preheat the oven to 325° F. Boil the cabbage leaves in lightly salted water for 5 minutes, until they are flexible. Drain and pat dry on a cloth. Cut out the central stalk if it is tough.

Take the sausage meat out of its skin and crumble it. Mix with the roast beef or pork, eggs, bread crumbs, garlic, nutmeg, and all but 1 tablespoon of the Parmesan cheese, adding salt and pepper to taste. Place the mixture in the centers of the cabbage leaves and fold them up to make parcels, securing with a cocktail stick. Put them on a baking sheet, dot with the butter, and sprinkle with the remaining Parmesan. Bake for 20 minutes.

Serve hot or at room temperature.

*CAPONNET AND CIPOLLE RIPIENE*

# CIPOLLE RIPIENE
STUFFED ONIONS

**FOR 4**

8 MEDIUM ONIONS

SALT AND PEPPER

7 OUNCES LUGANIGA SAUSAGE (SEE
    PAGE 77)

1 TABLESPOON OLIVE OIL

1 TABLESPOON BREAD CRUMBS

1 EGG, BEATEN

1 TABLESPOON RAISINS

1 TABLESPOON PINE NUTS

2 AMARETTI, CRUMBLED

1 TABLESPOON PARMESAN CHEESE,
    GRATED

SMALL PINCH FRESHLY GRATED NUTMEG

PINCH GROUND CINNAMON

*Very often in Piedmont baked onions are served with* caponnet *(see opposite) and sometimes the same stuffing is used for both. Here the stuffing is different, but it is Piedmontese despite the inclusion of spices, pine nuts, and raisins, which are of southern origin.*

Preheat the oven to 350° F. Peel the onions. Cook them in lightly salted boiling water for 10 minutes and then drain.

Take the sausage meat out of its skin and crumble it. Heat the olive oil in a skillet, add the sausage meat, and fry until browned. Leave to cool, then mix with the bread crumbs, egg, raisins, pine nuts, amaretti, Parmesan cheese, nutmeg, and cinnamon, adding salt and pepper to taste.

Cut the top off of each onion and remove the center with a spoon to make a container. Fill them with the stuffing and bake for 20 to 25 minutes. They can be served hot or at room temperature.

# SALSA DI POMODORO ALLA NAPOLETANA
NEAPOLITAN TOMATO SAUCE

**FOR 6**

1/3 CUP EXTRA-VIRGIN OLIVE OIL

2 GARLIC CLOVES, CRUSHED

2 1/4 POUNDS RIPE TOMATOES,
    PEELED, SEEDED, AND CHOPPED (OR
    USE 2 1/2 CUPS TOMATO PULP—SEE
    PAGE 118)

6 BASIL LEAVES

SALT AND PEPPER

*The name given to a dish or sauce usually denotes its place of origin or the place where it is usually cooked. Naples is synonymous with spaghetti, pizza, and naturally, therefore, with one of the basic tomato sauces. This sauce is known not only in Italy but anywhere in the world a Neapolitan immigrant has set up a business. It is indeed a delightful sauce, usually prepared with sun-ripened tomatoes. During winter, however, canned or bottled tomato pulp is used. Some people prefer to cook the sauce for only about 5 minutes if the tomatoes are very ripe, while others let it simmer for 20 to 30 minutes for a more concentrated flavor, even adding a spoonful of tomato paste. I prefer the briefly cooked version. The general Italian basic tomato sauce involves frying onion, carrot, celery, and parsley before adding the tomatoes and basil.*

Heat the oil in a pan and gently fry the garlic for a few minutes without allowing it to color. Add the tomatoes and fry, stirring constantly, for 5 minutes, allowing just the excess liquid to evaporate.

Add the basil and salt and pepper to taste and the sauce is ready to use for the most wonderful plate of spaghetti or many other dishes.

# GATTÒ DI PATATE

POTATO CAKE

**FOR 6**

2¹/₄ POUNDS FLOURY POTATOES

1³/₄ OUNCES *PROSCIUTTO COTTO*, CUT
   INTO CUBES

³/₄ OUNCES BUFFALO MOZZARELLA, CUT
   INTO SMALL CUBES

3¹/₂ OUNCES PROVOLA (SMOKED
   MOZZARELLA, SEE PAGE 244) CHEESE,
   CUT INTO SMALL CUBES

1³/₄ OUNCES PARMESAN CHEESE,
   GRATED

4 EGGS, BEATEN

2 TABLESPOONS FINELY CHOPPED
   FLAT-LEAF PARSLEY

BUTTER

4 TABLESPOONS DRIED BREAD CRUMBS

4 TABLESPOONS OLIVE OIL

SALT AND PEPPER

Gattò *is derived from the French* gâteau, *which this resembles in shape when baked. It is very common in Naples, where many French-influenced recipes are cooked even today—a legacy of the Bourbon occupation in the eighteenth century.*

Preheat the oven to 350° F. Boil the potatoes until tender, then drain and peel them. Pass them through a sieve to make a purée. Mix the potato purée with the prosciutto, mozzarella, provola, Parmesan, beaten eggs, parsley, and some salt and pepper.

Grease a round 10-inch cake pan with butter, and dust with some of the bread crumbs. Pour the potato mixture into it and press gently with a fork to give some shape. Sprinkle with the remaining bread crumbs and then drizzle with the olive oil. Bake for 30 minutes, until browned on top.

The cake is very good warm but also excellent cold.

# FRITTELLA PALERMITANA
ARTICHOKES, PEAS, AND FAVA BEANS FROM PALERMO

**FOR 2 AS A MAIN COURSE, 4 AS AN ACCOMPANIMENT OR A PASTA SAUCE**

4 TO 5 SMALL YOUNG ARTICHOKES
1/3 CUP OLIVE OIL
1 LARGE ONION, THINLY SLICED
5 OUNCES SHELLED FRESH PEAS
5 OUNCES SHELLED FRESH FAVA BEANS
1 TEASPOON SALTED CAPERS, SOAKED IN WATER FOR 10 MINUTES, THEN DRAINED
1 1/4 CUPS WATER
SALT AND PEPPER

*Made when the new season's vegetables have just appeared, this dish is the epitome of Sicilian springtime. A specialty of Palermo, it is extremely simple to make. Sometimes a teaspoon of white wine vinegar is added after the vegetables have been cooked. Without the vinegar it can be used as a pasta sauce. It can also be made into a more substantial dish using potatoes. Sicilians usually cook this dish until the vegetables are very soft. However, I prefer it cooked my way so that the vegetables remain separate. If you do overcook it, try serving it on pasta with some freshly grated pecorino cheese.*

Prepare the artichokes by removing the stems and outer leaves (see *carciofo*, page 105). Small, young artichokes have hardly any choke and should need very little preparation. Cut the artichokes into quarters.

Heat the oil in a saucepan; add the onion and fry briefly, until softened. Add the peas, fava beans, artichokes, capers, and some salt and pepper, then pour in the water and stir well. Put the lid on the pan and cook over medium heat for about 20 minutes or until the vegetables are tender, stirring from time to time.

ABOVE: *FRITTELLA PALERMITANA* AND *PANELLE DI PALERMO* (TOP)

# PANELLE DI PALERMO
CHICKPEA FRITTERS

**FOR 4 TO 6**

4 1/2 CUPS WATER
2 1/4 CUPS CHICKPEA FLOUR
1 TABLESPOON FINELY CHOPPED FLAT-LEAF PARSLEY
SALT AND PEPPER
OLIVE OIL FOR FRYING

*These are traditionally served with frittella palermitana (above). Like many Sicilian dishes, it has a strong Arab influence.*

Bring the water almost to a boil in a large pan, then take off the heat and gradually add the chickpea flour, mixing very well to prevent lumps from forming. When all the flour has been added, put the pan back on the heat and cook for about 30 minutes, stirring all the time. Add the parsley and season with salt. Pour the mixture onto a wet marble surface or baking sheet and flatten with a spatula to about 1/2 inch thick. When cool, cut into squares with a knife or into rounds with a pastry cutter. Shallow-fry in olive oil until golden brown on both sides. Serve hot, with a sprinkle of freshly ground black pepper.

# GIARDINIERA
## MIXED GARDEN PICKLE

**MAKES ENOUGH TO FILL A 2¼-QUART JAR**

1¼ POUNDS MIXED VEGETABLES
  SUCH AS PICKLING ONIONS, GHERKINS,
  CAULIFLOWER, CARROTS, CELERY ROOT,
  AND PUMPKIN

9 CUPS WHITE WINE
  VINEGAR

4½ CUPS WATER

3½ TABLESPOONS SALT

2 TABLESPOONS SUGAR

SMALL HANDFUL OF BAY LEAVES

SMALL HANDFUL OF CLOVES

CHILI PEPPER, TO TASTE (OPTIONAL)

A FEW JUNIPER BERRIES (OPTIONAL)

*Few people prepare their own* giardiniera *nowadays because commercial versions are readily available. However, the homemade variety is by far the best and can be kept for a long time in the brine. I encountered this particular recipe in Emilia-Romagna, where they love it served as an* antipasto, *dressed with olive oil. The vegetables, especially root vegetables such as carrots and celery root, can be cut with a serrated knife to give an attractive pattern. Red and yellow peppers are usually pickled separately, since they require a shorter cooking time and are used on their own in various dishes.*

Peel the vegetables as necessary, then cut them into bite-sized chunks. Put the vinegar and water in a large pan with the salt and sugar and bring to a boil, stirring to dissolve the salt and sugar. Add the vegetables and simmer for 30 minutes, until tender.

Transfer the hot pickle to a 2¼-quart sterilized preserving jar (or several smaller jars), tucking in the bay leaves, cloves, and chili and juniper berries, if using. Seal the jar and store in a cool place. The pickle can be used straight away.

# CREMA DI CANNELLINI
## CREAM OF CANNELLINI BEANS

**FOR 4**

1¼ CUPS DRIED CANNELLINI BEANS

1 OUNCE DRIED PORCINI MUSHROOMS

6 TABLESPOONS BUTTER

1 LARGE ONION, FINELY SLICED

1 CHICKEN STOCK CUBE, CRUMBLED

2 SAGE LEAVES

SALT AND PEPPER

4 SLICES BREAD, CRUSTS REMOVED,
  CUT INTO SMALL CUBES

*For this very creamy soup, which is served topped with croutons, the ingredients are available all year round; it makes a welcome starter for a delicate meal.*

Soak the cannellini beans in plenty of cold water overnight and then drain. Cover them with fresh water, bring to a boil, and simmer for at least 1½ hours or until soft. Drain well. Meanwhile, soak the porcini in lukewarm water for 30 minutes, then drain them, reserving a little of the water, and chop finely.

In another pan, place 4 tablespoons of the butter and fry the onion in it until golden. Add the porcini and fry for a couple of minutes, then add the drained beans and enough water to reach about ¾ inch above the level of the beans. Stir in the reserved porcini soaking water, add the stock cube and sage leaves, and cook gently for 15 to 20 minutes. Remove the sage leaves, and purée everything in a food processor or blender to obtain a velvety, creamy soup. Reheat and add salt and pepper to taste.

Lightly toast the bread and then fry it in the remaining butter. Serve the soup garnished with the croutons.

# CAPONATA
## SICILIAN VEGETABLE STEW

**FOR 6**

1 LARGE ONION, CHOPPED

3 TO 4 CELERY RIBS, INCLUDING LEAVES, CHOPPED

5 TABLESPOONS OLIVE OIL

2$\frac{1}{4}$ POUNDS EGGPLANTS, CUT INTO 1-INCH CHUNKS

1 TABLESPOON SALTED CAPERS, SOAKED IN WATER FOR 10 MINUTES, THEN DRAINED

20 GREEN OLIVES, PITTED

1 TABLESPOON SUGAR

1 TABLESPOON WHITE WINE VINEGAR

1 TABLESPOON CONCENTRATED TOMATO PASTE

SALT AND PEPPER

*In this typical Sicilian dish the vegetables are fried and then simmered in a sweet-and-sour sauce. The origins of the word* caponata *are unclear, although some say it is Catalan. It could derive from the Latin* caupona, *meaning* osteria *(bar), where you would always find a* caponata *ready to eat. Whatever its origin, this dish, served cold as an* antipasto, *is now popular all over Italy. It can also be eaten warm as an accompaniment to meat and poultry or used as a pasta sauce.*

Blanch the onion and celery in lightly salted boiling water for a few minutes, then drain.

Heat the oil in a large frying pan, add the eggplant chunks, and fry until brown and tender (don't overcrowd the pan; you will probably have to cook them in batches). Add the onion, celery, and all the remaining ingredients. Stir well, then cover and cook for about 15 minutes, removing the lid of the pan toward the end of cooking. Should the sauce require extra moisture, add a tablespoon or two of water during cooking. Season to taste with salt and pepper.

# INSALATA DI RINFORZO
REINFORCED SALAD

FOR 6

1 HEAD CAULIFLOWER

ABOUT 20 BLACK OLIVES

7 OUNCES PICKLED YELLOW OR RED
PEPPERS

7 OUNCES *GIARDINIERA* (SEE PAGE
134)

2 TABLESPOONS LARGE SALTED CAPERS,
SOAKED IN WATER FOR 10 MINUTES,
THEN DRAINED

VIRGIN OLIVE OIL

8 ANCHOVY FILLETS

FINELY CHOPPED CHILI PEPPER
(OPTIONAL)

*A typical Neapolitan dish made at the beginning of the Christmas season, this is called* rinforzo *(reinforcement) because it is topped up with fresh ingredients each time any is used. It can be eaten as an* antipasto *or a snack with bread, and is very appetizing indeed.*

Cut the cauliflower into florets and cook in lightly salted boiling water until *al dente*, then drain. Put the cauliflower, olives, pickled peppers, *giardiniera* and capers in a bowl and sprinkle with olive oil, then transfer to large screw-top jar. Decorate with a lattice of anchovy fillets, then seal the jar and store in a cool place. The salad should last throughout the festivities.

# INSALATA DI CAMPO

WILD SALAD

**FOR 4**

10 OUNCES TRIMMED WEIGHT OF
THE FOLLOWING WILD LEAVES, OR ANY
COMBINATION OF THEM: DANDELION,
ARUGULA, WILD GARLIC, TENDER
NETTLE LEAVES, CORN SALAD, OR
WHATEVER YOU FANCY

SMALL BUNCH SCALLIONS

4 TABLESPOONS EXTRA-VIRGIN OLIVE OIL

4 ANCHOVY FILLETS, SMASHED

1 GARLIC CLOVE, VERY FINELY CHOPPED

2 TABLESPOONS BALSAMIC VINEGAR

SALT AND PEPPER

*A popular springtime activity for many people is roaming the fields to collect the first tender leaves of the dandelion and other wild herbs for a hearty salad. With all the pollution nowadays, however, it is necessary to go to remote fields deep in the countryside to be sure of collecting something worth eating.*

Thoroughly wash all the leaves and pat or spin them dry. Chop the scallions into small chunks and arrange in a serving dish mixed with the leaves.

In a small bowl put the oil, anchovies, garlic, and balsamic vinegar with salt and pepper to taste. Mix well and pour over the salad. Toss to mix and serve.

# MOZZARELLA CAPRESE

MOZZARELLA, TOMATOES, AND BASIL, CAPRI-STYLE

**FOR 4**

1 POUND BUFFALO
MOZZARELLA, SLICED

2 LARGE RIPE TOMATOES, SLICED

10 BASIL LEAVES

4 TABLESPOONS EXTRA-VIRGIN OLIVE OIL

SALT AND PEPPER

*The best way of serving buffalo mozzarella as a starter is to combine it with ripe tomatoes, good olive oil, and fresh basil. This is often called* insalata caprese.

Arrange the slices of mozzarella on a plate, alternating them with the slices of tomatoes and basil leaves. Drizzle with olive oil, then season with salt and pepper.

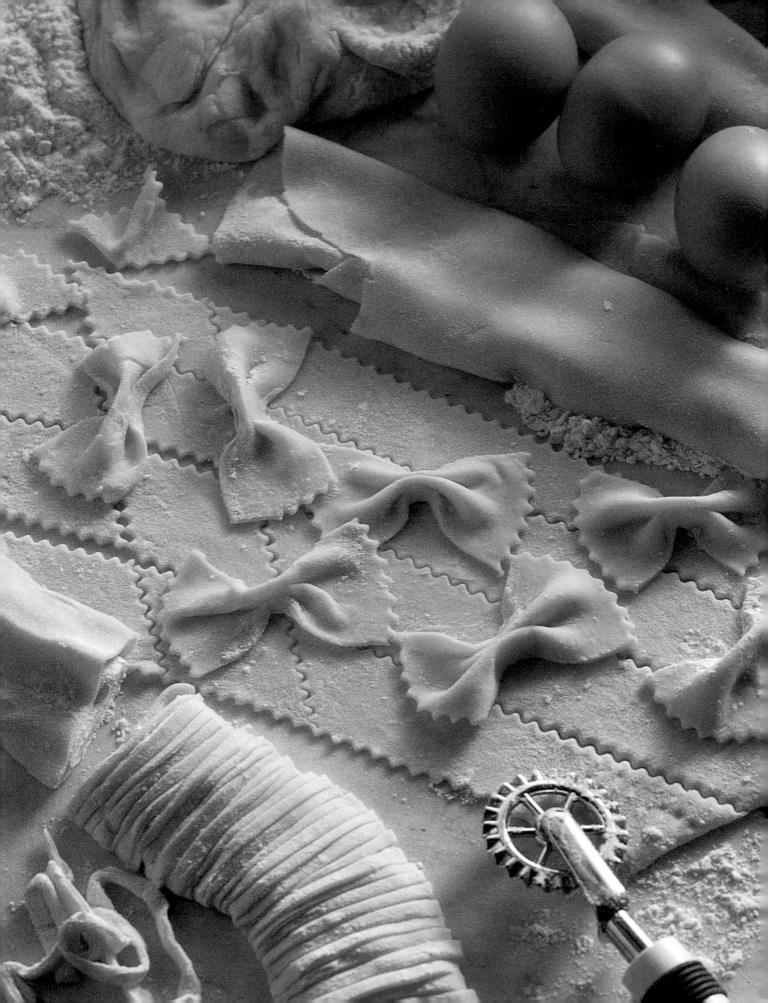

# PASTA

PASTA

I think I do have to begin this chapter with an apology to the reader. Pasta is such a rich, complex, and diverse subject that it really deserves an entire book of this size all on its own. That would allow a proper study of all the more than six hundred shapes and regional sub-varieties in the intricate Italian pasta tapestry, as well as the myriad sauces used with them. In the limited space available here, I have tried to provide a fairly comprehensive selection of some of the most important points and types of pasta.

It is frustrating that the exact historical origins of pasta are unknown. For a long time it was thought that Marco Polo brought it back from China, but the recent discrediting of his journals—which are now said to have been written without ever leaving Venice—means that this theory has been abandoned. Despite this, however, it is known that pasta was eaten in Italy by the Romans long before Marco Polo's time. The noodle they ate was called *laganum*, although it is not clear whether it was boiled, fried, or baked.

Pasta is now strongly perceived as a staple of Italy in general, but it started its life largely as a southern Italian—or even Sicilian—food. In Sicily, *macaroni* was introduced by the Greeks or Arabs, who were frequent visitors to the island. During the Renaissance, pasta flourished as a food mainly due to the fact that southern Italy was invaded by many marauders, who pillaged the local people

of much of their produce. As a result, the filling, flour-based food became a vital staple for feeding hungry families, as it was cheap to produce and easy to store. Naples and the surrounding area became, in time, the birthplace of a huge pasta-making industry using the (then) pure water from the hilly hinterland, the locally grown grain, and the wonderful Mediterranean climate to dry the pasta.

Over time, pasta has traveled with emigrating Italians all over the world, and it is a central part of many Western diets and is valued for its vitamins and as a source of complex carbohydrates, as well as for its culinary versatility. Unless you dress pasta with high-fat sauces, it is one of the most balanced foods you can eat, made up of 60% carbohydrates, 25% fat, 15% protein, minerals such as iron, and vitamins B1, B2, and niacin. Since it is high in complex carbohydrates, it releases energy slowly through the body, making it a good source of energy.

Today, *pasta alimentare*, the flour-and-water dough used to make dried pasta, is produced in factories and dried in special drying rooms over a period of about 12 hours, rather than in the sun. The demand for pasta is now so great that factories are in production 24 hours a day and the grain for the flour has to be imported to Italy from Russia, Turkey, Canada, and America. *Pasta alimentare* can only be made from durum wheat semolina (*Triticum durum*), which is quite different from *T. vulgare*, the soft grain from which bread is made. Only durum wheat has the structure needed to make pasta strings and shapes. The dough it produces has to be elastic and firm enough not to break up while cooking, and absorbent enough to soften on the outside but still remain *al dente*, or resistant to the bite, on the inside.

The other main type of pasta is *pasta all'uovo*, or egg pasta. Unlike *pasta alimentare*, this is usually made by hand and sold fresh, although commercially made versions can be bought in supermarkets, and versions made with durum wheat are dried. However, the best fresh pasta is made at home, where the freshness of the ingredients and storage can be carefully controlled to produce the finest pasta—to be dressed with the very best ingredients. Contrary to popular opinion, you do not need a pasta machine to make pasta at home, although if you make it a lot, you might like to indulge in a small machine, which rolls the pasta to the required thickness and allows you to cut the sheets into a variety of shapes.

The shape of any pasta, whether dried or fresh, is as significant as the dough itself. Many different shapes have been created over the last three hundred years since the early *maccheroni*—which literally translated means "quite expensive" – was first formed. Strings of pasta looking like little worms, hence the name *vermicelli*, came later. It is vital to combine certain sauces with certain shapes, so that the texture of the sauce is complemented by the shape of the pasta itself (see the note on Matching Sauces to Pasta Types at the end of this introduction).

Large pasta companies employ people to test new shapes and the feeling of the pasta on the palate. A pasta manufacturer called Voiello even recently commissioned car designer Giorgetto Giugiaro to make a new shape to hold more sauce. The result was an ergonomic and functional shape (see *marille*). Nowadays many shapes are cut out of sheets of pasta by machine, although some are purely decorative and miss the point of crafting the shape to suit a sauce.

Pasta can be divided into the following five main categories, according to the dough used and its culinary function.

### 1 Pasta di semola di grano duro secca
(dried durum wheat semolina pasta)
This is the basic dried pasta made from a flour-and-water mixture, using durum wheat semolina. The

dough is forced through a die to make long pasta shapes, such as *spaghetti*, which are cut to length and then dried, packaged, and sold. It keeps for a long time if stored correctly. Good dry pasta should still be flexible when bent and should have a glowing amber color.

Dried pasta can be further broken down into three categories:

(a) *Pastina* or *pasta corta minuta* (very short pasta): this pasta is often used to make the tiny shapes used in broths and soups. Extra protein is sometimes added to the dough in the form of gluten to make *pastina glutinata* for use in soups for children.

THE GRAIN FIELDS OF PUGLIA GROWING HARD DURUM WHEAT FOR THE CELEBRATED PUGLIESE PASTA

(b) *Pasta corta* or *pasta tagliata* (short pasta): this is larger than the type used for broth and includes most of the familiar shaped pasta like *farfalle* and *fusilli*. It is usually hollow, so that it cooks more evenly and is dressed with a tomato sauce (most short pasta is eaten with just enough sauce to coat it—this is known as *pasta asciutta*) or baked in timbales, known in Italy as *sformati*, *timpani*, and *timballi*.

(c) *Pasta lunga* (long pasta): in the past, pasta like *spaghetti* and *tagliatelle* were cut in long strings that were originally sold in traditional blue paper packaging (as were sugar and salt—indeed many modern manufacturers have gone back to this

nostalgic look). However, this very long cut of pasta had to be broken when cooked, otherwise it would be too difficult to eat. Most long dried pasta is eaten as *pasta asciutta*, like short pasta, with just enough sauce to coat each strand, although some very fine varieties like *capelli d'angelo* (angel's hair) are suitable for broths.

## 2 Pasta di semola fresca
(fresh durum wheat pasta)
This is made from a dough of fresh semolina and water, and is usually handmade. It is mostly produced and used in the South of Italy, particularly in Puglia. It takes a bit longer to cook

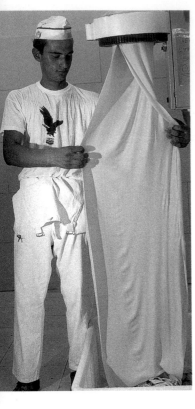

LEFT: EXTRUDING
A PASTA SHEET
FOR THE MAKING
OF *ORECCHIETTE* AT
THE PAP FACTORY
IN PUGLIA

than fresh egg pasta. The most frequently used shapes are *fusilli*, *cavatelli*, *strozzapreti*, and *orecchiette*, with Sardinia producing the well-known *malloreddus* or *gnocchi sardi*.

### 3 Pasta all'uovo secca (dried egg pasta)

This combination of durum wheat semolina and eggs is only produced commercially, as the very firm dough needs to be worked by machine to combine the ingredients sufficiently. It is usually cut in ribbons of various sizes, which are arranged in nests or *matassa* (plaits), to avoid the strands being damaged. It is dried for 12 hours so that it will keep. Stuffed pasta like *tortellini* or *ravioli* can also be made with this dough but, while commercially produced dried egg *tagliatelle* is a good standby, industrially produced stuffed pasta is never very appealing.

### 4 Pasta fresca all'uovo (fresh egg pasta)

Fresh egg pasta is made using free-range eggs and 00 (*doppio zero*) flour, the same tender wheat used to make cakes, rather than durum semolina. The dough is very malleable and can be formed into many shapes. Emilia-Romagna is the center of egg pasta production and is home to *lasagne*, *tortelli*, and *tortellini*.

### 5 Pasta speciale (special pasta)

As pasta has become more and more popular, many variations in shape, flavor, and color have been created. Green pasta (*pasta verde*) is made by adding a well-drained spinach purée to the dough; black pasta (*pasta nera*) with the ink of cuttlefish (for use with fish sauces); red pasta (*pasta rossa*) is made with tomato purée; and pink pasta (*pasta alla barbabietola*) with beetroot; while brown pasta is made by adding cocoa powder, and is eaten as a dessert. Pasta is also flavored with mushrooms, such as *porcini*, as well as with truffle and sometimes wine. From Lombardy and Piedmont come other special pastas made from a combination of 00 (*doppio zero*) flour and buckwheat flour (see *pizzoccheri*).

### HOW TO COOK PASTA

Pasta has to be cooked in plenty of boiling salted water—allow $4^1/_2$ cups water and 1 tablespoon salt for every $3^1/_2$ ounces pasta. Add the salt to the boiling water just before the pasta. It is also important that the pan used is large enough for the water to remain at a good rolling boil to ensure that the pasta moves around as it cooks, helping to prevent it from sticking together. Because pasta exudes starch as it cooks, the amount of water used in relation to the pasta is significant. If there is too little water in the pan, the liquid becomes clogged by the starch and the pasta does not cook properly.

Try to let the pasta fall gently out of your hands into the water rather than feeding it in clumps, which will encourage it to stick together. Gently curl long strands down into the water. Once the pasta has been added to the boiling water, put the lid on the pan to get the temperature of the water back to the boiling point as quickly as possible. As soon as it has reached boiling point again, remove the lid and loosen the pasta with a fork. Never add oil to the water unless you are cooking large sheets of lasagne which may stick together.

Timing is all-important in cooking pasta; a minute more or less can have an enormous influence on the quality of a dish. Fresh egg pasta cooks in a couple of minutes, or even less if it is very fine like *capelli d'angelo*. When using fresh egg pasta, make sure the sauce is ready before you start to cook the pasta, and that your guests are seated at the table and ready to eat. Pasta is cooked when it is *al dente*, that is, tender but offering a little resistance and firmness to the bite. Interestingly, Neapolitans like their *vermicelli* almost undercooked, or *fujenni*.

When the pasta is cooked, take the pan off the heat and add a cup of cold water to stop the cooking process, then wait for half a minute before draining it. Do not rinse the pasta under running water or you will strip it of flavor and nutrients. If cooking pasta for use in timbales, make sure it is slightly undercooked so it does not overcook in the oven. Reserve the drained cooking water, as this can be

BELOW:
MACHINERY NOW
REPRODUCES THE
ORIGINALLY HAND-
MADE SHAPE FOR
*ORECCHIETTE*

used to adjust the texture of the sauce (just-drained
pasta continues to absorb moisture, so a sauce that
was the right consistency before being added to the
pasta can suddenly seem too thick). When serving
pasta it should neither be drowned in sauce, nor too
dry.

## MATCHING SAUCES TO PASTA TYPES

Although the combinations are almost limitless, the
following are some good guidelines on how best to
optimize the effect on the palate and the digestion.
• Thin egg ribbons, like *tagliolini*, are mostly
served with truffles, butter, and Parmesan cheese,
or light, fresh tomato sauces.
• Thicker ribbons, like *tagliatelle*, are good with
sauces of tomato, mushroom, cheese, cream, ham,
and fish, and with *ragù bolognese*.
• Long, flat, dried pasta, like *trenette* or *linguine*,
best suit pesto and sauces of tomato, meat, and
fish.
• Long pastas like *spaghetti*, *lasagnette* and *festoni*
are best with tomato-based *ragùs* and for use in
timbales and *pasticcios*.
• Tubes, both long and short, like *rigatoni*, are
made for long-cooked tomato and other *ragùs*.
• Short shapes of pure semolina pasta, like
*cavatelli* and *orechiette*, are very good with
vegetable sauces like those using broccoli,

cauliflower, Belgian endive, artichoke, etc., and
seafood sauces.
• Stuffed pastas, like *ravioli* and *tortellini*, need
only simple sauces like the juices from a roast, or
butter and sage, or a light tomato sauce.

## EATING PASTA

When eating long pasta, as soon as it arrives in
front of you, loosen it on the plate to distribute the
sauce evenly. Lift a few strands and push them to
the side of your plate to make some space to turn
the fork, then twist
the pasta strands
around the fork.
Put the curled ball
of pasta elegantly
into your mouth.
Never allow
strands to hang
from your mouth,
and do not cut
long strands with
your teeth. The
use of a spoon with
the fork is
considered
impolite by
Italians.

# A-Z OF PASTA

**AGNOLINI** / STUFFED PASTA
*Agnolini* is a small, stuffed egg
pasta, similar in shape to *cappelletti*,
which can only be made by hand.
Fillings of ground roast meat, eggs,
and Parmesan cheese are placed in
the center of circles of pasta, which
are then folded over the fillings to
make semicircles. The corners of the
semicircle are bent round until they
touch, to form little rings.
*Agnolini* come from Lombardy and
Emilia-Romagna, and are mostly
eaten in a good chicken broth (*in
brodo*), but are also dressed with
sage and butter. Similar filled pastas
include *agnoli*, *tortellini*, and
*raviolini*.

**AGNOLOTTI** / STUFFED PASTA
A great deal of confusion is caused
by the variety of names given to this
pasta in different parts of Italy.
*Agnolotti*, very much like *ravioli*,
are little square cushions of stuffed
egg pasta. The Piedmontese, who
claim them as their own, fill
*agnolotti* with cooked greens, such
as spinach, Swiss chard, and
cabbage, mixed with egg, Parmesan
cheese, and cooked sausage. The
original idea was to use any leftovers
of meat and sausage to make a very
economical dish.
    *Agnolotti* are usually eaten
either with melted butter, sage, and
Parmesan cheese, with a light
tomato sauce, or even better, with
the deglazed juices from a roasted
joint. Similar pastas include the
Sardinian *angiulottus* and
*culingiones*, the Tuscan *tordelli*, the
Ligurian *ravioli*, and *tortelli* from
Emilia-Romagna. The fillings vary
from region to region with, for
example, the Sardinians using
pecorino cheese, spinach, saffron,
nutmeg, and eggs as a stuffing, while
the famous Emilia-Romagnan
*tortelli* are filled with pumpkin (see
*tortelli di zucca*, page 160). Rather
confusingly, a smaller version of
*agnolotti* is called *tortellini*, while a
larger is called *tortelloni*. See also
*ravioli*.

**ALFABETO, LETTERE** /
ALPHABET PASTA
This is simply a durum wheat
semolina pasta extruded from a
special die and cut very short into
the shapes of letters of the alphabet.
They are used in soups and are
often made with extra gluten for
children.
    When I think of *alfabeto*, I am
reminded of when I arranged the
wedding meal for my stepson and
daughter-in-law. I decided to add
their initials and some love hearts to
the soup, and had to go through
hundreds of packets of alphabet
pasta to get the letters "S" and "G"
(Sarah and Granby). The
disappointment came when only a
few people noticed as they reached
the bottom of their bowl of soup.
    Alphabet pasta is just one of an
endless variety of tiny pasta
scribbles for soups, and is, naturally,
a special favorite with children.

**AMATRICIANA** / PASTA SAUCE
Pasta *alla amatriciana* is a specialty
of the Lazio region, particularly the
town of Amatrice, after which it is
named. The main ingredient of the
sauce is *guanciale*, air-dried pork
cheeks (see page 76), with a little
*polpa di pomodoro* and spiced with
some chili peppers. Versions are
often made simply using *prosciutto*.
It is traditionally served on
*bucatini* and dressed with pecorino
cheese.

**ANELLI, ANELLINI** / RING-
SHAPED PASTA
This is a ring-shaped durum
wheat semolina pasta which is
very popular in Sicily but quite
difficult to obtain in other
regions. It comes in various sizes;
the smallest, *anellini*, is used in
soups. The largest version has a
diameter of about $5/8$ inch and is
mostly used by the Sicilians to
make their traditional *sformato*, a
pasta and tomato sauce cake.

**ANOLINI** / STUFFED PASTA
This smallest type of *tortellini* is
typical of the cuisine of Parma.
Because they are so tiny, they are
usually handmade, formed
around a woman's little finger. The
thinnest possible *sfoglia*, or pasta
sheets, are needed for their
manufacture. The stuffing is usually
chicken mixed with bread crumbs,
Parmesan cheese, and a touch of
nutmeg.

**BAVETTE, BAVETTINE, LINGUE
DI PASSERO** / LONG, OVAL-
SHAPED PASTA
*Bavette* or *lingue di passero*
(sparrows' tongues) is a long pasta
like a thick, flattened *spaghetti*,
with an oval section rather than
round, giving a lovely mellow
sensation on the palate. Its shape
makes it particularly good with
pesto and seafood sauces. Smaller
sizes are called *bavettine*,
*linguettine*, and *linguette*, while a
Genovese version is called *trenette*
and is almost exclusively eaten with
pesto.

**BIGOLI** /
MANTUAN
NOODLE
This popular pasta,
originally from
Mantova in Emilia-
Romagna, is a whole-
wheat wheat egg
pasta that looks like a
large, fat *spaghetti*.
In the past, the pasta
dough would have
been handmade and
forced through a

LEFT: ALPHABET
PASTA FOR SOUP

BOTTOM: *CIRIOLINE
FROM UMBRIA (SEE
BIGOLI)*

**ABOVE: CUTTING PASTA BY MACHINE**

little machine called a *torchio* or *bigolaro*, but today it is also produced commercially. Among many specialties from the region using *bigoli*, there is the Venetian dish called *bigoli in salsa*, in which it is served with a sauce of onions, olive oil, and anchovies.

Similarly shaped handmade pastas include the variously named *pinci*, *ciriole*, *cirioline*, and *stringozzi*, or *strengozzi*, as it is called in Umbria and Tuscany. These pastas are quite large, with a diameter of about 1/6 inch. Unlike *bigoli*, they are made from a dough of durum wheat, water, and a little olive oil, and are long and have an irregular shape obtained by rolling and stretching the dough. In Umbria, *strengozzi* are served with Norcia truffle, or ragùs of wild boar, rabbit, mushroom, and, naturally, tomato. Great care has to be taken when cooking it, since it is made without eggs and it breaks up readily.

**RIGHT: SERVING CUSTOMERS THEIR PASTA**

**BOCCOLOTTI MEZZANI, SEE ZITE**

## BUCATINI / HOLLOW NOODLE

Mostly used in Campania, Lazio, and Liguria, this long pasta is slightly larger than *spaghettoni* but has a *buco*, or small hole, through the middle, making it easier to cook. *Bucatini* is good with both *amatriciana* and *carbonara* sauces. In Naples this pasta is eaten with meat *ragù*. Similar pastas include *perciatellini* and *fidelini bucati*. Larger versions include *perciatelli* and *ziti*.

**CANDELE, SEE ZITE**

## CANNARONI RIGATI / LARGE PASTA TUBE

This is one of the larger pasta shapes that are preferred by the southern Italians. *Cannaroni* or *canneroni* can be *lisci* (smooth) or *rigato* (fluted), but always have the same tubular shape and are usually at least 1 1/2 to 2 inches long. They are popular in a number of regions and have many different names, from the larger *cannolicchi* and *denti di cavallo* (horse's tooth) to the smooth *sciviotti* and *occhio di lupo* (wolf's eye). It is used with a variety of sauces, as well as in soups, including the famous *minestrone*.

## CANNELLONI / LARGE STUFFED PASTA TUBES

This archetypal pasta from Emilia-Romagna is universally well-known, as its fame has been spread all over the world via Italian restaurants and trattorias. Today it is not only Italian manufacturers who make this large tubular pasta—it is made in many other countries as well, and is sold fresh, dried, and ready-cooked in chilled cabinets and freezers everywhere.

*Cannelloni* was originally made with a sheet of rectangular pasta that was cooked as usual in boiling water, drained, and rolled around a filling of meat, vegetables, or even fish, then baked in a tomato sauce and topped with *mozzarella* or sometimes with a béchamel sauce and Parmesan cheese. Now pasta manufacturers have developed ready-made tubes about 5 inches in length, which are easier to fill and can be cooked in the same way.

**CANNOLICCHI, SEE CANNARONI RIGATI**

## CAPELLI D'ANGELO / ANGEL'S HAIR PASTA

Resembling long strands of blond hair, hence the name *capelli d'angelo* (angel's hair), this long pasta is also known as *fidelini* or *capellini* and is the thinnest form of spaghetti you can find. It is at its best with delicate sauces, and with butter and Parmesan cheese, but it is also good in a light broth. It cooks very quickly so you will need to keep a close eye on the cooking time. There is also a black version, colored with cuttlefish ink, which is mostly used with seafood sauces.

**CAPPELLACCI, SEE TORTELLI**

## CAPPELLETTI, CAPPELLETTINI / LITTLE HAT

Resembling a hat (*cappello*), from which it gets its name, this handmade egg pasta is the trademark of Emilia-Romagna. There is a smaller version called *cappellettini*. *Cappelletti* are similar to *tortellini* but differ mostly in that the filling is made of beef, pork, and veal fried in butter, with some cubed Parma ham and Parmesan cheese. In Bologna they are eaten dressed with the juices from a roast or with a tomato sauce. They are also eaten *in brodo*, cooked in chicken broth. The freshly made variety take only about 5 to 7 minutes to cook, while the inferior mass-produced ones need at least double that time.

## CARBONARA / PASTA SAUCE

Like *amatriciana* sauce, pasta *alla carbonara* is another specialty of the Lazio region, making use of *guanciale*, air-dried pig cheek. The pork (nowadays usually replaced with *pancetta*) is cubed and fried in oil until crisp. This is then stirred into a seasoned mixture of beaten eggs and grated pecorino cheese, and a little of the pasta cooking water. The freshly drained pasta, traditionally *bucatini*, is then stirred into the sauce so that the egg mixture just coats the pasta but does not cook.

## CÂSONSÉI / STUFFED PASTA

Originating in Lombardy, this stuffed pasta is a specialty of the Valcamonica Valley. A rectangle of pasta is folded several times to make a dumpling shaped like a plaited loaf, which is then filled with potatoes, greens, *mortadella*, pork sausage, Parmesan cheese, eggs, garlic, bread crumbs, and parsley. Once the dumplings have dried out, the dumplings are cooked for 7 to 8 minutes and served with melted butter and more grated Parmesan cheese.

The Veneto produce *casonziei*, a stuffed egg pasta similar to *casônséi*, but folded into a circular plait rather than a rectangular one. The filling is made of spinach, *prosciutto*, San Daniele ham, eggs, Parmesan cheese, and a little butter and ground cinnamon. There are many similar types of pasta with the same basic filling but a slightly different shape.

## CAVATELLI, CAVATIEDDI, CAVATIDDI, CECATELLI / PUGLIESE HANDMADE PASTA

This typical southern Italian specialty is made of durum wheat semolina and water. *Cavatelli* are made of pieces of dough about 3/4 to 1 1/4 inch long, which are pressed and pushed with the thumb to make a curved and slightly hollowed oval shape. The name comes from *cavare*, meaning "to dig," because of the movement needed to make the shape, although it is called *strascinati* in Basilicata.

This pasta shape is now also popular in the North because it is ideal for vegetable sauces like those made with broccoli, arugula, zucchini, and eggplant. In the southern regions of Puglia and Sicily, *cavatelli* is served with a rich tomato sauce made with the very best local ingredients. It also goes well with seafood, especially mussels.

## CHIFFERI / ELBOW PASTA

This manufactured durum wheat semolina pasta is in the shape of a curved tube about 1 1/4 to 1 1/2 inches in length and looks like an elbow. It probably gets its name from the Austrian bread or biscuit called a *Kipferl*, which is curved into a croissant-like shape. There is a smaller version of this shape called *mezzi gomiti* (half elbows) as well as the similarly shaped *gobboni* (with a hump), *stortoni* (curved), and *gozzettoni*. All these varieties come with both smooth (*lisci*) and fluted (*rigatoni*) surfaces. In northern and central Italy this pasta is used in soups like *minestrone* while *rigati*, the comparable version of *chifferi* used in the South, are served with sauces.

## CHIOCCIOLE, LUMACHE, LUMACHELLE / SNAIL-SHAPED PASTA

Mostly eaten in Campania and Liguria, these are types of pasta in the shape of a snail's shell, and can be either smooth or fluted. They come in a range of sizes—the smaller ones are used in soups while the larger variety is eaten with tomato-based sauces.

## CHITARRA, MANFRICOLI, TONNARELLI / SQUARE SPAGHETTI

Called *maccheroni alla chitarra* in Abruzzo, *manfricoli* in Umbria, and *tonnarelli* in Lazio, this long pasta is much like *spaghetti*, except that it has a square rather than round section. It is made by laying a flat sheet of pasta over a special cutter made of many closely spaced steel wires, called a *chitarra*. The sheet of pasta is pressed through the wires with a rolling pin. The thickness of the pasta is equal to the distance between the wires, so that when it goes through the *chitarra*, it is cut in long, square strands.

Ideally it is eaten with a slow-cooked tomato and lamb *ragù*, a light tomato sauce dressed with pecorino cheese, or with a vegetable sauce. I have created a sauce based on *bagna caôda* and roasted peppers, which suits it well.

## CIALZONS / SWEET STUFFED PASTA

This sweet Friulian version of *casonziei*, made especially in Carnia, is the result of Austrian influences. The filling of spinach, raisins, candied peel, cinnamon, and chocolate is contained in a semicircular pocket of pasta. The *cialzons* are cooked for 7 to 8 minutes, then served dressed with melted butter, sugar, and ground cinnamon.

A savory version is made with a filling of potatoes, parsley, onion, mint, sugar, bread crumbs, cinnamon, and even a little grappa, and served with melted butter and Parmesan cheese.

CIRIOLE, SEE BIGOLI

## CONCHIGLIE, CONCHIGLIONI, CONCHIGLIETTE / PASTA SHELLS

This shell-like pasta shape from Campania has a ribbed surface and thus collects plenty of sauce. Because of its structure, however, it also takes about 14 to 16 minutes to cook. A larger version of the same shape, called *conchiglioni*, is often stuffed, usually with spinach and ricotta, and served with a tomato sauce. *Conchigliette* is a small version of *conchiglie* used in soups, and made with extra gluten for children. See *alfabeto*.

## CORZETTI / LIGURIAN HANDMADE PASTA

This Ligurian specialty pasta, typical of the Polcevera valley, uses a dough made with both egg and

LEFT: MACHINE-MADE *ORECCHIETTE* BEING SORTED FOR PACKING (SEE *CAVATELLI*)

water (only 1 egg per 2½ cups flour). A small, round piece of dough is then pressed with both thumbs to make a figure-eight shape about ¾ to 2 inches in size. It is served with a sauce of walnuts, cream, Parmesan cheese, and wild marjoram, or with a meat *ragù*. There is also a variety of *corzetti* called *stampati*, meaning "pressed," that is made with a special wooden tool with a design carved into it which is transferred onto the pasta.

## CULINGIONES / SARDINIAN RAVIOLI

This Sardinian contribution to stuffed pasta is rectangular in shape and filled with fresh pecorino cheese, Swiss chard, nutmeg, eggs, and grated, aged pecorino cheese. In some areas the little pockets are pinched shut in artistic ways. The pasta is served dressed with tomato sauce and more grated pecorino cheese.

## DENTE DI CAVALLO, DENTE DI PECORA, SEE CANNARONI RIGATI, MACCHERONI

## DITALI, DITALINI, DITALONI, TUBETTI / THIMBLE PASTA

A dried pasta from Campania, *ditali* is closely associated with Neapolitan cooking. Its name describes its shape, that of a little thimble, and these short pasta tubes come in a variety of sizes.

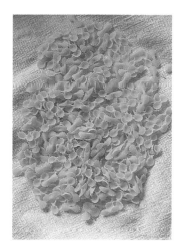

The smallest, called *ditalini*, is used in broths; the larger *ditali* is used in thicker vegetable soups; while the largest, *ditaloni*, are dressed with a variety of sauces. The smooth variety is used for more delicate sauces, while the *rigati*, or ridged, type are dressed with tomato and chili sauces.

## ELICOIDALE, SEE FUSILLI

## FAGIOLINI, SEE MACCHERONI

## FARFALLE, FARFALLINE, FARFALLETTE, FARFALLONI / BUTTERFLY, LITTLE BOW PASTA

Shaped like a butterfly, this pasta shape is usually commercially manufactured, although it can easily be made by hand using fresh pasta. To make it, cut long ribbons of pasta 1¼ to 1½ inches wide from a sheet of dough and divide the ribbons into sections about ¾ to 1¼ inches long. Pinch each rectangle of pasta in the center, pushing the edges together in the middle to make the butterfly shape. *Farfalle* is mainly eaten in northern Italy, dressed with light tomato sauce or cream and ham.

A small version, variously called *farfalline*, *canestrini*, and *tripolini* and of about ⅝ inch in length, is used *in brodo*, while *farfallette*, called *stricchetti* in Bologna, are slightly larger at 1¼ inches long and are used in thicker soups. *Farfalle* and the largest version, *farfalloni* (about twice as long), are only used dressed with tomato sauces, or butter, ham, and peas.

## FETTUCCE, FETTUCCINE, SEE TAGLIATELLE

## FIDELINI, SEE CAPELLI D'ANGELO

## FIDELINI BUCATI, SEE BUCATINI

## FORMATO / SHAPED

From *forma* meaning "shape," the term *formati* is used to encompass all the varied pasta shapes.

## FUSILLI / SPIRAL PASTA

*Fusilli* was first made in Campania by hand and was probably the first semolina pasta to have been made with a dough of just semolina and water, like Sicilian *maccheroni*. The technique has not changed much over the centuries, and today *fusilli* is still made by hand in Campania and Puglia and sold for a high price. The easiest way to buy *fusilli* nowadays is in its dried form.

Commercial imitations of *fusilli* have produced spiral shapes in many colors. Similar pastas to *fusilli* include *elicoidale*, *spirale*, and *eliche*, a southern version of *fusilli* with a substantial consistency that is dressed with meat and tomato sauces, and is now used all over Italy.

To make the traditional *fusilli*, roll a long, thin sausage of pasta between your hands or on a board, then twist it around a needle so that it makes a spiral shape. Gently slip the spiral off the needle and leave it to dry. *Fusilli* are delicious with meat *ragùs* and simple tomato sauces (see *salsa di pomodoro alla napoletana*, page 131).

## GARGANELLI / HANDMADE PASTA

This handmade egg pasta can be found only in Emilia-Romagna, where it was created. It is widely used there, either eaten *in brodo* or dressed with a light Bolognese *ragù*. The egg pasta dough is made in the usual way, but with the addition of grated Parmesan cheese and grated nutmeg. To make the *garganelli*, a special gadget is needed, which gives the outside of the pasta a ribbed texture. The dough is rolled out, then cut it into 1½-inch squares, which are wrapped around a slightly conical tool like a knitting needle and pressed onto a ribbed wooden block like a butter pat, leaving a fluted hollow pasta shape of about 2 inches in length and

½ inch in diameter with two pointed ends, like a quill.

## GIGANTONI, SEE MANICHE

## GNOCCHI, GNOCCHETTI /
LITTLE DUMPLINGS

It is very difficult to distinguish between *gnocchetti* and other similar pastas like *cavatielli*, *conchiglie*, *chiocciole*, or *lumache*. All were created as a result of the practice of boiling small, shapeless pieces of colored semolina-and-water dough in water and then serving them with butter and Parmesan cheese.

With the entry of potatoes into the culinary world, *gnocchi* started to be made with flour and potatoes instead of the standard semolina dough, and it is this that distinguishes them, making *gnocchi di patate* one of the first handmade pasta specialties. From this, a whole industry has developed around short pastas shaped in the form of little curls, snails, or shells.

*Gnocchetti* are round pasta shapes with a cavity, originally made with the thumb (see also *cavatelli*). Depending on their size, they are also called *conchigliette*, *coccioline*, and if they are very small, *margheritine*, which are used in soups. The larger ones, about ⁵⁄₈ inch in diameter, are called *tofarelle* or *mezze cocciolette* or *margherite*, and are often served with *pesto alla genovese* or light tomato sauces. *Conchiglie* or *arselle* are the largest examples and can be up to 1½ inches in diameter; they are mostly used in Campania.

Finally, there are two other types of *gnocchi* that are very different from those mentioned above. The first is *gnocchi alla romana*, which is made from cooked semolina, egg, Parmesan cheese, and butter, and baked in the oven. The other is the exceptionally high-quality *gnocchetto*, also called *malloreddus* in Sardinia, which is cooked for at least 15 to 18 minutes, then dressed with a tomato sauce and pecorino cheese. They come in three or four sizes, ranging from ¼ to 1¼ inches thick, and are concave with a ribbed back. They are also made in the shape of huge shells by Sardinian women, who gather to make them for special occasions and celebrations.

## GOBBONI, GOZZETTONI, SEE CHIFFERI

## GRANDINE / TINY DOT PASTA

*Grandine*, literally meaning "hailstone," is, as its name suggests, shaped like a very small round dot. It is made by cutting the thickest freshly made *spaghetti* into lengths of only a few millimeters. It is used in soups and broths only.

## LASAGNE, LAGANE, LAGANELLE
/ FLAT PASTA SHEETS

In Naples this wide, flat sheet of semolina-and-water pasta is called *laganelle*, the name used by the Romans, although it is not known whether in ancient times the pasta was fried, baked, or boiled. In Campania *lasagne* is called *lagane*, in Calabria, *laganedde*, and in Basilicata, *laane*. Whatever the name used to describe it, *lasagne* is a long sheet of pasta rolled to a thickness of about ¼ inches, and cut in widths of about ⅛ inch, although *laganelle* are ½ inch wide.

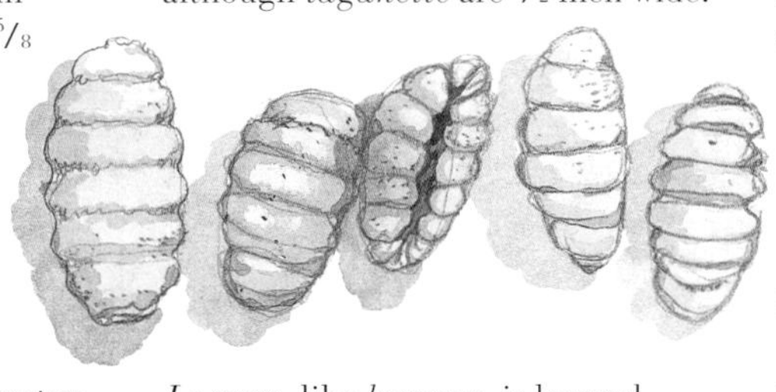

*Lagane*, like *lasagne*, is layered with *mozzarella*, tomato sauce, and plenty of freshly grated aged pecorino cheese or *ricotta salta*, and sometimes even *salami*. To help make the layers and produce a lighter and more airy dish, some *lasagne* are given a curled or corrugated edge; these are known as *lasagna riccia*, which are 1½ inches wide, and *lasagnetta doppio riccio* (half as wide) a smaller curly-edged lasagne.

The widest industrially made *lasagna* is called *lasagnoni*, and is usually 3¼ to 4 inches wide and about 8 inches long. This is the only type of pasta that requires a little oil in the water when cooking to prevent the sheets from sticking together. A smaller version of this curly pasta is called *arricciata tripolini* or *signorine*, and is only ¼ inch wide, while *mafalde* or *fettuccelle ricce* is ⅝ inch wide and *manfredi*, *trinette*, and *mezza lasagna* are all ¾ inch wide. All these pastas are eaten with tomato sauces and *ragùs* of beef, pork, lamb, or game. They are also used to make *pasticci*.

Due to its versatility, *lasagna* has become one of the most popular dishes considered to be "convenience food," not just in Italy but worldwide. It can be, and is most often, prepared in large quantities industrially, and then distributed to supermarkets either chilled or frozen.

## LASAGNETTE / PASTA SHAPE

Also known as *festoni*, *riccioline*, *reginette*, and *lasagnette ricce*, these are long, flat, wide pasta ribbons with curled edges, which prevent the ribbons from sticking together during cooking and make them ideal for collecting more of the sauce. This type of pasta is not cut like *tagliatelle* but extruded through a die. *Lasagn-ette* is mostly eaten in southern Italy with Neapolitan-style *ragùs*, or in Puglia with game sauces or cheeses such as ricotta or pecorino.

## LETTERE, SEE ALFABETO

## LINGUE DI PASSERO, LINGUINE, LINGUINETTE, SEE BAVETTE

## LISCI / SMOOTH

The term used to describe pasta that is smooth on the surface, i.e. without any ridges.

## LUMACHE, LUMACHELLE, SEE CHIOCCIOLE

## MACCHERONE, MACCHERONCELLI / MACARONI

Historians cannot agree about the origins of *maccheroni*. Some think

LEFT: FRESH *GNOCCHI*

*maccheroni* was first made in Sicily and is the result of Arabic influence, while others attribute it to the Ligurians. Indeed, centuries ago Genoa had the monopoly in the grain trade in the Mediterranean, hence its long tradition of pasta making.

Regardless of its exact historical origins, *maccheroni* is synonymous with Italy. The term indicates a number of short pasta tubes, either smooth or fluted, like *maccheroncelli*, *sedani rigati*, *maniche*, and many others. In the South, and especially in Naples, *maccheroni* is a generic term for all types of pasta. For example, the *frittata di maccheroni*, a pasta omelet so beloved of the Neapolitans, may use any type of pasta, including *vermicelli*, *linguine*, and *bucatini*.

*Maccherone* includes pasta shapes such as *cannolicchi medi*, *cannolicchi grandi*, *sciviottini*, *fagiolini*, *fischiotti*, *dente di pecora*, *dente di cavallo*, and many more. *Maccheroni*, like *penne* and *ziti*, is used in timbales of cooked pasta and other ingredients which are baked in the oven (see recipe, page 161). *Maccheroni alla chitarra* (see *chitarra*), *maccheroni bobbiesi*, *macceruna di casa*, and *maccheroni a ferritus* (from Sardinia) are all made by turning a fresh egg pasta dough around or through a special iron tool, and are similar to *fusilli*, but are not twisted. These are usually eaten with sauces based on meat, sausages, and tomatoes.

## MALFATTI / DUMPLINGS
Literally meaning "badly made," the name for these little *gnocchi* refers to their irregular shapes. Apart from flour and eggs, they may contain chopped spinach or Swiss chard and either *mascarpone* or ricotta cheese.

## MALLOREDDUS, SEE GNOCCHI

## MALTAGLIATI / IRREGULAR PASTA
Literally meaning "badly cut," *maltagliati* is made by cutting irregular shapes from a thinly rolled sheet of pasta. Mostly found in Emilia-Romagna, small pieces are used in *pasta e fagioli* and larger pieces are dressed with a wide variety of sauces, including simple tomato sauces and those made with roasted meat juices. See also *taccozze*.

## MANFREDI, SEE LASAGNE

## MANFRICOLI, SEE CHITARRA

## MANICHE, GIGANTONI / LARGE TUBE PASTA
This is a large, straight, hollow pasta tube about 2½ inches in length and ⅜ inch in diameter. The outside can be smooth or ribbed, the latter resembling rigatoni. In Manica, the tubes are slightly curved. They are especially popular in the South, where large pasta shapes are preferred, and they are eaten with meat sauces or as part of a timbale. (see recipe, page 161).

## MANILLI DE SEA, SEE TACCOZZE

## MARILLE / PASTA SHAPE
*Marille* was created by a car designer, Giorgetto Giugiaro, under commission from a pasta company in Campania. The idea was to design a pasta shape that would absorb and retain an abundant amount of sauce, so that each piece of pasta would become a juicy morsel in its own right. The pasta was designed on a drawing board, and is made of two tubes joined together. It is ribbed on the inside and smooth on the outside, with an aerodynamic wing attached to the side of one of the tubes. It holds the sauce inside it and is especially delicious dressed with a good tomato sauce and Parmesan cheese.

## MARUBINI / STUFFED PASTA
This is a large, round, *ravioli*-type pasta with a serrated edge. It is a specialty of Cremona and comes with two types of filling. The first consists of walnuts, Parmesan cheese, eggs, bread crumbs, and nutmeg. These are usually cooked in a good chicken broth, and are either

served in it or drained and dressed with melted butter and Parmesan cheese. The other filling is a meat filling like that used to fill *ravioli*.

## MEZZANI, SEE ZITI

## MEZZI GOMITI, SEE CHIFFERI

## MILLERIGHE, SEE RIGATONI

## OCCHIO DI LUPO, SEE CANNARONI RIGATI

## ORECCHIETTE, SEE CAVATELLI, CAVATIEDDI

## PAGLIA E FIENO, SEE TAGLIATELLE

## PANSÔTI / STUFFED PASTA
This stuffed pasta, typical of Liguria, is either a triangle or shaped like tortellini. The classic stuffing is *preboggion*, a mixture of wild local greens, including borage, with Parmesan cheese. It is traditionally served with *tocco di noce*, a walnut sauce.

## PAPPARDELLE, SEE TAGLIATELLE

## PASTICCIO, PASTICCIATA, PASTA 'NCASCIATA / PASTA PIE
The origins of the *pasticcio* probably lie with medieval Tuscan chefs mimicking the pies of Elizabethan England, and in those days the *pasticcio* would probably have contained meat. Nowadays, however, most consist of a pastry

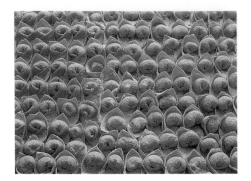

shell with a filling of cooked pasta, like *tortellini*, layered with cheeses and tomato sauce. Every region now has its own variation, like the *pasta 'ncasciata* of Sicily, which more closely resembles a timbale.

## PASTINA PER BRODO / PASTA FOR SOUP

This very soothing dish is mostly to be found in private homes rather than in restaurants. It is also more a part of life in northern Italy, where it forms part of supper, accompanied perhaps by some cheese and bread. The *brodo* (broth) can be chicken, veal, beef, or other meats cooked for some time with some onion, celery, and carrot. In this stock are cooked the following types of pasta, which have been specifically designed to cook in a short time: *anellini* (little rings), *avemarie*, and *tubettini* (short tubes), *conchigliette* (small shells), *cuoricini* (tiny hearts), *diavolini* (little devils), *farfalline* (baby butterflies), *grandine* (hailstones), *lumachine* (small snails), *pepe* (peppercorns), *pepe bucato* (peppercorns with a hole), *perline* (pearls), *puntine* (points), *quadrettini* (squares), *stelline* (stars), as well as *seme d'avena* (oat grains), *d'orzo* (barley), *di riso* (rice), *di mele* (apple seed), *di melone* (melon seeds), and *di peperone* (pepper seeds), and many, many others. See also *alfabeto*.

## PENNE / QUILL-SHAPED PASTA

*Penne* are tubes of pasta cut at an angle so that they have pointed ends, like a quill. After *spaghetti*, this is arguably the next best-known pasta shape in the world. It comes in two varieties, *penne lisce* (smooth) and *penne rigate* (ribbed) and in many different sizes. The smallest are *pennettine* and *pennine*, and the largest, *penne di ziti*, *penne a candela*, and *penne di natale*—which has a huge length of 6 to 7 inches.

*Penne* is most popular in Liguria and Campania, where there are many recipes for sauces, including the Campanian sauces based on tomatoes with meat and chili. The smaller varieties, called *pennette*, are best served in a much lighter fresh tomato sauce with basil and little cubes of *mozzarella*, which melt when they come into contact with the hot pasta. *Penne* are also used for timbales.

Another dish, *penne all'arrabbiata* ("angry penne"), is *penne* with a very hot chili sauce, the name suggesting the ferocity of the heat, which can, of course, be adjusted according to taste. It is perhaps due to the popularity of *penne all'arrabbiata* in both Italy and now abroad, that *penne* has become so popular throughout the world.

## PERCIATELLI, PERCIATELLINI, SEE BUCATINI

## PICCAGGE, SEE TAGLIATELLE

## PINCI, SEE BIGOLI

## PIZZELLE, SEE TACCOZZE

## PIZZOCCHERI / BUCKWHEAT NOODLE

*Pizzoccheri* is a long pasta typical of a valley in Lombardy called Valtellina, where the dough is made with one-third 00 (*doppio zero*) flour and two-thirds buckwheat flour. The best way to use *pizzoccheri* is to let it cook with potato cubes, green beans, or cabbage, and then layer it with *bitto* (a cheese, see page 238), Parmesan cheese, melted butter, and garlic, and bake it.

## PUTTANESCA / PASTA SAUCE

This typically Roman sauce gets its name from the Italian, for whore. The spirited combination of extra-virgin olive oil, black olives, chili, capers, and tomato goes very well with *spaghetti al dente*. Dishes using this sauce are never served with cheese.

## RAGÙ / RICH PASTA SAUCE

From the French *ragoût*, or meat stew, this term has been adopted for long-cooked rich sauces, especially in Emilia-Romagna for their universally renowned *ragù alla bolognese*, and in Naples for their *ragù alla napoletana* (a sauce of tomatoes, meat, herbs, and other flavorings). *Ragù bolognese* is mainly used to flavor *tagliatelle* in the North, and the Neapolitans use their *ragù* mostly on large pasta shapes like *rigatoni*, *candele*, and *ziti*.

## RAVIOLI / STUFFED PASTA

After *spaghetti*, *ravioli* is probably one of the most successful of pastas worldwide. You can find genuine *ravioli* in almost every respectable restaurant and with every filling you could desire. *Raviolini*, one of the smallest of the square stuffed pastas, is usually eaten *in brodo*, and *ravioloni*, the largest, is traditionally dressed with melted butter, sage, and Parmesan cheese. These little pasta parcels are called *ravioli* in most regions, with the exception

LEFT: FRESH FILLED *PANSÓTI* (SEE PAGE 149) FROM LIGURIA

LEFT: *PENNE*

of Piedmont, where they are called *agnolotti*.

My own version of *raviolo* is called *raviolo aperto* (see page 160). Two large squares of pasta the size of a plate are cooked in water, one is laid on the bottom of the plate, and the filling, which can be meat, fish, or mushrooms, cooked separately, is placed in the center and covered loosely with the other pasta square.

**RIGHT: *RAVIOLI***

### RIGATI / RIDGED
The term used to describe pasta that is ridged.

### RIGATONI / RIDGED TUBE PASTA
*Rigatoni* is a variety of large pasta tubes that are ribbed on the outside, and are served with meat *ragù* or other strong sauces, or baked in the oven. All of the pasta shapes included in this group are quite large, about 2 to $2^1/_2$ inches in length and $^1/_4$ to $^3/_4$ inch in diameter. *Rigatoni* is only produced commercially as a dried pasta.

Because of its large size, *rigatoni* is most popular in southern Italy. There it is eaten mostly on Sunday, dressed with a slow-cooked tomato sauce in which a large piece of beef has also been cooked. The meat is sliced and eaten as part of the second course with vegetables. *Rigatoni* is also eaten with a simple tomato sauce, or baked in the oven to make timbales. Variations include *giganti*, *maniche*, *schiaffoni*, *millerighe*, *tortiglioni*, and *paccheri*, meaning "a slap in the face." See also *chifferi*.

### RISTORANTI, SEE SPAGHETTI

### ROTOLO / PASTA DISH
A specialty of Emilia-Romagna, *rotolo* is made from a very large sheet of egg pasta, which is usually covered with a mixture of spinach and ricotta cheese, then rolled over like a Swiss roll, wrapped in a cloth, and cooked in boiling salted water

for at least 30 minutes. It is served cut in slices, with either a very light sauce of fresh tomatoes, basil, and Parmesan cheese, or with melted butter and Parmesan. The filling can be varied to include spinach and meat, or simply a meat *ragù*.

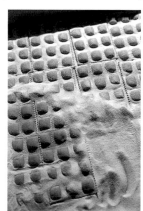

### RUOTE, ROTELLINE / WHEEL-SHAPED PASTA
Made in the shape of a wheel, this is an example of a pasta that has no special use except to be pretty. It is mostly served with a tomato sauce, but for me it is a little gimmicky.

### SCIVIOTTI, SEE CANNARONI RIGATI, MACCHERONI

### SEDANI / TUBE PASTA
Literally translated, *sedani* means celery, because the shape of this pasta resembles a small rib of celery. Probably from the same group as *maccheroni*, it is mainly used in southern Italy, and is a hollow pasta which can have either a smooth or ribbed surface. The smaller sizes are eaten with a tomato sauce, while a meat *ragù* usually dresses the larger sizes, which are known variously as *cannolicchi*, *fischiotti*, or *dente di pecora* (sheep's tooth). See also *maccheroni*.

### SEMI DI... / SEEDS OF...
There are a variety of pastas *per brodo* that are shaped like seeds and grains, such as those of wheat (*semi d'avena*), barley (*semi d'orzo*), melons (*semi di melone*), chicory (*semi di cicoria*), and pepper (*semi di peperone*). They are exclusively used in soups (see *alfabeto*, *pasta per brodo*).

### SFOGLIA / SHEET OF PASTA DOUGH
*Sfoglia* is the term used to describe the ultimate reason for working a pasta dough with plenty of elbow

grease until you have obtained a silky consistency. The dough is then flattened with a rolling pin to an almost transparent sheet. It is from this *sfoglia* that you can then cut out any desired shape, from *lasagne* to *tagliolini*.

### SPAGHETTI, SPAGHETTINI, VERMICELLI, VERMICELLINI / LONG STRAND PASTA
The area around Naples has the type of air, climate, and water that makes it ideal for producing *vermicelli*, meaning "little worms" (the term favored for *spaghetti* in the South), which can still be seen drying in the sun there. The dough for Neapolitan pasta is a mixture of hard durum semolina flour and water. The cooking time varies from 4 to 5 minutes for fine pasta and 8 to 9 minutes for the larger types—and even 12 to 13 for the largest. Neapolitans like their pasta quite undercooked, and a typical portion there would be $4^1/_2$ ounces per person, while in other places $3^1/_2$ ounces per person is more usual.

Nowadays *spaghetti* is made everywhere, in all the regions of Italy and all over the world. The commercial manufacture involves pushing dough through an extrusion system to make the noodles. These can either be smooth (*liscio*) or a brass die can be used to give a slight roughness to the pasta, enabling more sauce to be caught on it. *Capelli d'angelo* is the thinnest *spaghetti*, closely followed by *spaghettini*, similar to the *vermicellini* of Naples, with a diameter of $^1/_{16}$ inch. *Spaghetti* and *vermicelli*, also called *ristoranti*, in Naples have a diameter of $^1/_{11}$ to $^1/_{10}$ inch. The largest, *spaghettoni* or *vermicelloni*, range from $^1/_{12}$ to $^1/_{10}$ inch in diameter. Anything thicker than this would be difficult to cook well, so the next largest pasta in this group, *bucatini* or *perciatelli*, have the slight variation of a hole through the length of each strand.

It is still possible to buy *spaghetti* at the original length of 16 to 20 inches, but it is more common now

to find spaghetti at 8 to 10 inches long, about half its original length, as this is much easier to handle. The longest handmade *spaghetti* you can get, a staggering 30 feet in length, comes from Abruzzi. They are locally called *strangolapreti* or *strozzapreti* ("priest choker"), borrowing the name of another specialty.

*Spaghetti* can be eaten with a variety of sauces, from the simple *aglio, olio e peperoncino* (garlic, oil, and chili) to a refined sauce of langoustine or sardines beloved by the Sicilians. *Spaghettini alle vongole* (with clams) is a sublime dish, and even more heavenly is the *spaghetti* that I cooked in Puglia dressed with fresh roe of seaurchin (see recipe, page 156). I would, however, never eat *spaghetti* with a Bolognese sauce, because this is traditionally better suited to *tagliatelle*. I have developed a way of frying leftover *spaghetti* so that the strings at the bottom of the pan stick slightly and produce a lovely crunchy effect. The whole lot can then be turned over to reveal a delicious pasta crust.

**SPIRALI, SEE FUSILLI**

**STELLINE, SEE PASTINA PER BRODO**

**STORTONI, SEE CHIFFERI**

### STRANGOLAPRETI, STRANGULAPRIEVETE, STROZZAPRETI / LONG PASTA, DUMPLINGS
Priests in Italy are assumed to eat

well and also to possess even more than the normal healthy Italian appetite, hence these names (all meaning "priest strangler") for various types of pasta, related specialties, and dishes in the different regions. In Puglia, the term is used for a type of twisted pasta; in Abruzzi *strozzapreti* for extra-long *spaghetti*; in Naples and Campania *strangulaprievete* is applied to potato gnocchi; and in the North it mostly describes a type of *canederli*, or bread dumpling. See also *spaghetti*.

**STRASCINATI, SEE CAVATELLI, BIGOLI**

**STRINGOZZI OR STRANGOZZI, SEE BIGOLI**

### TACCOZZE, TACCONI, PIZZELLE, MANILLI DE SEA / PASTA SHEETS
These are all types of flat pasta made by hand from a dough of flour and water, which are widely used in many parts of Italy. From Marche, Campania, and Umbria comes *taccozze* or *tacconi*, which are 1$^1/_2$-inch squares of very thin *sfoglia*. The dressing varies from a meat *ragù* or tomato sauce to the juices from the roasting pan. Very similar but larger 2$^1/_2$ x 2$^3/_4$-inch rectangles called *pizzelle* are found in Puglia. The dough for these is made with salted water and durum semolina.

The largest variety, measuring 4$^3/_4$ inches square, comes from Liguria and is called *manilli de sea* (*sea* meaning "silk"). Indeed it is so thin and large that it looks like silk cloth. It is eaten dressed with pesto, mushroom, or meat sauces. Another, irregularly-shaped version of *taccozze* is *maltagliati*, which is made with an egg pasta dough.

### TAGLIATELLE, TAGLIOLINI, TAGLIARINI, FETTUCCE, FETTUCCINE, PICCAGGE, PAPPARDELLE / FLAT PASTA RIBBONS
These long, flat pasta ribbons come in a variety of widths and go under a number of names depending on the

region, but they are all basically *tagliatelle* or *fettuccine*. *Fettuccine* is associated mainly with central Italy around Rome, while its close relative, *tagliatelle* (*fettuccine* is a little narrower and thicker) is northern, with Bologna as its main center. Generally speaking, the further south you go, the thicker the pasta ribbons.

*Tagliare* means "to cut," hence the name for this Emilia-Romagnan pasta, which is cut with a knife from a very thin *sfoglia* of egg dough. Pasta ribbons can easily be made by hand by simply cutting slices of any width from a single sheet of pasta. To do this, simply roll up a sheet of pasta and cut it to the width desired, then unroll each little disc of pasta to reveal the long strands. Most of the *tagliatelle* eaten today are commercially produced, and sold dried and packed in nests to give a homemade feel.

*Tagliatelle* and similar pasta ribbons, like the thinner *tagliolini* and *tagliarini*, can be dressed with *ragùs* of meat, tomato, or seafood (for the smaller varieties), as well as pesto and mushroom sauces. A mixture of green and yellow varieties of *tagliolini* are used give the effect of "straw and hay" described by the name of the traditional dish *paglia e fieno*, which is usually dressed with a creamy ham and cheese sauce.

*Fettuccine* is the name given to pasta ribbons $^5/_8$ inch wide, and these are generally eaten dressed with meat or mushroom sauces. Smaller *fettuccine* of just $^3/_8$ inch in width are typical of Lazio, and especially of Rome, where they are eaten with tomato sauces and *all'alfredo*, with a cream and pepper sauce.

The *piccagge* of Liguria are $^1/_2$-inch-

LEFT:
*STROZZAPRETI*

BELOW:
*TAGLIATELLE*

ABOVE: MAKING *TROFIE* BY HAND IN LIGURIA

RIGHT: *ZITI AND SPAGHETTI*

wide ribbons made with egg dough, and often dressed with an artichoke sauce. Another specialty of Liguria is *trenette avvantaggiate*, which is only ¹/₈ inch wide and is made with a mixture of 00 (*doppio zero*) flour and *farina integrale* (wholemeal flour). This gives the pasta a darker color, and it is usually served dressed with the famous pesto sauce.

The widest pasta ribbons are *lasagne piccole*, which are ³/₄ inch wide and *lasagne grandi*, 1 to 1¹/₄ inches wide, which are popular in Emilia-Romagna and northern Italy. Traditionally baked in layers with meat *ragùs*, but also lately with vegetables, the pasta and *ragu* layers are interleaved with tomato sauce, soft cheese, and Parmesan cheese.

*Pappardelle* are pasta ribbons of various widths used in the Veneto and Tuscany. In Veneto the sauces are based on chicken giblets and tomatoes, while game sauces are favored in Tuscany, as in *pappardelle al sugo di lepre*, based on braised hare and sometimes wild boar.

### TAJARIN / PASTA RIBBON

This Piedmontese pasta is a local version of *tagliolini*, which is ¹/₈ inch wide and probably the smallest type of fresh cut pasta. It is traditionally cut from the *sfoglia* with a knife and is either served *in brodo* or with a sauce of white Alba truffle.

### TONNARELLI, SEE CHITARRA

### TORTELLI, TORTELLINI, TORTELLONI, TORDELLO, CAPPELLACCI / STUFFED PASTA

Depending on the region, *tortelli* may be either square or round, and are filled with all sorts of ingredients, like pumpkin, meat, sausage, or herbs. The diversity ranges from *tordello*, a Tuscan half-moon *raviolo* made from an egg pasta and filled with a mixture of Swiss chard or spinach, ricotta, pecorino cheese, veal, brains, and spices, to *tortelli di magro* (meaning lean, without meat) which is usually filled with ricotta, spinach, eggs, and cheese. *Tortellini* is a smaller version of the same pasta, while *tortelloni* is the largest. The sweet *tortelli di San Giuseppe*, filled with ricotta, sugar, and spices, are fried in oil.

*Cappellacci* are a handmade round or triangular version of this type of pasta, originally from Emilia-Romagna. The filling used is generally baked pumpkin and *mostarda di Cremona* (see page 269), Parmesan cheese, egg, crushed amaretti biscuits, and nutmeg, giving an interesting, sweetish savory taste which is unusual for Italy. *Cappellacci* are served with melted butter, sage, and more Parmesan cheese. There are versions with fillings of ricotta and other vegetables, such as spinach or Swiss chard. See also *agnolini*, *agnolotti*, and *ravioli*.

### TORTIGLIONI, SEE RIGATONI

### TRENETTE / LONG PASTA

Trenette is a flat and long Ligurian pasta, similar to *bavette* but slightly larger. It is eaten exclusively with Genovese pesto sauce.

### TROFIE / SPIRAL PASTA

Handmade using a dough of 00 (*doppio zero*) flour, and water, sometimes with the addition of potato purée, *trofie* are pieces of dough twisted to look like little spirals with pointed ends. To make these Ligurian specialties, roll some fresh dough in the palm of your hand until it is long and thin, like *spaghetti*. Cut it into 1¹/₂-inch chunks and roll them again with your fingers to make the spiral shape and the pointed ends. They are eaten mostly with pesto sauce

but are also very good with other sauces, which are called *tocchi* in Liguria, including *tocco di noce*, a walnut sauce, which is also used to flavor *pansôti al preboggion* (see page 167). See also *bavette* and *fettuccine*.

### TUBETTI, TUBETTINI / SMALL TUBE PASTA

These small pasta tubes are used in soups such as *minestrone* and for *pasta e fagioli*. They are available all over Italy and can be either ribbed (*rigati*) or smooth (*lisci*) on the outside. The size varies, and the larger variety is served with tomato sauce. *Tubettini* are the smallest of the range and are used *in brodo*.

### VERMICELLI, SEE SPAGHETTI

### ZITE, ZITI, ZITONI / TUBE PASTA

Today *ziti* is only made commercially, using durum wheat semolina and water. It is generally more popular in the South than the North, and over the years has somehow become the symbol of the South, and of Naples in particular.

It is a tubular pasta up to 2 inches in length, with a diameter of about ¹/₂ inch and a smooth surface. Cut in shorter tubes, it makes *ditali*, and cut in slightly longer tubes, *maccheroni*. If the sections are cut obliquely it makes *penne*.

If the *ziti* have a large diameter they are called *mezze zite* or *boccolotti mezzani*, while the largest are called *zitoni* or *candele*. If broken into irregularly shaped pieces they can be cooked and eaten either with a strong meat *ragù* or mixed with strong cheeses like *caciocavallo*, *provola*, *pecorino* or *mozzarella*, and sometimes sliced eggplant, to make *pasticci*.

*LINGUINE CON ARAGOSTA* SERVED WITH A GARNISH OF A WHOLE COOKED LOBSTER SHELL ON A RARE, OLD PLATTER FROM **G**ROTTAGLIE

# Pasta Fresca all'Uovo
FRESH EGG PASTA

**MAKES ABOUT 1 POUND**

HEAPING 2¹/₂ CUPS OO (*DOPPIO ZERO*)
  FLOUR, PLUS MORE FOR DUSTING
3 EGGS
PINCH SALT

*This is the basic recipe for handmade egg pasta.*

Sift the flour onto a work surface (marble is ideal), forming it into a volcano-shaped mound with a well in the center. Break the eggs into this and add the salt.

With your hands, incorporate the eggs into the flour, gradually drawing the flour into the egg until it forms a coarse paste. Add a little more flour if the mixture seems too soft or sticky. With a spatula, scrape together all the dough.

Clean your hands and the work surface. Lightly dust the work surface with flour again and then knead the dough with the palms of your hands, giving it plenty of shoulder power. Work the dough for 10 to 15 minutes, until the consistency is smooth and elastic. Wrap the dough in plastic wrap or foil and leave it to rest for about 30 minutes.

Lightly flour the work surface and a rolling pin. Gently roll out the dough, rotating it by quarter turns, to obtain a round sheet of pasta with a thickness of ¹/₁₂ to ¹/₈ inch. Cut the sheets into the desired pasta shape, as described in the other recipes.

# Linguine con Aragosta
LINGUINE WITH LOBSTER

**FOR 4**

1 LIVE LOBSTER WEIGHING ABOUT 2¹/₂
  POUNDS, OR 2 LOBSTERS WEIGHING
  ABOUT 1¹/₄ POUNDS EACH
¹/₃ CUP EXTRA-VIRGIN OLIVE OIL
¹/₂ GARLIC CLOVE, FINELY CHOPPED
1 GLASS WHITE WINE
1¹/₂ POUNDS TOMATOES, PEELED,
  SEEDED, AND CHOPPED
14 OUNCES *LINGUINE*
SALT AND PEPPER
1 TABLESPOON COARSELY CHOPPED FLAT-
LEAF
  PARSLEY

*You will find this "posh" pasta dish in most of the coastal regions, cooked in many different ways. This is the simplest.*

Bring a large pan of lightly salted water to a boil. Put in the lobster; cover and simmer for 15 to 25 minutes, depending on size. Remove the lobster and leave to cool, then cut it in half lengthwise and remove the 2 gills (near the head), the dark vein running down the tail, and the small stomach sac in the head. Do not discard the green, creamy liver in the head. Take out the tail meat, then crack open the claws and remove the meat. Cut it into small chunks.

Heat the oil in a pan and briefly fry the garlic without letting it brown. Add the wine and boil for a few minutes to allow the alcohol to evaporate, then stir in the tomatoes and simmer for 10 minutes. Add the lobster meat, the liver, and the shells, and heat through gently.

Cook the *linguine* in the water in which the lobster was boiled, then drain. Season the sauce with salt and a generous amount of pepper. Remove and discard the shells and mix the sauce with the linguine. Serve sprinkled with parsley.

# LINGUINE CON RICCI DI MARE

## LINGUINE WITH SEA URCHINS

**FOR 4**

**40** FRESHLY CAUGHT SEA URCHINS

**14** OUNCES *LINGUINE* OR *LINGUE DI PASSERO* (SEE *BAVETTE*, PAGE **144**)

**4** TABLESPOONS EXTRA-VIRGIN OLIVE OIL

**2** GARLIC CLOVES, FINELY CHOPPED

**1** SMALL CHILI PEPPER, FINELY CHOPPED

SALT

**1** TABLESPOON CHOPPED FLAT-LEAF PARSLEY (OPTIONAL)

*It is essential to use sea urchins that have been fished in immaculately clean waters, so be sure to buy them from a really good fishmonger you can trust. You could always fish for the sea urchins yourself, of course, as does my friend, Paola Navone, when on holiday.*

Open the sea urchins and remove the roe (see page 24).

Cook the pasta in boiling salted water until *al dente*. Meanwhile, heat the oil in a pan and gently fry the garlic and chili for a few minutes without letting them brown. Drain the cooked pasta, mix it well with the oil, garlic, and chili, then transfer to a serving dish and top with the sea urchin roe and the parsley, if using.

# Pasta e Fagioli

## PASTA AND BEAN SOUP

### For 4

1¼ CUPS DRIED CANNELLINI BEANS
   OR 2 CUPS FRESH BEANS

⅓ CUP EXTRA-VIRGIN OLIVE OIL

2 GARLIC CLOVES, FINELY CHOPPED

1 SMALL CHILI PEPPER, FINELY CHOPPED

2 CELERY RIBS WITH LEAVES, FINELY
   CHOPPED

1 CARROT, FINELY CHOPPED

2 LARGE TOMATOES, PEELED, SEEDED,
   AND CHOPPED, OR 1 TABLESPOON
   TOMATO PASTE

SALT AND PEPPER

2 BASIL LEAVES, PLUS EXTRA FOR
   GARNISH

10 OUNCES MIXED PASTA

*There are many regional variations on this dish but I like the traditional peasant way best. In fact, I always judge a chef by the way he or she prepares* pasta e fagioli. *It is very easy to make, provided you use the correct ingredients in the correct way. This recipe is the Neapolitan version, in which they use cannellini beans instead of borlotti beans. It's a good way of using up odds and ends of different pasta shapes, known as* munnezzaglia *in Neapolitan dialect.*

If using dried cannellini beans, soak them in enough water to cover for 12 hours. Drain, cover with fresh water, and cook for about 2 hours or until tender. If using the fresh variety, simply simmer for 30 to 40 minutes until cooked. Remove about a quarter of the cooked beans from the pan and purée in a blender; set aside.

Heat the oil in a pan add the garlic, chili, celery, carrot, and tomatoes, and fry for a few minutes. Add 4½ cups water with salt to taste, then stir in the whole and puréed beans with 2 basil leaves. Bring to a boil, then add the pasta and simmer for 8 to 10 minutes, until *al dente*. Leave to rest for a few minutes, then garnish with basil leaves, and serve.

# VINCISGRASSI
## MEAT AND VEGETABLE LASAGNE

*This is my version of* vincisgrassi, *the classic* lasagne *from the Marche region. I have adapted it to use more readily available ingredients, substituting a Bolognese* ragù *for the traditional sauce made with testicles, liver, and cockerel giblets. I've also added layers of fried vegetables, which make the whole dish lighter but still interesting. It is worth cooking it for a large number of people for special occasions.*

*If you cannot get fresh porcini, substitute chestnut mushrooms.*

Wash the spinach, put it in a pan with just the water clinging to its leaves, and cook for a few minutes until wilted. Squeeze out all the excess liquid. Chop roughly and mix with 1 egg, 1 ounce of the grated Parmesan, and nutmeg and salt to taste. Stir in the bread crumbs to bind the mixture together, then form it into small balls. Heat some olive oil for deep-frying and fry the spinach balls until golden brown. Drain on paper towels and set aside.

Lightly beat together the 2 remaining eggs. Dust the eggplant slices with

**FOR 10**

2 POUNDS FRESH SPINACH

3 EGGS

5 OUNCES PARMESAN CHEESE, GRATED

FRESHLY GRATED NUTMEG

SALT AND PEPPER

ABOUT 1 TABLESPOON BREAD CRUMBS

OLIVE OIL FOR FRYING

2 LARGE EGGPLANTS, CUT INTO SLICES
 ¼ INCH THICK

SEASONED FLOUR, FOR DUSTING

1 POUND LARGE PORCINI, SLICED

6 SMALL, THIN ZUCCHINI

1 RECIPE BASIC PASTA
 DOUGH (SEE PAGE 155)

1 RECIPE BOLOGNESE *RAGÙ*
 (SEE PAGE 163)

14 OUNCES FONTINA CHEESE, THINLY
 SLICED

seasoned flour, dip them in the beaten egg, and then shallow-fry them in a good layer of olive oil until golden. Drain and set aside. Shallow-fry the porcini in olive oil, then season with salt and pepper.

Cook the whole zucchini in boiling salted water until just tender; drain.

Preheat the oven to 400° F. Roll out the pasta dough and cut it into sheets of *lasagne*. Cook the *lasagne* in a large pot of boiling salted water for 3 to 4 minutes or until *al dente* and put on a dish towel to drain.

Take a deep 8 by 12 inch baking tray and spread a third of the *ragù* over the bottom. Cover with a layer of *lasagne*, then a third of the fontina and Parmesan, then half the fried eggplant and mushrooms. Add more sauce and another layer of *lasagne*, then arrange the whole boiled zucchini on top lengthwise. Cover with another third of the cheese and the remaining eggplant and mushrooms. Finish with a layer of sauce, then the spinach balls and the remaining cheese. Bake in a hot oven for 30 minutes, until golden brown on top. Remove and leave to set for 10 minutes before cutting into squares to serve.

# GNOCCHETTI SARDI AL RAGÙ
SARDINIAN GNOCCHI WITH SAUCE

**FOR 4**

4 TABLESPOONS OLIVE OIL

14 OUNCES KNUCKLE OR SHOULDER
 OF PORK, ON THE BONE

1 ONION, FINELY CHOPPED

1 GLASS DRY WHITE WINE

A FEW BAY LEAVES

A FEW JUNIPER BERRIES

3 CUPS TOMATO PULP (SEE
 PAGE 118)

1 TABLESPOON TOMATO PASTE

SALT AND PEPPER

1 POUND *MALLOREDDUS* (SEE
 *GNOCCHI*, PAGE 148)

2 OUNCES SARDINIAN HARD PECORINO
 CHEESE, GRATED

*In Sardinia these little* gnocchi *are known as* malloreddus.

Heat the oil in a large heavy-bottomed pan, add the meat, and brown on all sides. Add the onion and cook gently until soft, then stir in the wine, bay leaves, and juniper berries. Simmer until the wine has evaporated, then add the tomato pulp and tomato paste; lower the heat and cook gently for about 1½ hours. Season with salt and pepper to taste. Remove the meat from the pan and cut it into small strips, discarding the bone. Return the pieces of meat to the sauce.

Cook the pasta in lightly salted boiling water for 12 to 14 minutes or until *al dente*. Drain and mix with the sauce. Serve with pecorino cheese.

RAVIOLO APERTO CON FUNGHI SURROUNDED BY TORTELLI DI ZUCCA AND AGNOLOTTI PIEMONTESI AL BURRO E SALVIA (SEE PAGE 164)

# RAVIOLO APERTO CON FUNGHI

OPEN RAVIOLO WITH MUSHROOMS

**FOR 4**

1¼ POUNDS MIXED WILD
   MUSHROOMS, CLEANED
4 TABLESPOONS BUTTER
1 GARLIC CLOVE, FINELY CHOPPED
1 TABLESPOON TOMATO PASTE
1 TABLESPOON CHOPPED FLAT-LEAF
   PARSLEY
SALT AND PEPPER
1 SMALL GLASS WHITE WINE
8 SHEETS FRESH PASTA DOUGH,
   6 INCHES SQUARE (SEE PAGE 155)
1¾ OUNCES PARMESAN CHEESE,
   GRATED (OPTIONAL)

*This is a modern pasta dish found in very good restaurants. The filling can vary from fish and meat to vegetables and, in this case, mushrooms.*

Cut the mushrooms in half if large; otherwise leave them whole. Heat the butter in a pan, add the garlic, and fry gently fry until softened but not browned. Add the mushrooms and stir-fry for 5 minutes, then add the tomato paste, parsley, and salt and pepper to taste. Pour in the wine, bring to a boil, and let it reduce for a few minutes.

Cook the pasta in boiling salted water until *al dente*, then drain. Carefully lay 4 sheets of pasta on 4 hot serving plates. Divide the mushroom mixture between them, reserving some of the sauce. Top the mushrooms with the remaining sheets of pasta and brush the top with the remaining sauce. Sprinkle with the Parmesan cheese if desired and serve immediately.

# TORTELLI DI ZUCCA

PUMPKIN RAVIOLI

**FOR 6**

4 POUNDS PUMPKIN
6 AMARETTI, FINELY CRUMBLED
3½ OUNCES PARMESAN CHEESE,
   GRATED
1¾ OUNCES *MOSTARDA DI CREMONA*
   (SEE PAGE 269), CUT INTO VERY
   SMALL CUBES
4 TABLESPOONS BUTTER
12 SAGE LEAVES

*The pasta dough here is softer than the basic dough on page 155, making it particularly suitable for these delicate ravioli.*

Preheat the oven to 400° F. Cut the pumpkin into large slices and bake in the oven for about 40 minutes, until soft. Scrape the flesh off the rind, put it in a colander to drain, and then squeeze out most of the moisture. Mix with the amaretti, half the Parmesan cheese, and the *mostarda di cremona* fruits to make a compact paste.

Make the pasta, following the method on page 155, adding enough water to make a soft dough. Roll out into very thin sheets and cut out discs about 2½

FOR THE PASTA DOUGH:
HEAPING 5 CUPS 00 (*DOPPIO ZERO*)
    FLOUR
4 EGGS

inches in diameter. Place a little of the filling to one side of each disc, then fold into half-moons, pinching the edges together to seal.

Cook the *tortelli* in plenty of boiling salted water for 6 to 7 minutes, until *al dente*, then drain. Put the butter and sage leaves in a large pan and heat until the butter is foaming. Add the cooked *tortelli* and mix to coat with the butter. Transfer to serving plates and sprinkle with the remaining grated Parmesan cheese.

# TIMBALLO DI ZITI

## BAKED TIMBALE OF ZITI PASTA

**FOR 10**

2¼ POUNDS LONG *ZITI*
SALT AND PEPPER
½ CUP VIRGIN OLIVE OIL
1½ POUNDS LEAN GROUND PORK
9 OUNCES NEAPOLITAN SALAMI (SEE
    PAGE 83), SLICED, THEN CUT
    INTO THIN STRIPS
2 LARGE ONIONS, FINELY CHOPPED
FRESHLY GRATED NUTMEG
1 GLASS DRY WHITE WINE
7½ CUPS TOMATO PULP (SEE
    PAGE 118)
12 OUNCES HARD *CACIOCAVALLO* OR
    MATURED PROVOLONE CHEESE, GRATED
8 EGGS, BEATEN

*This is a typical dish served at weddings in the province of Caserta in Campania. It is relatively elaborate if you want to make it in the shape shown in the picture but is worth doing for a large number of guests, whether or not it is for a wedding*

Cook the pasta in boiling salted water for 4 minutes, until pliable but not too soft, then drain and set aside. Heat the olive oil in a large pan; add the pork and the salami and brown the meat, stirring from time to time to break up the lumps of ground pork. Add the onions and some nutmeg and cook until the onions are tender, then add the wine and boil until evaporated. Stir in the tomato pulp and cook gently for 2 hours. Add salt and pepper to taste and allow to cool a little.

Preheat the oven to 350° F. Line a deep baking dish with some of the pasta. Mix the rest of the pasta with the sauce and stir in the beaten eggs and all but 2 or 3 tablespoons of the grated cheese. Fill the baking dish with the mixture, sprinkle the remaining cheese on top, and bake in the oven for 40 minutes. Carefully turn it out onto a serving dish and cut into slices to serve.

# ORECCHIETTE CON POMODORINI

## ORECCHIETTE WITH CHERRY TOMATOES

**FOR 4**

1¼ POUNDS VERY RIPE FRESH
  CHERRY TOMATOES OR CHERRY
  TOMATOES PRESERVED IN BRINE

4 TABLESPOONS EXTRA-VIRGIN OLIVE OIL

1 GARLIC CLOVE, FINELY CHOPPED

5 BASIL LEAVES, TORN INTO STRIPS

1 POUND *ORECCHIETTE* PASTA

2 OUNCES PECORINO CHEESE, GRATED
  (OPTIONAL)

SALT AND PEPPER

*Nowadays you can buy* pomodorini *preserved in brine from Apulia. The cherry tomatoes taste so sweet and have such an intense color and flavor that they hardly require any other ingredients.*

If you are using preserved tomatoes, drain off the brine. Squash the cherry tomatoes lightly with the tip of a knife. Heat the oil in a pan, add the garlic, and fry gently for a few minutes, then add the tomatoes. Stir-fry for a few minutes, then add the basil and some salt and pepper.

Cook the pasta in boiling salted water until *al dente*, then drain and mix well with the sauce. Sprinkle with pecorino cheese if desired and serve immediately.

# PENNE CON PINOLI E MELANZANE
PENNE WITH PINE NUTS AND EGGPLANT

FOR 4

14 OUNCES EGGPLANT, CUT INTO
SMALL CUBES

1/3 CUP EXTRA-VIRGIN OLIVE OIL

1 GARLIC CLOVE, FINELY CHOPPED

1 TABLESPOON *ESTRATTO DI POMODORO*
(SEE PAGE 118) OR 3 TABLESPOONS
TOMATO PASTE

1 TABLESPOON PINE NUTS

10 LARGE SALTED CAPERS, SOAKED IN
WATER FOR 10 MINUTES, THEN
DRAINED AND CHOPPED

1 SMALL CHILI PEPPER, FINELY CHOPPED

20 BLACK OLIVES, PITTED

14 OUNCES *PENNE* PASTA

2 OUNCES MATURE PECORINO CHEESE,
FRESHLY GRATED

Soak the eggplant cubes in lightly salted water for 1 hour, then drain, squeeze out the water, and pat dry on paper towels. Fry them in the oil with the garlic until brown. Add the tomato paste, pine nuts, capers, chili, and olives and fry gently for 10 minutes. Add a little water if the mixture is too dry.

Cook the pasta in boiling salted water until *al dente*, then drain and mix well with the sauce. Serve with the grated pecorino.

# TAGLIATELLE AL RAGÙ BOLOGNESE
TAGLIATELLE WITH BOLOGNESE SAUCE

FOR 4

1 POUND FRESH *TAGLIATELLE*
OR 14 OUNCES DRIED
EGG *TAGLIATELLE*

2 OUNCES PARMESAN CHEESE, GRATED

FOR THE *RAGÙ*

3 1/2 TABLESPOONS BUTTER

1 3/4 OUNCES GROUND *PROSCIUTTO* FAT
OR *PANCETTA*

1 LARGE CARROT, FINELY CHOPPED

1 CELERY RIB, FINELY CHOPPED

1 ONION, FINELY CHOPPED

4 OUNCES GROUND LEAN VEAL OR BEEF

4 OUNCES GROUND LEAN PORK

1 GLASS DRY RED WINE

BEEF OR CHICKEN STOCK

3 TABLESPOONS TOMATO PASTE

SALT AND PEPPER

*This is by far the best-known Bolognese recipe which, to be genuine, has to be made with fresh tagliatelle and not spaghetti.*

To make the *ragù*, heat the butter in a large pan, add the prosciutto fat or pancetta, carrot, celery, and onion, and fry gently for about 10 minutes. Add the ground meats and stir with a wooden spoon to break them up into smaller chunks. Cook for about 15 minutes to brown the meat, then add the wine and boil for a few minutes to allow the alcohol to evaporate a little. Stir in a little stock to prevent the mixture from sticking to the pan. Stir in the tomato paste and dilute with a few tablespoons of stock to give a sauce-like consistency. Simmer for 1 1/2 hours, adding more stock if the mixture becomes dry. At the end of the cooking time, add a little more stock to obtain a smooth consistency. Season to taste with salt and pepper.

Cook the *tagliatelle* in boiling salted water until *al dente*, then drain and mix with the sauce. Serve with the Parmesan cheese.

# ORECCHIETTE CON BROCCOLI
## ORECCHIETTE WITH BROCCOLI

**FOR 4**

1 POUND BROCCOLI FLORETS
SALT
¹/₃ CUP EXTRA-VIRGIN OLIVE OIL
2 GARLIC CLOVES, FINELY CHOPPED
1 SMALL CHILI PEPPER, FINELY CHOPPED
1 POUND APULIAN *CAVATELLI* PASTA
FRESHLY GRATED PECORINO CHEESE
   (OPTIONAL)

*In Puglia, broccoli and orecchiette are almost inseparable. The combination of pasta and the very strong flavors of local broccoli, tomatoes, olive oil, and chilies makes it a really wonderful dish.*

Cook the broccoli in lightly salted boiling water until tender, then drain. Put the oil in a pan over a low heat, then add the garlic and chili and cook gently for a few minutes until softened. Add the broccoli florets and mix well. Season with salt to taste.

Cook the pasta in boiling salted water for 14 to 18 minutes, until *al dente*, then drain, mix with the broccoli sauce, and serve, accompanied by grated pecorino cheese if desired.

# AGNOLOTTI PIEMONTESI AL BURRO E SALVIA
## PIEDMONTESE RAVIOLI WITH BUTTER AND SAGE

**FOR 6**

10 OUNCES SPINACH OR SWISS
   CHARD LEAVES
SALT AND PEPPER
10 OUNCES *BRASATO* (SEE PAGE 71)
   OR OTHER LEFTOVER COOKED MEAT
4 OUNCES COOKED CHICKEN BREAST
4 OUNCES COOKED SAUSAGE, OR
   FRESH SAUSAGE SUCH AS *LUGANIGA*
2 EGGS
3 OUNCES PARMESAN CHEESE, GRATED
1 RECIPE BASIC PASTA DOUGH
   (SEE PAGE 155)
4 TABLESPOONS BUTTER
10 SAGE LEAVES
FRESHLY GRATED NUTMEG

*This Piedmontese stuffed pasta dish was created to use up leftover cooked meat. There are many different versions but this one is typical of Ivrea, where I was brought up.*

Cook the spinach in boiling salted water until tender, then drain and squeeze out excess liquid. Mince or very finely chop all the meat and the spinach. Put them into a bowl and stir in the eggs, one-third of the grated Parmesan, the nutmeg, and salt and pepper to taste. Set aside.

Dust a work surface with flour and roll out 2 long thin sheets of pasta. Place teaspoons of the filling at 1-inch intervals in rows along one sheet of pasta, then cover with the other sheet and press gently round each pile of filling, making sure the pasta sticks together all around it. Cut into squares with a serrated pastry wheel.

Cook the pasta in plenty of boiling salted water for 6 to 7 minutes, until *al dente*, then drain. Put the butter and sage leaves in a large pan and heat until the butter is foaming. Add the cooked *agnolotti* and mix to coat with the butter. Transfer to serving plates and sprinkle with the remaining grated Parmesan cheese.

# Strangozzi all'Acciuga e Peperone
## STRANGOZZI WITH ANCHOVY AND PEPPERS

**FOR 4**

2 TABLESPOONS EXTRA-VIRGIN OLIVE OIL

1 GARLIC CLOVE, FINELY CHOPPED

1 SMALL CHILI PEPPER, FINELY CHOPPED

3 ROASTED RED PEPPERS, PEELED AND SLICED

8 ANCHOVY FILLETS, FINELY CHOPPED

1 POUND *STRANGOZZI* OR SIMILAR HARD DURUM WHEAT PASTA SUCH AS *PINCI* OR *BIGOLI*

SALT

1 TABLESPOON COARSELY CHOPPED FLAT-LEAF PARSLEY

Heat the olive oil in a pan; add the garlic, chili, and roasted peppers and fry gently until they are slightly browned. Add the anchovies and let them dissolve over a gentle heat.

Cook the pasta in boiling salted water until *al dente*, then drain, reserving a couple of tablespoons of the cooking water to dilute the sauce. Add the pasta and reserved cooking liquid to the sauce and toss well, then mix in the parsley and serve. You may add salt if you wish, but be careful because the anchovies are salty.

# PASTA CON LE SARDE
PASTA WITH SARDINES

**FOR 6 AS A MAIN DISH, 8 AS AN APPETIZER**

12 FRESH SARDINES

4 OUNCES WILD FENNEL LEAVES
(SEE PAGE 214)

1 ONION, FINELY CHOPPED

2 TABLESPOONS CURRANTS

2 TABLESPOONS PINE NUTS

6 ANCHOVY FILLETS, CHOPPED

1³/₄ OUNCES *ESTRATTO DI POMODORO*
(SEE PAGE 118), DISSOLVED IN A CUP
OF LUKEWARM WATER

1 TEASPOON FRESHLY GRATED NUTMEG

1 POUND *MACCHERONCINI* OR
*BUCATINI* PASTA

SALT AND PEPPER

FLOUR FOR DREDGING

OLIVE OIL FOR FRYING

Cut the heads and tails off the sardines, gut and bone them, then open them out flat. Coat them lightly in flour. Heat a good amount of olive oil in a large frying pan and fry the sardines until golden brown on each side. If they are very fresh, this should take only a couple of minutes. Lift the fish out of the pan, drain on paper towels, and keep warm.

Cook the fennel in boiling water for about 20 minutes or until soft, then drain, reserving the cooking water. Finely chop the fennel. Heat 2 tablespoons of olive oil in a large pan, add the onion and fry gently until softened. Stir in the fennel, currants, pine nuts, anchovy fillets, *estratto di pomodoro*, and a little of the fennel water and mix well. Take 6 of the sardines and break them into the mixture in the pan. Mix well to make a fairly thick sauce and heat through. If the sauce is too thick, add a little more fennel water. Season with the nutmeg and some salt and pepper, being careful with the salt as the sardines can be salty.

Cook the pasta in boiling salted water until *al dente*, then drain and mix well into the sauce. Serve in a large dish, decorated with the remaining sardines.

# RAGÙ ALLA NAPOLETANA CON PENNE
PENNE WITH NEAPOLITAN *RAGÙ*

**FOR 6**

6 SLICES BEEF TOP ROUND, WEIGHING
ABOUT 4 OUNCES EACH

SALT AND PEPPER

1 GARLIC CLOVE, THINLY SLICED

1 BUNCH FLAT-LEAF PARSLEY, COARSELY
CHOPPED

3¹/₂ TABLESPOONS PINE NUTS

4 TABLESPOONS GOLDEN RAISINS

2 OUNCES *PROVOLA* OR PARMESAN
CHEESE, GRATED

2 TABLESPOONS LARD

³/₄ OUNCES PARMA HAM FAT

2 GLASSES RED WINE

2 TABLESPOONS TOMATO PASTE

1 POUND *PENNE* PASTA

*For many Neapolitan families Sunday is not Sunday without* ragù. *A piece of beef or pork—or even some-times lamb—is slowly cooked in tomato sauce for at least 2 hours in order to extract all the flavor from the meat and to concentrate the tomato sauce. The result is usually stunning.*

Season the beef with salt and pepper. Mix together the garlic, parsley, pine nuts, raisins, and grated cheese, then divide the mixture between the slices of beef and roll them up. Secure each roll with a wooden toothpick.

Heat the lard and Parma ham fat in a heavy-bottomed saucepan, add the beef rolls and brown them all over. Then add the wine and tomato paste and enough water to cover the meat by three-quarters. Cook slowly for about 2 hours, checking occasionally to make sure it is not getting too dry and adding more water if necessary. When the meat is tender, adjust the seasoning to taste.

Cook the pasta in boiling salted water until *al dente*, then drain. Serve the meat and sauce on the pasta.

# PANSÔTI AL PREBOGGION

PASTA STUFFED WITH MIXED GREENS

**FOR 4**

**FOR THE SAUCE:**

1 CUP WALNUTS, BLANCHED AND PEELED

½ CUP PINE NUTS

BREAD CRUMBS FROM 1 FRESH BREAD ROLL

1 VERY SMALL GARLIC CLOVE, FINELY CHOPPED

A FEW MARJORAM OR THYME LEAVES

4 TABLESPOONS STRAINED GREEK YOGURT

EXTRA-VIRGIN OLIVE OIL

SALT AND PEPPER

**FOR THE *PANSÔTI*:**

2¼ POUNDS MIXED GREENS (SEE RIGHT)

9 OUNCES *RICOTTA* CHEESE

2 OUNCES PARMESAN CHEESE, GRATED

2 EGGS

1 RECIPE BASIC PASTA DOUGH (SEE PAGE 155)

*The name* pansôti *comes from* pansa, *a Ligurian dialect word meaning "tummy." These small, tummy-shaped ravioli are filled with a typical Ligurian mixture of wild herbs and vegetables such as fresh borage, Swiss chard, and dandelion. You can substitute spinach and other greens if you like. It is most unlikely that you will be able to buy these ravioli freshly made, so make them yourself; they are delicious.*

First make the sauce: with pestle and mortar pound the walnuts, pine nuts, bread crumbs, garlic, and herbs a until they are reduced to a thick paste. Gradually work in the yogurt and enough oil to achieve a smooth, fairly thick sauce. (Alternatively, purée all the ingredients together in a blender.) Season to taste with salt and pepper.

TOP: *PANSÔTI AL PREBOGGION*
BOTTOM: *PESTO ALLA GENOVESE CON TROFIE* (PAGE **228**)

For the *pansôti*, cook the greens in a little boiling water until tender, then drain and squeeze out the excess water. Chop the greens very finely and combine with the *ricotta*, Parmesan cheese, eggs, and some salt and pepper. Mix well to a fairly stiff paste.

Roll out the pasta into long sheets about 1½ inches thick. Cut out circles 3 inches in diameter, divide the filling between them, then fold them in half to make half-moon shapes, pressing the edges together well to seal. You could also make triangular *pansôti* by cutting the pasta into 3-inch squares.

Lightly warm through the walnut sauce. Cook the *pansôti* in boiling salted water for 5 to 6 minutes, until *al dente*, then drain and mix with the sauce. Serve immediately.

# Rice & Grains

RISO E GRANO

Grains have been known to mankind since the beginning of time, and today they are still a basic food that sustains the world's population. In fact, the importance of grains in the world's diet continues to grow, despite Western developments in agriculture and the production of alternative foods. Although climatic changes and political upheavals threaten to disrupt the lives of half the population of the world, people survive thanks to the cultivation of a few grains. Every society has made the choice of which particular grain to cultivate, depending on what is suited to the local soil, water, and farming skills.

All types of grains are important to Italians, but probably the most important is wheat, which is used in the making of bread and that all-important Italian food staple, pasta (to which I have devoted a special chapter all its own because of its complexity). Rice is also important. Piedmont, Lombardy, and Veneto are the main areas in which rice is grown, and it is from these regions that the most interesting recipes originate.

Rice was brought to Italy about one thousand years ago, although there are many theories about how it came to be introduced to Italy. One theory is that Islamic expeditions in the Mediterranean, as a result of the slave trade with East Africa, led to it's introduction into Sicily. The Romans are also believed to have used rice, but it was only in the Middle Ages that it began to be taken seriously. The plague of 1345–52 left widespread devastation throughout Europe, and a reliable agricultural food was needed to build the recovery of the population.

Over the next five hundred years, rice brought a better diet to the people of Italy, where the ideal conditions for its cultivation were discovered in the Po Valley, which is straddled by four northern Italian regions. The valley is blessed with an abundance of the vitally important element of water, which is needed to grow the rice plant successfully. It flows through the valley from the Alps and lakes, and the Po valley was one of the first places where an irrigation system of canals was used. These systems ensured that the water needed to submerge the plants was constant and abundant.

The film *Riso Amaro* (Bitter Rice), one of the neo-realist films of the fifties, made it perfectly clear how arduous life was for those involved in the cultivation of this crop. The *mondine*, or "rice women," were at the receiving end of an industry that kept them in conditions of squalor and deprivation. The modern techniques used today in the cultivation of rice no longer require such human sacrifice, and the entire process, from planting to harvesting, is now done by machine. Today, the roughly 990,000 acres used to cultivate rice in Italy produce about 60 percent of the total European crop.

Another, but by no means less important, grain used in Italian cuisine is corn or maize, or *granoturco* (Turkish grain), so called because it was believed to have come from Turkey. In fact, corn was discovered in America by Christopher Columbus, who got something of a surprise when he arrived here as he believed he had landed in India. Instead of finding rice he found corn, a plant never seen before by Europeans. Impressed by the quantity consumed by the locals, Columbus introduced the grain to Europe, where it was first used for physical adornment. The Spanish were the first to attempt to cultivate corn as a food and their trade connections took it as far as Venice. The Venetians were more than happy to plant a grain that was so well suited to the local agricultural conditions, and it proved to yield a much heavier crop than any other grain planted in the area.

ABOVE: A MONDINA PLANTING *RISOTTO* RICE IN PIZZAROSTO NEAR VERCELLI

small amount of sauce, meat or cheese, however, it was found to make a valuable contribution to a well-balanced diet. The word *polentone* is still used by southerners as a derogatory term to describe people from the North, because they are such keen consumers of *polenta*.

In Italy it is now not only very fashionable to eat corn, cooked in many different ways in the form of *polenta*, but it is also used to feed animals. The yolk of an egg from a corn-fed chicken is bright yellow and tastes wonderful. Pigs fed on corn yield the tastiest meat, which is used in the production of some of the best hams and salami.

Before the advent of versatile corn, the *polenta* eaten by the Romans was based on a flour made from *farro* (a type of spelt), probably the longest-surviving grain grown in Italy. Today, however, there is a revival in the popularity of *farro*, especially in Umbria and Lazio, where it is used to make fashionably popular peasant food. In fact it is very much in vogue to rediscover *cucina povera*, the food on which poor people of the past survived, and today local chefs prepare wonderfully tasty soups using *farro*, *miglio* (millet), and *grano saraceno* (buckwheat), which have been the foundation of country cooking for many centuries past.

RIGHT: THE RICE FIELDS NEAR VERCELLI FROM ABOVE

It came to be used in the making of what was then known as *pollen* or *puls*, a sort of porridge previously made from other grains such as millet or buckwheat, and the ancestor of *polenta*. For many years *polenta* made with corn was the staple diet of farmers, who ate it unadorned. However, it was later discovered that a diet too heavily dependent on this porridge alone would bring about the deficiency disease pellagra. If it was eaten with a

# A-Z OF RICE & GRAINS

## AVENA / OATS

This cereal belongs to the same family as wheat, but has a very different function in Italian cooking. Oats are mainly grown in areas with good rainfall due to the fact that, like rice, it needs a lot of water to grow. In Italy, it its mostly grown in Naples and Puglia, and is mostly used as feed for animals. It is, however, also ground into oatmeal, a

popular food for young children, and is used flaked in porridge. Oats are widely recognized as having good health-giving properties.

## CRUSCA / BRAN

*Crusca* is the outer part of wheat, a sort of brown cuticle. The bran husk used to be separated from the grain by polishing, then given to the animals. However, its high fiber content makes it an important ingredient for a healthy diet. See *integrale*.

## CUSCUS / COUSCOUS

Couscous was introduced into Italy from North Africa via Sicily and Sardinia. Some people associate the introduction of couscous with the French occupation of Algeria, while others think it was introduced much earlier when the Arabs invaded Europe. Couscous is not actually a grain in its own right, but is made from tiny pellets of semolina. It is traditionally cooked for about two hours in a special pot called a

*cuscussièra*. During this rather long cooking time, a spicy *ragù* of lamb, chicken, or vegetables can be prepared for serving with it, or it can be eaten on its own dressed with a hot chili sauce. A fish stew is its traditional accompaniment in Sicily, and the *cùscus* itself is flavored with saffron.

## FARINA / FLOUR

This generic term, probably derived from *farro* (spelt), denotes the product of milling any dry seed, grain, or pulse. While the word *farina* on its own is only used to describe wheat flour, other ground grains are described in the same way, hence *farina di mais* (corn flour or polenta), *farina di orzo* (pearl barley flour), etc.

With the addition of liquid and spices, flour was found to be an endlessly versatile ingredient, which could be made into pasta, bread, biscuits, or used as a thickening agent for sauces and soups. Flour is graded by its fineness and its suitability for different types of cooking: *farina 00* (*doppio zero*) is used for fresh pasta and cakes; *tipo 0* is used for bread. See *grano duro*, *frumento*.

## FARRO / TYPE OF SPELT

One of the most wholesome grains available, *farro* is a type of the ancient grain spelt, which was used by the Romans for making bread and pasta. Its versatility made it the staple ingredient in the diet of the Roman soldier. *Farro* is now cultivated in Umbria, Tuscany, and Lazio, where it is still used to produce traditional dishes that have recently become popular on the broader culinary stage.

One of the best-known specialty dishes, *minestra di farro* or *farricello*, comes from Lazio, where it is made into a soup. Another way of preparing it is to cook it whole with beans, a method popular in Garfagnana, the mountainous region of Tuscany. Personally, I prefer to use it in a kind of stew flavored with sun-dried tomatoes, olive oil, parsley, and basil, which I serve with vegetables.

## FREGOLA / TYPE OF COUSCOUS

This is a type of small-grained *cuscus* from Sardinia, which is made from fragmented, toasted hard wheat, and is served in soups and *ragùs* of fish or meat.

## FRUMENTO / SOFT WHEAT

This cereal belongs to the *Triticum* genus, of which *farro* is also a member. This variety of wheat is a tender grain. It is densely cultivated in the extensive Po Valley, where it is popularly used to make bread.

## GERME DI GRANO / WHEAT GERM

If you put wheat grains in water for a brief period they will germinate. This sprouted seed is very precious because it contains large amounts of valuable nutrients. It is popularly used in the preparation of wholefoods.

## GRANO DURO / HARD WHEAT

The type of wheat known as hard durum wheat is ground into a fine semolina before being worked as pasta. In southern Italy, the warm dry climate is ideal for the cultivation of hard durum wheat. See also *semolino*.

LEFT: *AVENA*

LEFT: PUBLIC GRAIN MEASURES IN NORCIA

## GRANO SARACENO / BUCKWHEAT

This grain, belonging to a different family from wheat, originated in Mongolia and was brought to Europe by the Moors in the Middle Ages, hence its Italian name. In the sixteenth century it was used all over Italy to make bread, but now there are only two small areas where it is grown. One is Valtellina, a valley in Lombardy, where it is used to make a type of pasta called *pizzoccheri* (see page 150), as well as a type of coarse, rustic *polenta*. This *polenta taragna* uses a mixture of corn and buckwheat flours, together with the local cheese *scimud* or *bitto*. The other buckwheat-growing region is the Veneto, where it is also still used to make *polenta*.

## GRANOTURCO, MAIS / CORN

Corn was discovered by Columbus in America, but was only popularized some time later by the Spanish conqueror Cortès, who first introduced it into Spain around the

year 1500. The northern Italians and French were very impressed with the cereal, which grew abundantly in difficult, dry conditions.

While it was originally used to feed animals, it later became popular with the peasant population, who found that it could be dried and ground into a flour that could be used to make *polenta*, bread, and biscuits. It was then widely used as a substitute for wheat flour, although the corn itself was also eaten fresh on the cob, either boiled or roasted (see *pannocchia*, page 114).

## INTEGRALE / WHOLE

The word *integrale*, meaning complete or whole, is used to describe a grain or flour in which the bran as well as the grain is milled. There are many whole-grain foods, including *pane integrale* (whole-wheat bread), *farina integrale* (whole-wheat flour), *grissini integrali* (whole wheat breadsticks), and *pasta integrale* (whole-wheat pasta).

Although whole-wheat products are high in vitamins and have plenty of roughage, my opinion is that this is achieved at the cost of taste, as whole-wheat foods are not as appetizing as those made with ordinary white flour.

## MIGLIO / MILLET

This cereal was very popular with the Greeks and Romans, who used it largely for making bread and for thickening soups. Today, millet has been almost entirely replaced by corn, as this has a more palatable taste and is much easier to cultivate. Millet is now mainly grown as a fodder for cattle.

*Migliàccio*, an ancient cake, was originally made with *miglio* and the blood of a freshly slaughtered pig, but is now made using other flours, without the blood. In Emilia-Romagna, *migliàccio* is made with cornmeal, while in Tuscany it is a sweet *focaccia*, made with raisins, and in Naples it is a baked *polenta* eaten with stewed vegetables.

## ORZO / BARLEY

I can remember that when I was a child we had a sort of "coffee" for breakfast made from barley grains. When roasted and soaked in water or milk, barley produces a brownish liquid that resembles coffee. Another derivative of barley that delighted us as children during the summer was a drink called *orzata*, which was made with germinated barley, and ground almonds preserved in sugar and water. *Orzo perlato*, or pearl barley, is used in soups in the Alto Adige and Friuli regions, where the Austrian influence can still be felt.

PASTA, SEE PAGES 138–167

## POLENTA / PORRIDGE

In Roman times *polenta* was a porridge made from the flour of various grains and pulses, such as fava beans, spelt, etc. Today the name usually refers to a porridge of yellow or white corn flour. *Polenta* can, however, be used to describe any type of porridge as long as the grain or pulse of origin is used to specify what it is made from, e.g., *polenta di fagioli* (bean polenta), etc.

*Polenta* is best made in a copper pan by cooking the cornmeal with water until it achieves a fairly solid consistency. It takes about 40 minutes to cook, depending on the coarseness of the grains, and requires constant energetic stirring to prevent it from sticking to the bottom of the pan. The *polenta* can then be poured onto a wooden board and served in the middle of the table, where everyone can take as much as they like. It is usually eaten with a meat, mushroom, or vegetable *ragù*. *Polenta*, usually eaten as a substitute for bread, can be eaten cold or hot, or cut in slices and fried. It is also popular layered with cheese and a tomato sauce to make *pasticcio*, a sort of timbale.

An easy-cook variety called *polenta svelta* has been created in order to reduce the cooking time. It is made by pre-cooking ordinary cornmeal, which is then dried and milled again. The results are not as tasty as the original, but it is fine when butter and cheese are added to make a *polenta concia* (see recipe, page 96).

The best *polenta* can be found in northern Italy, where it has been a staple food for a long time. It is traditionally eaten in winter as it is a wonderful comfort food. Vicenza in Veneto is the best place to eat *polenta e baccalà*, which is simply air-dried cod cooked in milk with cornmeal. The other specialty of Veneto and parts of Lombardy is the controversial *polenta e osei*, *polenta* with sparrows.

### POLENTA TARAGNA, SEE GRANO SARACENO

### RISO / RICE

The rice eaten by Italians is produced almost entirely in Italy. The variety cultivated by the Italians is ideally suited to making *risotto*, the most Italian of rice dishes. The main characteristic of *risotto* rice is that it is able to absorb moisture and swell up to three times its initial volume when cooked, while still retaining a bite in its center. In other words, it has to be *al dente* like pasta to make it palatable.

The plant's Latin name is *Oryza sativa*. It is planted in the spring and reaches maturity after about 140 to 180 days. During this time, great care must be taken to keep it steeped in water and to protect it from pests. The rice is harvested between September and October. It is then completely dried and the grains are sorted, washed, and

separated from their husks before finally being polished to produce a perfect white grain. The polishing is a very delicate operation because only the smallest amount of the surface of the grain should be removed so that the vitamins from the outer skins are not entirely eliminated. Ideally rice should be eaten whole, with the husk on, but this would impair its vital quality of absorbency.

Types of Italian rice can be categorized according to their qualities and use:
*Riso comune* (common rice) is the

lowest-quality rice grown in Italy. It is a small round grain and tends to lose a lot of starch when cooked. It is ideal for soups and desserts and only needs 12 to 13 minutes cooking time. Varieties include *balilla*, *originario*, *elio*, *selenio*, and *trio*.
*Riso semifino* (semi-fine rice) has similar characteristics to common rice but has a larger grain. As a result it also needs a slightly longer cooking time (14 to 15 minutes). The varieties include *Italico*, *lido*, *alfa*, *argo*, *cripto*, *comellino*, *Piemonte*, *monticelli*, *Maratelli*, *Padano*, *Romeo*, *Rosa Marchetti*, *rubino*, and *vialone nano*. *Riso semifino* is at its best when used in timbales, *arancini* (rice croquettes, see recipe, page 179), and dry rice dishes, as well as in soups such as *minestrone*.
*Riso fino* (fine rice) has a larger grain but is a little more difficult to digest due to its size and the fact that it loses little starch when cooked. It takes 16 to 17 minutes to cook and is ideal for *risotto*, rice salads, and other main-course dishes. The varieties include *Europa*, *ariete*, *giara*, *molo*, *pierina marchetti*, *RB*, *ribe*, *ringo*, *riva Smeraldo*, *veneria*, *Senit belgioioso*, and *Santi Andrea*.
*Riso superfino* (superfine rice) is the Ferrari of rices, and includes varieties such as *arborio*, *baldo*, *volano gritna*, *koral*, *onda*, *silla*, *strella*, *miara*, *Indio*, *carnaroli*, *corallo*, and *Roma*. The large grains take around 18 to 20 minutes to cook and are perfect in *risotto* and salads as well as special timbales and *arancini* or *polenta*.

A typical rice dish from the area around Piacenza is *bomba di riso*. It is made with plainly cooked *risotto* rice, such as *vialone nano*, mixed with melted butter and Parmesan cheese. One or two pigeons are roasted with sage, butter, white wine, and a little tomato purée. The meat is removed from the birds and

LEFT: COOKED AND GRILLED *POLENTA*

## MAKING A RISOTTO

I have been making *risotto* for 40 years, so the following tips should help you to cook it perfectly. The best rice for *risotto* is *arborio*, *baldo*, *carnaroli*, *vialone nano*, or *Roma*. Anything else will not do. Make sure that you do not wash the rice before cooking it as this removes the valuable starch that makes the *risotto* creamy. The principle of *risotto* is to cook the rice slowly by letting it gradually absorb stock or wine that is added little by little until the rice is cooked. It is important to stir *risotto* continuously to prevent it from sticking to the bottom of the pan.

Before starting the *risotto*, make the stock. Depending on the recipe, you will need about 5 cups of chicken, beef, fish, or vegetable stock. Once it is made, keep the stock on the stovetop so that you can easily transfer the liquid to the *risotto* pan. It is important to keep the stock at boiling point, so that the rice does not stop cooking when the stock is added.

In a separate, large, heavy-bottomed pan, sweat a finely chopped onion in butter and olive oil along with any desired spices and herbs, and cook until the onion is soft. Stir in the rice and allow it to be coated in the oil and butter. Then start to add the liquid. If you are using wine, allow it to evaporate/be absorbed completely before adding the stock. Start by adding a ladleful at a time, stirring continuously, for about 15 minutes. When most of the stock has been used, test a grain of rice to check its consistency and add more stock as necessary. The rice is done when it is tender on the outside but has a firm bite in the center. Be sure to take the rice off the heat just before you think it is ready because it will continue to cook in its own heat. The ideal consistency for *risotto* is soft and runny (but you should be able to pick it up with a fork). *Risotto* should never be cooked until it is solid.

Finally, add some butter and grated Parmesan cheese and beat the *risotto* energetically to make sure all the ingredients are thoroughly mixed and the *risotto* looks creamy and shiny.

piled in the middle of some of the cooked rice in a mold, then covered completely with more rice. This is cooked for 15 to 20 minutes in a bain-marie, then uncovered, and baked in the oven for a further 20 minutes until golden.

### RISOTTO

This unique dish can be found in good Italian restaurants throughout the world. The appeal of *risotto* is that it can satisfy any palate, provided, of course, that it is made properly. It is no surprise that it is in the rice-growing regions of Piedmont, Lombardy, and Veneto that the classic *risotto* dishes such as *risotto* with truffles or *risotto* with porcini have their origins. Other regions, such as Tuscany, Campania, Sicily, and even Sardinia, have contributed some tasty dishes to the genre, but they cannot equal the great northern dishes.

There are various ways of using up leftover *risotto*. *Arancini* (see page 179) adds beaten egg to the cold mixture with a little grated Parmesan cheese, parsley, and bread crumbs. This is mixed well and formed by hand into little balls. These are then deep-fried until golden, and served hot.

### SEGALE / RYE

This ancient grain is very similar to wheat, and the flour ground from it is used to make bread, biscuits, and *grissini* (see page 293). It has plenty of roughage and is full of nutrients. Rye bread is particularly popular in the northern regions of Italy, especially those bordering Austria, where it is often flavored with cumin or fennel seeds.

### SEMOLINO, SEMOLA / SEMOLINA

Ground durum wheat, called *semolino*, is mainly used for making pasta, but is also used to make couscous, soups, and *gnocchi*, dumplings from Rome. *Gnocchi alla romana* are made with semolina that has been heated with milk and a pinch of nutmeg to form a firm mixture. When it is cool, beaten egg is added. The *semolino* is then spread out on an oiled surface and patted flat with a spatula. Coin-sized rounds are then cut from the mixture and placed on a buttered baking tray. More butter and Parmesan cheese are dotted over the top, then the *gnocchi* are cooked in a very hot oven for 10 to 15 minutes or until a golden crust has formed on top. Seasoned with freshly ground pepper, the *gnocchi* are served either as a first course or as a side dish with a meat stew.

PASTIERA DI GRANO

# PASTIERA DI GRANO
GRAIN TART

**FOR 10 OR MORE**

FOR THE PASTRY:

HEAPING ½ CUP SUPERFINE SUGAR

10 TABLESPOONS BUTTER OR COOKING
    FAT, PLUS MORE FOR THE PAN

3 LARGE EGG YOLKS

HEAPING 2½ CUPS FLOUR

FOR THE FILLING:

7 OUNCES WHOLE WHEAT, OR 1 POUND
    CANNED COOKED WHEAT (CALLED *GRAN
    PASTIERA*

2¼ CUPS MILK (IF USING
    FRESH WHOLE WHEAT)

MINCED ZEST OF 1 LEMON

1 TEASPOON GROUND CINNAMON

2 TEASPOON VANILLA-FLAVORED SUGAR

MINCED ZEST OF ½ ORANGE

10 OUNCES RICOTTA CHEESE

4 LARGE EGGS, SEPARATED

1 SMALL WINE GLASS ORANGE-FLOWER
    WATER

5 OUNCES CANDIED CITRON PEEL, FINELY
    CHOPPED

1 CUP SUPERFINE SUGAR

CONFECTIONER'S SUGAR FOR DUSTING

*This recipe will probably appear in every book I write because it is my mother's, and has always been a tradition in my family. It is very much an Easter cake, made with grains of wheat—symbol of wealth and prosperity—and in large quantities, as the cakes are given as presents to friends. The Neapolitans drink the locally produced wine, Lacrima Christi, to accompany this delicious tart.*

If using fresh grain, two days ahead soak it for 24 hours in several changes of water. The next day, simmer the grain in the milk with the zest of half a lemon for 3 to 4 hours over very low heat. When it is cooked (or if using canned), stir in a pinch of cinnamon, the vanilla sugar, and the remaining lemon zest and the orange zest. Set aside overnight for the flavors to mingle.

Make the pastry: in a large bowl, work together the sugar, butter, and the eggs until smooth, then add the flour and gradually incorporate to make a smooth pastry. Set aside in a cool place for 1 hour or more.

Preheat the oven to 375° F. Grease a 14-inch diameter flan pan with butter.

Finish the filling: beat the ricotta with the egg yolks and the orange-flower water. Add the candied peel and the flavored grain to the mixture. Beat the egg whites together with the sugar until stiff and fold them very gently into the mixture.

Roll out two-thirds of the pastry and use to line the flan pan, covering the bottom and sides with an equal thickness. Pour in the filling. Roll out the remaining pastry and cut it into long strips and form a lattice top for the tart. Bake for about 45 minutes until light golden. Allow to cool and then dust with confectioner's sugar.

# RISOTTO CON ASPARAGI
ASPARAGUS RISOTTO

**FOR 4**

2 POUNDS FRESH ASPARAGUS

ABOUT 4½ CUPS VEGETABLE STOCK

4 TABLESPOONS OLIVE OIL

6 TABLESPOONS BUTTER

1 SMALL ONION, FINELY CHOPPED

1½ CUPS *CARNAROLI* OR
    *VIALONE NANO* RICE

1¾ OUNCES PARMESAN CHEESE, GRATED

SALT AND PEPPER

Trim the asparagus and cook it in boiling salted water until tender. Drain, reserving the cooking liquid. Cut the asparagus into ½-inch chunks, leaving the tips whole. Mix the asparagus cooking liquid with enough stock to make 7½ cups. Prepare the risotto in the usual way (see page 175), adding the chopped asparagus, but not the asparagus tips, just before the rice. Garnish with the asparagus tips before serving.

# PANISSA
BEANS AND RICE

**FOR 6**

10 OUNCES DRIED BORLOTTI BEANS

4 TABLESPOONS OLIVE OIL

1 LARGE ONION, FINELY SLICED

4 OUNCES *PANCETTA*, CUT INTO
SMALL CUBES

2 OUNCES PARMA HAM, CUT INTO
SMALL CUBES

1³/4 CUPS *RISOTTO* RICE SUCH AS
*CARNAROLI* OR *ARBORIO*

¹/2 CUP RED WINE, PREFERABLY NEBBIOLO
(SPANNA)

9 CUPS CHICKEN STOCK (BOUILLON CUBES
ARE FINE)

SALT AND PEPPER

*Originally from Vercelli, this is a* risotto *with beans, not to be confused with* paniscia, *a similar but much more complicated dish from the town of Novara. Ideally it should be made with fresh borlotti beans but because they are hard to come by, especially outside Italy, you could use the dried ones.*

Soak the beans in plenty of water overnight, then drain. Put them in a saucepan, cover with fresh water, and simmer for about 2 hours or until tender; drain.

Heat the olive oil in a pan, add the onion, *pancetta*, and Parma ham and fry for 5 to 6 minutes. Add the rice and beans and stir well. Add the red wine and continue as for making *risotto* (see page 175). Serve hot, without cheese.

# RISOTTO ALLO ZAFFERANO
SAFFRON RISOTTO

**FOR 4**

1¹/2 CUPS *VIALONE NANO* RICE

4 TABLESPOONS OLIVE OIL

6 TABLESPOONS BUTTER

1 SMALL ONION, FINELY CHOPPED

10 STRANDS SAFFRON OR 3 SMALL
PINCHES SAFFRON POWDER

7¹/2 CUPS VEGETABLE STOCK

SALT AND PEPPER

Make the *risotto* in the usual way (see page 175), adding the saffron powder to the stock. This is traditionally served with *ossobuco alla milanese* (see page 95).

RIGHT: *RISOTTO CON ASPARIGI*
(TOP) SEE PAGE **177**; *OSSOBUCO ALLA
MILANESE* SERVED WITH *RISOTTO ALLO
ZAFFERANO* (BOTTOM)

# RISOTTO AI FUNGHI
MUSHROOM RISOTTO

**FOR 4 TO 6**

10 OUNCES FRESH *PORCINI*
    MUSHROOMS
6 TABLESPOONS BUTTER
1 LARGE ONION, FINELY SLICED
2³/₄ CUPS *CARNAROLI* RICE, OR
    *VIALONE NANO* OR *ARBORIO*
7¹/₂ CUPS CHICKEN STOCK
2 OUNCES PARMESAN CHEESE, GRATED
SALT AND PEPPER

*Ideally you should use* porcini *to make this* risotto. *However, they have only a limited season and are difficult to buy, especially outside Italy. If you cannot find freshly picked* porcini, *then the combination of cultivated mushrooms and dried* porcini *should give a good result, although naturally not to be compared to the real thing.*

Carefully clean the mushrooms (see page 185) and then slice them.

Heat half of the butter in a pan, add the mushrooms and onion, and sauté until soft. Prepare the *risotto* in the usual way (see page 175). Remove from the heat and leave to rest for 1 minute, then add the remaining butter and the Parmesan cheese and stir vigorously to obtain a very creamy, but not too liquid and not too firm, *risotto*. Serve on hot plates, sprinkled with a little black pepper.

# ARANCINI DI RISO ALLA PALERMITANA
RICE BALLS PALERMO-STYLE

**MAKES 20**

12 OUNCES GROUND BEEF
¹/₂ RECIPE *SALSA DI POMODORO ALLA
    NAPOLETANA* (SEE PAGE 131)
SALT AND PEPPER
2³/₄ CUPS *CARNAROLI* OR *ARBORIO* RICE
6 EGGS
1 TABLESPOON FINELY CHOPPED FLAT-LEAF
    PARSLEY
3¹/₂ OUNCES HARD PECORINO CHEESE,
    GRATED
5 OUNCES SOFT *CACIOCAVALLO*
    CHEESE, CUT INTO SMALL CUBES
FLOUR FOR DREDGING
DRIED BREAD CRUMBS
OLIVE OIL FOR DEEP-FRYING

*Perhaps the most famous* arancini *come from Sicily, where they were given the name because they are the same size as a small orange. As they are so nice to eat, rather like a little ball of* risotto, arancini *have been adopted in all the quick-service bars, where you can have them piping hot at lunchtime. They are ideal for parties or picnics because they can also be eaten at room temperature.*

Cook the ground beef in the tomato sauce for 30 minutes, then add salt and pepper to taste. Cook the rice in 9 cups lightly salted boiling water for 12 minutes only and then drain. Spread it out on a work surface and leave to cool. Beat 4 of the eggs together with the parsley and pecorino cheese and mix thoroughly with the rice. Take some of the mixture and thickly cover the palm of your hand with it. Put a tablespoon of the meat sauce and a few cubes of *cacciocavallo* cheese in the center. Close your hand and seal with a little more rice to make a ball the size of a small orange. Repeat with the remaining mixture.

Beat together the 2 remaining eggs. Roll the balls in flour, then in the beaten egg, and finally in the bread crumbs. Deep-fry them in plenty of olive oil for about 5 minutes, until golden brown. To achieve more crispness, after frying you could bake them for 5 minutes in an oven preheated to 450° F.

# POLENTA E BACCALÀ

POLENTA AND SALT COD

FOR 6

3$^1/_4$ POUNDS SALT COD, TAKEN
   FROM THE MIDDLE PART OF THE FISH
$^3/_4$ CUP EXTRA-VIRGIN OLIVE OIL
1 ONION, FINELY SLICED
2 GARLIC CLOVES, COARSELY CHOPPED
14-OUNCE CAN CHOPPED TOMATOES,
   OR 3 LARGE RIPE TOMATOES, PEELED
   AND COARSELY CHOPPED
8 BASIL LEAVES
3 TABLESPOONS COARSELY CHOPPED
   FLAT-LEAF PARSLEY
1 GLASS RED WINE
SALT AND PEPPER

FOR THE *POLENTA*:
9 CUPS WATER
1$^1/_2$ TABLESPOONS SALT
2 HEAPING CUPS COARSE CORNMEAL

*Synonymous with peasant comfort food, this can often be found on winter Fridays in small towns, where there will probably be a street market.* Baccalà *is a preserved fish (see page 16) which used to be cheap food eaten in the valleys where supplies of fresh fish were hard to come by. But today it is eaten everywhere because of its remarkable taste, and it is more expensive than fresh cod. The recipe for salt cod I find most suitable for eating with* polenta *is this one from Livorno. Sometimes you may find salt cod on sale already desalted. Otherwise you will have to soak it in water for 36 hours.*

If necessary, cut the salt cod into smallish pieces; this helps it lose more salt while soaking. Soak it in plenty of cold water for 36 hours, changing the water about every 6 hours. Drain and remove the bones and fins, then cut the cod into 1$^1/_2$ by 2$^1/_2$-inch chunks.

Cook the *polenta* in a copper pan with a rounded bottom, if possible. Put the water and salt in the pan and bring to a boil. Sift the cornmeal through your hand, letting it fall into the water a little at a time while stirring constantly to avoid lumps. Cook for 40 minutes, stirring all the time, until the *polenta* is pulling away from the sides of the pan.

Heat ½ cup of the olive oil in a pan, add the onion and garlic, and fry until soft. Add the tomatoes, basil, and parsley and simmer until the sauce begins to thicken. Heat the remaining oil in a separate pan, add the salt cod, and fry for 6 to 7 minutes on each side. Pour the tomato sauce and the red wine over the fish and season with black pepper and some salt if necessary. Cook gently for 20 minutes, then serve with the *polenta*.

# POLENTA TARAGNA

BUCKWHEAT POLENTA

FOR 6

11 CUPS WATER
1$^1/_2$ TABLESPOONS SALT
3 HEAPING CUPS *POLENTA TARAGNA*
   (SEE RIGHT)
10 TABLESPOONS BUTTER
5 OUNCES *BITTO*, *ASIAGO*, OR FRESH
   *TOMA* CHEESE, VERY FINELY SLICED

*This is a mixture of two types of flour, corn and buckwheat, which the inhabitants of Valtellina, a valley in Lombardy, very much prefer to plain* polenta. *It is tasty but requires a longer cooking time than standard* polenta. *If you cannot find the ready-mixed flour you can make it yourself, mixing 1 part cornmeal with 2 parts buckwheat flour.*

Put the water and salt in a large heavy-bottomed pan and bring to a boil. Sift the *polenta taragna* through your hand, letting it fall into the water a little at a time while stirring constantly to avoid lumps. Cook for 1 hour, stirring all the time, until the *polenta* is pulling away from the sides of the pan. Stir in the butter and then the cheese slices. Either serve immediately, alone or as an accompaniment to stews, or leave to cool, cut into slices, and then fry in butter or broil.

# PIZZOCCHERI
## BUCKWHEAT PASTA WITH POTATOES AND CABBAGE

**FOR 6**

2 LARGE POTATOES, PEELED AND CUT INTO
   SMALL CUBES

1 POUND SAVOY CABBAGE, CUT INTO
   STRIPS

2 GARLIC CLOVES, SLICED

6 SAGE LEAVES

7 TABLESPOONS BUTTER

10 OUNCES *BITTO*, *TOMA*, OR
   *ASIAGO* CHEESE, THINLY SLICED

3 OUNCES PARMESAN CHEESE, GRATED

SALT AND PEPPER

FOR THE *PIZZOCCHERI*:

2 1/4 CUPS BUCKWHEAT FLOUR

SCANT 1 CUP 00 (*DOPPIO ZERO*) FLOUR

2 EGGS

4 TABLESPOONS MILK

PINCH SALT

*Probably the only buckwheat pasta used in Italy,* pizzoccheri *comes from the Valtellina, a valley in Lombardy not far from Milan, and is popular in many northern regions. Traditionally served with cabbage, potatoes, and cheese, as here, it is quite a rich dish which could be served as a main course. It is, however, especially loved by vegetarians. If you can find ready-made* pizzoccheri *you will need 12 ounces.*

To make the pasta, pile the two flours up into a volcano shape on a work surface and make a well in the center. Add the eggs, milk, salt, and enough water to make a fairly firm dough. Knead for 8 to 10 minutes, until smooth and elastic, then cover and leave to rest for 20 minutes. Roll out with a rolling pin to 1/4 inch thick and cut into strips about 2 1/2 inches long by 1/2 inch wide. Either use immediately or store in the refrigerator for up to 2 days.

If using freshly made pasta, cook the potatoes and cabbage in lightly salted boiling water until almost tender, then add the *pizzoccheri* for the last 6 to 8 minutes. If using dried pasta, cook everything together until tender.

Meanwhile, fry the garlic and sage very gently in the butter, then remove from the heat. Drain the *pizzoccheri* and vegetables, arrange a layer of them in a preheated dish, and cover with some of the cheese slices. Reheat the butter, garlic, and sage until the butter is foaming. Pour a little of the hot butter and garlic over the cheese and sprinkle with some of the Parmesan cheese. Repeat these layers, then pour the remaining butter and garlic over the top. Leave for 1 to 2 minutes and then mix everything from top to bottom to check that the cheese has melted. Spread the mixture on a warmed plate, season with salt and pepper and serve immediately.

# FUNGI

FUNGHI

For most Italians, when you talk about mushrooms their mind goes immediately to *porcini* (*cèpes*). This mushroom grows only in the wild, from midsummer through fall, is picked by local gatherers and then sent to checking centers so that you may safely buy them in shops and markets. *Porcini*-hunting usually involves outings in the very early morning (only because you need to be first on the territory), armed with a basket, a knife, and possibly a stick.

While in other countries in the fall most people parking their cars near woods are simply taking the air, walking their dogs, or having a picnic, in Italy parked cars in such a vicinity means mushroom-hunters are about. Due to the overwhelming popularity of this pastime, the government has instituted laws that allow people to pick only a limited quantity of mushrooms—with levels varying from area to area but usually not exceeding 3 kg per person per day, and of specified measurements to prevent the depletion of the immature mushrooms. Heavy fines are attached to the disregard of these laws.

The history of gathering fungi in Italy is a long one. The Romans (who else!) were very fond of mushrooms, and one of the most precious was the favorite of the Emperor Caesar—which is why it is still today called Caesar's mushroom (see *amanita cesarea*, page 186). Mushrooms grow all over Italy, especially in high valleys. The best areas are, however, the valleys of Piedmont, Lombardy, and the Veneto, and more especially Trentino, Liguria, and Emilia-Romagna, with Borgotaro as one of the most famous centers for the best *porcini*. Quantities of mushrooms are also found in Tuscany, Umbria, Basilicata, and even Calabria, where the high plains of Sila, which is similar to parts of Switzerland, harbor good-quality *porcini* and other mushrooms, like the saffron milkcap, and even the white truffles usually only associated with Piedmont, Emilia-Romagna, and Umbria. The regions that offer perhaps the widest variety of mushrooms are Veneto and Trentino-Alto Adige. In the market of Trento in mushroom season one can find up to sixty different kinds of mushroom.

For reasons of safety, all the mushrooms sold in markets and shops are first checked for edibility by the local authorities, to avoid potentially dangerous errors. Despite this, however, every year in Italy there are fatalities, mainly among families picking their own mushrooms with ignorant confidence. The culprits on these occasions are usually the *Amanita phalloides* or the *A. virosa*, which is easily mistaken for its edible relatives. Unfortunately, there is no antidote for its toxin, and often the indications of poisoning come too late for anything to be done.

Mushrooms and truffles have great gastronomic importance in Italian cuisine. In fact, fungi are an industry of some

I do firmly recommend that you have a mushroom expert go with you for the first few outings, and that you prepare by studying some good books on the subject. Under no circumstances should you pick mushrooms at random. Some of them are very beautiful and look very innocent and edible. You may, however, inadvertently pick the one that provides you with your last meal!

Fungi can be divided into three major groups or families: gilled mushrooms, tubular mushrooms, and tubers such as truffles, each of which has its own distinctive characteristics and growing habits. Mushrooms have Latin names, like flowers or plants, so that they can be identified internationally. The same fungus can have more than one Latin name, however, depending on how many people claim its discovery. Hopefully, the simple guide that follows will help make the categories easier to understand.

The gilled mushrooms form the largest family, with literally hundreds of fungi making up the group. The main characteristic of the family, as its name suggests, are the lamellae, the gills beneath the cap. It is in these gills that the mushroom develops its spores, minute seeds, which individually are invisible to the naked eye. To see the spores, leave the cap gill-side down on a piece of paper and, after a couple of hours, an imprint will be left from the microscopic spores released from the gills. This imprint is unique in form and color to each individual mushroom, and can indicate as distinctively as a fingerprint the mushroom from which it came. The majority of mushrooms fall into the gilled category, but the most widespread is the common field mushroom.

The second type of fungus is no less prolific than the gilled mushroom and is also very much a mushroom. It is called boletus and, unlike the gilled mushroom, it has closely packed little tubes beneath the cap. These tubes are invisible in the youngest fungi, when the plant is still immature, but they develop with age, and it is here that they harbor the spores, allowing the mushroom to reproduce. The mushrooms that fall into this group include the famous *porcino* (*cèpe*), which together with the *cantarello* (chanterelle) and *spugnola* (morel) represent probably the best edible fungi in the world.

economic importance to the nation. Hundreds of companies produce industrially or artisanally dried and preserved mushrooms for local consumption, but also increasingly for export. In fact, many mushrooms are now imported from Eastern Europe and North Africa to keep the export industry supplied with sufficient raw materials.

People often think that mushrooms are complicated, and fear collecting and eating poisonous ones by mistake. However, while some are difficult to identify in the wild and definitely require an expert eye, many are very distinctive and can be picked with confidence. Of course, it is worth having a visual reminder of what you are looking for before you go mushroom hunting, so that you can quickly identify any that you find, but you should be guided by the location and conditions as much as anything.

RIGHT: BLACK
TRUFFLES

The third type of fungus is a tuber. Tubers produce their spores on their surface, and these are distributed not by the wind or rain but by insects. The truffle is the most famous member of this group and the very best of the group have a fine and distinctive aroma and flavor and carry very high prices. Truffles look like potatoes and grow underground. They are notoriously difficult to find, so dogs and pigs are used to sniff them out. Those truffle-hunters who use pigs have to be able to present good rewards, or the pigs are likely to eat the truffles.

The life-span of a mushroom depends on the prevailing weather conditions so it can either be very short or very long, lasting from less than a day to a few days from the time it first appears through to maturity. The best mushrooms are those that are about halfway through their life-cycle. Avoid the smallest, even though they may look tender and very tempting. Conversely, as mushrooms mature the flavor deteriorates and the proteins begin to degenerate. They also attract more worms as they age.

When out collecting mushrooms, make sure you take a knife with you so that you can remove any

worm-infested areas or decayed parts on the spot. This prevents their spread from one mushroom to another. It is best to carry mushrooms in a basket so that they are well-ventilated and so that the spores can fall as you walk, allowing the mushrooms to propagate new fungi rather than losing spores their being lost in the kitchen. Of course, as you are dealing with the natural environment you should be clean and tidy and treat any suspect or unknown specimens with respect. Do not touch them unless you know what they are, as some mushrooms are even poisonous to the touch.

When preparing mushrooms for cooking, do not wash them, but instead wipe them with a clean damp cloth. The only exception is when cleaning chanterelles and morels: with these, sand is sometimes embedded in the gills and they have to be thoroughly cleaned under running water. Some of the flavor will be lost, but you cannot have it both ways. When cleaning mushrooms, great care should be taken to ensure that worm-infested or decayed parts are cut out. Both fungi collected from the wild and those bought from shops or market stalls should be used straight away, whether they are being used fresh or preserved. They only keep for a short time in the refrigerator.

There a few golden rules to remember when using fungi. First of all, make sure that they have been properly identified by a competent authority as edible. Secondly, never accept mushrooms as a present from someone you do not know to be an expert. Thirdly, remember that some people are allergic to certain edible fungi, so avoid eating too many of any new variety and remember not to drink alcohol with fungi as the two can sometimes react badly when combined. Lastly, mushrooms should be cooked and eaten when they are collected; do not keep leftovers, as the proteins in the mushroom degenerate quickly.

Despite all these caveats, fungi are still a wonderful natural gift, as long as you understand them. My favorite way of cooking them is simply sliced and sautéed in butter or olive oil, with a little garlic, parsley, and sometimes some chopped chili pepper.

# A-Z OF FUNGI

## AGARICO DELIZIOSO /
SAFFRON MILKCAP *Lactarius deliciosus*

One of the most beautiful of the *Agaricacae* family of mushrooms, the saffron milkcap belongs to the subspecies *Agarico lactarius*, and when cut or broken it exudes a yellowy, milky substance, as its name implies. The saffron milkcap reaches about $1^1/_4$ to $2^1/_2$ inches in height and has a fairly thick and meaty, flat, orange-to-green-colored cap made up of concentric circles, with a depression in the center. The edges of the cap are turned under, and the gills on the underside are quite tight and of the same saffrony color as the straight hollow stem. In Calabria it is called *sanguinello* or *fungosanguigno* because of the reddish tinge to its milk.

The flesh is utterly delicious, nutty in flavor and slightly resinous. Make sure when buying or collecting it that it is free of worms. To check, just cut the mushroom in half. It needs to be well cooked or it will be indigestible. Although it is not suitable for drying, it can be frozen. However, the best way to enjoy it is cooked in olive oil, with a little garlic, parsley, and chili pepper.

The saffron milkcap is unfortunately often confused with the toxic powderpuff milkcap (*Lactarius torminosus*), which, although similar in shape, has white gills, a white stem and flesh, and exudes a white milk. Its surface is also different—it is covered in hairs rather than smooth. The powderpuff milkcap grows singly or in small groups near pine trees and grass all over Italy in late summer and early fall.

## AGARICO NUDO / BLEWIT
*Clitocybe nuda*

A fairly common but beautiful fungus of the agarics, the blewit can be found from fall through early winter in deciduous woods and fields that are adjacent to woods. It usually grows singly, but can sometimes grow in little groups.

The whole of the young fungus is usually violet in color, turning brown with age. The round flat cap can reach up to 5 inches in diameter, with the irregular edges rolled under. The flesh is quite firm, with a nutty flavor and delicate perfume. It is slightly poisonous when raw but is perfectly edible when cooked. Try braising them in butter until the moisture from the mushroom has evaporated, then season with chives, salt, and pepper, and eat as an accompaniment to meat or fish.

Although the blewit cannot be dried, it can be preserved by pickling and freezing.

## AMANITA

This is the name of the most famous genus of fungi, embracing a wide range of mushrooms from the most delicious, the *Amanita caesarea*, to the most poisonous— including *A. phalloides*, *A. virosa*, *A. pantherina*, and *A. verna*. All these are deadly mushrooms for which there is no antidote. The family also includes the very beautiful *A. muscaria* (fly agaric), which is red with white spots and is considered to be a hallucinogen, but can possibly cause death.

## AMANITA CESAREA, OVOLO, COCCO, FUNGO IMPERIALE /
CAESAR'S MUSHROOM *Amanita caesarea*

Named after the Roman emperor Caesar, who was very fond of it, the *Amanita caesarea* is probably one of the most sought-after mushrooms in Italy. Probably exceeding the very popular *porcino* (*cèpe*) for extreme delicacy of taste and splendid colors, it grows under oak and chestnut trees in very warm, dry areas, especially in the South, but is particularly popular in northern Italy, where it can be bought in specialist shops.

It can grow up to $3^1/_2$ inches in height and has a bright orange cap of up to 8 inches in diameter, with slightly paler orangey-yellow gills and flesh. When mature, a yellow ring or skirt appears on the stem. As it grows, the mushroom resembles a thick white egg out of which the orange "yolk" of the mushroom breaks, hence its Italian name *ovolo* or *cocco*, meaning "egg." Be cautious when collecting it, because when it is small and undeveloped, it is very similar to other very poisonous mushrooms from the same genus (see *Amanita*).

Italians love to eat this mushroom raw, finely sliced in salads with slices of truffle and dressed with extra-virgin olive oil and a few drops of lemon juice.

## ARRICCIATA / RUFFLES, CAULIFLOWER MUSHROOM
*Sparassis crispa, S. radicata*

The cauliflower fungus does not look like a mushroom at all. It grows at the base of old pine trees during the fall, reaches more than 20 inches in diameter, and weighs several kilos. It develops from a single thick, short stem hidden at the base of the tree, into a series of tightly packed branches with little off-white lobes at the end, which make it look like a huge cauliflower or brain (hence its other English name, "brain fungus"). It is not a common fungus and cannot be bought easily in Italy, except in local markets such as Trento where, in the fall, up to

LEFT: *AGARICO DELIZIOSO*

LEFT: *OVOLI*

sixty different types of mushroom are on sale in any one day.

Great care has to be taken when cleaning the *arricciata* and, depending on their size, it is advisable to cut them into chunks to check for insects, pine needles, and small stones. If they have been growing in a sandy area it is also necessary to wash them. Before being cooked they should be briefly blanched in boiling salted water. They can then be fried in butter or cut in small chunks, sautéed with a mixture of other types of mushrooms, or dipped in beaten egg and deep-fried. They can also be cut in chunks and skewered along with small pieces of chicken for barbecuing over charcoal.

### BOLETO BAIO / BAY BOLETE
*Boletus badius, Xerocomus*
Many Italians wrongfully doubt the edibility of this fungus belonging to the boletus genus (beneath the cap it has pores instead of gills) since, when cut, the flesh turns a little blue on coming into contact with the air. Otherwise it looks quite ordinary and is sometimes confused with other boletes, some of which are edible and others poisonous, and it is also sometimes confused with *porcini*. It can, though, be distinguished by the fact that it grows in the northern and central regions of Italy in summer and fall under beech and pine trees, where there is grass or moss. Its surface looks like brown velvet or leather when dry, although it turns slippery and sticky when wet. It grows in large families so there are always plenty to take home.

The cap grows up to 6 inches in diameter and is quite firm and meaty when young, turning spongy when fully developed. The undeveloped pores are tight and cream colored, gradually turning from pale to deep green as they age. The fairly solid edible stem is pale brown with stripes and can grow up to 5 inches high.

When preparing the fungus,

discard any infested by worms. Only perfect examples should be collected and eaten. They are good dried, but should first be cut in slices. Although it does not have the same intensity of flavor as *porcini*, it is still valuable as a flavoring for sauces and soups, etc. Young boletes freeze well and are good for pickling. They can also be puréed, simply sautéed in butter or oil, or dipped in beaten egg, tossed in bread crumbs, and shallow-fried. Make sure you know the origin of bay boletes before you buy them because, more than any other mushroom, they absorb pollution and nuclear fall-out — especially radioactive strontium.

### BOLETO ELEGANTE, LARICINO / LARCH BOLETE *Suillus grevillei*
Although it looks similar to other boletes, the *elegante*, as its name suggests, looks much better than it tastes. It is not one of the most sought-after fungi, but it has its merits, not least of which is its abundance. It can be found mainly from summer through fall under larch and pine trees, where the ground is free of brambles and other heavy shrubs. This fungus is always a little moist, whatever the weather conditions, but fully developed specimens should not be picked after rain as they can become waterlogged.

The yellow-orange cap reaches up to 6 inches in diameter and the stem up to 5 to 6 inches in height. The ring around the stem is the remainder of a veil, and under the cap are bright yellow pores. Take care not to confuse it with some very toxic species of *Cortinarius*—if you want to collect it yourself make sure you have a professional

mycologist with you. The larch bolete grows in the Alps and Apennines, where pastureland borders larch and pine woods. It is common in Calabria on the Sila flatlands.

In my opinion, most mushrooms should not be cooked for too long, but a recipe of Rosetta, a local forest warden, changed my mind. She peeled the mushrooms, removed the viscous skin, then chopped and fried them for half an hour in extra-virgin olive oil, with garlic, chili, and parsley, until all the moisture had evaporated. They were delicious. Incidentally, salt should always be added at the end of the cooking of mushrooms so that they do not sweat too much.

### BOLETO GIALLO, PINAIOLO / SLIPPERY JACK *Suillus luteus*
Even in dry weather, the cuticle (skin) of this fungus is always viscous and wet. It also belongs to the boletes, and mainly grows in pine woods during the spring and fall. It grows freely and can be found in large groups. The wet cuticle is a brownish-purple color and should be removed during preparation of the fungus. The cap is about 5 inches in diameter, with yellow pores on the underside. The tubular stem is 3 to 4 inches high and whitish in color. It also has a ring around it from the remains of the veil. It can be used in the same way as the *boleto elegante*, but is also good sautéed and in soups.

### BULE, BRISA, SEE PORCINO

### CANTARELLO / CHANTERELLE *Cantharellus cibarius*
This mushroom is also known as *galletto*, *gallinaccio*, *gialletto*, *cantarello*, *finferlo*, *margherita*, and *garitula* in Italy, and *girolle* in French. The fact

*RIGHT: WINTER CHANTERELLES*

that almost every region in Italy has a different name for this fungus shows how popular it is. It is, however, equally highly appreciated all over the world. Like the *porcino*, the chanterelle is available during the summer and fall from most specialist food shops, although at quite a high price. As well as for its subtle flavor, the chanterelle is popular because of its pretty, bright yellow-to-apricot color, its size, attractive shape, and firm, chunky texture. It looks like a funnel with an irregularly shaped cap, its fairly loose gills running down onto the short stem, which is just over an inch high. It is quite abundant, growing in large groups on mossy ground in dank woodland.

The chanterelle's fragrant yellowish-white flesh is delicious simply fried in butter with a few chopped shallots and chervil or parsley. Some people add cream to this dish, but I think it smothers the delicate flavor. It is also good with scrambled eggs or in an omelet, but can also accompany steamed fish and meat dishes. The chanterelle can be preserved in many ways, including pickling in vinegar to be eaten as part of an *antipasto*, as well as freezing and drying, although this method is more effective for retaining the shape and color of the mushroom than the flavor. I have discovered a way to sweet-cure them so they can be used as a decoration for exotic desserts (see *finferli al liquore*, page 201).

### CARDONCELLO, CARDARELLO, FUNGO DI FÄROLA / TYPE OF OYSTER MUSHROOM *Pleurotus fuscus*

This extremely popular fungus grows wild only in southern Italy, and mainly in the Basilicata and Puglia. It can grow at altitudes of up to 6,000 feet and prefers to be among the fallen needles of the umbrella pine. It is an irregularly shaped fungus belonging to the *Pleurotus* genus, and grows in abundant clumps on thick tree stumps or wood that is decaying beneath the soil. Under its meaty

head, which ranges in color from pale brown to gray, are its loose off-white gills, which run down to the top of the stem.

Like other types of oyster mushroom (see *pleuroto*), it is commercially grown in sacks filled with wood chips injected with the spore of the fungus and stored in temperature- and moisture-controlled rooms. This farmed product is not very different from the wild one, as its main characteristics lie in its firm, bulky flesh and crunchy texture rather than its aroma or flavor.

It is this textural quality that makes the *cardoncello* so ideal for preserving. The Pugliese cook it in wine vinegar before grilling it *alla brace* (over charcoal) and then preserving it in jars with Pugliese extra-virgin olive oil and garlic, parsley, and chili. Another popular Pugliese method is to bake the mushrooms, sprinkled with fresh bread crumbs, parsley, salt, and pepper, and plenty of extra-virgin olive oil, in a fairly hot oven for half an hour.

### CEPPATELLO, SEE PORCINO

### CHIODINO, FAMIGLIOLA BUONA / HONEY MUSHROOM *Armillariella mellea*

In the fall, this mushroom can be bought for a modest price at every Italian market. As a fungus it is greatly feared by foresters and owners of orchards or fruit trees because of its parasitic habit of feeding on not only decaying wood but the sap of living trees, which threatens their survival.

Its Italian names, *chiodino* and *famigliola*, refer to its shape, *chiodo* meaning "nail,"

and pattern of growth—*famigliola* means "small family," indicating that it grows in tight bunches. Its Latin name, *mellea*, means "honey," hence its name in English, although this is a reference to its color rather than its flavor.

The little fungus heads grow close together on a very long stem and start off being round and honey-colored with a black top and center. The gills are initially white, but turn to a creamy brown when the cap opens. The best time to pick them is when they are closed, otherwise they are fragile and break easily.

When you find them, they will be available in abundance. Once it took me and a friend just a couple of hours to collect about 350 pounds from the stump of an enormous beech tree which had a surface of only 30 or 35 square feet. However, this mass of mushrooms left a very unpleasant smell in my car. Be sure to avoid picking the very similar—but very poisonous sulfur tuft, *Hypholoma fasciculare*, which grows in similar circumstances to the honey mushroom, often right next to it, but can be distinguished by its sulfurous yellow color and green-to-dark-brown gills.

The honey mushroom can only be eaten after it has been cooked, as it also is also poisonous when raw. Despite this, the *chiodino* is an excellent and versatile fungus, which is excellent pickled in vinegar or preserved in extra-virgin olive oil along with some spices for flavoring. It can also be frozen, as long as it has been thoroughly cleaned, with only one-third of the stem still attached to the head.

Before using it, cook the honey mushroom in slightly salted water for a few minutes, then discard the water as the toxins may be left in it. The fungus can then be added to tomato sauces for *polenta*, used to make delicate risottos, or as a flavoring for pasta. My

LEFT: *CHIODINI*

favorite way of eating the blanched mushroom is sautéed in extra-virgin olive oil with garlic and chili, and then dressed with lemon juice, salt, pepper, and parsley as a cold salad.

## COLOMBINA MAGGIORE /
GREEN, VARIEGATED BRITTLEGILL *Russula virescens, R. variata*
There are literally hundreds of varieties of the particularly pretty *Russula* genus, many of them edible. The fungus has an infinite range of colors and it is easily confused with other species, both poisonous and edible. It can be difficult even for experts to distinguish them, so I would advise against collecting them unless you are in the company of a real expert.

It is a delicate mushroom with a cap that is red, yellow, green, or even pale blue and purple. It usually appears in deciduous woods during August and September. The field variety is usually white with a straight, hollow stem that can be either white, yellow, or a pinkish color. If you find it in a shop, check that it has been passed by the forestry authority for edibility, and prepare as for the *agarico delizioso*.

## COPRINO CHIOMATO / SHAGGY
MANE *Coprinus comatus*
This curious, but fairly common, fungus from the Agaricacae family grows from spring to fall in large clusters on rich soil and along

country lanes. It has a hollow stem and a shaggy oval cap, which is covered with a rash of brown spots. It is quite delicious, but should only be eaten when closed, as once it is fully open and ripe the gills turn black and the mushroom becomes inedible. In order to prevent the white gills from turning black once collected, pull off and discard the stem (which is not very useful anyway).

The shaggy mane is difficult to find in markets, but grows on pastures and hills all over Italy. It is delicious stewed in butter with scrambled eggs and parsley, but avoid drinking alcohol when you eat it as this could make you quite ill.

**ELATA, SEE SPUGNOLA**

**FAMIGLIOLA BUONA, SEE CHIODINO**

**FUNGO DI FÄROLA, SEE CARDONCELLO**

**FUNGO IMPERIALE, SEE AMANITA CESAREA**

**FUNGO OSTRICA, SEE PLEUROTO**

**GELONE, SEE PLEUROTO**

**GIALLA, SEE SPUGNOLA**

**LARICINO, SEE BOLETO ELEGANTE**

**LEPIOTA BRUNA, SEE MAZZA DI TAMBURO**

## LINGUA DI BUE /
BEEFSTEAK FUNGUS *Fistulina hepatica*
Each country names this fungus according to its impression of it, hence its Latin name means liver, its Italian name means ox tongue, and in English its name is beefsteak. Indeed, this fungus is generally known as "the poor man's steak."

*Lingua di bue* is a polypore, meaning that

the underside of the cap is made up of a vast number of pores. It is of the bracket variety of this genus, and grows like a shelf on old oak trees and occasionally old chestnut trees. Although the fungus feeds on the tree, in the case of the oak the fungus returns a resinous liquid which turns the tree's wood a reddish color, making it much sought-after by the furniture trade.

It grows from late summer to early fall and reaches up to 10 to 12 inches in diameter. Its flesh is dense, moist, and very heavy, with some mushrooms weighing around $4^1/_2$ pounds. The surface of the cap is sticky and dark red, while the underside is pinkish in color. When cut, it secretes a blood-like liquid which colors any sauce in which it is cooked.

I think the ideal way of cooking this fungus is to take the young mushroom, clean it thoroughly (it is not usually infested with worms), and slice it thin. Rub a pan with half a garlic clove, then add some butter and oil and melt the butter over moderate heat. Add the beefsteak fungus and fry for 5 minutes, then add a couple of spoonfuls of heavy cream, some salt, and some finely chopped fresh dill.

**LOFFA, SEE VESCIA MAGGIORE**

## MAZZA DI TAMBURO, LEPIOTA BRUNA /
PARASOL MUSHROOM
*Lepiota procera*
The Italian name for this mushroom means "drumstick," referring to the way the undeveloped mushroom looks like a ball attached to a long stick. When ripe, the cap can reach 8 inches in diameter on a thin stem of up to 12 inches in height, hence the English-language name, parasol.

The *mazza di tamburo* belongs to the

*Lepiota* genus, and thus has very thick gills, which are cream-colored, turning pinkish with age. The cap can be oval or round and is borne on a thin brownish stem. As the mushroom grows and the hat opens out, its woolly surface starts to flake from the top, sprinkling the brown skin with white. It is widespread from late summer through fall, growing singly or in very small groups under pines, in fields near woods, and sometimes on large lawns. There is a similar but much smaller mushroom that is poisonous—so take care to pick the right one.

The parasol must be checked carefully for worms before being sliced and sautéed or cooked in a variety of other ways. One of the best is the method used in Veneto, where this fungus is particularly popular. Beat together an egg, a little chopped parsley, and some pepper, then detach the open caps from the stems, dip them in the egg mixture, and fry them on both sides in a generous amount of olive oil and serve sprinkled with salt and a little lemon juice. An unusual use of the fibrous stems is to dry them, then grind the dried stems to an aromatic powder.

### ORECCHIETTA / WOOD EAR
*Auricularia auricula*
This mushroom gets its other English name, Judas Ears, from the fact that it usually grows on elder trees, the tree from which Judas Iscariot hung himself. The Italian name refers to the fact that it is shaped like a human ear. It is brown with a velvety texture on the surface, and is shiny inside. It grows in colonies, one above the other, throughout the year, and even in winter if the weather is mild and humid. It does not have pores or gills. Instead its spores are produced inside the mushroom and it propagates itself on the bark of the tree when the bark is wet.

It is much sought-after in China, where its gelatinous consistency is an integral ingredient in many stir-fried dishes. In Italy it does not see much use, although it is cooked *trifolati*, that is, sautéed in oil or butter with garlic, chili, and parsley. Make sure you cook it over low heat, though, as a pocket of hot vapor can build up inside the fungus and explode, splattering you with hot fat.

I have cooked it with great success in my restaurant, in tandem with honey mushrooms, in butter, stock, and brandy as a sauce for poached turbot. If you collect a large number, you can dry them and use them later, rehydrating them until they reach their original size. You can also buy them dried in specialist Asian food shops.

### OVOLO, SEE AMANITA CESAREA

### PINAIOLO, SEE BOLETO GIALLO

### PIOPPARELLO, PIOPPINO
*Pholiota aegerita*
This is as common as the honey mushroom and is enjoyed all over Italy, but especially in the South. It appears in the early spring and late fall on tree stumps of all types of tree, but especially the poplar and willow. Its flat head changes from brown to beige, but has a little more coloring in the middle. It is carried on a long, thin stem with a whitish ring around it. The beige gills are tightly packed and darken with age. It grows in groups called *famigliole* (small families) and is easy to collect and clean on the spot by cutting off three-quarters of the fibrous stem. The *piopparello* has recently been cultivated, so it can be found on sale all year round. These look very pretty in the market, as the little heads are still closed and dark brown, but they lack the flavor of the wild variety.

The *piopparello* has been used in Italian kitchens at least since the time of the Romans, and possibly even before. The best way of cooking it, however, remains almost exactly the same. In the South it is combined with tomatoes to make a pasta sauce, as well as cooked *trifolato*, that is, sautéed in oil with garlic, chili, and parsley. It also can be cooked in the same ways as the honey mushroom.

BELOW: *PLEUROTO*

### PLEUROTO, GELONE, FUNGO OSTRICA / TYPE OF OYSTER MUSHROOM *Pleurotus ostreatus*
This fungus is now commercially cultivated and can be found all year round on supermarket shelves packed in hygienic plastic trays—far from its natural habitat of decaying fallen trees and tree stumps, which give it a lovely aroma and more powerful flavor.

Like the *cardoncello*, it belongs to the large *Pleurotus* genus, the most common of which is the *ostreatus*, so-called because it resembles an oyster. It attaches itself to beech and elm trees—which it has the potential to destroy—forming numerous shelves. Given the right conditions of moisture and warmth, it can grow all year round, even in winter if the weather is mild. It is flat, with a short stem to the side attaching it to the tree. The stem itself is as sought-after as the fungus, which varies in color from dark gray, almost blue, to creamy gray.

There is a variety called *cornucopioide* (cornucopia), which is funnel-shaped and pale cream in

LEFT: *ORECCHIETTE*

color. The gills beneath the flat tongue are slightly gray, tending to yellow or cream.

The *pleuroto* is an excellent mushroom and is delicious dipped in beaten egg and bread crumbs then deep-fried, brushed with olive oil and then grilled over charcoal, and *trifolati* (briefly sautéed in olive oil with garlic, chili, parsley, and lemon juice), then served in a salad. It also responds well to preserving in numerous ways, from pickling to freezing.

## POLIPORO SOLFOROSO, POLLO DEL BOSCO / SULPHUR SHELF *Laetiporus sulphureus*

This magnificent fungus grows to an astonishing size and weight out of the bark of oak and willow trees. It is splendidly colored—sulphur-yellow on its underside and an orangey-yellow on top. It is very meaty and grows in shelves in groups of three, the top one reaching up to 16 inches in diameter and the whole group weighing several pounds.

It belongs to the Polypore group, which indicates the myriad pores that cover the underside of the fungus. These pores carry the spores, which form a white stain on the bark of the tree when the fungus is reaching maturity and becoming old and woody.

Some believe the *poliporo* is inedible, but I regularly serve it in my restaurant, sautéed with other mushrooms. It is only edible when just picked, preferably still dripping its pale juices. Also belonging to this family are the Umbrella Polypore and *Grifola frondosa*, which are only edible when small and tender. The slightly acidic but very tasty and tender, chicken-like flesh of the latter has gained it the name "hen of the woods."

## PORCINELLO GRIGIO, PORCINELLO ROSSO / BIRCH, ASPEN (RED-CAPPED) SCABERSTALK *Leccinum scabrum, L. insigne, L. aurantiacum*

The *porcinello rosso* (*Leccinum insigne, L. aurantiacum*) appears from July to early fall and belongs to the boletes, growing in symbiosis with birch trees, hence its English-language name. There are a few similar varieties, all of which are edible, although they all have a slightly different coloring and grow from conifers or oak trees. All members of this genus are bulky and fibrous, with a white stem covered with blackish-brown tints. The cap is an orange-red color, with one branch of the genus, the *porcinello grigio* (*L. scabrum*), tending to a darker gray/brown. The *grigio*, however, is not as firm or as tasty as the *rosso*.

Especially when growing straight from the ground around the roots of a tree, the young *porcinello rosso* has a phallus-like appearance. It has a stem of 2 inches in diameter and a height of up to 8 inches, with a white scaly surface surrounded by a round, tight, bright red cap. The cap later develops into a rather large and solid round of up to 8 inches in diameter, with very compact dark gray pores that fade with age.

It is sought-after for its very firm and solid flesh, which tends to discolor to bluish-pink when cut, and turn black while cooking. It is, however, definitely still edible, with a wonderfully crunchy texture. It is much-used in northern Italy, where it is abundant in the woods on the slopes of the pre-Alp valleys. It is seen as a culinary treat, much like *porcini*, although it cannot be eaten raw.

## PORCINO, CEPPATELLO, BULE, BRISA / CÈPE *Boletus edulis*

*Funghi* in Italy really means *porcino*, the king of all the edible mushrooms. Its popularity is the result of both its culinary usefulness and its looks. There are a number of varieties of this fungus from the Boletaceae family, and all but a few are excellent. The first one to avoid is *Tylopilus felleus*, which is so bitter it is inedible, and the second is *B. delus satanas*, which is both poisonous and ugly. The ones to seek out are the following:

*B. reticulatus*: appearing from early May to June, then again from August to September, its name comes from *rete*, meaning "net," because of the typical net-like pattern on its stem.

*B. pinicola*: in my opinion the best of all the *porcini* because of its dark chocolate-brown color, its extremely meaty cap, and solid stem. It appears from the end of summer through to fall, growing on common and red pines in coniferous woods.

RIGHT: *PORCINI*

*B. aureus*: often confused with the excellent *pinicola*, this is equally delicious. It is most common in the South, the best coming from Calabria, Sardinia, and Campania, where the climate is warm and oak trees are abundant. The more intense red-brown color of its cap differentiates it from other species of *Boletus*.

A common characteristic of these three varieties is that the spores start out creamy white, then turn from pale-green to dark green as the mushroom reaches maturity, and the cap opens to a diameter of up to 12 inches. The stem is bulky, even when the mushroom is small, which is why it has the name *porcino*, meaning "piglet."

An entire industry has grown up around this fungus, which sustains both commercial and cottage ventures because the demand for it

## DRIED MUSHROOMS

While most fungi and truffles are eaten fresh in season—prepared in any of hundreds of different ways according to ancient and local customs—out of season they are still available preserved. Dried mushrooms are mostly used in sauces, and are also used to boost the flavor of fresh mushroom dishes. Mushrooms are also preserved in oil, and these are traditionally eaten in *antipasto* like a pickle. The most recent means of preserving mushrooms is freezing them, and this conserves a great deal of their flavor, although the texture gets lost in the process. Frozen mushrooms are, however, still very good for sauces, soups, and stews.

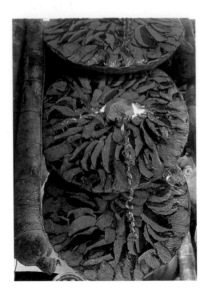

LEFT: DRIED MUSHROOMS

is so great. All are situated near the growing areas, so that the time between collection and transportation is as short as possible. The best source for the mushrooms is the hilly part of Emilia-Romagna, but they can also be found easily all over Piedmont, Lombardy, Veneto, and Trentino, Tuscany, Umbria, Lazio, Campania, Marche, Abruzzi, Calabria, the Altipiano della Sila, Basilicata, Puglia, and Sicily. They are also in evidence, although less prolific, in Emilia-Romagna and Sardinia. All these regions have developed industries that specialize in preserving the mushrooms, either by preserving them in oil or by drying them.

Because the demand is so high, *porcini* are also imported from countries as far away as Poland, Russia, Turkey, Romania, and Yugoslavia—even Morocco and Tunisia. However, these foreign introductions can never match the fragrance and flavor of the home-grown variety, so Italian families tend to preserve their own so that they can be sure of the quality.

In the kitchen, the *porcino* has a position of honor. When it is in season, specialist restaurants feature it cooked in many ways. The large, but still young, caps are always

grilled over charcoal, or cut in slices, dipped in beaten egg and bread crumbs, and then deep-fried. It is probably the only mushroom that stays creamy white even after cooking, and the texture and taste are unmatched. *Porcini trifolati* (see *orecchiette trifolate*, page 198) is a fantastic dish, but *porcini* are also wonderful in stews or soups, in sauces for pasta, or as an accompaniment for *polenta*, as well as in risottos, or as a side dish to meat and sometimes fish.

The smallest and firmest *porcini* make a wonderful salad. First clean and finely slice the *porcini*, then arrange them on a plate and sprinkle with extra-virgin olive oil, lemon juice, salt, and pepper, and serve with *grissini*. If you want to store them in the freezer, the best way is to cut them into slices about $\frac{1}{4}$ inch thick and sauté them with a little chopped onion and lots of butter for 10 minutes. Divide the mixture into small trays, allow it to cool, and freeze. When frozen, the butter will insulate the mushrooms from the ice.

### PRATAIOLO / MEADOW MUSHROOM *Agaricus campestris*

The common button mushroom is mainly commercially cultivated in dark humidity- and temperature-controlled rooms. The spores are mixed with sterilized straw and dung and spread over large trays. After 2 or 3 days they start to shoot and are cut by hand when they reach the required size. They are grown all year round, regardless of the season. This commercially produced mushroom, tasteless as it is, has many uses in the kitchen on a daily basis.

The wild version of the *prataiolo*, or meadow mushroom, which the French call *rose de pré* (field rose), is very delicate and enjoyable. It appears from August through November, growing close to the ground among short grass in pastureland, especially where there are horses.

The *prataiolo* is part of the *Agaricaceae* genus, which includes many other edible varieties that grow in very similar conditions. Among the best are *Agaricus sylvicola*, which grows among conifers, and the silvery white *A. macrosporus*, which prefers high-altitude pastureland and has a ring or skirt around the stem and pinkish gills that darken with age. Another mushroom in the family, which has been successfully cultivated, is *A. bisporus*, which can grow a cap up to 4 inches in diameter and is slightly brown on top. The largest in the group is *A. arvensis*, or horse mushroom, which is a real giant—

LEFT: *PRATAIOLI*

growing a cap of up to 12 inches in diameter, with the same ring around the stem and the typical pink gills that turn almost black with age.

If you pick any of these mushrooms yourself, take care to avoid the very similar *Agaricus xanthodermus*, which has the same white color, ring or skirt around the stem, and the same pink gills. As its English name, "yellow stainer," indicates, however, it colors yellow when touched. You can also spot it by the yellow stain at the base of the stem. One of the reasons it is important not to cut mushrooms, but instead to twist them gently, without pulling up the mycelium, or root, is that this allows you to check stem details.

Meadow mushrooms are very versatile in the kitchen and have a wide range of uses, from raw in salads to sautéed in butter, in an omelet, or *al funghetto* (pan-fried with garlic and parsley). The only thing I would never do is peel them, otherwise all the taste is lost; instead, wipe them with a damp cloth and cut away the earthy or sandy base with a knife.

**RIGHT: *SPUGNOLI***

## PRUGNOLO / ST GEORGE'S MUSHROOM *Lyophyllum georgii, Tricholoma gambosum*

This is one of the earliest mushrooms to appear and for this reason is called St. George's mushroom in England, because it usually makes its first appearance around the 23rd of April, St. George's day. It grows on old pastureland that has not been disturbed by cultivation for many years, and has a tendency to grow in a circle like the *gambe secche*, fairy-ring champignons. In fact, they often share the same ring because the mycelium, or root, spreads in a circle beneath the earth, thereby expanding the diameter every year.

Another of its names, *gambosum* (like a big leg), refers to its tight bulky stem thinning towards the top, where it carries a compact cap. It is off-white in color, with dense flesh, and has a slightly flowery scent and a very subtle flavor. It is

an excellent mushroom, and can be found in large numbers.

To find it, look for circles of dark green, as this is one of the best indicators that the mushrooms are hidden in the grass, allowing them to be spotted at a distance. It mostly grows on the slopes of the hilly pre-Alps or in lush fields, and is mostly used in the North of Italy. It is delicious sautéed in butter with a little garlic and some chopped parsley or chives, in tomato sauces to dress pasta, or parboiled and then dressed with extra-virgin olive oil and lemon or plum *aspretto* (vinegar) in a salad.

In the US, the only species of the *Tricholoma* genus that is considered safely edible is *flavovireus*, but this is often difficult to distinguish from poisonous varieties.

## SPUGNOLA, GIALLA, ELATA / BLACK, COMMON MOREL *Morchella conica, M. esculenta*

This is a fairly sophisticated mushroom and, although it is not as popular as others in domestic kitchens, it is much used and loved by professional chefs and connoisseurs—the only exception is in Emilia-Romagna where no such division exists. One of the reasons for the uncertainty about its pedigree could be the fact that it belongs to a family of mushrooms that includes potentially poisonous varieties. Some are poisonous when raw, but are perfectly safe when cooked, but *Gyromitra esculenta* is very poisonous even after it has been cooked.

The curious sponge-like texture and unusual taste of the morel make it highly prized, especially in France. The first of the three main varieties of morel is the *Morchella conica*, which has a small, conical

cap made up of a dark brown, honeycombed or spongy flesh. Varying from 2 inches to as much as 6 inches in height, its stem is white and it grows in mixed scrubland or hills near pine woods, where the soil is fairly bare. Because it is hollow inside, it sometimes collects stones or pine needles as it grows. Unlike true mushrooms, morels belong to the Ascomycetes family, producing spores inside the spongy cells, called asci. The second of the three varieties is the *M. esculenta*, which is very similar to the *conica* except that the spongy cap is slightly lighter in color, making it more highly valued by the cook than its darker counterpart. The third member of the family, is the toxic *Gyromitra esculenta*, which differs from the other two in having a more irregularly shaped dark brown cap. As all three are so similar, be sure to get the advice of an expert to avoid picking the poisonous one. If you buy your morels, however, you can be sure that they will be the right ones.

Morels in particular need to be thoroughly cleaned to get rid of the stones and earth they collect inside their caps. The best method is to blanch them in hot water for a minute, as this washes away not only the dirt but also any latent toxins. Since it is hollow, the morel is ideal for stuffing, but is also delicious in sauces for pasta, in risottos, with scrambled eggs, and as an accompaniment for game and poultry. One of the most useful features of the morel is that it can be dried very successfully and, once rehydrated, it returns to its original shape and size.

## STECCHERINO DORATO / SPREADING HEDGEHOG *Hydnum repandum*

This mushroom is one of the

oddities of nature, a wonderful fungus that has neither gills nor pores and does not belong the Ascomycetes family either. Instead it has spikes underneath its cap, which produce spores—hence its Italian name *steccherino*, from *stecchi*, meaning "little sticks," and *dorato*, meaning "gilded," and its English-language name "hedgehog."

It grows from summer through to fall in moist, shady places, under trees in woods where there is short grass or moss. It can be bought from markets in northern and central Italy. The cap is pale orange, irregularly shaped, and quite meaty. The stems are also very uneven, with tight and very fragile spikes running from the cap to the base. These spikes are only loosely attached and fall off if touched. The flesh, which is slightly paler than the color of skin, is similar to that of chanterelles, and can be cooked in the same way.

## Tartufo / TRUFFLE *Tuber aestivum, T. melanosporum, T. magnatum pico*

Ancient Romans used to think that this subterranean fungus, called a tuber, which grows under or in the proximity of trees was the fruit of

lightning. They could not find any other explanation for something so delicious that even pigs were inebriated by it. For centuries afterward, the truffle has been considered unlike other fungi, a food that only cultured people could enjoy. Indeed, the aura surrounding this fungus has been so elevated that it has become an elitist food to be enjoyed only by those with money. In Italy, however, even with the high prices, almost every Italian eats truffle at least once a year, even if it is only a few shavings on a plate of pasta.

There are three varieties of truffle, all belonging to the same genus:

**Tartufo bianco,** *Tuber magnatum pico* (white Alba truffle)
The Lange area of Piedmont is the capital of the white truffle, or Alba, as it is known in Italy. Although it also grows in Emilia-Romagna, the Marche, Umbria, Tuscany, and Calabria, these cannot compare with the Piedmontese Alba, with its intensely pungent scent. Because it is the best and most sought-after truffle, it is also the most expensive, costing up to 5,000,000 lire or $4,000 per kilo.

It is only eaten raw, thinly shaved with a special cutter called a *mandolino*, and lightly sprinkled over a dish to give a hint of its precious flavor. Indeed, it is so intense that if placed in a refrigerator its scent will impregnate all the food in it. I store white truffle in the cellar with fresh free-range eggs, so that after a day or so the eggs will have absorbed so much of the

aroma that they will taste of truffle.

Along with the majority of recipes for truffle, a cheese dish has been developed in Piedmont—where the truffle is king—known as *fonduta*, a sort of creamy hot mixture of egg, milk, and *fontina* cheese over which truffle is shaved before the whole mixture is scooped up with bread, like a Swiss fondue. Other classic preparations for truffle include risottos, pasta like *tagliolini*, baked or fried eggs, raw beef salads, and *porcini* salads. Truffle is also used to flavor oils (see page 217) and butter,

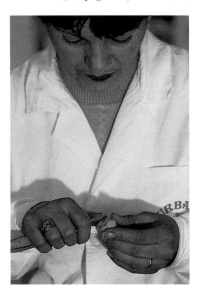

as well as to make truffle cream for *crostini* and, indeed, any other savory dish you might want to try it with.

**Tartufo nero di Norcia** or **invernale,** *Tuber melanosporum* (winter, black, or Périgord truffle)
This tuber grows from winter to late spring in Umbria and specifically around Norcia, as well as in Piedmont, Emilia-Romagna, and Calabria. A similar truffle can be found in Campania around Bagnoli Irpimia, but unfortunately it has a

LEFT: WHITE TRUFFLES PRESERVED IN BRINE

LEFT: DORIANA CLEANING TRUFFLES

FAR LEFT: *TARTUFI BIANCHI D'ALBA*

strong smell of carbolic acid and is therefore not sought-after (although it is consumed by the locals).

The *melanosporum* has much smoother skin than its summer counterpart, but it is its scent and taste for which it is valued. It is hunted by trained dogs (mostly mongrels), who are rewarded with biscuits. In the past, pigs were used to track down truffles, but pigs were so fond of them that it was difficult for the truffle hunter to persuade them not to eat the truffle.

It has recently been discovered that it is possible to encourage cultivation of truffles by impregnating the roots of selected young oak trees with the spores. It still takes ten to twelve years before the truffles can be collected though, a long time to wait and remember where the truffle should be growing. Despite this innovation to increase production, the prices remain high, as demand escalates beyond what nature is capable of supplying.

The black truffle can be used shaved like the white truffle, but it is mostly used in sauces, pâtés, and dishes *en croûte*, to keep the maximum flavor. In Umbria, they cook it chopped in butter as a sauce for pasta.

**Scorzone,** *Tuber aestivum* (summer truffle)
Called *scorzone* (bark-like) in Italian because of its tough, warty black skin, this tuber grows harmoniously on the roots of trees like chestnuts, beeches, and hazelnuts. It first appears in the early summer and

continues until late winter. One of the main problems with this truffle, as with all others, is that it is difficult to find, and then only by dogs. However, it does sometimes grow near the surface so that its knobbly skin and other protuberances extend above the soil. The skin has pyramidal warts, but its flesh is creamy, maturing to brown with white veins. Due to its poor scent and taste it does not have a great commercial value. This poor cousin among truffles is often used in tandem with truffle oil to boost its flavor.

### TROMBETTA DEI MORTI, CRATERELLO /
#### HORN OF PLENTY
*Craterellus cornucopioides*
The macabre Italian name *trombetta dei morti*, meaning "trumpet of death," is a poor indicator of the beauty and flavor of this funnel-shaped, thin, and fragile fungus. Black on the inside and grayish black outside, it is very delicate and grows only an inch or so high. It is easy to find, though, as it grows prolifically in little groups in mixed woods and on almost bare ground from summer to fall.

To clean it, cut away the base of the fungus until you can see through the funnel to any trapped leaves and insects. It can then be sautéed gently in butter and used to accompany steamed fish, especially a dish of

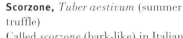

poached fillet of sole, where its black color and delicate scent and flavor give the most dramatic contrast to the white fish. It is popular with professional chefs and can be used in the same way as the chanterelle.

### VESCIA MAGGIORE, LOFFA /
#### GIANT PUFFBALL *Calvatia gigantea* (sometimes *Langermannia*)

This is perhaps the biggest of all the fungi, growing up to 2 feet in diameter. Of all the members of the puffball family, which include the pear-shaped *Lycoperdon pyriforme*, the pearly-surfaced *L. perlatum*, and many others, most of which are edible, the giant puffball is the most satisfying because, if in good condition, its firm white flesh will feed an entire family.

It can be found among nettles, in pastureland, and sometimes in woods and even flower borders—I once found one in Hyde Park in London, hidden among the flowering shrubs. It grows from summer to fall, depending on the weather. It is usually attached to a single root that you should take care not to damage when you pick it. If it very fresh and young it gives a satisfying deep, hollow sound when tapped gently with your fingers. Be careful to avoid the inedible common earthball (*Sceroderma citrinum*), which is often found on footpaths.

It can be used in many ways, including cut in cubes and sautéed in butter, or sliced then dipped in egg and bread crumbs and fried, or, as I like it, cut in large slices or simply in half, brushed with garlic-flavored olive oil, and grilled over charcoal for a couple of minutes on each side, then served sprinkled with salt and finely chopped parsley.

# TAJARIN AL TARTUFO
## TAGLIERINI PASTA WITH TRUFFLE

**FOR 8**

1³/₄ POUNDS FRESH OR DRIED *TAJARIN*
PASTA (SMALL RIBBONS ABOUT
¹/₈ INCH WIDE)

SALT

9 TABLESPOONS BUTTER

3 OUNCES WHITE ALBA TRUFFLE, CUT
INTO SHAVINGS

3 OUNCES PARMESAN CHEESE, GRATED

¹/₂ GARLIC CLOVE

*The simpler the better, they say. This is not only better, it scores high for simplicity and sophistication.*

Cook the pasta in a large pot of boiling salted water until *al dente*.

Meanwhile, rub a skillet with the halved garlic clove. Put the butter and a few truffle shavings in the pan and heat gently.

Drain the pasta, reserving a little of the cooking water. Add the pasta to the butter and truffle, mixing well, then add salt to taste. Stir in some of the pasta cooking water if the mixture is too dry. Add the Parmesan cheese, mix well, and serve topped with the remaining truffle shavings. Serve immediately.

# PORCINI SOTT'OLIO
## PORCINI IN OIL

**MAKES ENOUGH TO FILL TWO
1¹/₂-PINT JARS**

3¹/₄ POUNDS VERY FRESH, FIRM,
YOUNG *BOLETUS EDULIS* MUSHROOMS

9 CUPS STRONG (6%) VERY GOOD-
QUALITY WHITE WINE VINEGAR

4¹/₂ CUPS WATER

4 TABLESPOONS SALT

10 FRESH BAY LEAVES

10 CLOVES

20 BLACK PEPPERCORNS

1 CHILI PEPPER

GOOD OLIVE OIL (NOT VIRGIN)

*The art of pickling mushrooms so they can be eaten out of season is widespread in Italy. Almost every family makes at least one jar to be saved for grand occasions such as Christmas. They are served as part of an* antipasto *and people don't mind the vinegary taste, which overpowers most of the initial mushroom flavor.*

*I must stress that when preserving mushrooms at home it is important to take precautions against botulism, a deadly bacteria which can develop in the center of food that has not been properly cooked or preserved. Vinegar and salt are ideal preserving agents and I devised this recipe using both to ensure perfect preservation. Home preserving is subject to variations, however, so I cannot assume responsibility for any unfortunate little incidents. But my friends and I are still alive and enjoying fungi!*

Thoroughly wash the preserving jars and dry them in a low oven. Scrupulously clean the mushrooms to remove all the impurities (see page 185). Cut them open to check for worms. Cut any large *porcini* in half so they are all the same size.

Put the vinegar, water, salt, bay leaves, cloves, peppercorns, and chili in a pan and bring to a boil. Add the mushrooms and cook for 20 minutes from the moment the mixture comes back to a boil, then drain. Put the mushrooms on a very clean linen cloth and under no circumstances touch them with your hands. Using a sterilized spoon, put the mushrooms (without the bay leaves and spices) in the sterilized jars so that they are quite tightly packed but not pressed down. Pour in enough olive oil to cover the mushrooms by ¹/₂ inch, making sure it reaches every surface of the mushrooms. Seal the jars tightly. The *porcini* will keep like this for a month but should be refrigerated once opened.

OPPOSITE: *TAJARIN AL TARTUFO*

# FUNGHI CONCIATI
## CURED MIXED WILD MUSHROOMS

FOR 4

1¼ POUNDS MIXED WILD MUSHROOMS

4 TABLESPOONS WHITE WINE VINEGAR

SALT

½ CUP EXTRA-VIRGIN OLIVE OIL

2 GARLIC CLOVES, SLICED

1 CHILI PEPPER, FINELY CHOPPED

2 TABLESPOONS FINELY CHOPPED FLAT-
LEAF PARSLEY

*For this recipe a good mixture of whatever you find in the market—or in the woods if you are a knowledgeable mushroom lover— will do. Chanterelles, meadow mushrooms, hedgehog, and oyster mushrooms are all welcome.*

Carefully clean the mushrooms (see page 185) and cut any large ones in half. Bring a large pot of water to a boil with the vinegar and 1 tablespoon salt per 1 quart water. Add the mushrooms and boil for 8 to 10 minutes, then drain and leave to cool.

Heat the oil in a pan, add the garlic and chili, and fry gently for a minute or two without letting the garlic brown. Add the mushrooms, stir well, then add the parsley and salt to taste. Serve cold as a salad or appetizer, or with cold meats.

# CAPRETTO AI CARDONCELLI
## BAKED KID WITH *CARDONCELLI*

FOR 6

1 POUND *CARDONCELLI* MUSHROOMS

½ CUP EXTRA-VIRGIN OLIVE OIL

1 LARGE ONION, FINELY SLICED

1 CHILI PEPPER, COARSELY CHOPPED

1 LEG OF KID, WEIGHING ABOUT
3¼ POUNDS, CUT INTO CHUNKS

FLOUR FOR DREDGING

1 POUND RIPE TOMATOES OR 2 CUPS
*POLPA DI POMODORO* (SEE PAGE **118**)

1 SPRIG ROSEMARY

1 SMALL SPRIG WILD MARJORAM

SALT

*This recipe is from Apulia, where both kid and mushrooms are commonly available in season.* Cardoncelli *can be replaced by oyster mushrooms or shiitake.*

Preheat the oven to 350° F. Carefully clean the mushrooms (see page 185) and cut any large ones in half.

Heat the oil in a casserole and gently fry the onion and chili until the onion is translucent. Dredge the meat in flour, add to the oil, and brown on all sides. Stir in the mushrooms and cook gently for 10 minutes, then add the tomatoes, rosemary, marjoram, and salt to taste. Cover the casserole with a lid, transfer to the oven, and bake for 45 minutes, until the meat is tender.

# ORECCHIETTE TRIFOLATE
## WOOD EARS SAUTÉED WITH GARLIC AND PARSLEY

FOR 4

14 OUNCES FRESH WOOD EAR
MUSHROOMS

4 TABLESPOONS BUTTER

1 GARLIC CLOVE, FINELY CHOPPED

1 SMALL CHILI PEPPER, FINELY CHOPPED

½ CUP CHICKEN STOCK

2 TABLESPOONS COARSELY CHOPPED
FLAT-LEAF PARSLEY

SALT

*These mushrooms are also called Judas ears, from the Latin* Auricola judae. *They are remarkable gelatinous fungi, growing mostly on old elder trees. If you cannot find fresh ones, you can rehydrate the dried version. This is available from Chinese food stores and is known as black fungus.*

Carefully clean the mushrooms (see page 185) and cut any large ones in half.

Put the butter in a pan with the garlic and chili. Allow it to melt and then add the mushrooms. Stir-fry for 1 minute, then add the stock and cook gently for 15 minutes or until most of the liquid has evaporated. Stir in the parsley and salt to taste; serve either as an appetizer or as an accompaniment to chicken or game.

# CAPPELLE DI FUNGHI ALLA GRIGLIA
## BROILED PORCINI TOPS WITH GARLIC

1 LARGE *PORCINO* MUSHROOM PER
PERSON

GARLIC CLOVES, CUT INTO THIN STRIPS

OLIVE OIL

SALT

CHOPPED FLAT-LEAF PARSLEY

Remove the stems from the mushrooms and discard. Make small incisions in the mushroom caps and insert the strips of garlic. Drizzle with olive oil and place under a hot broiler for about 10 minutes, until tender. Sprinkle with salt and chopped parsley, then serve.

# INSALATA DI DUE TUBERI

TWO-TUBER SALAD

**FOR 4**

1¼ POUNDS WAXY POTATOES
1½ OUNCES WHITE ALBA TRUFFLE
SALT AND PEPPER
EXTRA-VIRGIN OLIVE OIL

*The potato is a tuber in its own right, whereas the truffle is actually a fungus but is also called a tuber—in this case* Magnatum pico, *the white Alba truffle.*

Peel the potatoes and boil them until tender but still quite firm. Slice thinly and place on a serving dish. Drizzle some olive oil over, season with salt and pepper and then shave the white truffle over the potatoes. Serve immediately.

# OVOLI IN INSALATA CON TARTUFO
## SALAD OF CAESAR'S MUSHROOMS WITH TRUFFLES

FOR 4

6 STILL-CLOSED (IN THE SHAPE OF AN
  EGG) CAPS OF *OVOLI* (*AMANITA
  CAESAREA*) MUSHROOMS
1$^1/_2$ OUNCES PARMESAN CHEESE, IN ONE
  PIECE
$^1/_3$ CUP OLIVE OIL
JUICE OF $^1/_2$ LEMON
SALT AND PEPPER
1$^1/_2$ OUNCES WHITE ALBA TRUFFLE,
  BRUSHED AND READY TO BE SLICED

*I include this recipe with the knowledge that you will find it difficult to find
the two main ingredients outside Italy. The* ovolo (Amanita caesarea) *and the
white truffle are both in season in Italy from September through October and
only very good restaurants offer this rather sophisticated but wonderfully
simple dish. Serve as an appetizer with* grissini.

Clean the mushrooms with a knife and rub them with a wet cloth if they are still
dirty. Cut the mushrooms into very thin slices directly onto each serving plate,
displaying the beautiful orange color and the shape of the gills. Shave the
Parmesan on top very thinly.

Mix together the olive oil, lemon juice, and salt and pepper to taste to make a
dressing and pour it over the salad. Finally, shave the Alba truffle on top and
enjoy a dish fit for kings! (Julius Caesar was very fond of this mushroom.)

# FINFERLI AL LIQUORE
## CHANTERELLES PRESERVED IN SWEET VERMOUTH

MAKES ENOUGH TO FILL A
1$^1/_2$-PINT JAR

2$^1/_4$ POUNDS FRESH CHANTERELLE
  MUSHROOMS
4$^1/_2$ CUPS SWEET VERMOUTH
SMALL CINNAMON STICK
PINCH SALT
2 TABLESPOONS SUPERFINE SUGAR
APRICOT LIQUEUR

*This recipe is for mushroom fanatics who would have mushrooms even for
dessert. Well, here is an idea which can serve as a decoration for* panna cotta,
tiramisu, *and other cream-based desserts. The best chanterelles to use for this
preserve are very firm and not too large. Bear in mind, however, that they
reduce in volume by half when cooked.*

Carefully clean the mushrooms (see page 185). Put the vermouth in a pan with
the cinnamon, salt, and sugar and bring to a boil. Add the mushrooms and keep
them pressed down with a wooden spoon to ensure they are submerged in the
liquid. Boil for 15 minutes or a little longer if necessary, depending on size. They
must be completely cooked; taste one to see if it is cooked in the middle.

Drain the mushrooms (the vermouth, unfortunately, has to be discarded) and
use a spoon to put them on a very clean cloth to cool and dry. Try not to touch
them with your hands (to avoid bacteria). Put them in a sterilized preserving jar
with a sterilized spoon, pressing them down gently with the spoon. Pour in
enough apricot liqueur to cover the mushrooms completely and then seal the jar.

Once opened, keep them refrigerated and always under liquid. Use just a few
to decorate desserts.

# CROSTINI AI FUNGHI

MUSHROOM CROSTINI

**FOR 4**

1 POUND MUSHROOMS (SEE RIGHT)
4 TABLESPOONS BUTTER
1 GARLIC CLOVE, CRUSHED
4 SAGE LEAVES
2 TABLESPOONS *VIN SANTO* OR
   EQUIVALENT WINE (NOT TOO SWEET)
SALT AND PEPPER
1 TABLESPOON COARSELY CHOPPED
   FLAT-LEAF PARSLEY
8 SLICES *PANE DI CAMPAGNA*
   (COUNTRY-STYLE WHITE BREAD),
   TOASTED

*Porcini mushrooms or other boleti such as bay or birch, are best for this recipe, but a mixture of these would do. You could also use cultivated mushrooms with the addition of dried porcini for flavor.*

Carefully clean the mushrooms (see page 185) and then chop them finely. Melt the butter in a pan, add the garlic and the sage leaves, and fry gently for 2 minutes. Add the mushrooms and sauté, stirring from time to time, until they are tender and most of their moisture has evaporated. Add the wine and salt and pepper to taste and stir-fry for a couple of minutes. Stir in the parsley and spread the mixture on the toasted bread.

# ZUPPA DI FINFERLI CON CANEDERLI

CHANTERELLE SOUP WITH DUMPLINGS

**FOR 4**

5 OUNCES SMALL, FRESHLY PICKED
   CHANTERELLE MUSHROOMS
1 SMALL SHALLOT, FINELY CHOPPED
2 TABLESPOONS BUTTER
6¼ CUPS CHICKEN STOCK
1 SMALL BUNCH CHIVES

FOR THE DUMPLINGS:
2½ CUPS FRESH WHITE BREAD CRUMBS
3 EGG YOLKS
2 TABLESPOONS FINELY CHOPPED
   FLAT-LEAF PARSLEY
2 OUNCES PARMESAN CHEESE, GRATED
1 SLICE *SPECK* (SEE PAGE 84), CUT
   INTO STRIPS, THEN INTO VERY
   SMALL CUBES
SALT AND PEPPER

*This typical South Tyrolean or Alto Adige recipe reflects the Austrian culinary influence. The dumplings may be varied but are usually based on dried bread crumbs and egg. Here they accompany chanterelles in a delicate broth.*

To make the dumplings, mix the bread crumbs with the egg yolks, parsley, Parmesan cheese, *speck*, and some salt and pepper to give a pliable consistency. Shape them into balls the size of large olives.

Carefully clean the mushrooms (see page 185) and cut any large ones in half. Sauté the shallot in the butter and as soon as it starts to color add the chanterelles. Sauté for 5 minutes, then add the stock and bring to a boil. Add the dumplings to the boiling soup. Simmer for 5 minutes and then serve topped with the chives, cut into small tubes with scissors.

# FUNGHI IN TEGAME

SAUTÉED WILD MUSHROOMS

## FOR 4

1³/4 POUNDS MIXED WILD MUSHROOMS
SUCH AS CÈPES, CHANTERELLES, HORN
OF PLENTY, BAY BOLETES, SHAGGY
MANE, OYSTER MUSHROOMS

3 TABLESPOONS BUTTER

2 TABLESPOONS EXTRA-VIRGIN OLIVE OIL

1 GARLIC CLOVE, FINELY CHOPPED

1 SMALL CHILI PEPPER, FINELY CHOPPED

SALT

2 TABLESPOONS COARSELY CHOPPED
FLAT-LEAF PARSLEY

*Whether you are a knowledgeable fungi gatherer or buy them in specialized shops, you can use any sort of wild mushroom for this dish. Sometimes I cook ten different varieties and the result is always stunning because of the wonderful combination of flavors. Serve sautéed mushrooms alone as an appetizer, with scrambled eggs, or as a side dish to accompany meat or poultry.*

Clean the mushrooms by scrubbing them with a small, soft brush. Don't wash or peel them unless absolutely necessary. Cut them into bite-sized pieces.

Heat the butter and oil in a large skillet and briefly fry the garlic and chili. Add the mushrooms and stir-fry over high heat. Once they begin to soften, add salt to taste and the parsley and serve immediately.

# OILS, VINEGARS, HERBS, SPICES & FLAVORINGS

## OLI, ACETI, ERBE, SPEZIE E SAPORI

Whenever I travel abroad, the first place I visit in any town or village is the marketplace, because it reveals so much about the gastronomic life of any area or culture. In some of the countries that I have visited, like India, Bali, Turkey, Egypt, and Morocco, the spice markets are separate from those selling other food products. I do not fully understand the subtleties of the combinations of the spices in the recipes from these countries, but it seems to me that certain flavors predominate. In Indian food it seems to be cumin, while in Chinese cooking it is soy sauce and ginger, and in Thai cooking, lemongrass, cilantro, and chili. If I had to classify the central flavors of Italian cooking in the same way, I would have to say garlic and basil, with some rosemary and oregano.

Spices used to be called *droghe* (drugs) in Italy, because medicines, like spices, were also made from the seeds, flowers, and berries of plants, and used to be sold in *drogherie* (drugstores *cum* grocers) which specialized in *coloniali*,

products originating in the colonies. Spices first came to Europe from India and China many centuries ago. Italian cuisine, however, seems to have concentrated more on the herbs and spices grown domestically, allowing the exceptions of cinnamon, nutmeg, and cloves. Other spices like saffron have adapted to the climate and are grown in Italy, even if it is not their natural home.

Salt is probably the most used flavor enhancer and preservative in cooking. It is an essential ingredient in almost every kitchen. It was once so valuable in Italy that it was handled by the government and was sold exclusively at tobacconists, along with tobacco and quinine (when malaria was common in Italy). In fact, the English word "salary" comes from the practice of the ancient Romans paying their soldiers with salt. Salt is mostly produced in Trapani, Sicily, by the evaporation of seawater. Today, sea salt is sold in its traditional coarse form, as well as in more refined varieties so it

can be poured onto food rather than ground over it or added in its crystal form.

The most common companion to salt is, of course, pepper. As well as being ground into a almost everything we eat, it is also used whole or crushed. Today, pink and green peppercorns have become fashionable. Despite their popularity, though, it is black peppercorns that are still the most often used, and these are among the most valued spices in Italian cooking.

Rosemary and sage are also commonly used all over Italy and are even sold—or even given away—by some butchers along with particular cuts of meat. Many Roman dishes include rosemary along with mint. The Neapolitan zucchini dish, *zucchini alla scapece*, would be nothing without fresh mint (and garlic). In spring, Sicily produces a lot of wild fennel, which is mainly used in *pasta con le sarde* (see page 166). Fennel seeds are also frequently used throughout the whole of the South of Italy, sometimes being added to sausages to make the Tuscan specialty *finocchiona*. They are also used with good olive oil in the South to make *taralli*, little round, crunchy savory crackers to accompany *antipasti* instead of bread.

*Peperoncino*, hot chili pepper, is a popular spice in southern Italy and Calabria in particular. There, it is used in the simple but delicious *pasta all'arrabbiata* (with tomatoes, chili, and garlic) and *aglio, olio, e peperoncino* (garlic, oil, and chili), and in stews and sausages, as well as salami—a tradition also shared by Campania and Puglia.

The Italian classics, however, are still basil and garlic, which, with the addition of pine nuts, Parmesan, and extra-virgin olive oil, make the famous pesto sauce. Basil and tomatoes, another

traditional combination of flavors, whether raw or cooked, is hard to beat. Of the other herbs used in Italian cooking, parsley is the most widely used and has a central role in *salsa verde* (see page 224), a sauce that has become very fashionable abroad, much like *rucola*, or wild arugula, which has become a central ingredient in today's green salads, although it is also eaten on its own, with tomatoes, and as a component in various types of *carpaccio*. *Foglie di sedano* (celery leaves) are used to add a marvelous aroma to chicken or beef *brodo*, and in various types of summer salads.

Oregano is perhaps the most misused herb outside Italy, because although it is associated with Italian cooking, it is not often used in the same dishes abroad as it is in Italy. Italians use spices and herbs to improve good-quality ingredients, while cooks in countries where the natural ingred-ients are not of such a high quality use the powerful flavor of oregano to hide or pep up flavors.

Of the other flavorings used in Italian cooking, the most important are the oils and vinegars—and of the oils, the one that epitomizes Italian cooking is olive oil. The olive was first cultivated in Iran

TOP LEFT: AN OLIVE GROVE IN LIGURIA

LEFT: MARIA, A CALABRIAN WOMAN, SETS HER HARVEST OF CHILIES TO DRY IN THE SUN

**ABOVE: THE**
***SECOLARI—***
**THOUSAND-YEAR-**
**OLD OLIVE TREES**
**IN THE GROUNDS**
**OF THE MASSERIA**
**SAN DOMENICO,**
**PUGLIA**

about 5,000 years ago, and from there spread to Italy. The climatic conditions in Italy mean that the olives grown there produce very fine olive oil and Italy is one of the largest producers of it, second only to Spain. Italian olive oil, is subject to strict legislation to guarantee its quality and purity. Olive oil's international status has recently been secured by the recognition that it is one of the most beneficial fats available, even helping to keep blood cholesterol levels low. A major contributor to the Mediterranean diet, it is used in the southern European countries as butter is used in the North. Italians have in their larders at least two types of olive oil—virgin for dressing salads, and an ordinary olive oil for sauces and other cooking—together with one seed-oil for frying.

The other indispensable condiment is vinegar, which is mostly made from wine, but has more recently begun to be made from anything containing alcohol, including cider and beer. All this is only possible thanks to a bacterium called *acetobacter aceti*, which when introduced into the beverage transforms the alcohol into vinegar. As well as being delicious in salad dressings, vinegar gives a distinctive flavor to marinades, and like salt, sugar, and alcohol, makes an excellent preservative. Vinegar can be used to pickle a large number of vegetables, including artichokes, mushrooms, eggplants, zucchini, tomatoes, sun-dried tomatoes, peppers, asparagus, and many others, to make wonderful additions to the classic Italian *antipasto*.

# A-Z OF OILS, VINEGARS, HERBS, SPICES & FLAVORINGS

### ACETO / VINEGAR

Vinegar is produced by a bacteria called *acetobacter aceti*, which turns alcohol into acetic acid. A lot of oxygen is needed to aid this process, which is why a bottle of low-alcohol wine left open turns quite quickly into vinegar. In Italy a good vinegar has, by law, to have a minimum of 6% acetic acid and a maximum of 1.5% alcohol residue. Vinegar can also be produced using a colony of bacterial fungi, called a mother, which looks like a gelatinous mass and builds up on the bottom of vinegar-making containers.

Vinegar has various uses in the kitchen, mainly to preserve food. A vinegar with 6% acidity is strong enough to preserve vegetables and fruit, although it does have the disadvantage of leaving behind a strong flavor, which either needs to be washed off or watered down, or the food needs to be stored in oil after being cooked in the vinegar. Vinegar can also be used in small quantities to sharpen sauces, or in marinades for fish and meat. More unusually, there are parts of Italy where vinegar is poured over strawberries with sugar to lift the flavor, and where it is added to water and sugar to make a refreshing summer drink.

### ACETO BALSAMICO / BALSAMIC VINEGAR

This special vinegar was once used to cure illness, hence its name. *balsamico*, meaning "like a balm." It is probably the most expensive vinegar in the world, partly because of the complex and lengthy process needed to make and mature it, and partly because only a small quantity is produced each year. *Aceto Balsamico Tradizionale di Modena* is the name given to the only genuine balsamic vinegar, brewed by 30 or 40 families in the Modena area who only produce 8,000 liters a

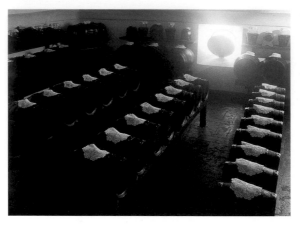

year. Together, these families form the *Consorzio*, a special association that safeguards the quality of the vinegar. It is sold at a high price in small, specially designed bottles, each containing only 10 cl, and should have been aged for at least thirty years.

It is made by reducing the must of the white Trebbiano grape until it achieves a deep brown color and syrupy consistency called *saba*. This liquid is poured into open-topped oak barrels and left to mature in well-ventilated attics, where the seasonal extremes of cold and heat encourage the evaporation of the vinegar, concentrating the flavors. The reduced liquid is transferred, using a process called *solera*, into successively smaller barrels each year of the maturing process. The first is made of chestnut wood, the next smaller barrel is made of cherry wood, the third of ash, then one of mulberry. This cycle is repeated until the vinegar has been aged for the requisite period. Some vinegars are aged for up to fifty years, to become rich and treacle-like. The batteries of barrels used are precious components of the estates of the producing families, and are accordingly traditionally left to the eldest son.

Due to the explosion in demand for balsamic vinegar, an inferior product also called *aceto balsamico di Modena*, but without the all-important *Tradizionale* label, has been created. This second-class version, however, is still quite good, having been aged for a minimum of

5 years and sometimes up to 10, 15, or even 20 years for the best. If you want to be sure of the quality, depend on the price for guidance; the cheapest can be no more than a normal vinegar with burnt sugar syrup added for coloring. Try to spot the differences.

Balsamic vinegar can be used for marinades, for brushing foods to be grilled, or to make vinaigrettes for salads or to add to sauces. I like just to savor it by itself in small quantities—a few drops are excellent on a piece of fresh Parmesan or on boiled vegetables or steamed lobster.

### ACETO DI FRUTTA, ASPRETTO DI FRUTTA / FRUIT VINEGARS

Modern cooks have shown a great interest in exotic vinegars made with fermented fruit such as plums or berries. Such vinegars are expensive, however, because of the need to ferment the fruit first to make a wine before then turning it into a vinegar, which in turn requires a lengthy ageing process of up to 6 months. It is stored in barrels in cold cellars hewn out of rock, where the temperature causes the wine to reach only 4 to 5% oxidation. The addition of extract made from the fruit enhances the flavor.

These fruit vinegars can give extra

LEFT: A "*BATTERIA*" OF WOODEN CASKS FOR THE AGEING OF *ACETO BALSAMICO TRADIZIONALE DI MODENA* IN THE WONDERFUL ATTIC OF SIGNORA GIACOBAZZI IN SPILAMBERTO, MODENA

BELOW: TASTING *ACETO BALSAMICO TRADIZIONALE DI MODENA*

flavor to salads, although care should be taken to choose the right type — for example raspberry vinegar is wonderful on a salad of bitter leaves. One of the best ways to use them is in sauces to accompany game. Try pouring fruit vinegars over broiled meat or combining them with melted butter for fish.

ABOVE: THE LABEL FOR A BOTTLE OF ACETO BALSAMICO TRADIZIONALE DI MODENA

### ACETO DI VINO / WINE VINEGAR

Today, almost the whole production of wine vinegar is undertaken by large manufacturers mainly for use in the preservation industry. White or red wines can be used to make wine vinegar, called *aceto di vino bianco* or *aceto di vino rosso*. You can buy wine vinegars that have been made with just one variety of grape, but this has more to do with being able to charge a higher price than producing a better product. If the vinegar has been properly made, allowing the alcohol in the wine to oxidize to 6% acidity, then the type of wine used is not important.

Wine vinegars are generally used to make salad dressings, and Italians tend to make their wine vinegars into *aceti aromatici* by adding herbs or other flavoring ingredients, like rosemary, dill, basil, tarragon, bay, garlic, shallots, and chili.

### ACQUA DI ROSA / ROSE WATER

The petals of the highly perfumed, wild, red *Rosa canina* are imported from Arabic countries, Romania, and Bulgaria to make rose water, which is used to flavor cookies and pastries. It is also essential for the preparation of *rosolio*, a gentle and old-fashioned liqueur which has recently become fashionable again.

### AGRODOLCE / SWEET-AND-SOUR

This term describes a method of cooking which imparts a sweet-and-sour taste to certain types of food. The sweetness is usually provided by sugar or honey and the sourness by vinegar or lemon juice, in combination with other flavorings like garlic, herbs, and spices. Vegetables like onions, eggplants, artichokes (see *carciofi in agrodolce*. page 129), zucchini, and cauliflower are often given this treatment, as are some sauces for meat and game.

### ALLORO, LAURO / BAY

The aromatic leaves of the evergreen sweet bay tree (*Laurus nobilis*) have always been a popular herb in the kitchen. Bay plays an important part in *aromi* (the Italian version of bouquet garni), court-bouillon, and soups. My mother used to use a sprig of bay to pierce liver before it was wrapped in caul fat for frying. I use bay leaves when boiling chestnuts and in marinades for fish and meat. Try to get fresh leaves as they have a stronger flavor than dried.

### ANETO / DILL

Dill is a relative newcomer to Italian cuisine. Because of its physical similarities to fennel, is it is known in Italy as *finocchio fetido* or *bastardo*. It has thin bushy leaves and an intense aroma, whether used fresh or dry, and is used in sauces for fish and vegetables as well as with preserved gherkins to give them a distinctive flavor. I like dill finely chopped in a salad with peeled and thinly sliced cucumber, a little salt and pepper, some olive oil, and some milk.

### ANICE / ANISEED

Aniseed comes from a plant very similar to fennel (*Pimpinella anisum*), that bears bunches of greenish-yellow flowers which produce the seeds when mature. Indeed, it is difficult to distinguish between the two plants growing in the wild. The essential oil of the seeds, called *anetolo*, has an intense flavor which is used in the making of liqueurs and confectionery, as well as medicinally. The seeds are often used in baking, especially in the famous Sardinian sweet biscuits called *anicini* (see page 288), and to be found with baked dried figs in Campania and Puglia. They are also used to flavor some savory dishes, particularly salads and broiled fish.

### ANICE STELLATO / STAR ANISE

The star-shaped fruit of this Asian plant, quite unrelated to aniseed, produces seeds which have an intense aniseed flavor—about 20 times as strong as aniseed itself. Because of its potency, it is imported for use in the preparation of liqueurs like Sambuca, as well as in the confectionery and pharmaceutical industries. The ground seeds are an ingredient of Chinese five-spice powder, so popular in Asian duck and pork dishes.

### AROMI / BOUQUET GARNI

The melding of a few flavors like herbs and spices is called *aromi*, and the means of achieving this is the equivalent of a bouquet garni. A *mazzetto di aromi* or *mazzetto odoroso* usually consists of a mixed bunch of parsley, rosemary, sage, thyme, bay, and sometimes marjoram, tied up in a bundle so that they may be discarded easily after use. *Aromi* are often sold in fruit and vegetable shops, and are used to enhance soups, sauces, marinades, and stews.

### ASCOLANA, SEE OLIVA

### BASILICO / BASIL

In my opinion this is by far the best of the herbs. Although originally

RIGHT: BASIL GROWING IN LIGURIA

from India, since the Romans brought it from Greece it has been adopted throughout Italy to take up a central position in Italian cuisine. The bushy annual with small leaves grows up to 20 inches high on a tall stem. To keep the growth bushy and the flavor of the leaves sweet, nip off the flower at the top of the plant. I think it should always be used fresh or preserved, as when it is dried it loses much of its character. To preserve basil, take just the leaves, unwashed and completely dry, and keep them under olive oil in an airtight jar. My father used to add salt and chili too. Basil leaves can also be used to flavor extra-virgin olive oil, and this can then be used to make dressings for salads.

There are two types of basil grown in Italy, mainly in Liguria, home of the famous pesto sauce (see page 228). One variety has small, very pungent leaves and the other has larger leaves and is grown in the summer (and under glass in Campania). Basil is principally used in tomato sauces, on pizzas, and in salads.

### BORRAGINE, BORAGINE, BORRANA / BORAGE

This unusual plant, with its pretty pale blue-and-yellow flowers (used for decorating salads and desserts) and large, deep-green, hairy leaves, is very popular in two Italian regions, Campania and Liguria. In Campania it is used as a vegetable like spinach. I like to boil the leaves until tender, then sauté them briefly in extra-virgin olive oil with garlic and a little chili, and sprinkle them with lemon juice just before serving. In Liguria, where borage grows freely with many other herbs, it is cooked in a similar way and is an essential part of *preboggion*, a mixture of wild herbs used as a filling for *pansôti* (see page 167).

### CACAO / COCOA

It was Hernando Cortés, the Spanish conquistador, who first brought back the precious cocoa bean from South America at the beginning of the fifteenth century. The fruit containing these seeds grows on trees found mainly in central South America and equatorial Africa. They are grouped in pods embedded in a yellow pulp which is allowed to ferment before the beans are removed in order to develop the flavor. After drying in the sun, the beans are then sent to chocolate factories, where they are roasted and milled to produce a thick deep brown paste ready for further refinement to produce chocolate, or treated with alkalis to remove much of the fat, or cocoa butter, and make it into the soluble powder we know as cocoa. Cocoa is widely used as a flavoring in cake- and pastry-making, as well as in confectionery and in drinks.

### CAFFÈ / COFFEE

One of the most remarkable happenings at the beginning of the Perestroika era in Russia was the sanctioning of the opening of Western-style cafés in Moscow, and President Gorbachev personally endorsed the enjoyment of having an espresso from a Gaggia machine. That the café could become a symbol of Western culture and be politicized is indeed remarkable. The exciting drink which Italians consume in vast quantities is obtained by infusing the powder of a roasted bean produced by an evergreen plant. Coffee was brought into Italy by the Arabs in the sixteenth century; the first coffee shop was opened in Venice in 1640, where Turkish-style coffee was available. Indeed the term *caffè* in Italian refers to both the drink and the place.

The coffee plant is tropical, originally from East Africa but now cultivated also in Costa Rica, Honduras, Colombia, and above all Brazil, where it was established by European settlers and made Brazil the largest producer in the world. It is necessary to blend various types of beans to get the right flavors, and generally most blends are of the arabica and robusta varieties. The way the beans are roasted dictates the different style of coffee. Americans like a light roast, producing a pale brown drink with light aroma and full of caffeine (a potent stimulant that can be toxic if abused). The general European roast is darker, giving a stronger aroma and less caffeine

LEFT: LIGURIAN BASIL BEING GROWN FOR THE MAKING OF PESTO IN FINALE

LEFT: PACKING BASIL AT A LIGURIAN GROWER

BELOW: *BICERIN* CHOCOLATE AND COFFEE AT THE BARATTI E MILANO CAFFÈ IN TURIN

content. Italians love their coffee beans roasted to a very dark brown, almost burned, giving a very concentrated flavor and a certain bitterness, which is balanced by adding sugar. The dark-roasted Italian-style coffee has a lower caffeine content because caffeine is reduced during the longer and hotter roasting process.

There are several ways of brewing coffee: either simply in a jug like tea, or by allowing hot water to percolate through the coffee grounds, or with pressure produced by boiling the water in a *caffettiera* with a screw top, or in the modern systems by very high-pressure steam in a special machine.

Coffee is used in various forms in the kitchen, especially in baking and confectionery. It is a delight in summer to order a *granita di caffè* in any bar in southern Italy and be presented with a small glass full of iced coffee. In a concentrated form, coffee is used in liqueurs, to fill chocolates, and in powdered form in some pastries, like *cannoli* (see page 256).

Instant coffee is not often used in Italy, where the fresh espresso and cappuccino are drank for breakfast and at any time of the day, but especially after meals—perhaps *corretto* with a dash of grappa in the North and a dash of anis in the South.

## CAMOMILLA / CAMOMILE

This herb is commonly found growing on open fields. The centers of its small flower are used to make tisanes and teas which have a calming effect, aiding sleep and digestion. Italians often drink a cup of camomile tea after a meal.

## CANNELLA, CINNAMOMO / CINNAMON

The Italian name for this spice comes from *canna*, meaning "little cane," indicating the fact that cinnamon comes from a piece of bark. Cinnamon comes from India, Sri Lanka, and China. The Chinese variety is often considered to be the best, with a stronger aroma and flavor. Cinnamon first found its way to Europe many centuries ago from the Far East via travelers and explorers. It is used all over Italy in savory dishes, such as sauces for meat and game, and even in risottos (see *risotto all'isolana*, page 226). It is also familiar in mulled wine and as a flavoring in sweets like *cannoli* (see page 256) and cream fillings for sweet flans. Ground cinnamon is also sprinkled over fresh fruit.

## CAPPERO / CAPER

The caper is the bud of a plant with very pretty, thick round or oval leaves. The harvesting of the buds starts in late springtime in Sicily, when the weather is already hot.

The little islands of Lipari and Pantelleria, south of Sicily, produce capers of excellent quality and in sufficient quantities to be able to export as well. The smallest capers are the most sought after, because of their pungent flavor and tenderness. The larger they grow, the less flavor they have.

Like olives, capers are bitter and inedible when raw, and need first to be cured before being eaten. They can be cured in vinegar, brine, or dry salt. I think the best preserving medium is either brine or dry salt. If using brine, make a solution of 20% salt, add the capers, and leave them to soak for a couple of days, then drain them and layer them in a jar with coarse sea salt, finishing with a top layer of salt. When you want to use them, soak them in a bowl of water for about 15 minutes.

The best way to use capers is to add them to a dish, either chopped or whole, towards the end of the preparation, so that they keep their flavor and do not turn bitter. Capers can be used to flavor salads, tomato sauces, pasta, or cooked vegetables like artichokes or fava beans. They can also be used to add piquancy to tuna fish sauces, as in *vitello tonnato* (see page 87), and to make a butter and lemon juice sauce for steamed fish.

## CAPSICO, SEE PEPERONCINO

## CARDAMOMO / CARDAMOM

This exquisite spice is mainly used in the cooking of India and the East, but was popular in Amalfi, Pisa, Genoa, and Venice during the time of the Doges. The flavor of the cardamom comes from the black seeds inside the pale-green, oval pod. However, in Italy it is mostly used in the form of an oily liquid extract in the manufacture of liqueurs and confectionery, as well as in the specialty called *panforte* (see pages 281 and 296), which dates back to the Middle Ages. I myself often make a cardamom-flavored ice cream.

## CERFOGLIO / CHERVIL

The leaves of this delicate plant, which looks like flat-leaved parsley except that it is much smaller and paler, are used all over Italy during

the summer when it grows freely. Chervil is very aromatic when fresh and is especially good with steamed vegetables, on salads, in delicate soups such as *stracciatella* (a broth with egg beaten into it), and in other egg dishes, especially scrambled eggs. It should always be used uncooked and only added to hot dishes just before serving.

## CHIODI DI GAROFANO / CLOVES

Brought to Italy around the time of the Crusades, cloves are still popular in Italy. The clove (from the Latin *clavus*, like the Italian *chiodi*, meaning "nail") is an unopened bud of the *Eugenia carophillata*, an evergreen tree that grows up to 45 feet high. The buds are picked and dried in the sun so that they keep their pungent aroma, and are used in many recipes, including *vino brûlé* (mulled wine), roast meats, game sauces, marinades, stocks, cooked fruit, and in preserving fungi and gherkins. Clove powder and oil are also widely used both in the pâtisserie industry, and as a medicine (for its anaesthetic qualities).

## CINNAMOMO, SEE CANNELLA

## CIOCCOLATO / CHOCOLATE

Chocolate, the substance that has the power to make children and grown-ups equally happy, is made from the cocoa bean (see *cacao*). Lots of refinement and blending, plus the possible incorporation of milk, cream, sugar, vanilla extract, and more cocoa butter (the fat extracted from the cocoa bean) are done either industrially or on an artisanal basis. Italy is quite famous for good chocolate—the industry and artisans are spread in all the regions and they mostly use the

best-quality cocoa beans from Ecuador, the Ivory Coast, and Ghana. A company in Turin, Peyrano, still imports the cocoa beans and makes the very lengthy transformation to

produce bars of *cioccolato* or *cioccolatini* (small chocolates), with the addition of all sorts of flavorings, such as orange, mint, vanilla, and many more. The chocolate is poured by hand into classic molds, allowed to cool, and wrapped in multicolored metal foil. For specially shaped chocolate, like Easter eggs or bunnies, or Santa Clause, the best bittersweet chocolate is needed to prevent the figures from breaking or melting too easily.

As well as for confectionery, chocolate is also used in and on desserts and cakes, and in the South with baked figs or to coat crystallized fruit like clementines, cherries, walnuts, and hazelnuts. The chocolate used for this is called *copertura* (couverture) and comes in big blocks which are melted down for use. Sweetened drinking chocolate called *cioccolata* is very popular in Italy, and is at its best when served in one of the beautiful old cafés of Turin.

## CORIANDOLO / CORIANDER, CILANTRO

Italians only use the seeds of this herb and not the wonderfully aromatic leaves so common in the cooking of Southeast Asia. Coriander seeds are added to salamis, such as *mortadella*, and are used to make syrups for the

manufacture of liqueurs, and by the baking industry.

## CREN, RAFANO / HORSERADISH

This curious plant ( *Armoracia rusticana* ) grows wild all over Italy during the summer. It is harvested for its pungent tap root late in the season so it can be kept through the winter. The strong leaves easily can be confused with those of the dock, and the thick root— which can grow up to 18 inches in length—has to be dug out carefully to avoid breaking it. It is very hard and has be grated for use. When doing this, take care to wear glasses or goggles of some sort as the juices in the radish are very pungent and will irritate the eyes on contact.

Horseradish is mainly used in Veneto, Trentino, and Alto Adige, where there is a cookery tradition influenced by the southern Tyrol in Austria. As well as being used as a condiment and in sauces for boiled meats like pork, chicken, veal, and beef, and with fish (particularly smoked), and on salads, it is often mixed with a potato purée together with heavy cream. I particularly like it freshly grated on rare T-bone steaks (see *bistecca alla fiorentina*, page 70).

## CRESCIONE / WATERCRESS

Watercress grows wild at the banks of small rivers, but is mainly grown commercially. It is in season from spring to autumn, when the weather is mild. This herb, which has only recently found a place in Italian cuisine, has a peppery flavor which is delicious in soups and salads.

## CUMINO / CUMIN

Cumin is a very aromatic spice that comes from the fruit of a plant called *Carum carvi*, which is similar to aniseed. It grows in the summer around the edges of fields and is used to flavor breads, potato dishes, and sauerkraut. It is only used in the northeast of Italy, in Trentino, Friuli, and Veneto.

## DIAVOLILLO, SEE PEPERONCINO

LEFT AND TOP: TRADITIONAL CHOCOLATE PACKAGING

## HOW CHOCOLATE IS MADE

At the Peyrano chocolate factory in Turin, the raw dried cocoa beans are picked over and then toasted over olive wood.

The toasted beans are then milled between huge rotating cylindrical stones and the resulting chocolate liquor is chilled to produce solid blocks of raw chocolate. This is then subjected to a long series of further refining and blending processes, mixing in sugar and other flavorings, including Piedmontese hazelnuts when making the *gianduiotti* (see over) shown.

The chocolate is poured by hand into the classic molds and, when set, wrapped and packed again by hand.

## DRAGONCELLO, SERPENTARIA, ESTRAGONE / TARRAGON

This strongly flavored summer herb with long narrow leaves is much used in modern Italian cooking, probably as a result of French influence. It mainly features in sauces for fish, eggs, and poultry, although it is also used in salads and as a garnish. A typical sauce based on melted butter, lemon juice, and finely chopped tarragon is ideal with poached trout or boiled chicken. Added to vinegar, tarragon imparts a distinctive flavor to any salad dressing. Based on a French idea, I have created a sorbet made with lemon juice, water, sugar, and plenty of finely chopped fresh tarragon.

## ERBA CIPOLLINA / CHIVES

Although they have been well known for many centuries, chives have only recently been rediscovered in modern Italian cuisine. This energetic herb grows in bushy clumps and has long, thin dark-green hollow stalks that reach about 12 inches in height and are topped with pretty violet flowers. Its mild flavor falls somewhere between that of garlic and onion, giving it a wide variety of uses. The stalks are used finely cut in egg dishes, added to soft cheeses, salads, consommés, and on *crostini* with tomato.

## FINOCCHIO / FENNEL

As well as using the bulb as a vegetable (see page 112), both the leaves and seeds of the fennel plant are widely used in Italy, where it can be found growing wild in the South beside country roads. Its flavor is less sweet than that of the very similar aniseed, to which it is related. The seeds are longer, and a distinctive pale green when dried.

Fennel is popular in the cooking of Tuscany and the South, to flavor pork dishes and the famous Tuscan salami called *la finocchiona*, as well as other fresh and preserved sausages. In Puglia and the South it is often used to make *taralli*, the local savory crackers, as well as bread and sweet cookies.

## GIANDUIOTTO / HAZELNUT CHOCOLATE

Probably among the best produced in Italy, these little triangular chocolates contain a high percentage of hazelnut paste, produced from Piedmontese hazelnuts, which are celebrated for not easily becoming rancid. The chocolate melts instantly in the mouth and has an extremely fine flavor. *Gianduiotto* was created to celebrate the local folkloric figure called Gianduja, who represents the city of Turin at carnivals and other festivities. Gianduja's hat is triangular in shape, hence the distinctive shape of the chocolates. A famous specialty called *bicerin*—said to be the favorite drink of Cavour, the hero of Italian unification, can be tasted in the wonderful classic Turin cafes. For this, a *gianduiotto* is added to a cup of hot espresso coffee, resulting in a deliciously rich beverage.

## GINEPRO / JUNIPER

This common plant, similar to the pine but much more prickly, grows mainly around the coasts in Italy as well as in the Tuscan Apennines, Sardinia, and the pre-Alps. The juniper berry is green, ripening to black, and has a slightly resinous flavor that is at its best when the berries are fresh and lightly crushed before use. Well-known for its use in the distillation of gin, it is widely used in marinades and meat dishes, especially game.

**LAURO, SEE ALLORO**

## LIQUIRIZIA / LICORICE

In Italy this perennial plant grows mostly in the South. In Sicily and Calabria it is harvested after about 4 or 5 years of growth, when it has reached a height of about 3 feet. Its flavor is extracted commercially by cooking the root until it forms a black syrup, which is then mixed with sugar and starch to make the sweet licorice, mostly used in the confectionery industry. I remember when I was quite young I used to buy small batons of licorice root, which we children chewed to extract the sweet juice.

**MACIS, SEE NOCE MOSCATA**

## MAGGIORANA / MARJORAM

A close relative of oregano, marjoram is enjoyed in most Italian regions for its minty fragrant aroma, but is especially popular in Liguria where it grows freely in the hills. It is used to flavor the famous stuffed breast of veal, *cima alla genovese*, and *torta pasqualina* (see page 301), as well as other roast meats and stews, especially with rabbit, and in salads. Marjoram is also the

**LEFT: WILD FENNEL GROWING IN SICILY**

**ABOVE: WILD FENNEL BUNDLES IN FLORENCE MARKET FOR DRYING**

**LEFT: DRAGONCELLO**

predominant herb in *preboggion*, a paste of mixed herbs used to fill *pansôti*, ravioli dressed with a walnut sauce (see page 167). Marjoram is also easily cultivated and is often grown on windowsills and in pots on balconies.

### MENTA, MENTUCCIA, NEPITELLA, NEPETELLA / MINT

Italians use three of the many varieties of mint available, and further confusion arises from the fact that the same name has been given to two types of mint grown in different regions. The most common form of mint is peppermint, *Mentna piperita*, a very invasive plant that grows up to 3 feet high and has dark-green oval, pointed leaves. This plant does not propagate by seeding, but via its roots, which spread so quickly over the ground that it has to be contained by containing the area with stones pushed deep under the earth. The other commonly used variety is the small-leafed mint called *mentuccia* (*M. romana*) which is often confused with *nepitella* (*Calamintha nepeta*), a slightly less popular small-leafed mint, the wild version of which is known as *nepetella*. Only in Tuscany and Umbria is the *nepitella* used in cooking, mainly with mushrooms and stews.

Oils extracted from mint are used in the making of sweets, syrups, sugar candies, and chewing gum. Mint syrup added to ice makes a particularly refreshing granita. It is also infused in water or milk to make refreshing drinks. My mother used to put mint leaves in 95% pure alcohol for a couple of days so that she could make a wonderful drink made up of two parts sugar dissolved in equal parts of the mint liqueur and water. We children were only allowed a thimbleful of this drink, which had to be further diluted with fresh water for us, but

even so it was wonderful.

As well as sweets and drinks, mint is also used in salads (especially of fish), with tripe, or with fried zucchini (see *zucchini alla scapace*, page 124) and artichokes, as in *carciofi alla giudea*. Today, mint is as much loved by modern Romans as it was by the ancients — it is stuffed in chickens and used to flavor cooked beans and, in Umbria, leafy vegetables.

### MIELE / HONEY

As everyone knows, honey is made by bees from the nectar of a variety of flowers, and is the oldest sweetener known to mankind. Most honeys are made from the nectar of all the flowers within the range of the hives, and these are called *millefiori* (thousand flowers). However, some honeys are made by bees who have collected nectar from only one type of flower. These are

called monofloral (single-flower) and are generally more expensive than ordinary honeys and have more delicate aromas and flavors, reflecting the qualities of the flowers used.

The most common single-flower honey is acacia, and this is common in the region of Veneto. Acacia honey does not crystallize or cloud when used. It is popular in the confectionery industry but is also delicious eaten on buttered bread. *Fior d'arancio*, orange blossom honey, is a specialty of Calabria and Sicily and has an intensive bitter-sweet taste which is popular in Sicily for making sweets similar to the Arabic specialty, Turkish delight.

*Castagno*, or chestnut honey, is a very dark and heavily scented honey with a slightly bitter flavor, and is made all over Italy when the chestnut tree is in bloom. Piedmont, with its hilly terrain, produces a lot of good-quality chestnut honey, and this makes delicious *croccante di nocciole* (see page 280).

*Lavanda*, or lavender honey, is an extremely delicate and highly perfumed honey that is mainly produced in Liguria, where wild and cultivated lavender grows abundantly. In Tuscany, *rosmarino*, or rosemary honey, is specially made, with producers regularly moving their beehives to areas where rosemary is abundant. In addition to these specialties, there are honeys made with the nectar of almond blossom, thyme, and cloves, although only in very small quantities.

Honey is easily digestible and includes many nutritionally valuable trace elements and proteins. It is mostly used in the preparation of cookies and creams, and to sweeten drinks. I add it to sauerkraut and spread it on roast pork to caramelize the skin. It is, however, at its most delicious in the Neapolitan specialty *struffoli* (see page 306).

### NEPETELLA, NEPITELLA, SEE MENTA

### NOCE MOSCATA, MACIS / NUTMEG, MACE

The nutmeg is the seed of the tropical tree *Myristica fragrans*, which grows up to 35 feet in height and which is native to the Molucca Islands of Indonesia, but is now mostly cultivated in the West Indies. It produces a yellowish fruit, similar to an apricot. The brown seed, which looks like an oval nut, is dried in the sun. The nut's membrane, or aril, which shrinks to a lacy covering and turns dark orange, is known as mace. This is usually ground to a powder and used

RIGHT: BEE HIVES IN PIEDMONT

for flavoring in the same way as nutmeg, although it has a subtly different flavor.

The actual dark brown nutmeg, although it is also sold ground as a powder, is better freshly grated over food so that its intense aroma can be fully appreciated. Since the introduction of nutmeg by Arabs during Roman times, it has always been part of Italian cooking, especially in the North, where it is used to flavor roasts, stews, sauces, mashed potatoes, and stuffings for ravioli.

## OLIO / OIL

Oils are made by pressing fruit, seeds, or nuts through a special press, or are extracted using a chemical process. In the past, oil production in Italy centered on olive oil, with the result that the country has gained the reputation for producing some of the finest quality olive oil in the world. However, many other oils are now produced in Italy, including *arachidi* (peanut), *semi di girasole* (sunflower), *semi di soya* (soya), *mandorle* (almond), *noci* (walnut), *nocciole* (hazelnut), *ravizzone* (rape seed), and *vinaccioli* (grape seed).

*Olio di arachide* (peanut oil)

came to be used in Italy at the same time as margarine was introduced from America. It is used for frying because it takes high temperatures well and is cheaper than olive oil. Like peanut oil, *olio di mais* (corn oil) is widely used in Italy as a cheap alternative to olive oil for frying.

## OLIO D'OLIVA / OLIVE OIL

This miraculous product is made by mincing and pressing the pulp of the olive, itself the fruit of an amazing tree. Olive trees are native to Mediterranean countries, and Italy is no exception. In the last 2,000 years, olive oil has become a symbol of Italian agricultural skill and expertise. It is not so much the quantity of the oil, although Italy is the largest producer of oil in the world after Spain, but the unique characteristics that make it the best-known olive oil in the world. With the exception of Piedmont and Lombardy, where the climate and soil are unsuitable, all of the other eighteen Italian regions grow olive trees, and these produce millions of tons of olives, which are used to make about 908,000 tons of oil, half of which is extra-virgin.

For the olive trees to produce this quantity they need a great deal of care, especially as 58% of the total area of 2,900,000 acres devoted to them is on hilly slopes. One of the most difficult provinces for growing olive trees is Liguria, where, high in the hills, the trees have to be planted on terraces and can only be reached on foot. The Ligurian oil is one of the lightest and it is produced exclusively from one type of olive, the Taggiasca, a relatively small olive which is collected from around December to January, when the olive is almost ripe.

They are immediately transported to the *frantoio*, or olive mill (of which there are about 9,000 in Italy), where they are reduced to a

pulp by two huge, rotating millstones. The pulp is then evenly spread on round mats, which are laid on top of each other like a huge sandwich and crushed by hydraulic presses until the last drop of oil is extracted. The liquid is collected in huge containers where it separates naturally into cold green oil on top of the water from the olives. (About 30% of the total liquid collected is oil and the rest is water.) The oil is separated from the water and filtered to remove any impurities. Olive oil is sensitive to sunlight, which can reduce the quality of the oil, so it is kept in complete darkness until it is bottled, usually in dark glass containers.

*Olio di Oliva Extra Vergine* (extra-virgin olive oil)
By law, an oil can only be called extra-virgin if it has less than 0.5% acidity. This can only be guaranteed if the olives are collected by hand when still unripe to prevent any bruising, which would cause the

ABOVE: EXTRA-VIRGIN OLIVE OILS FROM TUSCANY, UMBRIA, LIGURIA, AND PUGLIA

veins carrying the oil to be exposed to the air and result in oxidation. Also to avoid oxidation, it is paramount that the olives reach the mill in the shortest time possible, and that they are milled immediately by a process of cold-pressing. This need for careful treatment goes some way toward explaining the high price of extra-virgin olive oil. Cooking damages the proteins in extra-virgin olive oil, so it is better used cold as a dressing or in dishes such as *pinzimonio*, *fettunta*, and *bruschetta* (see pages

LEFT: A TRADITIONAL NEAPOLITAN OLIVE OIL CAN BE USED IN THE MAKING OF PIZZAS

LEFT: A SIGN OUTSIDE A SHOP IN NORCIA, UMBRIA

223, 226, and 224).

Tuscan oil is made with Frantoio, Leccino, Maurino, and Puntino olives, and is quite different from Ligurian olive oil. Tuscans like their oil fairly peppery and herby. Tuscan olives are collected as early as October, when they are still very green and their acidity is especially low. Because the olives are so young, however, they do not reach full size and so the yield of Tuscan olives is lower than the yield of those grown in other regions. As a result, the quantity of oil produced is also quite low, making it especially precious, and it is valued all over the world for its exceptional quality. In a bid to market their oil more aggressively, a group of producers has created a special bottle for it, labeled *laudemio*. In my opinion these oils are not superior to others, although they are of a very high quality.

Tuscany has hosted the first world congress for olive oil producers, called Oleum, where experts from all over the world meet to discuss their problems and achievements. There are also many professional oil tastings organized to try to discover which is the best olive oil. The Pugliese, who are the largest producers of oil in Italy, have been a little jealous of these Tuscan initiatives regarding olive oil, but are pleased that it has led to general guidelines being drawn up to help eliminate dubious production methods and products.

Pugliese oil is made from Corantina, Frantoio, Oliarola Barese, and Leccino olives, although it is not always a combination of the oil from all four varieties and is sometimes a mixture of just two or three. Whatever the combination, however, Pugliese oil usually has a sharp, fruity flavor because it is made with fully ripened olives whose acidity is at the highest permitted level, due to the fact that

they are picked as late as January.

In Sicily, olive oil is made from Nocella Etnea, Tonda Iblea, and Bianco Lilla olives, which produce an oil very similar to the Pugliese variety, whereas the Marche uses a wide variety of olives— Frantoio, Moraiolo, Leccino, Rosciale, Maurino, Pendalino, and Carbonella—to blend their distinctive oil, which is considered to be one of the best in Italy.

*Olio Vergine di Oliva* (virgin olive oil)
Virgin olive oil is produced in the same regions as extra-virgin, using more mature olives and giving a greater yield. It has a higher acidity level and a lower price. It is mainly used for light cooking in which the oil is not overheated, and for mayonnaise and vinaigrettes. It is an excellent oil and can be mixed with extra-virgin olive oil when a richer color and flavor are required.

*Olio d'Oliva* (olive oil)
This is the simplest of the oils, usually made using a hot pressing method to extract the oil and sometimes using the "cake," the crushed cold-pressed olives that remain after the extraction of extra-virgin olive oil. It is frequently used for cooking, as it is suitable not only for preserving but also for frying, because it maintains its qualities when heated to a high temperature. *Fritto misto alla piemontese* and *fritto misto di mare* are always fried in olive oil to give the dishes extra flavor. The rest of the "cake," which after the hot pressing is called *sansa*, is passed on to commercial producers who chemically extract the remaining 5 to 10% oil from it

for cosmetic and other purposes.

In the last few years there has been a growing demand for oils flavored with truffle to make *olio al tartufo*, which is used to dress cold meat dishes, fish, and egg dishes. Other ingredients that are also used to flavor olive oil include chili (*olio al peperoncino*), garlic (*olio all'aglio*), rosemary (*olio al rosmarino*), and mixed herbs (*olio alle erbe*). All of these oils, except the truffle oil, can be made at home simply by adding the relevant ingredients to a bottle of olive oil, although care should be taken with the garlic, which will need to be discarded after a day or two.

## OLIVA / OLIVE
If you were to eat an olive picked straight from the tree you would discover that it is extremely bitter— whether ripe (black) or unripe (green), it is inedible. It is the salt-curing process that makes olives palatable.

Olives grown for consumption are generally different varieties from those grown for oil production, with the exception of Taggiasca, which is grown in Liguria for both. Edible olives, called "*da tavola*," are mostly grown in the South and include varieties such as the fairly large, green Ascolana in the Marche; the Pugliese Cerignola, Maiatica, and Molellara; and the Bella di Spagna, Santa Agostino, and Santa

Caterina from Spain, all of which are picked when green and unripe, but which turn from deep violet to black when ripe.

Olives are cured by fermentation, which usually takes place naturally, courtesy of the micro-organisms in the skin, called lactic bacteria, that preserve the olive from decay. The oldest method of preserving small green olives is by soaking them in water for ten days, changing the water daily, and then preserving them in salt water and storing them in a cool place. Larger olives, such as the Ascolana and Cerignola, are treated with caustic soda and lime before they are preserved in brine to sweeten them.

A Sicilian olive called Olive Bianche goes through a prolonged curing process with a very strong salt solution, which leaches the color from the olives. They are then repeatedly washed to clean away all the salt, and stored in a light brine. Commercial producers of olives pasteurize, or even sterilize them, before selling them cheaply in large cans. Olives are sold in this way either whole, pitted, or stuffed with peppers or pimentos. Black Baresane olives are also sweetened with caustic soda and lime before being sterilized and canned.

Famous for its sharpness and very widely used in Italian cooking is the *oliva di gaeta*, a black olive cured in water for one day and in salt for another day, then soaked in water for 40 days, and finally kept in a boiled mild brine. These olives are excellent for *antipasto*. One of my favorite olives is the small, black, cured variety, which are baked (or dried in the oven) for a more concentrated flavor.

Italian markets sell a huge range of olives, sometimes more than 20 different varieties, whole and stuffed. Most are eaten with bread as part of an *antipasto*, but some are only suitable for cooking in one of the countless Italian recipes employing olives, especially those from Sicily, where the olive is an indispensable ingredient in famous dishes such as *caponata* (see page 135).

Some olives can be stuffed at home, and the range of possible fillings includes ground meat or tuna fish with capers, parsley, bread crumbs, and beaten egg. The stuffed olives are then dipped in beaten egg and rolled with bread crumbs before being deep-fried until golden (see *olive ascolane*, page 223). Recently, recipes such as olive pâté have been developed, and this is used to boost the flavor of sauces and as a topping for *bruschetta*.

## ORIGANO / OREGANO OR WILD MARJORAM

This small-leaved, long-stemmed herb grows up to $2^{1}/_{2}$ feet high and produces bunches of bushy pinkish flowers when mature. This typical Mediterranean plant can be found growing wild on hillsides, although it is now often commercially cultivated. It has a strong minty flavor and is one of the few herbs that is actually improved by drying. Most recipes that include oregano come from the South, where it is almost as popular as basil.

It goes particularly well with eggplants, especially the preserved variety, and with tomatoes as part of the famous *pizzaiola* sauce (see page 57). It is also added to breads and cookies, sprinkled over pizzas, and used to flavor olives. However, contrary to the widespread belief outside Italy that it makes the sauce more Mediterranean, it should *never* be added to Bolognese sauce.

## PANPEPATO / PEPPERED BREAD

*Panpepato* is a sweet bread that is made in a number of Italian regions, and was the predecessor of Tuscan *panforte*. It gets its name from the addition of copious amounts of ground black pepper to the more usual ingredients of almonds, hazelnuts, walnuts, pine nuts, candied orange and lime peels, wheat flour, and honey. The bread is then cooked in a medium oven for 40 minutes and allowed to cool. Sometimes the loaf is also covered in a layer of dark chocolate. (See recipe, page 230.)

## PAPRICA, PAPRIKA, SEE PEPERONCINO

## PEPE / PEPPER

Of all the exotic spices, pepper has been the most enthusiastically received in Italy. It is believed that Alexander the Great brought it back from India, where it is still grown today. The corns are the fruit of a vine-like plant that climbs to a height of 30 feet, although it is usually cut back to 12 feet so that it is easier to pick, and so that it produces compact clusters, each bearing 70 to 80 peppercorns. India, Pakistan, and Indonesia are all producers of pepper.

White peppercorns are mainly used in pale sauces and in dishes in which the distinctive flavor is needed. To make white peppercorns, the corns are collected from the trees, then soaked in water to loosen the outer skin. When it is soft, the outer skin is rubbed off and the corn is left to dry in the sun. For black peppercorns, the fresh corns are fermented with the skins on,

LEFT: PUGLIESE OLIVES IN THE FLORENCE MARKET

RIGHT: A VARIETY OF CHILIES STRUNG FOR DRYING

then drained before being dried in the sun. Green peppercorns are simply fresh or preserved peppercorns, and do not have as much flavor as the dried versions. A fourth variety, the pink peppercorn, is not in fact a real peppercorn at all, but comes from a different tree and lacks the pungent, sharp flavor of real pepper.

To make the most of pepper, it is important to grind it as you need it, because it loses its delicate aroma and piquant taste if stored ready-ground. It is also important to buy the best-quality peppercorns possible, and to store them correctly. The best white pepper comes from Madras in India, while the best black is from the Moluccan Islands and the best green peppercorns are from Madagascar.

In Italy, pepper is used whole in salami to add spice, and on hams, such as the air-cured rolled bacon *pancetta arrotolata*, which is covered in coarsely ground pepper. It is also used in stocks and soups, in which the long cooking of the whole corn helps to develop flavor. Ground pepper is added to most sauces and is delicious on slices of *lardo di arnaz*, cured pork fat, broiled until translucent and then eaten on a piece of bread. Pepper is the main ingredient of a sauce called *peverada* (see page 228), which is a specialty of Treviso, and is heroic in *panpepato* (see page 230).

BELOW: PEPERONCINI

## PEPERONCINO, CAPSICO, DIAVOLILLO, PEPE DI CAYENNA /

CHILI PEPPER, CAYENNE PEPPER

It is thought that chili was brought to Europe from America by Christopher Columbus. It

quickly became known as *la droga dei poveri*, "the poor man's drug," because of its powerful taste that could flavor any food, however dull. It also had the extra benefit of stimulating digestion as well as acting as a disinfectant. In Italy, chili is very popular in the South, where it is used as a condiment and offered on the tables of restaurants along with the salt and pepper.

*Peperoncini* are part of the Capsicum (bell pepper) family, but instead of producing the large mild peppers, the plants bear small fruits of green or fire-red in the shape of little horns. The smallest chilies, called *diavolilli* (little devils) in Abruzzi, are the hottest, while other varieties include the round cherry-shaped red chili, the long, fat chili called *sigarette*, and the very common cayenne, a small pointed chili which is dried and powdered to make *pepe di cayenna* or *pepe d'India* (cayenne pepper), much like the Hungarian spice paprika, only hotter.

In Italy, chili is used in a number of recipes, including *spaghetti aglio, olio, e peperoncino* (spaghetti with garlic, olive oil, and chili), and *penne all'arrabbiata* (pasta quills with "angry sauce," a chili-hot tomato sauce). Until recently, chili has only traditionally been used in the South and the islands. Today, however, it has been embraced with more or less enthusiasm by the cooks of every Italian region. Piedmont uses it in Tumin (*Tomino*), a small fresh cheese that is preserved in vinegar and oil with garlic and lots of chili. In fact, it is so hot that is it sometimes called

*Tomino elettrico* because it feels like an electric shock on the tongue—hotter still is an explosive version called *atomici*!

Chili is also used in *tofeia*, a dish of beans and pork cooked with chili in a special terra-cotta pot, as well as in *salsa verde* (see page 224). The further south you go, the more this powerful "drug" is used. The peppers can often be seen hanging in long strings from balconies and windows, ready to be added liberally to sauces, salamis, sausages, stews, and vegetables.

## PREZZEMOLO / PARSLEY

There are two different types of parsley, both of which are used a great deal in every Italian kitchen, but especially those on the coast because of the herb's affinity with fish. The tightly curled type of parsley is usually used as a garnish, while the common *gigante d'Italia*—with its small, flat leaves—is the variety used for flavoring a large number of recipes.

Parsley is often used combined with garlic as the base of a number of sauces for pasta and seafood. It is also used in seafood salads and with sautéed kidneys, fried sweetbreads, soups, stocks, and vegetables, such as braised artichokes, carrots, and sautéed mushrooms. Parsley is also the main ingredient in the Piedmontese recipe *salsa verde* (see page 224) and is a crucial flavoring in eggplant fried *al funghetto*.

## ROSMARINO / ROSEMARY

This evergreen herb grows in all the coastal regions of Italy, and most

families with a garden or balcony grow a small bush for their own use. The aromatic rosemary needles, with an underside of velvety gray, are carried on woody branches, and the plant has an attractive blue flower in the summer.

The herb goes particularly well with any roasted meat. It can also be used, finely chopped, in marinades and in sauces, although it should be used carefully to avoid over-flavoring. If grilled over charcoal, rosemary gives a wonderful smoky flavor to meat and fish. It is best when used fresh as, once dried, its flavor changes slightly.

### RAFANO, SEE CREN

### RUTA / RUE
This bushy little plant (*Ruta graveolens*) has pretty gray-blue leaves which may be used in salads, but with caution because of its sharp bitterness. A branch of rue is sometimes put into grappa to add to its digestive qualities.

### SALE / SALT
Salt was the first preserving agent used by man and as a result was extremely valuable, in fact the word "salary" comes from *salario*, meaning that part of people's earnings that used to be paid in salt. Salt is most notably used in the preservation of fish such as cod, anchovies, and herrings. However, it is also used to preserve capers and, above all, to cure all the many and varied pork products.

There are three types of salt—the refined commercial salt, coarse treated sea salt, and very coarse untreated sea salt. Sea salt is still made in Trapani in Sicily and in

Sardinia by flooding flat areas with seawater and letting this evaporate in the sun. The resulting salt is then treated and refined to make it edible. Some Italians use coarse sea salt when cooking pasta, but I like it best on *focaccia*, when it gives the bread a lovely crunchy quality.

### SALVIA / SAGE
Along with basil, oregano, rosemary, and parsley, sage is one of the most popular herbs in Italian cooking, and is used in every region. It is a perennial plant with evergreen, oval leaves that are velvety to the touch. The gray-green leaves contain a fragrant oil that is delicious with white meat like veal, pork, and chicken. Among the most popular ways of using sage are with calves' liver sautéed in butter, and in *ravioli* or *tortellini*, along with meat, vegetables, and Parmesan.

### SENAPE / MUSTARD
Around May and June the fields of mustard start to turn deep yellow as the mustard plant flowers. After this, the seed pods form and fill with little black

or white seeds, which are then milled and reduced to a yellow or brown powder. This is then mixed with vinegar, wine, or sometimes garlic and anchovies to make a paste that can be used in cooking or as an accompaniment for meats, salamis, and fish. Some mustards are flavored with tarragon or other strong spices and are used in the making of sauces for game. I like the little, broccoli-like, unopened flowers of the mustard heads briefly boiled and then flavored with olive oil and lemon juice.

### TIMO / THYME
This very popular perennial herb grows wild all over the Mediterranean region. In Italy it is almost easier to find it growing wild on most hills than it is to buy it fresh in shops.

The flavor of the very small leaves of this little evergreen plant is quite intense. It suits all meat dishes, especially in marinades made to tenderize the meat, but is most suitable for lamb, pork, and game. It is part of the *aromi*, and has to be used sparingly because of it strength of flavor. Thyme is also used in the preparation of liqueurs such as *strega* and *cent'erbe*.

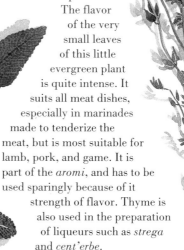

### VANIGLIA / VANILLA
Vanilla comes mostly from the tropical rain forests of Mexico and Central America. It is produced by a perennial vine that climbs to the top of huge trees of up to 100 feet in height. The thin beans, about 6 inches long, contain a sticky brownish substance that holds millions of tiny seeds. Before it can be used, the bean has to be cured

LEFT: *ROSMARINO*

ABOVE: *TIMO*

LEFT: *SALVIA*

and fermented for up to six months, then dried before it gives off any flavor or aroma. At this stage, however, it has developed a strong sweet smell.

To make the most of the flavor, the bean should be split open along its length in order to expose the seeds, which are scraped out and used for flavoring. If you cannot get hold of vanilla beans, then look for good-quality vanilla extract, which is very expensive and strong, and should be used with care. There is also a powdered version for dishes in which the seeds and color of the vanilla are not wanted. Synthetic versions of vanilla extract and powder are far weaker than the real thing.

Vanilla is used almost exclusively for making candies, chocolate, creams, ice creams, custards, and pâtisserie. It is also possible to use the beans to flavor sugar by placing one or two beans in an airtight jar until the sugar has absorbed the scent. This vanilla sugar can then be used for making custards, or for *panna cotta*, or added to all sorts of puddings and cakes.

### ZAFFERANO, ZAFFERANONE / SAFFRON

Saffron has enjoyed its reputation as the king of spices since Egyptian times, and was used as currency for trading by the Doges of Venice. Its high price is due to the fact that it has to be picked by hand and that it takes the stigmas of half a million *Crocus sativus* (which only flowers for two weeks) to make 2 pounds of saffron. Once picked, the stigmas are dried over a low heat, and this reduces their overall weight by

eighty percent. This, combined with the fact that it is widely used in medicine and as a dye, makes it extremely rare and very valuable.

The saffron stigmas are sold in small vials of just $^1/_5$ ounce in weight, or are reduced to a powder. It is best to use the strands as they give the best flavor and color. To use saffron, soak the strands in a little water to release the color and flavor before adding them to the dish with the soaking liquid. Saffron is used very parsimoniously in Italian cooking, the most famous recipe being the Milanese *risotto allo zafferano* (see page 178). It is also used in fish sauces and soups, which are really lifted by the warm color and aroma imparted by the

spice. I have developed an ice cream based on saffron to celebrate the Doges of Venice (see recipe, page 231).

Most saffron is grown in La Mancha in Spain, but Italian saffron comes from the Abruzzi region, and more recently Sardinia, where the longest, richest-colored stigmas of outstanding quality can be found. There is a much cheaper version of saffron called *zafferanone*, which only has a fraction of the aroma of the real thing, but the same coloring properties.

### ZENZERO / GINGER

The Romans tried unsuccessfully to introduce this root in Europe from the Middle East, although it originated in Asia. In the Middle Ages it began to be used in Tuscany,

along with many exotic spices like cardamom, nutmeg, coriander, cinnamon, and others, to make a bread called *panpepato* (see page 230) and this recipe is still used today to make *panforte*. The ginger plant, which has only a few leaves and pretty pink or red flowers from a cane-like stem, is cultivated in Africa, China, India, Jamaica, and Japan, although the best comes from Australia.

### ZUCCHERO / SUGAR

Sugar occurs naturally in almost all foods, although there are a few in which it appears in a very high concentration, and it is from these that sugar is extracted. Sugar cane, a perennial grass from the *Saccharum offifinarum* family, originated in India before spreading all over the world, and now it is mainly grown in the West Indies and Southeast Asia. Other principal sources of sugar are roots like sugar beet, which are cultivated all over Europe and now produce a respectable quantity of the world's sugar.

Making caramel from sugar is a science in itself and requires a fine judgement of both temperature and cooking time, to make candy like *croccante di nocciole* (see page 280) and burnt caramel for *crema caramello* (crème caramel).

# PINZIMONIO
CRUDITÉS WITH EXTRA-VIRGIN OLIVE OIL

**FOR 4**

2 BUNCHES SCALLIONS, TRIMMED

4 SMALL TENDER ARTICHOKES, OUTER
    LEAVES REMOVED, CUT INTO EIGHTHS

2 YOUNG BULBS FENNEL, CUT
    LENGTHWISE INTO EIGHTHS

INNER TENDER STALKS, PLUS HEARTS, OF
    4 YOUNG HEADS CELERY

8 SMALL NEW CARROTS

4 RAMEKINS OR SMALL DISHES FILLED
    WITH EXTRA-VIRGIN OLIVE OIL

SALT AND PEPPER

Pinzimonio, *also called* cazzimperio *in Rome, is the surprise put on your tables in good trattorias in Tuscany when the first tender vegetables of springtime are available and the newly pressed olive oil is still at its full, peppery strength.*

Put the vegetables in a large bowl containing ice cubes and a little water and place in the center of the table. Add to each dish of olive oil a teaspoon of salt and a teaspoon of pepper, which will collect at the bottom.

Each guest takes a piece of vegetable, dips it in the oil while trying to collect a little of the salt and pepper, and eats it accompanied by good bread.

# OLIVE ASCOLANE
STUFFED OLIVES

**FOR 48 TO 50 OLIVES**

3¹/₂ TABLESPOONS BUTTER

10 OUNCES GROUND PORK

10 OUNCES GROUND BEEF

GRATED ZEST OF ¹/₂ LEMON

FRESHLY GRATED NUTMEG

SALT AND PEPPER

1 GLASS DRY WHITE WINE

1 TABLESPOON TOMATO PASTE

3 OUNCES SALAMI, VERY FINELY CHOPPED

2 OUNCES *MORTADELLA*, VERY FINELY
    CHOPPED

2 OUNCES BLACK TRUFFLE, CUT INTO
    FINE SHAVINGS (OPTIONAL)

2 OUNCES PARMESAN CHEESE, GRATED

2 TABLESPOONS CHOPPED FLAT-LEAF PARSLEY

5 EGGS

FOR ABOUT 50 VERY LARGE GREEN OLIVES
    (PREFERABLY ASCOLANE OLIVES—SEE
    PAGE 217)

FLOUR FOR DUSTING

BREAD CRUMBS

OLIVE OIL FOR DEEP-FRYING

LEMON JUICE (OPTIONAL)

*Quite a lot of preparation is required for this dish but the result is extremely tasty and most useful for cocktail parties or to serve as an* antipasto.

Heat the butter in a pan, then add the ground meat, lemon zest, and some nutmeg, salt, and pepper and fry for a few minutes. Stir in the white wine and tomato paste and cook gently for 30 to 40 minutes. Leave to cool and then stir in the salami, *mortadella*, the truffle if using, the Parmesan, parsley, and 2 of the eggs. Put the mixture in a blender to obtain a fairly soft paste that still has a little texture.

Using a very sharp curved small knife, cut the flesh of each olive from the pit in a spiral fashion to obtain a loose case; the olive should open up like a continuous strip of peel. Stuff each olive case with a little of the filling, reshaping it as a large olive.

Beat the remaining eggs together. Dust the stuffed olives in flour, then coat them with beaten egg and roll in bread crumbs. Deep-fry in olive oil; to avoid using a lot of oil, do this in a small pan and fry them in small batches. If serving them hot, sprinkle with some lemon juice; otherwise they can be eaten at room temperature.

# BRUSCHETTA

**MAKES 6**

1 LOAF *CIABATTA* BREAD, SLICED
    **2** INCHES THICK

**2** LARGE GARLIC CLOVES, PEELED

**8** TABLESPOONS EXTRA-VIRGIN OLIVE OIL

**2** LARGE RIPE BEEFSTEAK TOMATOES,
    VERY FINELY CHOPPED

BASIL LEAVES

SALT AND PEPPER

*Originally from Abruzzo, this basic dish has conquered all of Italy and it would also seem that its sway is spreading all over the world. From the dialect word* bruscare, *meaning "to broil" or "to toast," the slice of very good toasted country bread is rubbed with garlic and flavored with the best extra-virgin olive oil available. The addition of tomatoes, basil, and salt makes it more than a bread to accompany antipasti.*

Preheat the oven to 400° F. Place the *ciabatta* slices on a baking sheet and bake for 10 to 15 minutes, until golden brown. Immediately rub the garlic cloves over the hot bread. The garlic should melt into the bread. Dribble about half the olive oil over the bread, then sprinkle the tomatoes on top and add a leaf of fresh basil. Season with salt and pepper and then drizzle with the rest of the olive oil.

Either serve immediately while still warm or serve cold as a party snack.

# SALSA VERDE
### GREEN SAUCE

**FOR 4 TO 6**

6 SALTED ANCHOVY FILLETS, SOAKED IN
    WATER FOR **10** MINUTES, THEN
    DRAINED

2 TABLESPOONS SALTED CAPERS, SOAKED
    IN WATER FOR **10** MINUTES, THEN
    DRAINED

2 GARLIC CLOVES

1 LARGE BUNCH FLAT-LEAF PARSLEY

4 BASIL LEAVES

EXTRA-VIRGIN OLIVE OIL

*At the Trattoria Italia in Castelletto Stura, Piedmont, this unusual* salsa verde *is put on each table regardless of whether or not it has been ordered. It is one of those trattorias one always hopes to find, with the mother (Ghibaudo Marianna) cooking the most delicious local specialties. Father and son serve in the restaurant and the rest of the family works behind the scenes. A huge bowl of impeccably cleaned vegetables is also presented at your table with a knife so you can prepare your own salad!*

Chop the anchovies, capers, garlic, parsley, and basil very finely with a knife (not in a food processor). Stir in enough olive oil to make a very dense sauce.

It can be eaten with buttered bread or *grissini* as an *antipasto*, or served with *bollito misto* (see page 92), also a local specialty.

# FRITTELLE DI BORRAGGINE
BORAGE FRITTERS

FOR 4 TO 6

10 OUNCES BORAGE LEAVES AND
   TOPS (WITH FLOWERS)
SALT
SCANT 1 CUP ALL-PURPOSE FLOUR
2 EGGS, BEATEN
MILK
OLIVE OIL FOR FRYING

*Borage is not very often used in Italy. A borage soup is made in Naples, and otherwise it is added to beans. Here is a new way of cooking it. These fritters have a surprisingly delicate flavor and are excellent served with aperitifs.*

Blanch the borage in boiling salted water for 3 minutes, then drain thoroughly and leave to cool. Sift the flour and a pinch of salt into a bowl. Whisk in the eggs and enough milk to make a fairly liquid batter. Dip a few borage leaves in the batter at a time and shallow-fry in plenty of hot olive oil until golden. Drain on paper towels. These fritters are best served warm but they are also good at room temperature.

# SALMORIGLIO
DRESSING FOR BOILED FISH

Mix together 3 parts extra-virgin olive oil and 1 part lemon juice. Add some freshly chopped parsley and pour over boiled fish.

# RISOTTO ALL'ISOLANA
RISOTTO ISOLA-STYLE

**FOR 4**

10 OUNCES *LUGANIGA* SAUSAGE
   (SEE PAGE 77)
1 ONION, FINELY CHOPPED
7 TABLESPOONS UNSALTED BUTTER
1³/₄ CUPS *VIALONE NANO* OR
   *ARBORIO* RICE
4¹/₂ CUPS CHICKEN STOCK
SALT AND PLENTY OF FRESHLY
   GROUND BLACK PEPPER
1 TSP GROUND CINNAMON
2 OUNCES PARMESAN CHEESE, GRATED

*Isola, south of Verona, is the area from which this remarkable risotto comes. The unique use of cinnamon reflects the influence of nearby Venice, which imported spices from the East during the Middle Ages.*

Take the sausage meat out of its skin and crumble it. Gently fry the meat and onion in 3 tablespoons of the butter until the onion is translucent and the meat is slightly browned.

Prepare the *risotto* in the usual way (see page 175), then remove from the heat, add the cinnamon and the rest of the butter, and stir to mix well. Serve topped with the Parmesan cheese.

# FETTUNTA
TUSCAN TOASTED BREAD

**FOR 4**

8 SLICES TUSCAN COUNTRY-STYLE
   UNSALTED BREAD
1 GARLIC CLOVE, PEELED
6 TABLESPOONS TUSCAN EXTRA-VIRGIN
   OLIVE OIL
SALT AND PEPPER

*From* fetta *(slices) and* unta *(oiled), this is exactly what it says. The Tuscans eat it with* antipasti *or by itself as a snack. In Lazio and other parts of the South it is called* bruschetta, *not to be confused with the tomato version on page 224.*

Toast the bread on both sides, then gently rub with the garlic. Drizzle with the olive oil, sprinkle with salt and pepper, and eat warm.

# PATÉ DI OLIVE NERE
BLACK OLIVE PASTE

**MAKES ABOUT 3 CUPS**

2 CUPS FIRM BLACK OLIVES
2 TABLESPOONS SALTED CAPERS, SOAKED IN
   WATER FOR 10 MINUTES, THEN DRAINED
4 ANCHOVY FILLETS
1 TEASPOON FRESHLY GROUND BLACK PEPPER
1 SMALL CHILI PEPPER, CHOPPED
   (OPTIONAL)
PINCH FRESH OR DRIED OREGANO
   (OPTIONAL)
¹/₂ CUP EXTRA-VIRGIN OLIVE OIL

*This makes a welcome spread for* crostini *or is served with bread as an* antipasto. *The paste can also be made with green olives, although the anchovies are then replaced by ground almonds.*

Pit the olives, taking care that no hard fragments remain.

Put all the ingredients except the oil in a blender. With the motor running, add the oil a little at a time until you have a spreadable paste. No salt is necessary because of the olives, capers, and anchovies, which are already salted. If you include the chili, reduce the amount of black pepper.

# PENNE ALL'ARRABBIATA
## PENNE WITH ANGRY (CHILI-HOT) SAUCE

### FOR 4

⅓ CUP EXTRA-VIRGIN OLIVE OIL

1 SMALL ONION, FINELY SLICED

FRESH OR DRIED CHILI PEPPER, AT YOUR
DISCRETION AND TASTE

1 GARLIC CLOVE, COARSELY CHOPPED

1¼ POUNDS TOMATOES, PEELED,
SEEDED, AND FINELY CHOPPED (OR
THE EQUIVALENT OF *POLPA DI
POMODORO*—SEE PAGE 118)

6 BASIL LEAVES OR 3 TABLESPOONS
COARSELY CHOPPED FLAT-LEAF PARSLEY

14 OUNCES *PENNE RIGATE*

SALT

*This sauce has gained worldwide popularity through the multitude of Italian restaurants and trattorias. It is also eaten in every region of Italy. Arrabbiata means angry, and the sauce is so called because of the abundance of chili it contains.* Penne *is the usual pasta for serving with it.*

Heat the oil in a pan, add the onion, chili, and garlic and fry for 1 minute. Stir in the tomatoes and cook, not too quickly, for 6 to 8 minutes, then add the basil or parsley and salt to taste.

Cook the pasta in boiling salted water until *al dente*. Drain and mix with the sauce, allowing it to absorb the flavors for a minute. No Parmesan cheese here!

*ARRABBIATA* SAUCE READY TO BE ADDED TO
THE PASTA

# PEVERADA DI TREVISO

## TREVISO PEPPER SAUCE

### FOR 4 TO 6

4 TABLESPOONS EXTRA-VIRGIN OLIVE OIL

1 ONION, VERY FINELY CHOPPED

1 CARROT, CUT INTO VERY SMALL CUBES

3$^{1}$/$_{2}$ OUNCES *SPECK* (SEE PAGE 84), CUT INTO
  STRIPS, THEN INTO SMALL CUBES

3 ANCHOVY FILLETS, FINELY CHOPPED

ZEST OF $^{1}$/$_{4}$ LEMON

10$^{1}$/$_{2}$ OUNCES VERY FRESH CHICKEN
  LIVERS, CLEANED, VERY FINELY
  CHOPPED

5 TABLESPOONS DRY WHITE WINE

1 TABLESPOON WHITE WINE VINEGAR

1 TO 2 TEASPOONS BLACK PEPPER, NOT TOO
  FINELY GROUND

$^{1}$/$_{2}$ CUP CHICKEN STOCK

2 TABLESPOONS FINELY CHOPPED FLAT-LEAF
  PARSLEY

SALT

*In and around the town of Treviso in northern Italy, this sauce, not to be confused with the totally different* peara *of Verona, is a must for serving with chicken, guinea fowl, pigeon, and most game. It comes in many versions but the abundant use of black pepper is its main characteristic. If you simmer it to evaporate the moisture it can also be used as a spread for* crostini.

Heat the oil in a pan, add the onion, carrot, and *speck*, and fry for a few minutes until the onion is translucent. Add the anchovies, lemon zest, and chicken livers and stir-fry for 5 minutes, then add the wine, vinegar, black pepper, and some salt and cook, stirring from time to time, for 5 minutes. Add the stock, reduce the heat, and simmer for 5 minutes.

Just before serving, stir in the parsley and adjust the seasoning with salt and pepper.

# PESTO ALLA GENOVESE CON TROFIE

## PESTO WITH TROFIE PASTA

### FOR 4

14 OUNCES *TROFIE* PASTA (SEE PAGE
  167)

### FOR THE PESTO:

2 CUPS FRESHLY PICKED BASIL LEAVES,
  PREFERABLY LIGURIAN SMALL-
  LEAFED BASIL

LARGE PINCH COARSE SEA SALT

1$^{1}$/$_{2}$ TABLESPOONS PINE NUTS, TOASTED

2 GARLIC CLOVES, ROUGHLY CHOPPED

1$^{3}$/$_{4}$ OUNCES PARMESAN CHEESE,
  GRATED (IF YOU PREFER A STRONGER
  SAUCE, USE *PECORINO* INSTEAD)

$^{2}$/$_{3}$ CUP LIGURIAN EXTRA-VIRGIN
  OLIVE OIL

*One of the most famous Italian sauces, pesto is served with pasta, minestrone, and other dishes. Here it is accompanied by* trofie, *a type of pasta twirl which is still handmade in Liguria; elsewhere the commercially produced version is very good. Another typical Ligurian pasta,* trenette, *is sometimes cooked with a few potatoes and green beans and then dressed with pesto. Many versions of this sauce exist; this is representative of them all.*

You could put all the ingredients for the pesto in a food processor and after a few seconds it is all over. However, the taste of real pesto is obtained using a pestle and mortar. Put the dry basil leaves in a mortar with the salt, pine nuts, and garlic. Rotate the pestle to grind all the ingredients, using the salt at the bottom of the mortar to help break them down. Work like this for a while until you see a pulp starting to form. Still working with the pestle, add the cheese a little at a time and pound until it has all been absorbed and a thick paste has formed. Now start to pour in the oil a little at a time and work with the pestle until it has all been absorbed.

Cook the pasta in boiling salted water until *al dente*, then drain, reserving 2 to 3 tablespoons of the cooking water. Put the pesto in a pan, dilute with the reserved cooking water and just warm through. Mix with the pasta and serve.

# FEGATO AL BALSAMICO
## CALVES' LIVER WITH BALSAMIC VINEGAR

**FOR 4**

8 THIN SLICES CALVES' LIVER
FLOUR FOR DREDGING
3 TABLESPOONS BUTTER
4 TABLESPOONS BALSAMIC VINEGAR
SALT AND PEPPER

*This delightful dish is very popular in the North, especially in Emilia-Romagna, where balsamic vinegar is made.*

Dredge the slices of liver with flour and shake off any excess. Melt the butter in a large pan. As soon as it is hot, increase the heat and fry the liver very briefly—about 1½ minutes on each side. Add the vinegar and stir to scrape up the browned bits from the bottom of the pan. Season the liver with salt and pepper and serve immediately.

# PATATE AL ROSMARINO
## POTATOES WITH ROSEMARY

**FOR 6 TO 8**

3¼ POUNDS WAXY POTATOES
SALT
A FEW SPRIGS ROSEMARY
4 SAGE LEAVES
ABUNDANT TUSCAN EXTRA-VIRGIN OLIVE
 OIL FOR FRYING

*Rosemary has such an intense flavor that it should be used carefully. Potatoes, however, can take strong flavors, especially when combined with peppery Tuscan olive oil, as in this recipe. Potatoes cooked in this way can accompany any meat dish.*

Peel the potatoes and boil them in lightly salted water for 10 minutes. Drain and cut into ¾-inch cubes.

Put a generous layer of olive oil in a large skillet over medium heat and add the potatoes. Cook until tender and brown, stirring often to ensure that the potatoes brown on all sides. Add the rosemary and sage half way through cooking and season with salt just before serving.

# PANPEPATO
PEPPERED BREAD

**MAKES 1 LOAF (FOR 6 TO 8)**

HEAPING 1/2 CUP ALMONDS, BLANCHED,
SKINNED, TOASTED, AND CHOPPED

HEAPING 1/2 CUP HAZELNUTS, TOASTED
AND SKINNED

HEAPING 1/2 CUP WALNUT HALVES

1/3 CUP PINE NUTS

1/3 CUP MUSCAT RAISINS, LEFT TO
SOAKED IN A FEW TABLESPOONS VIN
SANTO FOR 30 MINUTES, THEN
DRAINED

1/2 CUP COCOA POWDER

1/2 CUP MIXED CANDIED PEEL, CUT INTO
SMALL CUBES

1/2 TEASPOON GROUND CINNAMON

1/2 TEASPOON GROUND CORIANDER

1/2 TEASPOON FRESHLY GRATED NUTMEG

1 TEASPOON FRESHLY GROUND BLACK
PEPPER

1/3 CUP ACACIA HONEY

ALL-PURPOSE FLOUR

*This is another ancient specialty based on spices. In this case the name comes from the predominance of black pepper. Various versions exist in different regions, but Tuscany remains the main source of this delightful cake. This recipe comes from a pâtisserie in the town of Gubbio.*

Preheat the oven to 325° F. Mix all the ingredients together in a bowl, adding enough flour to obtain a fairly stiff mixture. Shape with wet hands into a round loaf and place on a buttered baking sheet. Bake for 30 minutes, then leave to cool before serving.

# GELATO ALLO ZAFFERANO
SAFFRON ICE CREAM

**FOR 6**

2¹/₂ CUPS MILK

PINCH SAFFRON POWDER

8 EGG YOLKS

HEAPING ¹/₂ CUP SUPERFINE SUGAR

³/₄ CUP HEAVY CREAM

*This is my own contribution to the ice cream world, rather than a traditional specialty. It was my aim to celebrate saffron, one of the most sought-after and expensive spices in the world. I believe it constitutes an expression of modern Italian cooking without being too clever.*

Bring the milk to a boil in a pan and add the saffron. Beat the egg yolks and sugar together in a bowl until foamy and then gradually pour in the milk, stirring all the time, to obtain a velvety mixture.

Pour the mixture into a bowl set over a pan of very hot water, making sure the water is not touching the bowl, and cook, stirring, until it begins to thicken.

Add the heavy cream, mix well, then transfer to an ice-cream maker and freeze. If you do not have an ice cream maker, pour the mixture into a shallow bowl, and place in the freezer for about 1 hour, until it is beginning to solidify around the edges. Whisk it well with a fork, then return to the freezer. Repeat this process 3 times and then freeze until firm.

# DAIRY PRODUCTS

## LATTE E DERIVATI

Milk is the first food mammals receive when they are born, and it continues to give warmth and nourishment until the youngster is able to take solid food. Today, I still dip bread into a bowl of milk when I want a comforting snack.

The amazing transformation of milk into cheese is almost as old as humanity. It is a miracle that is brought about by a coagulating agent, either from the stomach of a milk-fed calf or an artificial chemical or vegetable coagulant from the flower of the cardoon, or the milk of the fig plant, or even from some fungi. When the coagulant is added to the milk, the whey separates from the curds, producing a mass that can be strained, pasteurized, fermented, or aged, until it turns into what we know as cheese.

Everyone in Italy consumes quite a lot of milk daily. Children have their *scodella di latte* with cookies, and either at home or at a bar before going to work, adults have a cappuccino with a brioche for breakfast. Some of the milk is used fresh, some is turned into yogurt, and the rest is turned into cream, butter, and cheese. Lately cream has become very popular in cooking. Although it is pleasant to eat, I find it makes everything taste the same. In my restaurant, cream is not used widely. Cream is, however, important for pâtisserie and very

important in the making of ice cream, a product of which the Italians are very fond and knowledgeable. Italian soft cheeses like *mascarpone*, which is over 60% fat, are often used in desserts.

Each Italian region produces its own distinctive dairy products, which are hardly known in other regions. For example, on the eastern part of the Italian Riviera, *quagliata* (or as they call it in Ligurian dialect, *prescinsocua*), a coagulated milk similar to junket, is used mixed with pesto sauce or eaten on its own sweetened with sugar. In other parts of Italy, *cagliata*, a kind of Italian unfermented yogurt, is eaten with fruit.

One of the images of my childhood in Piedmont is the exodus of the cows to the mountains as soon as the snow had melted, the herds accompanied by a smiling, brown-faced cowboy or -girl. The cows would return in the fall after having spent a very productive summer. With their huge bells hanging around their necks, you could hear them far away in the valley. Everybody in the village turned out to see the spectacle of hundreds of cows returning, led by the *reine*—or Queen—and the major bull, both decorated with flowers and bows in the colors of the Italian flag. They really looked liked they were coming back from their vacation, and I can still smell the

strong-scented leftovers on the road, which people collected to put in their geranium pots!

Fortunately, the inhabitants of the Aosta Valley retain their sense of tradition in the annual *La Bataille des Reines*, among other festivals. It takes place near Aosta between the more belligerent cows, not the bulls. This demonstration of their determination is not a cruel spectacle; the farmers place bets on which cow will win—the losing cow just abandons the fields.

If, by chance, you find yourself in Aosta Valley in the Valle di Champoluc, take the cable car to the crest and visit my very good friend Nina Burgai. You cannot possibly miss her, she is one of the three inhabitants of this wonderful tranquil spot, where she runs a small hotel. As soon as you arrive she will probably offer you a coffee, into which she may put a knob of her own butter (as she always does for me). The butter is made locally at the altitude of 6,500 feet, where Nina's happy cows roam. The creamy milk is put in a large copper bowl and then into a small storehouse that sits over the burbling cold mountain stream. The butter has a unique fragrance and is like a light and foamy

ABOVE: SHEEP GRAZING ON SPRING PASTURE IN SICILY

cream when it is in the coffee; it is not oily and fatty as you might imagine. The taste and smell of all those minty grasses and herbs of the high mountain pasture are reflected in the foam—a unique experience.

Of course, the most important category of dairy products is cheese. During the cheese-making process, and depending on the kind of milk used and the results required, the cheese can be drained in perforated baskets made out of willow, plastic, or stainless steel and the resulting mass pressed together. It can then either be immersed in brine, or salt can be added directly to the cheese as a preservative, before it is left to age.

Because of its geographical position and its array of different landscapes, Italy has a great history of cheese-making. Starting from the luscious North, some of the Alpine slopes are carpeted with the juiciest and most aromatic pasture imaginable. Farther down toward the Po is the region of Emilia-Romagna, which is the home of what is perhaps the most prestigious—and certainly most famous—Italian cheese, Parmesan. From Liguria toward the Apennines, the vegetation becomes sparser and sparser until in Puglia and Calabria, Sicily, and Sardinia, the type of farming is totally different, and sheep's and goats' milk gradually replaces cows' milk in cheese-making. Most of the cheeses are hard for grating, but you will also find soft fresh cheeses such as *ricotta*, *caciotta*, and many others.

Just south of Rome and in the Naples region was originally buffalo territory and here there are hundreds of small artisanal producers of specialties using buffalo milk. Now, however, delicious *buffalo mozzarella* is produced all over southern Italy, as well as industrial versions using cows' milk made in the North.

As the Italian dairy industry has grown, laws have had to be implemented to enforce and the good

TOP RIGHT: [LEFT TO RIGHT] MATURE *PECORINO SARDO*, FRESH *PECORINO*, *PECORINO* WITH PEPPERS, ACCOMPANIED BY FRESH FAVA BEANS

RIGHT: GOATS ON THEIR WAY TO MARKET IN SICILY

FAR LEFT: CHEESES AND BUTTERS OF THE LANGHE IN PIEDMONT: INCLUDING *CASTELMAGNO, TOMA, RASCHERA, BIANCO SOTTO BOSCO, TOMINI* AND *CAPRINI*, WITH CHESTNUTS AND RED VINE LEAVES

LEFT: CHEESES FROM BATTIPAGLIA IN CAMPANIA: INCLUDING *BURRINO, PROVOLETTA, SCAMORZA AFFUMICATA, MOZZARELLA AFFUMICATA, RICOTTA SALATA, RICOTTA FRESCA, MOZZARELLA FARCITA, MOZZARELLA, BOCCONCINO* WITH *MASCARPONE*

quality and the origin of the best cheeses. *Consorzi* are cooperatives or agencies of producers of the same type of cheese. Their self-imposed systems of production control ensure that each member uses only the best local milk and makes the cheese in the traditional manner, in some cases by methods that have been followed for centuries. These cheeses are DOC (*Denominazione di Origine Controllata*), protected in just the same way as fine wines, in the equivalent of France's *appellation contrôlée*.

Usually DOC cheeses have their own brand or stamp on the rind and in many cases the cheeses are numbered and dated so that their authenticity can be checked more effectively. In the case of such cheeses, the milk that is used to produce them has to be from a certain type of cow. For example, the original brown cows whose milk was used to make Parmesan cheese could only be milked by human hands, rejecting the much more convenient but soulless machines. This is just one of the many reasons why Parmesan is so expensive.

Italian cheeses are classified first by the milk used, and then by their consistency, and sometimes by the methods used in their manufacture. Starting with milk, there are four different varieties:

*Cows' milk:* mostly available in the North and used for most of the familiar soft and hard cheeses, like *mascarpone*, *Gorgonzola*, and Parmesan.

*Buffaloes' milk:* produced almost exclusively in the regions of Lazio, Campania, Puglia, and Calabria, and almost all of it used to make *mozzarella*. The most famous *mozzarella di bufala* is made in the Battipaglia near Salerno. Nowadays, however, buffalo milk is either mixed with—or totally replaced by—cows' milk in much *mozzarella* manufacture, to make a more economical (but not necessarily better-quality) cheese.

*Goats' milk* and *sheep's milk:* the areas in which these milks are more widely produced are Tuscany, Lazio, and the entire South, including Sicily and Sardinia. There is a return to their production, due to increasing popular demand for *pecorino* and *caprino*.

The main cheese consistency categories are:
*Formaggi a pasta molle* (soft cheeses), which include all fresh cheeses. They have a content of more than 40% water and must be consumed soon

after production as they are best when eaten fresh. Cheeses in this group include *mascarpone*, *mozzarella*, *formaggella*, and *robiola*. *Formaggi a pasta dura* (hard cheeses), to which *stagionati* or aged cheeses belong, have a water content of less than 40%. The longer hard cheeses age, the more water evaporates and the harder the cheese becomes. It is then used grated for sprinkling on top of dishes and in cooking. Cheeses like Parmesan and *pecorino* belong to this category.

Fat content categorizes cheeses further with: *formaggi magri* (low-fat cheeses), with a fat content of less than 20%; *formaggi semi grassi* (half-fat cheeses), having a fat content of 20 to 42%; *formaggi grassi* (full-fat cheeses), with a fat content of over 42%. The fat content is determined by the milk used, which can be either *scremato* (skimmed), *parzialmente scremato* (semi-skimmed), *incro* (full fat), or *con aggiunta di panna* (with added cream).

Cheese can also be either pasteurized, indicating that it has been heat-treated to kill any bacteria, or left unpasteurized to make *pasta cruda*, cheeses that continue to develop as they age. *Formaggi fermentati*, fermented cheeses, belong to this second group and include cheeses such as *caciocavallo* and *provolone*, both of which are made with partially pasteurized milk.

Some cheeses are made for eating on their own, and are called *formaggio da tavola*, or table cheeses, while others are made for use in cooking and are called *formaggio per cucina*. When buying cheese for the table, you should always buy from the best shop so that you can be sure of good quality. If you are not sure, ask for information about how to keep or serve a cheese. If you are having a formal lunch, either serve one exceptionally good cheese or a selection of six cheeses, of which three should be soft and three semi-hard, including at least one blue cheese.

Cheese should be served when it is at the peak of its maturity, with a variety of breads and *grissini*, and a few curls of butter, toasted hazelnuts, walnuts, small bunches of red grapes, pieces of fresh pear, and celery. Keep cheese in the least-cold part of the refrigerator and take it out at least an hour and a half before serving. I personally only keep the very fresh cheeses like *ricotta* and *mozzarella* in the refrigerator.

# A-Z OF DAIRY PRODUCTS

## ASIAGO

This cheese has been made since medieval times, although it has only been eaten all over Italy since the beginning of this century. There are three varieties: *Asiago d'allevo*, *Asiago pressato*, and *Asiago grasso di monte*.

The first, *Asiago d'allevo*, is a half-fat hard cheese made from cows' milk, with a smooth crust. Quite a compact cheese, with holes in the paste, it has a light straw color and a sweet flavor. The milk for this cheese comes from the cows that graze on the Altopiano di Asiago, the Alpine pastures of Veneto. Formed into rounds with a diameter of about 12 to 14 inches, 4 to 5 inches in height, and weighing 18 to 27 pounds, it is one of the region's most interesting cheeses. It is aged for varying amounts of time: for six months, when it is known as *mezzo anello*; 12 months, when it is known as *vecchio*; 18 months, when it is called *stravecchio*; or for 2 years, when it is known as *vecchio di montagna*. Only *mezzo anello* is eaten at the table, otherwise the cheese is used for cooking and grating, especially with *polenta*, *pasticciata*, *raviolini*, and *sopa acquada*, among other dishes.

The second variety of *Asiago* is *Asiago pressato*, a semi-cooked, full-cream cows'-milk cheese with a fat content of 44%, which comes in drums with a diameter of 12 to 16 inches, weighing 24 to 33 pounds. It takes between 20 and 40 days to mature, and is mainly eaten at table. It is made in the whole of the Veneto area, and thus does not carry the guarantee of quality conferred by the DOC label.

The third variety of this cheese, *Asiago grasso di monte* is a full-fat soft cheese made only between June and September in the Altopiano di Asiago, from the full-cream milk of cows that graze on pastures 3,000 feet above sea level.

## BAGOSSO, BAGOSS, BAGOLINO

In the Caffaro Valley in the province of Brescia (Lombardy), cows' milk is used to produce these half-fat round cheeses, weighing about 32 to 36 pounds, which can be eaten fresh at 3 months or aged up to 24 months and used for grating or cut in slices and broiled. It is very much the local *formaggio da tavola*.

## BEL PAESE

This is probably the first cheese to be commercialized on a large scale. Produced by the company Egidio Galbani around the turn of the century, *bel paese* (meaning "beautiful land") is a soft cows' milk cheese with a creamy yellow color and a fat content of 45%. Used initially as a table cheese, it is now widely used for cooking because of its melting properties, especially in pasta timbales or in the modern *toast al formaggio e prosciutto* (ham and cheese toast). Due to the increasing popularity of other cheeses, the *bel paese* is disappearing more and more from Italian cheeseboards and restaurants.

## BITTO

From the province of Sondrio in Lombardy comes this well-known half-fat cooked cheese, which is mostly used for grating or for cooking, depending on its age (up to 1 year). The cheeses weigh between 39 and 55 pounds, and their taste is mellow and fragrant. *Bitto* is used in making *pizzoccheri* (see page 181), but it is also eaten as a table cheese, accompanied by the famous local wines, like Sassella and Grumello.

## BOCCONCINO

From the diminutive of *boccone* meaning "mouthful," this term is used in various connections, but always regarding food. *Bocconcino* has been generally adopted to indicate a small *mozzarella*, the size of a walnut, which is used for party food or for salads with tomatoes.

## BRA

This semi-hard, half-fat (32%) cheese made with semi-skimmed cows' milk comes from the town of Cuneo in the province of Piedmont. Its name is taken from the little town of Bra, which is reputed to be the commercial center of the production of the cheese. The cheese is sweet-tasting, mild, and flavorsome, with little holes in the paste and a white center. There are two versions: the fresh cheese, which is matured for 45 days and used as table cheese and for cooking; and the aged one, which is matured for one year to produce a semi-hard cheese which is good for grating. Bra comes in rounds with a diameter of 12 to 16 inches, 2³/₄ to 3¹/₂ inches high, and weighing around 13 to 24 pounds.

## BRANZI

This country cheese from the Brembana Valley in Bergano, Lombardy, is made from cows' milk and comes in two varieties: one made with full-cream milk mixed with semi-skimmed, and the other with just full-cream milk. The best is produced between June and July, when the cow, have grazed on lush mountain grass.

The curds are twice cooked at 113°F, then are broken. They are then put in wooden molds 16 to 18 inches in diameter and 3¹/₂ to 4³/₄ inches high, and pressed to squeeze out the whey. The molds are then topped up before being put into a salt brine for 3 to 4 days. The ageing takes place in a temperature-controlled room at 50 to 55°F and the cheeses are turned every second day for 3 to 6 months.

LEFT: *BEL PAESE*

*Branzi* is an excellent semi-soft cheese of exceptional quality and is mostly used at table or for cooking delicately flavored dishes.

### BRIS, BRÔS, BRÜS, BRUSSU

This cheese is a specialty of Piedmont, made with a variety of cheeses that are cut up in small pieces and then put in a jar to ferment for a few days. After this time, grappa is added to the jar, and this is then left to age for couple of weeks to make a creamy cheese for spreading on bread or *polenta* (see recipe, page 252). Because it is a preparation made by individual families, there is a great deal of variation of the exact recipe, with the addition of other flavorings like oil, pepper, wine, and chili. I think that the sharp tang of this cheese has been deliberately created so that it has to be washed down with the local wines, Barolo or Barbera.

### BURRATA

This is one of the most delicate fresh cheeses to have been developed in the last eighty years and, thanks to the family in Puglia that has created it, it now supports a whole cottage industry. It is a soft ball made up of layers of cows' milk cheese similar to *mozzarella*, although slightly creamier. It should be eaten within 24 hours of being made. This full-fat cheese is eaten as a dessert, served with a little salt, pepper, and sometimes a little extra-virgin olive oil.

### BURRINO, BUTIRRO

This ancient method of preserving butter was developed because the high temperatures in the South would otherwise only allow butter to be kept for a day or two. The principle in *burrino*, or *butirro*, as it is called in the area of Avellino and Sorrento, is to encase the butter in a sealed envelope of cheese.

A round casing is made with a *pasta filata* of cows' milk, as with *provolone* and *mozzarella*. The curds are worked initially by hand, as in the making of *mozzarella*, to spin it into strings which will result in layers in the finished cheese. When shaping the pear-shaped cheeses, an opening is left on top to allow the insertion of a ball of butter 1¼ to 1½ inches in diameter. This is then sealed and the cheese allowed to dry by hanging the balls in pairs on a cane. After one week the exterior will have hardened a little and the butter inside will confer a wonderful soft taste. Each pear can weigh from 7 to 14 ounces and can be kept for a month or two. The cheese is eaten cut in slices with bread, and the butter is used as such.

### BURRO / BUTTER

Butter is obtained by collecting the cream off the top of the milk. After allowing the cream to undergo a little natural fermentation to develop flavor, it is put in a revolving container and churned

until a clotted mass of the fat results, and the excess water is discarded. This mass is then pressed into rectangular shapes for packaging.

Italian butter is generally unsalted and is especially flavorsome, particularly when made with Alpine milk. Butter is often used in the making of cakes, cookies, and tarts, but is used in general cooking mainly in the North. Even there nowadays, however, it is suffering in competition with southern olive oil for reasons of health. Butter is the dairy product with the highest fat content, at least 82%, and the fat is highly saturated.

### CACIO / CHEESE

*Cacio* is a generic term for cheese, from the Latin *caseum*, and is mostly used in Tuscany. However, various cheeses take this initial name, as in *caciotta*, *caciocavallo*, or *cacioricotta*, to indicate a slightly aged *ricotta* almost turned into cheese.

### CACIOCAVALLO

Originally from Naples, *caciocavallo* is a uncooked cheese made with cows' milk. Using the *pasta filata* method (see page 244), the curds are worked when hot into a stringy mass, which is molded by hand into a pear shape, then hung to dry. Like *burrino*, they are tied in pairs (a *cavallo*, from which it possibly gets its name) over a stick. These are then hung from the ceiling for 3 to 12 months, depending on whether they are to be eaten fresh or grated, until dried and matured. The finished cheese weighs around 2¼ to 4½ pounds.

*Caciocavallo* is a specialty of southern provinces like Campania, Abruzzo, Puglia, Calabria, and Sicily, although it is also made in the North. In Sicily there is a special variety of *caciocavallo* made in Ragusa using cows' and sheep's milk, which is salted then aged for up to one year. It is used grated as a substitute for Parmesan.

### CACIOFIORE

This cheese from central Italy is made from full-fat sheep's milk using a vegetable rennet from wild artichokes. It is a soft fresh cheese, sometimes colored with saffron, to be eaten after 2 weeks, or to be used for cooking.

### CACIORICOTTA, RICOTTA SALATA / SALTED RICOTTA

A specialty from Puglia, this is a salted *ricotta* used for grating on Pugliese dishes. *Cacioricotta* is a hard, dense cheese that is used locally, grated on pasta dishes instead of Parmesan, or to make *calzone di cipolle*, an onion *calzone*.

## CACIOTTA

*Caciotta* is a semi-soft cheese made in various regions of Italy, using cows', ewes', or goats' milk. It is round and weighs about 2$^1/4$ pounds. When young and fresh it has a very mild flavor, which makes it ideal for children: if matured for about a month, the rind yellows slightly but the cheese stays white, although it has a stronger flavor. The most important regions for *caciotta* are Tuscany, Marche, Lazio, Umbria, and Puglia, although the cheese from Tuscany is the best-known and most sought-after. In many regions this name is used to

describe a different product, but always one to be eaten as a very young table cheese or for cooking. *Caciotta* is ideal to eat with fresh fava beans, accompanied by good bread and a glass of red wine.

### CAGLIATA, SEE QUAGLIATA

### CANESTRATO

*Canestro* means "basket," and *canestrato* is named after the mesh used to strain the curds. For thousands of years this mesh was made with woven straw or rush, but now it is unfortunately made of plastic. Mainly produced in Puglia, Sicily, and Sardinia, *canestrato* is a semi-cooked cheese made with cows' and ewes' milk and then pressed by hand into the basket. Round in shape, it weighs about 4$^1/2$ to 6$^1/2$ pounds and is imprinted with the weave of the basket. It is salted in brine then aged for 2 to 6 months, or even longer depending on whether it is to be used fresh or matured for grating. It is used in the same ways

as *caciotta*, and has a mild flavor that strengthens with age.

### CAPRINO / GOAT CHEESE

Italian goat cheeses are either made from raw goats' milk or with semi-cooked milk. The latter is left to mature for 2 or 3 months and is then used as it is. However, in Liguria and more especially in Piedmont, it is traditional to immerse the cheese in vinegar and oil, sometimes with added chili. In Alba, there is a new development whereby the little round cheeses, 1$^1/2$ inches across and $^3/4$ inch high, are preserved in oil with truffle.

There is also an aged version of *caprino* which has a slightly yellower skin but the same white center and delicate flavor. In the South and in Sardinia, where the tough dry grass is ideal for goats and produces a strong and flavorsome milk, a version called *meridionale* is made. It comes in little drums with a diameter of 3$^1/2$ to 7$^1/4$ inches, 1$^3/4$ to 5$^1/4$ inches high, and weighing 2$^3/4$ to 11 pounds, and is only aged for 20 to 30 days. This very white cheese with little holes has a hard rind. *Formaggini* or *robiolini* is another *caprino* from the area around Como in Lombardy, but the most famous comes from Valsassina and Montevecchio in the Lambro Valley in Lombardy.

### CASTELMAGNO

One of the most popular Piedmontese cheeses, this blue cheese is made in the area around the town of Castelmagno in the province of Cuneo. A semi-hard cheese with only 34% fat content, it is made from cows' milk and a little partially skimmed ewes' milk. The initial curd is hung for 24 hours in cloth to allow the whey to drain out. It is then placed in a large wooden container for 4 to 5 days before being divided into molds to mature. Each cheese weighs between 6$^1/2$ and 15$^1/4$ pounds and has a diameter

of 6 to 10 inches and a height of 4$^3/4$ to 8 inches. It is kept in stone cases at a constant temperature of 50 to 54°F for 4 to 6 months, during which time it develops its unique nutty flavor. It is an excellent white cheese, dotted with green mold, that is mostly eaten as a table cheese.

### CASUMARZU / SARDINIAN ROTTEN CHEESE

Sardinian *casumarzu* is a type of *pecorino*. One certainly needs a strong stomach to enjoy Sardinian *casumarzu*, because its main characteristic is that it contains little white maggots, which are considered a delicacy. The maggots are added to a matured *pecorino* cheese through a little hole in the top, then a few drops of fresh milk are added as well. The cheese is left to develop at room temperature and, when it is ready, the maggots (tasting of *pecorino*) can be scooped out with bread.

### CRESCENZA

It takes 100 quarts of full-cream pasteurized cows' milk to make from 32$^1/2$ to 37 pounds of full-fat (48%) *crescenza* cheese, depending on how long it has been drained. This typical Lombardian soft cheese was at one time made only in the winter months because of its tendency to turn sour. With the help of today's technology, however, it can be produced all year round. *Crescenza* is made by an elaborate procedure which takes place strictly at room temperature. The finished cheese is sold in 7$^1/4$-to 8-inch squares, 1$^1/4$ to 2$^1/2$ inches high and weighing 3$^3/4$ to 4$^1/2$ pounds, although it is also sold in 7-ounce chunks enveloped in a special waterproof paper. It should be eaten 5 to 8 days after it has been made. It has various roles in the kitchen, especially in the specialty of Camogli in Liguria called *focaccia al formaggio*, a delicious thin *focaccia* stuffed with melted *crescenza*. It also makes an excellent dessert cheese.

### DOLCELATTE / SOFT BLUE CHEESE

Literally translated, *dolcelatte* means "sweet milk," and the cheese is

LEFT: HAND-MILKING A GOAT IN PIEDMONT

BELOW: FRESH GOAT CHEESES WITH HERBS, PEPPER, AND ASH

simply a much milder version of *Gorgonzola*, created by an Italian commercial cheese-making company. It does not have an official denomination, but is one of the best-known Italian cheeses throughout the world.

## FIOR DI LATTE / MOZZARELLA-TYPE CHEESE

This cheese, similar to *mozzarella*, is industrially produced in the North of Italy while *mozzarella* is made in the South. The main difference between *fior di latte* and *mozzarella* is that the former is made from cows' and the latter generally from buffaloes' milk (see *mozzarella*). *Fior di latte* is sold in 5- to 7-ounce portions in plastic packets, together with a small amount of its own whey to keep it moist and fresh. It should be used as soon as it is removed from the whey, and can be eaten not only raw in salads, like *mozzarella*, but also on pizzas and pasta.

## FONTAL

*Fontal* is the industrial copy of *fontina* cheese (below), a very similarly shaped cheese with similar technical characteristics, but with only half of the flavor of *fontina*. It can be made anywhere outside the Aosta Valley, using cows' milk coming from any other areas.

## FONTINA

*Fontina* cheese is associated with the Aosta Valley in Piedmont. The tradition of its manufacture very ancient, and it has been produced since the twelfth century. The region is extremely proud of this product, which literally brings the fragrance of the pastures to the table. It is produced by a cooperative of *fontina*-makers from 74 towns in the valley.

The cows used to produce the milk come from the Val d'Aosta area, and they are very carefully controlled to maintain a high standard in the cheese. The milk from these herds has to be used immediately, at most 2 hours after being collected, which is why milk from cows high up in the Alps is transported to a central storage area in Aosta for distribution.

After the cheese has been pressed, it is carefully aged in temperature-controlled cellars. The cheeses are stored on slats and turned every day. The white mold that grows on its surface is cleaned off with a cloth and the cheese is dipped in a saline solution every other day.

*Fontina* is a full-fat, semi-soft cheese sold in wheels 14 to 18 inches in diameter, $3^{1}/_{4}$ to 4 inches high, and weighing 18 to 39 pounds. It has a strong orange-brown rind $^{1}/_{12}$ inch thick, while the cheese itself is a soft, elastic pale yellow sprinkled with copious holes. It takes 2 to 6 months to mature, depending on the maker. Its very sweet flavor makes it ideal for cooking, while its melting quality means it is ideal for fondue, although it can also be eaten raw. It has a high fat content of 45%, one of the highest in Italian cheese.

## GELATO / ICE CREAM

The practice of preserving snow in caves was brought to Sicily by the Arabs. In Sicily also, snow was mixed with citrus fruit pulp to make early sorbets. The Romans then developed the technique of mixing snow and ice with fruit and honey. In 1533, Caterina de Medici took this, among many other culinary novelties, with her to France when she married Henri II.

It was, however, a Sicilian, Francesco Procopio, who opened a café in Paris at which new techniques were used to produce real ice cream, based on cream, eggs, and sugar, as we know it today. However, the invention of this product has actually been credited to a French chef of the British King Charles I, in 1650.

Today ice cream is representative of Italy, where the best artisanal ice cream is produced. The most famous *gelaterie* are still to be found in Campania and Sicily. Also, like *pizzerie*, you can find Italian run ice-cream parlors all over the world.

## GORGONZOLA / BLUE CHEESE

Thousands of years old, this blue (*erborinato*) cows'-milk cheese originates in the town of Gorgonzola in Lombardy, although today it can also be made in Novara, Vercelli, Pavia, Cuneo Mortara, Milano, Brescia, Como, Cremona, and Bergano. It is a full-fat cheese (48%) and comes in a drum 10 to 12 inches in diameter, $6^{1}/_{4}$ to 8 inches in height, and 7 to 28 pounds in weight. The milk used to make it comes from herds that graze the nearby Alps. It was once produced by locals using unpasteurized milk, but today it is commercially made using pasteurized milk with fermentation aids and a selection of molds called *Penicillium glaucum*, which give the typical blue marbling and unique flavor. It is aged in temperature-controlled caves at 39 to 41°F over 2 to 4 months.

*Gorgonzola* is an excellent table cheese, but can also be used in sauces for pasta or *gnocchi*, or simply with plain *polenta*. *Torta di san gaudenzio* consists of alternating layers of *gorgonzola* and *mascarpone*.

## GRANA PADANO, PARMIGIANO REGGIANO / ITALIAN HARD CHEESE

It is almost impossible to divide these two cheeses, but the differences between the two are many. Although technically both cheeses are made in almost exactly the same way, there is a perceptible difference in flavor. The history of *parmigiano* and *grana* goes back to the twelfth century, when the Po Valley was turned from waterlogged soil to fertile land suitable for the grazing of cows and sheep.

*Parmigiano reggiano* used to be made only between 1 April and 11 November, but today both types of cheese can be produced throughout the year. However, the cows that produce the milk for *parmigiano reggiano* can be fed only on grass and hay, but the cows producing the milk for *grana padano* can be fed on many other foods as well. In general, it takes longer to age *parmigiano reggiano* than *grana padano*, and *parmigiano reggiano* does not contain any additives to aid fermentation.

*Parmigiano reggiano* can only be made in Parma, Reggio Emilia, Modena, Mantova on the right of the river Po, and Bologna on the left of the river Reno. *Grana padano* is made in the provinces of Alessandria, Asti, Cuneo, Novara, Torino Vercelli, Bergamo, Brescia, Como, Cremona, Mantova on the left of the river Po, Milano, Pavia, Sondrio, Varese, Trento, Padova, Rovigo, Venezia, Verona, Vicenza, Bologna on the right of the river Remo, Ferrara, Forli, Piacenza, and Ravenna. In other words *parmigiano reggiano* can only be

made in Emilia-Romagna, while regions such as Piedmont, Lombardy, Veneto, Trentino, and parts of Romagna are all allowed to make *grana padano*.

Because they are so dense, *parmigiano* and *grana padano* cannot be cut, but rather are forced apart with special knives. If the cheese is well made, a precise line will give a clean breaking point. Parmesan is not only grated over most Italian pasta dishes (except those containing fish), but it is also used to flavor omelets, grated and added to other ingredients as a filling, cut or shaved into slices and sprinkled on *carpaccio* and into salads. It is also delicious eaten with fruit such as pears, grapes, figs, walnuts, or hazelnuts, or even dressed with a few drops of balsamic vinegar.

## MANTECA

This is the Pugliese version of the *butirro*, a *scamorza* cheese filled with butter. See *burrino*.

## MANTECARE

This is a term especially used in Veneto and Lombardy for an operation involving the addition of a knob of butter and some grated Parmesan cheese at the end of making *risotto*, to make it creamy and shiny. It probably comes from the Spanish word for butter, *mantequilla*.

## MARZOLINO

Produced in the area around Siena by Sardinian shepherds who traditionally migrated to Tuscany, this fresh soft cheese similar to *caciotta*, was at one time made from ewes' milk given after the first fresh grass feeding in March. In the past,

also, a vegetable rennet made from a wild thistle was used to firm the curds; today, however, animal (sheep) rennet is employed. The cheese is still oval in shape, weighing $17^{1}/_{2}$ to 21 ounces, with a full and fragrant flavor, and it is mostly eaten as a table cheese. A similar cheese, called *baccellone*, is produced in the area around Pisa and is made in the spring when the fava beans, with which the cheese is traditionally eaten, are young and sweet (see also *pecorino*).

## MASCARPONE, MASCHERPONE

Initially only made in southern Lombardy, in the province of Lodi, *mascarpone* is now produced in various Italian regions. Made within 24 hours from pasteurized cream coagulated with citric or 5% tartaric acid, it is a very soft cheese, which must be consumed immediately. One hundred quarts of cream produce 90 to 110 pounds of *mascarpone* with a fat content of 50% and up.

*Mascarpone* is seldom used as cheese, but is extremely valuable as an ingredient for sweets and desserts, one of the most famous being *tiramisu*. It is also used, together with herbs, as a filling for *ravioli* or as a thickener for sauces. In the past it was packed in small fabric containers, but it is now sold in jars or plastic containers.

## MONTASIO

A DOC cheese from the Friulian region in the northeast corner of Italy, *Montasio* is also made in the provinces of Belluno, Treviso, Padova, Venice (with the main area of production around Pordenone), Gorizia, and Trieste. Its name comes from the area around the Montasio Massif in the Roccolone Valley. It is made using the milk from Red Pezzata and Alpine Brown cows, which are kept in immaculate pens on the steep hills in the area, away from any pollution from roads.

This hard cheese can be eaten fresh after just a two-hour maturation period, semi-fresh after four months ageing, or fully

LEFT: THE REGION OF EMILIA-ROMAGNA ONLY PERMITS THE WARRANTY STAMP ON PERFECT PARMESAN WHICH HAS BEEN AGED FOR A MINIMUM OF 18 MONTHS

# HOW PARMIGIANO REGGIANO IS PRODUCED

The milk is filtered, then left overnight so the cream can rise to the surface and be skimmed off. This skimmed milk, still 1.8 to 2.1% fat, is mixed with the unskimmed morning milk and then poured into huge double-walled copper cauldrons which allow steam to circulate, thereby regulating the temperature of the milk. The milk is brought to 90° to 91° F and stirred continuously while the rennet is added, and it turns into curds within 10 minutes. Each cauldron contains 250 gallons of milk, producing about 70 to 77 pounds of curds.

The curd is then cut or broken into tiny pieces, each the size of a grain of corn, and then cut even smaller. Throughout this procedure, the curds and whey are continuously stirred by a mechanical arm. They are then heated to 109° to 111° F for a few minutes and then the temperature is raised to 129° to 133° F. This process takes 45 to 50 minutes. The mixture is heated again for another 45 minutes to allow the curds to collect before they are lifted and placed in a large linen cloth, still bathed in the whey. The curd is then divided into two even cakes, each of which is put into a new cloth, placed in a metal mold, and covered with a round wooden lid, which is weighed down to squeeze out any remaining liquid.

 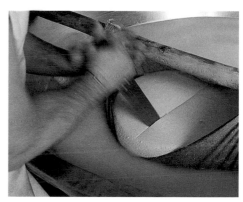

The cloth is changed again an hour later, the cheese turned over, and the curds reshaped in the mold. This process of turning is repeated every two hours, four or five times until a crust forms. The cheeses are then put into a saline solution, where they are left for one day for every kilogram of weight, and are turned over every day. After about three days, the cheese is set on wooden slats to dry. After being cleaned of any mold, it is left to develop a crust before being set in a temperature-controlled room at 72° F for 6 to 7 days. The cheese is then heaped into piles divided by wooden boards, and left in large, airy, high-ceilinged rooms called cathedrals for 6 to 7 months to dry. During this time, each cheese is turned over every 4 to 5 days. For the following 6 to 7 months, it is turned every 10 to 12 days. This long ageing process goes some way to explaining the expense of the cheese.

# MAKING MOZZARELLA CHEESE

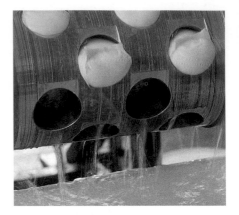

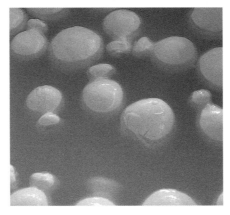

*Mozzarella* is a fresh, soft cheese, which should be consumed within 3 or 4 days of being made. The milk is heated to 91° to 93° F and rennet is added so that the milk forms curds and whey. The curds are then left to rest for twenty minutes before being cut into four parts. After another ten minutes, the curds are further cut or broken into walnut-sized pieces and left in the warm whey to mature. When a piece of curd placed in almost-boiling water breaks into strands (*pasta filata*), the curds are then ready for spinning.

The curd is taken out of the whey and left to drain on a special table. It is cut in small strips and immersed in water heated to 194° F. It is then spun by hand and shaped into individual portions varying in weight, including *bocconcini* (morsels) weighing 1 ounce, or *ciliegine* (little cherries) which are tiny, up to large, 1¼ -pound rounds or long braids. Once it has been shaped, the *mozzarella* is placed in cold water to cool and harden a little before being placed in salt brine for 30 minutes. Each piece of cheese is then packed in a waterproof container along with some salted water or a little milk and water so that it stays moist. A smoked version, called *provola*, has a harder yellowish-brown skin. The residue from the milk used in making *mozzarella* is used to produce the most wonderful *ricotta*.

matured after 12 months. It is a smooth cheese of creamy yellow color with medium-sized holes, and comes in small, round drums 12 to 16 inches in diameter, 2$^1$/$_2$ to 4 inches in height, and weighing 11 to 15 pounds. It is used at table, but also has a prominent place in Friulian cuisine, where it is grated over various dishes including *polenta* and *carpaccio*.

RIGHT: BUFFALO IN CAMPANIA

## MOZZARELLA
This southern Italian cheese is named after the technique of tearing apart or cutting (*mozzata*) the whey with the fingers to form balls of cheese. It is mainly produced in Battipaglia in the province of Salerno, but is also made in Caserta and the provinces of Naples, Puglia, and Lazio. Authentic buffalo-milk cheese is traditionally produced by only a few specialists, as there is not enough buffalo milk to meet the demands of commercial production.

What makes *mozzarella* so special is its unusually low fat content. The richness of flavor of the buffalo milk, with only 7 to 7.5% fat content, also gives *mozzarella* its distinctive taste. The cheese has been made since the thirteenth century, and the same techniques used then are still used today. It is said that in the past, in order to increase milk production, the buffalo were milked one by one to the tune of a lullaby, and each animal was individually named—real VIP treatment.

Fresh *mozzarella* has a sweet, nutty, and slightly salty flavor, and is perfectly white. It should also have a few holes inside, where tears of whey seeped out when the cheese was cut. In Lazio, especially around Rome, another version of *mozzarella*, called *provatura*, is made with a mixture of whole cows' milk and pasteurized sheep's milk. It is similar to the original cheese, but is harder in texture and has a yellowish color. A smoked version, called *scamorza*, is produced in Campania, Abruzzo, and Molise. *Scamorza* is also used to make *butirro*, (see page 239).

*Mozzarella* is delicious eaten raw, sliced and dressed with a little salt and pepper and a trickle of extra-virgin olive oil, or with slices of tomatoes and a few basil leaves in *mozzarella caprese* (see page 137). It can also be used cooked on pizzas and in timbales of pasta.

## MURAZZANO
This tasty, soft, fresh, full-fat (50 to 56%) cheese is made mostly with ewes' milk around the area of Murazzano, in Cuneo in the province of Piedmont. Formed into a cylindrical shape 4 to 6 inches in diameter, 1$^1$/$_4$ to 1$^1$/$_2$ inches high, and weighing about 10$^1$/$_2$ to 14 ounces, it is white and does not have a crust because it is immersed in brine during production. It should be eaten within 6 to 10 days of production. It is an exquisite table cheese and is delicious served with olive oil, salt, and pepper, or in hot sauces.

## PAGLIERINA
This soft, full-fat cheese from the area around Turin in Piedmont, is made from cows' milk and is shaped into rounds 4 to 8 inches in diameter and $^1$/$_2$ to $^3$/$_4$ inch in height. The little discs are briefly left to mature on straw mats, or *paglia*, from which the cheese gets its name. *Paglierina* should be eaten as soon as it is ready and makes a wonderful table cheese, especially when served dressed with olive oil and vinegar.

## PANNARONE, PANNERONE, PANERONE
This full-fat, sweet-flavored soft cheese from the Lodigiano area in Lombardy is known as "white Gorgonzola," because it has a similar flavor and shape as the famous blue cheese, as well as being made by a similar method, although without the mold. It gets its name from *panera*, which is Lombardian for the top of the milk from which it is made. Formed in drums 10 to 12 inches in diameter, 7 to 8 inches in height, weighing 10 to 26 pounds, it has a smooth, thin, slightly yellow crust and a creamy-white paste. This is one of the very few unsalted cheeses and it should be eaten as soon as it has matured, at about 8 to 10 days. It is an excellent table cheese that is generally only eaten locally.

## PARMIGIANO REGGIANO, SEE GRANA PADANO

## PECORINO
This cheese is so popular that almost every region makes its own version, each one adapted to suit local ingredients and culinary traditions. Wherever it comes from, *pecorino* is made in the same way. The difference in flavor between each one comes from the qualities in the local milks and the ageing processes. *Pecorino* is a semi-cooked hard cheese made with full fat milk. The drums are about 8 to 12 inches in diameter, 5$^1$/$_2$ to 8$^3$/$_4$ inches high, and weigh 7 to 54 pounds. It is a compact, white cheese which is aged for at least 8 months before being eaten at table or grated like Parmesan.

By law, *pecorino romano* can only be made in Lazio in the provinces of Rome, Frosinone, Grosseto, Latina, and Viterbo. Exceptionally *romano*-style *pecorino* is also made in Sardinia, in the provinces of Cagliari, Sassari, and Moro, where three-quarters of all *pecorino romano*-style cheeses are produced.

Sardinia's own *pecorino* is called *fiore sardo* or *cacio fiore*, and is produced in the same way as other *pecorinos*, except that it is formed into much smaller rounds, weighing 3$^1$/$_4$ to 11 pounds. It is ready to be eaten at table after only 2 to 3 months, although it needs to be aged for 6 months if it is to be hard enough for grating. Sardinian *pecorino* is very popular in Liguria, despite the fact that Liguria makes its own *pecorino*, where it is used to make pesto sauce. One *pecorino*, which is produced in the province of Ragusa, has whole black peppercorns in it.

### PRESCINSOEUA, SEE QUAGLIATA

### PRIMO SALE
Similar to *caciotta*, primo sale (meaning "first salt") is a fresh cows'-milk cheese made in several regions in Italy, including Liguria and Savona. It has to be eaten when extremely fresh and just after it has been through the salting process. In Sicily and the South there is a similar fresh cheese also called *primo sale*, the only difference being that is made with ewes' milk.

### PROVATURA
This large *mozzarella*-type cheese is made to be aged slightly, for a couple of days at least, to obtain a stronger flavor and texture. It is sometimes smoked and eaten as a table cheese, or used in cooking. See also *mozzarella*.

### PROVOLONE, PROVOLETTA, PROVOLONCINO
This peculiar cheese originated in the Basilicata in the province of Potenza, and from there it spread all over southern Italy and eventually to the North, where it now flourishes.

It is a compact, full-fat cheese made of cows' milk. After the rennet and relevant fermenting agents have been added, as with *caciocavallo*, the curds are spun in hot water and worked into a large pear-shaped or cylindrical cheese weighing at least 7 pounds. They can, in fact, reach 4 feet in height and a weight of 130 to 220 pounds. After they have been shaped, they are placed in giant containers and immersed in brine before being hung and bound by special strings which give them their distinctive shape.

The maturing process takes about

12 months, depending on whether the cheese is to be eaten fresh (*tipo dolce*) or aged for grating (*piccante*). The matured cheese is covered with a thin layer of wax to prevent contamination by bacteria. It is also known as *provoloncino* or *provoletta*, and by many other names depending on the region.

*Provolone* is eaten as a table cheese and is used in cooking, added in small cubes to stuffings for vegetables and pasta timbales, and also grated on pasta. It has a distinctive texture and flavor, the *tipo piccante* sometimes tasting quite sharp.

### QUAGLIATA, PRESCINSOEUA
This coagulated milk similar to junket is enjoyed all along the Eastern part of the Italian Riviera (in Ligurian dialect, it is known as *prescinsoeua*). It is used there mixed with pesto or eaten on its own, sweetened with sugar. In other parts of Italy *cagliata*, a kind of Italian unfermented yogurt, is eaten with fruit. I remember my grandmother sun-drying milk with a little lemon juice to produce her own.

### QUARTIROLO
This soft, full-fat cheese is made exclusively in Lombardy, in the areas of Como, Milano, Bergamo, Brescia, and Pavia. The best, called *Quartirolo di Monte*, come from Valsassina (Sassina Valley) and from the Quartirolo, and are square in shape like *taleggio*.

The cheese is made with the milk from cows fed on the fragrant grass of the high pastures of the Quartirolo. The unpasteurized milk is coagulated in small copper

cauldrons using rennet and milk enzymes. After the curds have formed, they are put in square molds, and the whey is drained off. The salting of the cheese takes place after a few days' maturation, when a white mold has formed. For the next 6 to 8 days, the cheese is repeatedly rubbed all over with salt, after which the cheese is ready.

When ready to eat, each cheese weighs about $3\frac{1}{4}$ pounds, and they are sold in quarters. The compact, white cream cheese has a delicate and fragrant flavor reminiscent of mushrooms.

### RICOTTA / SOFT CHEESE
As is suggested by its name, meaning literally "cooked again," this cheese is the product of other cheeses, using the residue left after the curd has been lifted. Fresh milk is added to this residue to give a higher yield, and then the mixture is brought to a boil. An acidic agent like lemon juice or rennet is then added, and when casein froth forms on the surface it is scooped off and allowed to drain. This froth is the *ricotta* cheese, and there are many types of it made all over Italy.

*Ricotta forte:* This *ricotta* from Bari in the province of Puglia is made in the basic way except that salt is added before the cheese is put in wooden containers to cool and dry. Over the next couple of months, the *ricotta* is moved from one container to another, worked by hand each time, until all the excess liquid has been forced out. It has a distinctive sharp flavor and is yellow in color. It is used in a variety of ways, including in *calzone* mixed with onions.

*Ricotta romana:* This is cooked a little longer than most others to give a more compact and refined *ricotta* that can be used in a variety of savory or sweet dishes.

*Fior di ricotta:* This is made with full-cream sheep's milk instead of

ABOVE: UMBRIAN *RICOTTA* IN HUSKS OF WHEAT

LEFT: FRESHLY MADE *RICOTTA*

the cheese residue, to produce a richer *ricotta*, higher in fat, which may be eaten raw but is mainly baked in *pastiera di grano* (see page 177), or used as a filling for other desserts.

*Ricotta marzotica:* This *ricotta* from Foggia in Puglia is named after the month of March because it is made, salted, and aged for 15 to 30 days during this month. Due to the springtime freshness of the grass, this *ricotta* is particularly delicate and ideal for filling *ravioli* or just for eating as a dessert.

## MAKING AND PRESERVING TOMINI

The curds are cut and drained, then the *tomini* are shaped by hand into rounds about 1/2 inch in diameter and 3/4 inch in height. They can be flavored with wine vinegar, before being bottled in oil with added flavorings such as herbs, chilies, or truffles.

*Ricotta calabrese condita:* This is a variation on the excellent Calabrian *ricotta*, made in the usual way except that salt and chili are added before it is dried in an oven to give it a very *piccante* flavor.

*Ricotta infornata:* Similar to the *calabrese condita*, this *ricotta* from Sicily is also dried and salted before being covered with ground black pepper.

*Ricotta salata:* This salted *ricotta* is allowed to mature and harden, so it can be used grated on a variety of dishes.

## ROBIOLA

This soft cheese, traditionally made with unpasteurized full-cream cows' milk, is now commercially produced using treated milk. Although it is a specialty of Lombardy, it is also made in Piedmont, where the cheese has an aromatic, spicy flavor. The drained curd is dipped in brine, then matured for 20 to 30 days. It must then be eaten immediately, as a table cheese. Smaller versions of the same cheese are called *robioline*.

*Robiola delle langhe* is a variation of the main cheese made with a mixture of cows' and goats' milk to give a very distinctive flavor. Another variation, *robiola di roccaverano*, was at one time made only with goats' milk, but is now made using only cows' milk. *Robiola* is one of the cheeses generally used to make *brôs* (see page 252).

## SCAMORZA

Made using the *mozzarella* technique, *scamorza* is produced industrially using mostly cows' milk. It is more consistent in texture than *mozzarella* and shaped in a way that allows it to be tied with a string or raffia. The cheeses always come tied in pairs, which are hung and sometimes smoked. It is eaten fresh as a table cheese one to three days after it is made. *Scamorza* is often also filled with butter for ageing, as in *butirro*.

## TALEGGIO

One of the best-known Italian cheeses, *Taleggio* is eaten at table all over Italy as well as abroad. It is made in the Italian pre-Alps, in the Taleggio Valley north of Bergamo, where the pastures are particularly juicy and aromatic, and in Savoy there is a consortium of producers who safeguard the quality of the cheese. However, this full-fat cheese (48%) is also made in Brescia, Como, Cremona, Milano, Pavia, Novara, and Treviso.

It is matured for 40 to 45 days, during which time it develops a pinkish crust. It is then sold in squares of 8 to 12 inches, about 2 1/2 inches high. The cheese itself is very soft, containing many tiny holes, and has a creamy white color. It should be eaten quite fresh, as it becomes increasingly acidic as it ages.

## TOMA, TOMETTA, TOMINO

This hard cheese, made with unpasteurized full-fat or semi-skimmed cows' milk, is produced in Piedmont, the Aosta Valley, and Liguria. The cheeses are shaped into cylindrical rounds 4 to 8 inches in diameter and 1 1/2 to 3 1/4 inches in height, with an average weight of 4 1/2 to 9 pounds. After it has been salted in brine, it is aged for 30 to 70 days.

It is essentially a table cheese, with all the flavors of Alpine pastures. When it is fresh it is called *tometta* and is sold in rounds of a similar shape to the *toma* and, like *paglierina*, 4 3/4 to 6 inches in diameter and 3/4 to 1 1/4 inches high. The most famous of these cheeses are the *carmagnola* of Pratonevoso and the *caprella*, which is made with goats' milk.

*Tomino* is another fresh *toma* that is sold in rounds 1 1/2 inches in diameter and 3/4 inch in height. It can be flavored with wine vinegar before being submerged in oil and spiced with either herbs or chili. The resulting cheese is called *tomini elettrici* because of its strong flavor. In the Langhe region, *tomini* are also immersed in oil before being flavored with Alba truffle to produce an exquisite cheese. The most famous of these preserved *tomini* are from Chiaverano, near Ivrea.

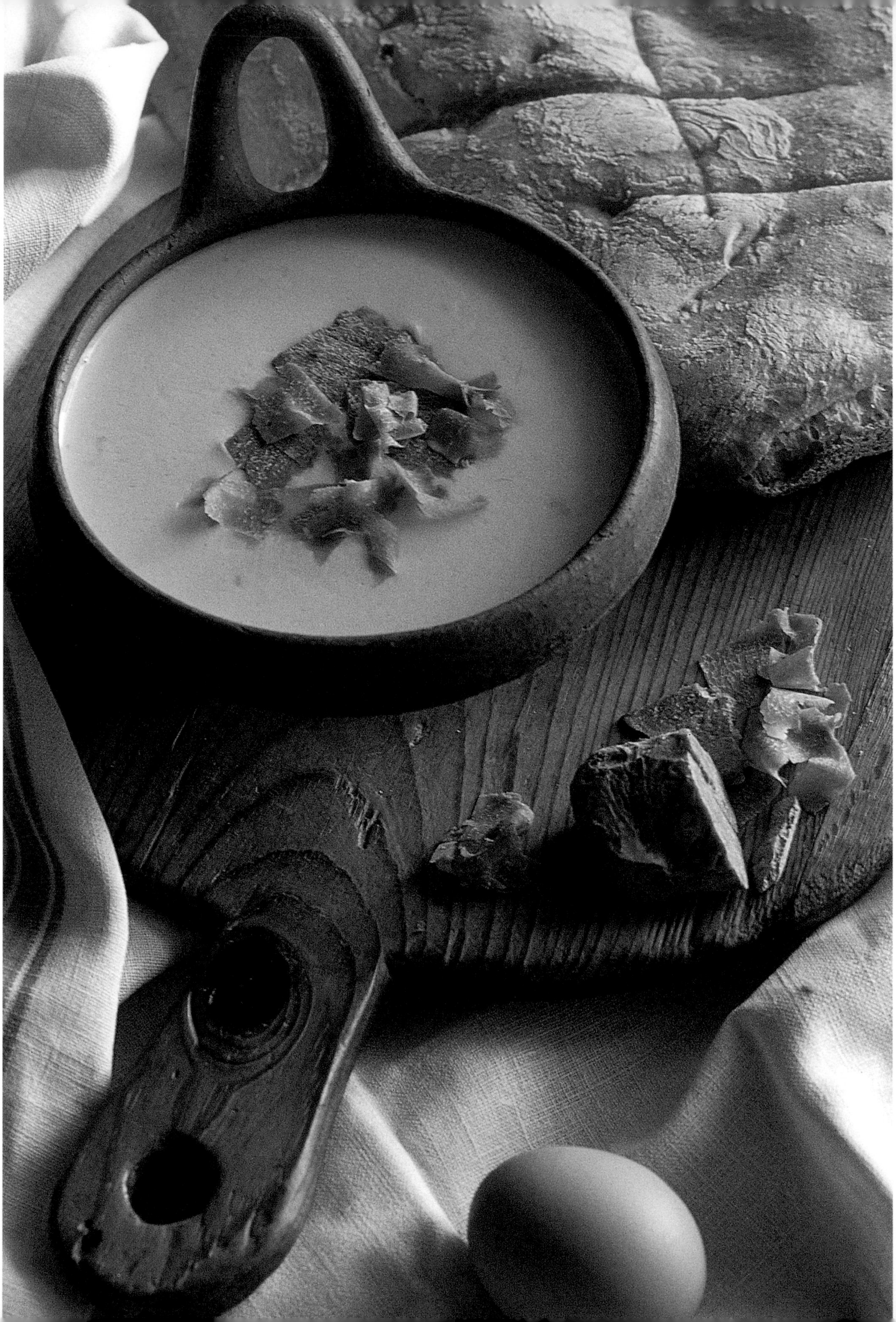

# FONDUTA CON TARTUFO
## CHEESE FONDUE WITH TRUFFLE

**FOR 4**

14 OUNCES *FONTINA* CHEESE, CUT
INTO SMALL CUBES
ABOUT 1¹/₄ CUPS MILK
6 EGG YOLKS
2 TABLESPOONS BUTTER
1¹/₂ TO 1³/₄ OUNCES WHITE TRUFFLE
SALT AND PEPPER

*Farmers in Piedmont used to dip bread in this heavenly-tasting sauce made with local ingredients:* fontina *cheese from the Aosta Valley (irreplaceable for this dish) and white truffles. Due to the incredibly high prices for truffles, this dish is now available only in the finest Piedmontese restaurants. A most elegant and delicious first course, it is very simple to make but requires extreme care in its preparation.*

Put the cubes of cheese in a bowl, pour in enough milk to cover, and let it soak for 2 to 3 hours.

Place the bowl over a pan of hot but not boiling water, making sure the water is not touching the base of the bowl. Stir gently until the cheese melts to form a smooth mixture. At this stage add the egg yolks, butter, a pinch of salt, and some pepper. Continue to stir until the mixture thickens to a creamy consistency.

Distribute between 4 small heated bowls. Shave some truffle over and eat with toasted slices of bread cut into strips.

# ASPARAGI ALLA EMILIANA
## ASPARAGUS EMILIAN-STYLE

**FOR 4**

1³/₄ POUNDS GREEN ASPARAGUS
(I PREFER THE GREEN TO THE WHITE)
3¹/₂ OUNCES PARMESAN CHEESE,
GRATED
6 TABLESPOONS BUTTER, MELTED
SALT AND PEPPER

*Asparagus is a wonderful vegetable which goes extremely well with dairy produce. In Emilia-Romagna, and especially in Parma, you can't resist using the local butter and Parmesan. This dish announces the arrival of summer.*

Peel the lower stem of the asparagus, discarding all the stringy parts. Boil in lightly salted water until the stalks are just tender but still *al dente*, ensuring that the tips are intact.

Drain the asparagus, then arrange the spears all pointing in the same direction on serving plates and sprinkle with Parmesan cheese. Season with salt and pepper to taste, then pour the hot melted butter over the tips and serve immediately.

OPPOSITE: *FONDUTA CON TARTUFO*

# TORTA RUSTICA DI RICOTTA
## SAVORY RICOTTA CAKE (SEE PAGE 304)

### FOR 6

1 1/2 TABLESPOONS BUTTER

3 TABLESPOONS BREAD CRUMBS

1 POUND VERY FRESH *RICOTTA*, PREFERABLY
  SHEEP'S-MILK *RICOTTA*

4 EGGS, SEPARATED

1 1/2 OUNCES PARMESAN CHEESE, GRATED

SCANT 1/2 CUP ALL-PURPOSE FLOUR

SALT AND PEPPER

3 1/2 OUNCES MIXED MELTING CHEESES
  SUCH AS *PROVOLONE*, *PECORINO*, AND
  *SCAMORZA*, CUT INTO VERY SMALL CUBES

3 1/2 OUNCES PARMA HAM, SALAMI, AND
  *SPECK*, VERY FINELY CHOPPED

*Ricotta is a wonderful vehicle for both sweet and savory flavors. It is very convenient because it is fairly low in fat and mixes perfectly with eggs to produce a delightful and not too heavy result. My mother used to conceal any leftover salami and cheese in this savory ricotta cake. It was our favorite!*

Preheat the oven to 400° F. Use the butter to grease an 8-inch ovenproof dish and dust it with the bread crumbs.

Put the *ricotta* in a bowl. Beat the egg yolks with the Parmesan cheese, flour, a little salt, and plenty of freshly ground black pepper. Fold this mixture into the *ricotta* and then add the cheese and ham.

Beat the egg whites until stiff and fold them gently into the *ricotta* mixture until it is smooth and light. Pour it into the prepared dish, smooth the top level and bake for 30 to 40 minutes or until a nice crust has formed.

Turn out onto a serving dish and eat warm. It is also good at room temperature.

# GNOCCHI ALLA BAVA
## GNOCCHI PIEDMONTESE-STYLE

### FOR 6

HEAPING 2 1/2 CUPS 00 (*DOPPIO ZERO*)
  FLOUR

HEAPING 2 1/2 CUPS BUCKWHEAT FLOUR

2 EGGS

ABOUT 3 TABLESPOONS MILK

5 OUNCES *FONTINA* CHEESE, THINLY
  SLICED

5 OUNCES FRESH *TOMA* CHEESE,
  THINLY SLICED

2 OUNCES PARMESAN CHEESE,
  GRATED

4 TABLESPOONS BUTTER

SALT AND PEPPER

*There are many variations on this dish, most of them from Piedmont. Alla bava means that when you lift the gnocchi from the plate with a fork they should form strings of melting cheese. Most gnocchi are made from potatoes or semolina; these, however, are made with two types of flour.*

Preheat the oven to 400° F. Put the flours into a bowl, then mix in the eggs and enough milk to obtain a firm dough. Roll a small part of the dough at a time into a cigar shape. Cut into small chunks about 1 1/4 inches long and run them lightly over the tines of a fork to leave an indent, rolling them off the fork onto a clean cloth. Cover and leave to rest for 30 minutes.

Bring about 5 quarts of lightly salted water to a boil and cook the *gnocchi* in it for a minute or two. They are ready when they rise to the surface. Scoop them out with a slotted spoon and arrange them in layers in an ovenproof dish with the *fontina, toma,* and a little of the Parmesan. Sprinkle the remaining Parmesan over the top, dot with the butter, and bake in the oven for 10 minutes. Serve immediately.

# MOZZARELLA IN CARROZZA

FRIED MOZZARELLA SANDWICH

**FOR 1**

**2** THICK SLICES *PANE DI CAMPAGNA*
(COUNTRY-STYLE WHITE BREAD)

**1** LARGE SLICE *BUFFALO MOZZARELLA*

MILK

**2** EGGS, BEATEN

SALT

FLOUR FOR DREDGING

OLIVE OIL FOR FRYING

*Originally from Naples and generally from Campania, this dish has spread all over Italy and is to be found mostly in bars as a lunch-time snack. It is delicious when freshly made and still crisp.*

Dip the bread in milk for a few seconds but do not soak. Drain, then place the *mozzarella* on one piece of bread and put the other on top to make a sandwich. Dredge in seasoned flour, then dip the sandwiches in the egg. Shallow-fry in a good quantity of oil for 5 minutes until golden, turning once.

# FORMAGGIO AL TARTUFO
TRUFFLED CHEESE

## FOR 6

7 OUNCES *RICOTTA*, PREFERABLY
  SHEEP'S-MILK *RICOTTA*
2 OUNCES PARMESAN CHEESE, GRATED
7 OUNCES *MASCARPONE*
³/₄ OUNCE FRESH ALBA TRUFFLE,
  GRATED (OR USE FRESH BLACK TRUFFLE
  AND A FEW DROPS OF TRUFFLE OIL)
SALT AND PEPPER

*If you cannot get hold of truffled cheese it is easy to make yourself—provided you have the most important ingredient, the truffle.*

Mix all the ingredients together very well, adding just a little salt and pepper, and leave for a couple of hours for the flavors to infuse.

# FORMAGGIO CONCIATO (BROS)
CURED CHEESE

## MAKES ENOUGH TO FILL A
## 1-QUART JAR

1³/₄ POUNDS MIXED CHEESES SUCH AS
  *ROBIOLA*, FRESH *TOMA*, GOAT CHEESE,
  FRESH *PECORINO*, OR *GORGONZULA*
1 CHILI PEPPER, VERY FINELY CHOPPED
4 TABLESPOONS GRAPPA
1¹/₂ TEASPOONS FRESHLY GROUND BLACK
  PEPPER
¹/₂ CUP EXTRA-VIRGIN OLIVE OIL
2 TABLESPOONS RED-WINE VINEGAR

*This is a typical Piedmontese specialty, made mostly at home. There is an infinite number of combinations but the idea is to use up leftover cheese, which is macerated in oil, grappa, and spices for some time to obtain a "hell of a cheese," as I call it. It is usually eaten either on toast or with sliced polenta. In Apulia there is a similar dish made with ricotta, called ricotta forte.*

Put all the cheeses into a bowl and break or cut them into small pieces. Add all the other ingredients and mix well. Put in a jar and then seal. Keep in a cool place and stir every 2 or 3 days. Do this for a couple of months until you have a spicy, strong cheese paste which can be kept for a long time. Good luck!

# CROCCHETTE DI PATATE
MOZZARELLA-STUFFED POTATO CROQUETTES

## FOR 4

1³/₄ POUNDS FLOURY POTATOES
4 TABLESPOONS FRESHLY GRATED PARMESAN
  CHEESE
3 EGG YOLKS
1 TABLESPOON FINELY CHOPPED FLAT-LEAF
  PARSLEY
SALT AND PEPPER
10 OUNCES *BUFFALO MOZZARELLA*,
  CUT INTO FINGER-SIZED STICKS
1 EGG WHITE, LIGHTLY BEATEN
DRIED BREAD CRUMBS
OLIVE OIL FOR DEEP-FRYING

*These little croquettes are stuffed with* mozzarella *cheese. A similar recipe uses rice instead of potatoes and is called* suppli *or* arancini *(see page 179).*

Boil the potatoes in their skins until soft. Drain and peel while still warm. Pass them through a ricer or sieve to make a purée, then add the Parmesan cheese, egg yolks, parsley, and salt and pepper to taste. Mix to make a soft dough.

Cover the palm of your hand with some of the potato mixture. Put a *mozzarella* stick in the middle and cover it completely with more potato. Shape into a cylinder, making sure the *mozzarella* is in the center. Repeat with the remaining potato mixture and *mozzarella*. Dip each croquette in the egg white, then roll in the bread crumbs and deep-fry for a few minutes until crisp and brown. Serve warm.

# RAVIOLI FRITTI SARDI CON MIELE

FRIED SARDINIAN PECORINO RAVIOLI WITH HONEY

**MAKES 8**

7 OUNCES *PECORINO* CHEESE, THINLY
    SLICED
OLIVE OIL FOR FRYING
CHESTNUT HONEY OR OTHER HONEY

FOR THE PASTRY:
HEAPING 2¹/₂ CUPS FLOUR, PREFERABLY
    00 (*DOPPIO ZERO*)
3 EGGS
SCANT ¹/₂ CUP SUPERFINE SUGAR

*These little pastries filled with* pecorino *cheese are a Sardinian specialty, served with honey. They are delicious after a light meal.*

Sift the flour, make a well in the center, and add the eggs and sugar. Gradually draw in the flour to make a smooth dough, similar to pasta dough. Roll it out to a thickness of ¹/₈ inch and cut out 16 circles about 5 inches in diameter.

Divide the *pecorino* cheese among half the dough circles. Brush the edges of the dough with water and cover with the remaining pieces of dough, pressing down gently around the edges to seal.

Heat a generous quantity of olive oil in a large skillet and fry the pastries until golden brown on both sides. Serve hot with honey.

# Panna Cotta
BAKED CREAM

**Serves 4 to 6**

1 LEAF GELATIN

2¹/₄ CUPS LIGHT CREAM

SCANT ¹/₄ CUP SUGAR

1 VANILLA BEAN

1 TEASPOON VANILLA EXTRACT

1 TABLESPOON DARK RUM

STRIPS OF CANDIED ORANGE PEEL OR

   FRESH BERRIES

*This is one of the most fashionable desserts both in Italy and abroad.*

Soak the gelatin leaf in a little cold water until soft.

In a heavy-bottomed pan, mix the cream with the sugar and vanilla bean and extract. Bring to a boil. Remove from the heat and add the soaked gelatin leaf and the rum. Stir well until the gelatin has dissolved. Pass through a fine sieve and pour into 4 to 6 dariole molds. Put in the refrigerator to set.

To serve, decorate with small pieces of candied orange peel or, if you prefer, with fresh berries.

# MARRONI AL MASCARPONE
## CANDIED CHESTNUTS WITH MASCARPONE

### FOR 4

2 EGG YOLKS

SCANT ¹/₂ CUP SUPERFINE SUGAR

1 TEASPOON VANILLA SUGAR

2 TABLESPOONS WHISKEY

4 TABLESPOONS LIGHT CREAM

14 OUNCES *MASCARPONE*

12 WHOLE CHESTNUTS IN SYRUP OR
   MARRONS GLACÉS

12 FRESH BAY LEAVES

*This is a dessert with abundant calories, to be served mainly in winter after a very light meal.*

Beat the egg yolks with the superfine sugar, vanilla sugar, and whiskey to obtain a smooth cream. Beat the light cream into the *mascarpone* to soften it and then gently fold in the egg yolk mixture. Put the mixture into a piping bag and pipe 3 equal mounds onto each dessert plate. Top with the chestnuts and then decorate with the bay leaves.

# PARMIGIANO CON LE PERE E NOCI
## PARMESAN CHEESE WITH PEARS AND WALNUTS

### FOR 4

7 OUNCES PARMESAN CHEESE

4 RIPE WILLIAMS PEARS

SCANT ³/₄ CUP FRESH WALNUTS, PEELED

GOOD *PANE DI CAMPAGNA* (COUNTRY
   BREAD)

*This combination is ideal for when new-season walnuts are available and are fresh enough to peel. The skin should come off easily in your fingers. Not really a recipe, this is just an idea for a dessert, and one that is very popular in Emilia-Romagna, where the famous cheese comes from.*

Break the Parmesan cheese into splinters. Peel, core, and slice the pears. Assemble the cheese, pears, and walnuts on each plate and serve with the bread.

# TIRAMISU

### FOR 6

3 EGG YOLKS

SCANT ¹/₂ CUP SUPERFINE SUGAR

1 TEASPOON VANILLA SUGAR OR A FEW
DROPS
   VANILLA EXTRACT

¹/₂ CUP LIGHT CREAM

1 POUND *MASCARPONE*

6 CUPS COLD STRONG ESPRESSO COFFEE

4 TABLESPOONS COFFEE LIQUEUR, SUCH
   AS KAHLÚA

20 *SAVOIARDI* COOKIES (SEE PAGE 299)

COCOA POWDER

*Another Italian specialty that has emigrated to Italian restaurants all over the world, this can be prepared in minutes, is not cooked, and yet has a high degree of sophistication and appeal. The name means "pick me up," and could well be a reference to the number of calories this dessert contains. Whoever invented it must have been in need of quick energy. There are many variations on tiramisu but I prefer this very simple one.*

Beat the egg yolks with the superfine sugar and vanilla sugar until thick and mousselike. Beat the light cream into the *mascarpone* to loosen it, then carefully fold in the egg yolk mixture.

Spread half the mixture in a large shallow serving dish. Mix the espresso coffee and liqueur together in a shallow dish and briefly dip in the *savoiardi* cookies one by one, putting them immediately on top of the layer of *mascarpone*. When you have used up all the cookies, spread the rest of the *mascarpone* mixture on top to cover them completely and then put in the refrigerator just until chilled. Before serving, dust the *tiramisu* generously with cocoa powder. You could make individual portions in glasses, cups, or other small containers.

# CASSATA

**FOR 4**

CONFECTIONERS' SUGAR FOR DUSTING

9 OUNCES MARZIPAN (SEE PAGE 279 OR USE READY MADE)

1 ROUND *PAN DI SPAGNA* (SEE PAGE 294), ABOUT 8 INCHES IN DIAMETER AND 1/4 INCH THICK

2 TABLESPOONS MARSALA

13 OUNCES *RICOTTA*

SCANT 1/2 CUP SUPERFINE SUGAR

1/2 TEASPOON VANILLA EXTRACT

3/4 OUNCE CANDIED ORANGE PEEL, CHOPPED

3/4 OUNCE CANDIED CITRON PEEL, CHOPPED

3/4 OUNCE BITTERSWEET CHOCOLATE, CHOPPED

ANGELICA AND EXTRA CANDIED PEEL

**FOR THE FROSTING:**

SCANT 1 CUP CONFECTIONERS' SUGAR

1 EGG WHITE

1 TEASPOON LEMON JUICE

1 TABLESPOON ALL-PURPOSE FLOUR

*There are two versions of* cassata, *both of which originate from Sicily. One is a cake made with marzipan,* ricotta, *and candied fruit, while the other is a later development made with ice cream. The name derives from the Arab* qas'at, *referring to the small bowl used to shape the dessert. The sloping sides of the container ensure that when the contents are turned out they have a conical shape. It was originally produced by nuns during Holy Week but is now available all year round. At Christmas, however, the cake is often made in a heart-shaped mold. A smaller version of* cassata, *called* cassatina, *is a common sight in Sicilian bars, cafés, and pastry shops.*

Dust with confectioners' sugar an 8-inch diameter pie dish with sloping sides. Divide the marzipan into two balls and knead one to a smooth dough, then roll it out until it is 1/4 inch thick. Use it to line the sides of the dish, cutting it to fit. Place the *pan di Spagna* on the bottom of the dish, trimming around the edges if necessary to make it fit. Sprinkle with the Marsala.

Put the *ricotta* in a bowl and crush it with a fork. Add the superfine sugar and vanilla extract and mix until it becomes slightly moist and binds together well. Pass the mixture through a sieve, then stir in the candied peel and chocolate. Spoon the *ricotta* mixture over the sponge in the dish.

Knead the remaining marzipan, roll it out, and place it over the filling. Turn the *cassata* upside down onto a serving plate so that the sponge that was at the bottom is now at the top.

To make the frosting, sift the confectioners' sugar into a bowl and mix in the egg white and lemon juice. Add the flour gradually to thicken it slightly. Mix well and pour immediately over the *cassata* to cover the top and sides. Decorate with candied peel and angelica, then leave for a couple of hours for the frosting to set.

# CANNOLI
## SICILIAN RICOTTA PASTRIES

**MAKES 15**

1 TABLESPOON LARD OR BUTTER

1 TABLESPOON SUGAR

3 TABLESPOONS DRY WHITE WINE

1 TEASPOON WHITE WINE VINEGAR

1 1/4 CUPS 00 (*DOPPIO ZERO*) FLOUR

1 TABLESPOON COCOA POWDER

1 EGG, BEATEN

VEGETABLE OIL FOR DEEP-FRYING

Cannoli *are probably the best-known Sicilian dessert. They used to be made only at* carnevale *(carnival time), and especially for the feast day of San Carlo. Nowadays they are eaten all year round, not only after meals, but also as a snack. They are special pastries, wrapped around a piece of cane and deep-fried, hence the name* cannolo, *from* canna. *The cane is removed after frying and the pastry is filled with a mixture of* ricotta *cheese, sugar, candied fruit, and chocolate. You will need 15 pieces of cane, 1 inch in diameter and 6 inches long, for this recipe, or use commercially made* cannoli *forms.*

Beat together the lard and sugar until light and creamy, then mix in the wine and vinegar. Fold in the flour and cocoa powder and knead to form a dough. Cover

**FOR THE FILLING:**

1¼ POUNDS *RICOTTA* CHEESE

HEAPING 1¼ CUPS SUPERFINE SUGAR

1¾ OUNCES CANDIED CITRUS PEEL, CHOPPED

1¾ OUNCES BITTERSWEET CHOCOLATE, CHOPPED INTO SMALL PIECES

with plastic wrap and place in the refrigerator for 30 minutes.

Roll out the dough to a large sheet about ¹/₁₂ inch thick and cut into 15 rectangles, each about 4 x 2½ inches. Wrap each piece of dough around a length of cane, sealing the join with beaten egg.

Heat the oil in a large deep pan, making sure there is enough to cover the *cannoli*. When the oil is very hot, add the *cannoli*, a few at a time, and deep-fry until crisp and golden brown, for only 1½ to 2 minutes. Drain on paper towels and leave to cool. Remove the canes, leaving a hollow pastry ready to be filled.

To make the filling, pass the *ricotta* through a sieve and beat with a fork. Mix in the sugar, candied peel, and chocolate. Fill each *cannoli* with the *ricotta* mixture. Serve cool but do not refrigerate.

A SELECTION OF CAKES AND PASTRIES IN MARIA GRAMMATICO'S STORE IN ERICE, SICILY: [CLOCKWISE FROM THE TOP LEFT] *CANNOLI*, MARZIPAN APPLES, ALMOND COOKIES, *CASSATA*, AND LITTLE BABY *CASSATINA*

# FRUIT & NUTS

## FRUTTA FRESCA E SECCA

When I was a child, one of the most exciting times of the year was the beginning of summer. Not only was it school holiday time, but there was also a sense of anticipation that the first of the summer crops of fruit were ripening. Having gone through the long winter eating pears and apples and preserved fruit in the form of *composta*, or compote, it was exciting to consider eating the new season's cherries for dessert instead.

These days, many fruits are available all year round. They are imported from all over the world, from Chile and Bolivia to South Africa. Unfortunately, this fruit is usually harvested when it is unripe so that it can ripen on its journey. This means, however, that it often lacks flavor, and that sun-ripened scent that comes only from fruit eaten a day after it has been picked.

Fruit is bought on a daily basis in Italy because it is ripe when it goes to market. This explains why stallholders are so anxious to sell their goods; it is almost essential to have sold out before the end of the day, as the fruit will be past its best if kept until the next. Street markets are very colorful in Italy, with the vendors shouting the praises of their wares as loudly as they can so they can beat off the competition. The atmosphere of the markets is electric and the customer benefits enormously from the wide choice of produce on sale.

Italians eat lots of fruit in many forms, fresh, preserved, or dried, and Italian meals usually end with fruit as the dessert. By happy accident, the regular consumption of fresh fruit—and lots of it—complies with modern attitudes about a healthy diet. I have the feeling sometimes that all Italians will live for hundreds of years if they eat like this. Unfortunately, other factors such as stress and man-made pollution work against this, so a natural balance is maintained. Perhaps Italians enjoy life more, though, and that is already something!

When I was a teenager I would return from school only to be sent straight off by my mother to buy the fruit for the evening meal. I knew which would be at market before I got there, as the local farmers always told us which fruits were about to ripen. I also knew who grew the best of each type, so our table was always graced by the most impeccable specimens. If I ever bought sub-standard fruit, the family would complain to me, an occurrence which definitely encouraged me to develop the art of buying and bargaining for the best.

Cooked fruit in the form of jam is also popular in Italy, and it is often eaten at tea time, known as *merenda*, with fresh bread and butter. It is also used to make jam tarts called *crostata di frutta*, a shortcrust pastry shell baked blind, then filled with jam and covered with a lattice of pastry and baked again, until the lattice strips are cooked. This too is eaten for tea or for dessert during the winter months, when little fresh fruit is available.

During a filming trip to Turkey I came across a method of preparing uncooked jam. Considering that all the vitamins contained in ripe fruit are usually lost during cooking, this should be the best way to preserve them. The only handicap is that the sun has to be very strong and continuous for a few days. You just take very ripe fruit, like peaches or plums, weigh them, liquidize them, and stir in an equal weight of sugar—then leave this in the sun, stirring a couple of times a day until you see that most of the liquid has evaporated and you are sure that the sugar concentration is sufficient to preserve the sun-cooked fruit. In a similar way, my grandma used to produce a six-times concentrate of tomatoes—the same principle same, but with different ingredients. Try to make the jam yourself if you are in a hot country—it is delicious.

*Frutta candita*, or candied fruit, is also very often used in the preparation of Italian cakes and sweets. In Calabria there is a large industry and artisanal manufacturing of all sorts of candied citrus peel due to the local abundance of tangerines, oranges, lemons, and citrons. These *candite* are important ingredients in all sorts of traditional dishes, from Milanese *panettone* to the various Tuscan spicy cookies and *panforte*, but above all in the Sicilian *cassata*, *cannoli*, and many other sweet dishes. In Lombardy, Emilia-Romagna, and Veneto, there is a curious but wonderful variation on candied fruit, in which all types of fruit are cooked in a heavy, sharp, and sweet mustard syrup. This *mostarda di Cremona* is served as an accompaniment to boiled meats. Finally, in Piedmont there is also the production of candied

chestnuts, which are given a lengthy processing in a vanilla-flavored sugar syrup to become *marroni canditi* or *marrons glacés*.

The production of *frutta secca*, or dried fruit, was originally an ancient means of preserving bumper crops of fruit. In all the regions of modern Italy, however, it has become quite an

important element in the renaissance of artisan industries. Fruit like apricots, pears, peaches, plums, and figs are dried either in the sun or in ovens, to be eaten as they are—as chewy nutritious snacks—or rehydrated by cooking in water or fruit juice, together with added spices like cinnamon, to make tasty desserts. Dried fruit is also cut in small pieces and used in the production of spicy breads and cakes.

More important even are dried nuts, which contain a very high degree of protein and fat, and are used in so many ways. For example, Piedmont and Campania offer the best climatic and soil configuration to cultivate the highly prized hazelnut. Hazelnuts have various uses in the confectionery industry, where they are incorporated in *torrone* (a nougat made of egg white, sugar, and

LEFT: ANGELO THE GARDENER WITH HIS LEMONS IN NAPLES

hazelnuts) or even turned into a paste to produce the Piedmontese chocolate called *gianduja* (see *gianduiotto*, page 214).

Emilia-Romagna and Campania are also the largest producers of walnuts, which are eaten as they are and also used in the making of cakes and cookies. The incomparable flavor of these walnuts finds one of its best expressions in Liguria, where it is used to make a sauce for pasta (see *preboggion*, page 167). When picked green, they are also used to make a liqueur called *nocino*, a specialty of Modena.

The almond is the most important of nuts in the South, where it is cultivated especially in Sicily. The Arab influences in the area have left a rich legacy of use of the highly nutritious almond. As well as being eaten whole, when reduced to a paste with added sugar and egg white, it becomes *pasta reale* ("royal paste") or marzipan. Cookies, cake fillings, *cassata*, *torrone*, and *croccante* (nuts covered with melted sugar) are also made with almonds, as are the curious Sicilian *frutta di marturana*, marzipan shaped and colored like different types of fruit. Among the most famous of the almond products are the *amaretti* cookie, now renowned all over the world, and the *panforte di Siena*, a spicy bread containing the entire array of nuts and dried fruit, which dates back to the Middle Ages.

The best example of the value placed on fruit and nuts is at Christmas, where at the end of a long and rich festive meal appear the special cookies which have taken the last few weeks to prepare, together with tangerines, lots of nuts, walnuts, *torrone*, and *marroni canditi*.

# A-Z OF FRUIT & NUTS

## ACTINIDIA / KIWI FRUIT
Italy has only discovered the kiwi fruit in the last ten years or so, during which time the country has become the biggest producer of the fruit in the world, as several regions have the ideal growing conditions of frost-free springs and falls, and rich, well-aired soils. The kiwi is most successfully cultivated in Piedmont, Veneto, Emilia-Romagna (the biggest producer), Campania, Lazio, Puglia, and Basilicata.

The most popular variety is the Hayward, but the Bruno, Kovyorch, and others are also popular. The overnight success of this fruit is partly due to its vitamin content. Kiwis contain seven times more vitamin C than lemon's and do not need sugar to make them palatable. This wonderful fruit is shaped like a large egg and is about the same size, and has fuzzy brown skin and a brilliant green pulp. It is mainly eaten raw as a table fruit, or used in fruit salads and on fruit tarts, but a large proportion of the crop also finds its way to the drink and confectionery industries.

## AGRUMI / CITRUS FRUIT
This is the generic term for all citrus fruits, such as lemons, limes, oranges, tangerines, grapefruit, etc., which are so much a part of the Italian culinary tradition. Many were first introduced by the Arabs in the South, where they are now grown extensively.

## ALBICOCCA, ARMELLINE / APRICOT, APRICOT KERNEL
Apricots were brought to Italy from China by the Arabs. It is a fruit with many varieties, including Cafona and Reale d'Imola. It ripens over three months between June and September, depending on the variety. The velvety orangey-yellow-skinned and large-pitted fruit has a juiciness and flavor rivaled only by the peach. Italy produces about 221,000 tons of apricots every year, making it one of the largest producers in the world. It is grown in the warm, sunny regions of Campania and Emilia-Romagna, two of the most fertile regions of Italy, as well as in Piedmont, Basilicata, and Sicily.

Apricots are mainly eaten fresh, but are also used to make a drink called *Nektar*, and are preserved in alcohol or in syrup, and made into jam which is used in pâtisserie as a glaze and to cover fruit tarts (see *crostata di cugna*, page 277). It can also be dried and eaten in winter as a part of a compote. Finally, the kernel of the pit, called *armellina*, is used for its intense bitter-almond flavor in *amaretti* and in the making of marzipan.

## AMARENA, MARASCA, VISCIOLA, CILIEGIA ACIDA / MORELLO CHERRY, MARASCHINO CHERRY, MONTMORENCY CHERRY, SOUR CHERRY
Even when ripe, the morello cherry still tastes sour, although it leaves a wonderful flavor in the mouth. It is this very bitterness that makes these cherries ideal for preserving and for making syrups and jams that are used in the making of pastries, drinks, and ice cream. The famous Maraschino liqueur is made with a variety of the sour cherry called Marasca. The best variety is the Montmorency, which is cultivated in the hilly regions of Italy and exported to Germany, where it is used to make the liqueur Kirsch.

## ANGURIA, COCOMERO / WATERMELON
This refreshing summer fruit has almost no nutritional value, with 95% of its flesh water and most of the rest sugar. A few successful varieties have been introduced to Italy from the Nile Valley in Egypt, from which they originate. They come in a variety of shapes—oval, oblong, and round—and a range of colors from dark to pale green. The fruit is usually eaten as a refreshing dessert or as a snack on the hottest of days, turned into ice cream or sorbet, or simply liquidized and served with ice as a drink.

## ARACHIDE / PEANUT
Peanuts are grown in Italy, mainly in Puglia and Campania, and are often eaten toasted and salted with drinks. The majority of the peanuts grown in Italy are used to make peanut oil for frying, while those used in the confectionery industry to make *torrone* are imported from Africa, India, and America.

## ARANCIA / ORANGE
Oranges have a relatively short history in the Mediterranean and it was only in the last century or two that the culture of oranges began in Sicily and Campania—now two of the main areas of production in Italy. For successful cultivation, oranges need sub-tropical temperatures and well-drained, rich organic soil with a modern system of irrigation.

The orange is an extremely versatile fruit, which can be eaten fresh on its own or squeezed for its juice. Certain varieties of orange can be turned into jam, and orange skin is used by the perfume and extract industries for its precious aromatic oils, as well as being candied for use in cakes and confectionery. Scented orange flower water is used in

ABOVE: ORANGES GROWING IN SICILY

LEFT: *ALBICOCCA*

RIGHT: ROASTING
CHESTNUTS WITH
BAY LEAVES.

baking, especially in *pastiera di grano* (see page 177). In Sicily, oranges are combined with smoked herring to produce an interesting salad, *insalata di aringhe, arance, e pompelmi* (see page 29).

Of the many varieties, the best are Biondo Comune, Navel, Bella Donna, and Valencia Late, which is much-used in the jam and confectionery industry, although the bitter Seville orange is best. The main varieties of blood orange, which all have a deep-red pulp, are the Tarocco, Sanguinello, and Moro.

**ARMELLINE, SEE ALBICOCCA**

**AVELLANA, SEE NOCCIOLA**

### BERGAMOTTO / BERGAMOT
Not to be confused with the flower of the same name, the bergamot is a citrus fruit which looks like a small, slightly pear-shaped orange. The small tree is grown only in Calabria and Sicily, and produces a bitter fruit. The skin of the fruit is candied for use by the pâtisserie industry and its oils are used to scent and flavor tea and liqueurs, and in the blending of perfumes—indeed, it is the main constituent of *eau de cologne.*

### CACHI, KAKI, CACHI-MELA, LOTO / PERSIMMON, SHARON FRUIT
I adore this tree, which can be found in most gardens in northern Italy, especially in Campania and Puglia, where it is mostly cultivated for local use. The trees grow up to 30 feet high and have thick, round, dark green leaves which fade before the fruit ripens. The round, green, apple-like fruit matures into a rich orange as it ripens, and inside its very thin skin there is a gelatinous but very juicy sweet pulp with two or three large oval seeds.

The fruit is only palatable when it is very ripe, but before this it has

BELOW: *CACHI*

a strong taste that is heavy with tannin. It is full of vegetable proteins and sugar, and rich in vitamins A, B1, and B2. One variety, called *cachi-mela, loto,* and *legno santo* ("holy wood") is cultivated in southern Italy, but originated in Israel, where it is called sharon fruit. Unlike the variety grown in the North, it is edible when it is still hard and green, and never gets soft like the other variety.

The *cachi* is almost exclusively eaten ripe as fruit. Some people do make jam with it, but its mild flavor means that it is not otherwise much used in cooking.

### CANDITO / CANDIED FRUIT AND PEEL
*Candito* is the name given to fruit or citrus rind that has been permeated by flavored sugar syrup. In the lengthy and complicated procedure, the sugar slowly replaces the water in the fruit, both preserving it and turning it into an edible sweet morsel. *Canditi* are used to make pastries in every Italian region. All sorts of fruit flans employ candied fruits of all types, including cherries, strawberries, chestnuts, pears, apricots, whole clementines, and even certain varieties of pumpkin.

The most important candied peel, however, is that of the citrus fruits, like oranges, mandarins, lemons, and especially *cedro,* or citron. Candied fruit, called *frutta candita,* is often served at the end of meals to be washed down with a little liqueur.

### CASTAGNA / CHESTNUT
No walk in the mountains during the months of October and November is complete without collecting a few pounds of chestnuts. This nut grows on huge trees that are also valued by the furniture industry for their precious wood. The sweet chestnut tree is common in the Apennines and pre-Alps and when the nuts are in season they are either roasted or boiled and

consumed in huge quantities.

As well as the common chestnut, there is another variety called *marroni,* which is much-used in the kitchen. *Marroni* have a spiky shell and grow singly, whereas ordinary chestnuts grow in clusters. They are used to make *marroni canditi* (*marrons glacés,* or candied chestnuts), which are very popular at Christmastime. *Marroni canditi* are very expensive because in the process of making them many get broken and only the whole ones are eventually sold.

In the past, chestnuts were used by the Italian peasant to enrich everyday meals such as soups, or eaten as a vegetable or fruit. Because the chestnut has a rather neutral taste, it can be used in many ways—boiled and puréed for savory stuffings, and served with milk, sugar, and whipped cream in the famous dessert *montebianco,* which can be further enriched by the addition of chantilly cream and alcohol. One of the classic recipes in which chestnuts are used is *caldallessa,* or *ballotta,* a dish of freshly boiled chestnuts served with wine in northern Italian trattorias or *enoteche* (wine bars) on November 2. The nuts may also be simply boiled with a few bay leaves for 40 to 45 minutes, then peeled and eaten on their own.

Chestnuts can also be roasted (*caldarroste*), either in a pan over charcoal or in the oven. Charcoal-roasted chestnuts are often sold on street corners in the winter. If you cook them in the oven, they will get an overall browning and will be easier to peel. Whichever method you use, make sure you make a small incision in the tough skin before cooking to prevent the chestnuts from exploding. If you roast them in a pan, you will need a special roaster with holes in the bottom. Turn the chestnuts over the heat from time to time so that they roast evenly and do not burn, although if they develop a few black spots it will give them flavor. Do not cook them for too long—30 minutes in a hot oven should be enough, or they will become hard and inedible.

Dried chestnuts need to be soaked for a day before being cooked in milk until soft, when they can either be eaten with salt as a savory side dish, or with vanilla, sugar, and cinnamon as a dessert. Ground, dried chestnuts can also be made into a flour, which is used to make an unleavened cake called *castagnaccio* (see page 282), for thickening soups, and is sometimes mixed with wheat flour to make of certain types of pasta. Chestnut flour is also mixed with water, sugar, and vanilla to make *crema di castagne*, a filling for sweet *ravioli*.

## CEDRO / CITRON

This citrus fruit looks like a large lemon which can weigh up to $2^1/4$ pounds and its rind can be up to $1^1/4$ inches thick. It is grown in Calabria, Campania, and Sicily for its peel, which is rich in aromatic oils, and is mainly candied for use by the confectionery industry. The candied peel is also used in the

famous Italian cakes *panettone* and *panforte*, in *cassata* and *cannoli* (see page 256), as well as in a tart filling made of *ricotta* and granules of *pastiera di grano*, and to make a drink called *cedrata*. The flowers of the citron plant produce a concentrated essence that is used to flavor confectionery and in the making of perfumes.

## CILIEGIA / CHERRY

Cherries are mostly grown in Campania, Puglia, Emilia-Romagna, and Veneto, all four regions exporting a huge number all over Europe. The main varieties grown are Durone Nero, Durone Nero di Vignola, Durone Nero di Anella, and Amarena. Their need for particularly well-drained soil and hand-picking at harvesttime makes them one of the most expensive fruits available. As well as being eaten on their own, cherries can also be preserved in pure alcohol or candied and colored for use in confectionery. Cherries are also cooked with sugar and vanilla to make a dessert, as well as used to make sauces for poultry and game.

**CILIEGA ACIDA, SEE AMARENA**

**CLEMENTINA, SEE MANDARINO**

**COCOMERO, SEE ANGURIA**

## CONFETTO / ALMOND CONFECTION

These sweets are offered to the guests in the celebration of baptisms, first communions, and weddings. The most common is an almond enrobed in hard white sugar. *Confetti* may also have an interior of hazelnut or chocolate—even a small aniseed, producing a round sweet—and may also be colored pink, red, silver, or gold.

## CONFETTURA, MARMELLATA / JAM, MARMALADE

The Italians make a preserve similar to marmalade using oranges, lemons, tangerines, mandarins, clementines, grapefruits, or limes. To earn the name *marmellata*, the preserve must be made with the pulp, juice, and rind of the fruit. By contrast, *confettura*, or jam, is made only with the pulp and juice of the fruit. The two are often confused, but to add to the problem there is a third type of preserve called *gelatina*, a fruit jelly made with the strained juice of the fruit.

To make perfect jams and marmalades it is essential that the balance of sugar and the ripeness of the fruit be right, so it is important to use the ripest and the most perfect fruit you can find. If you add less sugar than the fruit needs, more water is extracted from the fruit in the cooking process, making it stronger in flavor but also more prone to fermentation and mold. My mother used to make a jam called *mostarda* (or *cugnà* in Piedmontese) from freshly pressed red grape juice and pears, prunes, peaches, quinces, and even walnuts. The fruit was mixed with sugar and vanilla and then cooked until it resembled a deep brown jam with a thick consistency. The taste was heavenly and we used to spread it liberally on buttered bread and *crostata di cugna* (see page 277) for *merenda*.

LEFT: FRUITS OF THE FALL

LEFT: CITRON BEING SOLD BY THE ROADSIDE IN AMALFI

RIGHT: FIGS IN THE PALERMO MARKET

## CORBEZZOLO / STRAWBERRY TREE

A typical Mediterranean evergreen, this bushy strawberry tree grows wild around all the southern Italian and Sardinian coasts. The round and beautifully red fruit is covered with little red bumps that give it a spiky look. Although it is not used commercially, the fruit of the strawberry tree is both attractive and tasty. It is mostly used as fresh fruit and sometimes for jam.

## COTOGNA, CUGNA, MELA, PERA, COTOGNATA / QUINCE, QUINCE PASTE

In the past, the quince was often used in the kitchen, especially to make sauces for roasted meats. Today, although it is still cultivated and is available on the market stalls of Italy in autumn, it no longer holds the culinary position it once enjoyed. The small trees, with their regularly shaped leaves, bear pear- and apple-shaped fruit (hence the names *mela* or *pera*), with downy yellow skin that rubs down to a shine. It has a wonderful scent, although its flesh is too sour to eat raw and once cut it discolors rapidly, so a few drops of lemon juice need to be sprinkled over it.

It is possible to buy a commercially produced quince paste called *cotognata*, but this can also be made at home simply by peeling the fruit, quartering it, and cooking it in a little water with the zest of a lemon until the water has evaporated and the fruit is very soft. It may then be liquidized or mashed to a purée, mixed with the same quantity of sugar, and reheated over a medium heat, stirring all the time to prevent it from sticking, until it turns a lovely reddish-brown. Spread the mixture on a flat surface and allow it to cool and dry for a couple of days before cutting it into cubes and rolling it in coarsely crushed sugar. It can also be cooked with less sugar, but with juice and cinnamon, to make a compote or jam. In Veneto they add mustard seeds and syrup to quince to make a preserve that is eaten with boiled chicken (see *mostarda di Cremona*).

## CROCCANTE, SEE NOCCIOLA

## DATTERO / DATE

The date tree, which came originally from North Africa, can only be grown for fruit in very warm climates. The trees that decorate gardens in southern Italy produce only very small fruit, which never matures. Dates, which have a sugar content of 70% and are rich in vitamins A, B, C, and D, are among the most nutritious fruits available.

Although dates are not grown in Italy, they are often sold dried, especially at Christmas, with nuts, figs, and other preserved fruits. They are also eaten at other times of the year, both fresh and dried. The ancient Romans were very fond of dates, consuming them among the exotic delicacies served during their famous banquets, but also using them to flavor meat dishes. Today they are used in pâtisserie, usually filled with marzipan, but also as part of Tuscan spicy breads like *panforte*.

## FICO / FIG

The finest figs are those eaten ripe from the plant, a rarity these days as so much fruit is picked unripe for long transportation—a particular issue with figs, which are extremely perishable. Originally from Syria, the fig was spread all over the world by the Romans and it is now grown in Italy in the regions of Puglia, Calabria, and Sicily, where a few of the 700 available varieties are grown and eaten, either raw or preserved.

Figs can be either round or pear-shaped, and some of them reach a considerable size, weighing up to 1³/₄ to 2 ounces each. The skin is very delicate and the inside of the fruit is made up of thousands of pods that produce a very sweet, syrupy substance, giving the fruit its succulence. The best-known varieties grown in Italy are the Gentile Bianco, a Genovese variety which grows in Liguria, the Verdello, Brogiotto Bianco, and Ottato. Fresh figs are very popular eaten plain, with Parma ham (*prosciutto e fichi*), and in fruit salads and tarts.

Full of vitamins, the fig contains five times more calories by weight when dried than it does when fresh, and it is easier to transport and keep. Dried figs are obtained by drying the mature fruit in the sun, in an oven, or in an air-drier, whereby all the water in the fruit is evaporated. Another way of preserving figs is in a honey syrup, and these are exceptionally good eaten for dessert with a touch of cream.

My favorite recipe for dried figs is to bake them in the oven until brown, then cut them in half and serve with peeled almonds or other nuts. Figs soaked in a syrup of orange juice and honey and then boiled for about 5 minutes are also delicious, as are figs enrobed in chocolate.

## FICO D'INDIA / PRICKLY PEAR

This fruit, which originates from Latin America, can often be seen on postcards from southern Italy and Sardinia. The fruit is grainy and slightly scented, and the skin is covered in tiny sharp spikes, which give it its name. The whole, peeled fruit can be eaten, including the little seeds. There are a number of varieties, which come in a range of colors from yellow and white to red. They are eaten fresh, and are also used to make the alcoholic drink tequila.

## FRAGOLA, FRAGOLA SELVATICA OR DI BOSCO / STRAWBERRY, WILD STRAWBERRY

The strawberry grows outdoors, from spring through autumn, but is now cultivated all year round in greenhouses. It perishes very quickly and should not be handled too much as it bruises easily. The best types of strawberry are the Gorella (a conical variety that is available from May), the rounder Pocahontas, the long and pointed Belruby, and the Aliso, which grows mostly in the South, Emilia-Romagna, Piedmont, Veneto, and Campania.

Wild strawberries, called *fragole di bosco*, grow in woodland areas. They are much smaller than the cultivated variety and have a much stronger flavor. They fetch a much higher price than commercially grown strawberries and, despite attempts to cultivate them, the real thing still cannot be beat. Wild strawberries only need a little sugar and a few drops of lemon juice or

balsamic vinegar as an accompaniment if they are eaten on their own, but they are also wonderful in fruit tarts and in all the recipes calling for cultivated strawberries, such as confectionery, liqueurs, preserves, jams, and jellies. Strawberries may also be candied and used as a filling and decoration for many cakes, sweets, and desserts.

## FRUTTA SECCA / DRIED FRUIT

This is the generic term for all dried fruit, such as plums, peaches, pears, apples, apricots, and figs, as well as nuts like hazelnuts, walnuts, peanuts, and almonds.

## GELSO, SEE MORA DI GELSO

## KAKI, SEE CACHI

## LAMPONE / RASPBERRY

The fruit of a bushy plant that grows in the hills of Italy at an altitude of up to 4,500 feet, the raspberry needs a cool climate to grow well. Like strawberries, they are perishable and delicate, and should be handled as little as possible. They are made up of a cluster of tiny sacs, each of which contains a seed. The berry is attached to a conical white stem, from which it can only be pulled cleanly when the fruit is quite ripe.

The flavor of the raspberry is so intense that it is mostly used to make syrups and jellies for the confectionery

industry, but they are also delicious raw on tarts, on meringues, in fruit salad, or best of all, on their own. If cooked with sugar, they make a wonderful sauce for ice cream or creamy desserts, as well as making wonderful sorbets. Agricultural and technological advancements have made commercial cultivation of this fruit much easier, and much of the new abundant crop is frozen to make sauces, syrups, and gelatins.

## LIMA, LIMETTA / LIME

This citrus fruit has only recently been introduced to Italy, especially in Sicily where they are being grown experimentally. Smaller than a lemon, the lime has a dark green color and a highly scented rind which is used in drinks, as well as in sauces for fish. The juice is less pungent than that of the lemon, and is used in delicate dishes, again especially with fish. Very recently, also, a liqueur has been produced using the very intensely perfumed oils extracted from the skin.

## LIMONE / LEMON

Originally from Asia, the lemon found its way to Europe via the Middle East, and was probably introduced by the Arabs. Sicily produces 90% of Italy's lemons (717,000 tons per year), and the other 10% are grown in Calabria and Sardinia, with some of the best coming from the Amalfi coast in Campania. Lemon varieties tend to have quite funny names, like Femminello, Femminello di Santa Teresa, Monachello, and Interdonato.

Lemons are well known for being rich in vitamin C, and they are so acidic that their juice can corrode iron and is used as a disinfectant. In the kitchen, however, it is the ability of the lemon to flavor and to sour, as well as to prevent oxidation, that is most valued. Lemon juice is used to heighten the flavor of both sweet and savory sauces and to establish a

LEFT: PRICKLY PEARS GROWING IN SICILY

LEFT: *LAMPONE*

LEFT: STRAWBERRIES IN TURIN MARKET

good balance between fat and acid. It is also used instead of vinegar to dress salads, and is almost always squeezed over broiled, fried, and boiled fish to bring out the flavor of the fish. It is an indispensable acid agent for curing raw foods such as meat tartares (see *carne all'albese*, page 86), and for marinating fish.

The aroma and flavor of the lemon is strongest in its skin. The beverage, confectionery, and baking industries make good use of the oils extracted from the skin in juices, jams, and extracts. I often use lemon rind infused in hot water to make *canarino*, which is a wonderful tonic.

RIGHT: BOTTLES OF *LEMONCELLO*, A LIQUEUR MADE WITH AMALFI LEMONS, IN NAPLES

### LOTO, SEE CACHI

### MACEDONIA DI FRUTTA /
FRUIT SALAD
This term is used for salads of fresh fruits cut in pieces and left to macerate in orange or lemon juice with a little added sugar and perhaps a splash of liqueur, usually Maraschino. *Macedonia* can also consist of vegetables, either raw or cooked, dressed with vinaigrette or mayonnaise.

### MANDARINO, MANDARANCIO, CLEMENTINA, MANDARINETTO
/ MANDARIN, SATSUMA, CLEMENTINE
The mandarin has been joined by two very similar fruits, the satsuma and the clementine, but neither can match the flavor and juiciness of the seedless flesh of the thin-skinned original. This popular citrus fruit comes from China and is now cultivated with great success in Calabria and Sicily, which together produce 75% of the national yield. The rest is grown in Campania, Basilicata, Puglia, and Sardinia, although this is now being replaced, at least in part, by the new hybrids.

The clementine is smaller and the satsuma larger than the mandarin, and both have a wonderful, deep-orange skin and are rounder than the mandarin. The best-known varieties of mandarin are the Avena, Tardivo di Ciaculli, and Tardivo della Conca d'Oro, while the best-known clementine varieties are Comuni, Clementine Monreales, Clementine di Nules, and Clementine Orovales. The satsuma—a seedless version of the tangerine with more compact pulp—is used in the same way as the mandarin. Its culture is fairly recent in Italy.

The technique used in the culture of mandarins of continually watering the plants on a drip system allows thr trees to be adequately irrigated in the summer. The fruit is harvested between November and January for consumption about a month later. A variety of commercial operations have grown up around the cultivation of mandarins, including the production of juices, aromatic oils, pulp, and candied peel, all for use in the beverage, confectionery, and cosmetics industries. The fruit itself is generally eaten during the winter months, especially at Christmas.

The smallest variety of mandarin, called *mandarinetto*, used to be candied whole, resulting in a delicious confection with a slightly resilient skin and a very sugary center.

### MANDORLA / ALMOND
Common all around the Mediterranean and in Asia, the almond was introduced, along with the vine and the fig tree, into Italy by the ancient Greeks. The almond tree has many similarities with the peach tree, with leaves of the same shape, and the same type of wood. When it is growing and forming, the nut is contained within a pointed oval shell that is encased within a thick green outer skin, called *mallo*.

Due to its combination of proteins, minerals, and high fat content (50%), the almond has been a valuable food for thousands of years. A number of varieties, including Tuono, Filippo Ceo, and Ferrangnes, are cultivated in Sicily, Veneto, Puglia, Campania, and Sardinia.

There are two types of almond: the sweet and the bitter. The bitter almond is the smaller of the two and has the typical almond taste, which is used to boost the flavor of all products made with sweet almonds. It has to be heat-treated before use, however, as otherwise it is toxic.

Among the best-known almond products is marzipan (see *marzapane*, page 268 and *pasta di mandorle*, pages 279 and 297), which is much-used in the South. The almond is particularly favored in Sicily, where it is used to make the famous Sicilian *cassata* (see recipe, page 256), as well as cookies and *torrone*.

The very precious oil from almonds is used both in pâtisserie to flavor sweets, and in medicines and cosmetics for its softening properties. There is also a kind of milk that is extracted from the almond, which is used to make a drink called *latte di mandorle*. It resembles coconut milk and is extremely delicious.

Almonds are also used in the making of amaretto, a famous liqueur, and *amaretti* cookies (see page 279). Both of these products require a large number of bitter almonds and less of the balancing sweetness of the other variety. In the kitchen, almonds are often paired with trout. I sometimes use ground almonds instead of flour to thicken sauces. There is a term *mandorlato*, which indicates the presence of almonds, as in *torrone mandorlato*.

MARASCA, SEE AMARENA

MARMELLATA, SEE CONFETTURA

MARRONI, SEE CASTAGNA

## MARZAPANE, PASTA REALE / MARZIPAN

This paste of sugar, almond flour, and egg white is widely used in Sicily to make *cassata siciliana* and to bake a variety of cookies. It is also used as filling for tarts and dates. Marzipan has a sweetish taste, only sometimes betraying a hint of the bitter almonds, or *armelline*, added to enhance the almond flavor. In certain parts of the South, *marzapane* is called *pasta reale* ("royal paste"), indicating the regard with which it is held. A Sicilian creation called *frutta di marturana* is marzipan shaped into all types of fruit, which are then painted realistically by hand. See *pasta di mandorle*, page 297, and recipe page 279.

## MELA / APPLE

By far the most frequently eaten fruit in Italy—probably in Europe—is the apple. Of the total 220 pounds of fruit eaten by each

Italian every year, at least half is apples. There are over 250 varieties of apple, and it is considered one of the healthiest fruits, with its high level of fiber, vitamin C, and acidity.

Fifty percent of Italian apples are cultivated in the Trentino Alto-Adige, with Emilia-Romagna, Veneto, Piedmont, Lombardy, and Campania contributing the remaining half. Apple trees needs cool temperatures and little wind, which is why they are cultivated in tranquil valleys, and the flatlands of the North. The varieties grown in Italy are used to meet local needs, so they may be different from those grown in other parts of the world.

The first harvest in July includes varieties like Gravenstein, Ozark Gold, and the succulent Golden Red apple. These are followed in the fall by Golden Delicious, Red Delicious, the very red Stayman, the extremely green Granny Smith, and the huge Imperatore. My favorite apple is the Reneste/Reveste, a rusty yellow apple with a yellowish pulp and a highly developed flavor, which stays juicy and firm all winter. Most apples keep for quite a long time, up to a month if stored in a well-ventilated, temperature-controlled room.

Apples are eaten their own, and often used in the making of sauces, compotes, pies, tarts, and in other baking, as well as for juices and in the manufacture of brandy.

MELA COTOGNA, SEE COTOGNA

## MELAGRANA, GRANATA / POMEGRANATE

The pomegranate tree, with its pretty red blossom and fruit, is now largely grown for its ornamental beauty, although in the Middle Ages the fruit was used to make sauces and for stuffing game. The fruit used to be regarded as a sacred symbol of fecundity.

Although it is still grown all over Italy, it makes a minor commercial contribution in Sicily, where it is cultivated to serve the syrup industry. Especially in Renaissance times, *melagrana* was used in Tuscan cuisine as a flavoring in game and poultry dishes. Today it is mostly used as a tablefruit, but is sometimes pressed for juice to produce sorbet and to add to fruit salad.

The pomegranate is round, with a tough orange-red skin and a little crown on top where the stalk of the tree was attached. Inside, its flesh is divided into segments by a large number of yellow membranes, and each segment holds many transparent sacs of juice, each with a little seed. As a result, it is quite difficult to eat, and I tend to eat it with a spoon. First make four lengthwise cuts through the skin with a knife, as if cutting an apple into quarters. Then start to loosen the sections, collecting the fruit and juice in a bowl and discarding the bitter yellow membranes. The pink fruit is sweet with a slightly acidic aftertaste and a granular texture.

LEFT: A MARZIPAN HEART FOR CHRISTMAS IN ERICE, SICILY

LEFT: PLASTER MOLDS FOR MARZIPAN EASTER LAMBS

LEFT: IMPERATORE APPLES

LEFT: *MELAGRANE*

## MELONE, POPONE / MELON

Originating in southern Asia and equatorial Africa, the melon comes from the same family of plants as the pumpkin and zucchini. The plant spreads its tentacles over a wide area, feeding the round or oval fruit with the moisture it needs to reach about $2^{1}/_{4}$ pounds in weight. There are many varieties of melon, some growing and maturing in summer, and others in autumn, with the later fruit often kept for the winter months. Among the latter are the Invernale Giallo and Verde varieties, oval melons shaped like rugby balls, with a very thick yellow or green skin and a white, not-too-sweet pulp. They are mostly grown in Emilia-Romagna, Lazio, Puglia, Campania, and Sicily, and can be kept for several months.

Summer melons tend to be round with an orange skin, which can be either smooth or rough, with a net of raised green veins all over it. The summer varieties of Cantaloupe and Retato are round in shape, with a smooth green-gray skin and a net-covered yellowish skin respectively, and both contain an extremely juicy dark-orange, highly flavored, sweet pulp. They are grown in Emilia-Romagna, Campania, and Puglia.

Choosing a ripe melon can sometimes be a little difficult, but the best way to judge is to see if the center of both top and bottom are slightly soft and are giving off a definite aroma. The weight is also a good indication of a ripe melon, so the heavier it is, the juicier and riper it will be.

Melon is almost always eaten on its own or as part of a fruit cocktail, but it can also be used to make sorbet or a refreshing drink if liquidized. It can also make a lovely chilled summer soup if blended with some lemon juice, salt, pepper, and some chives. The best way of eating melon, though, is with a few slices of Parma ham, accompanied by a good white wine, beneath a pergola—that is what summer is all about.

*RIGHT: MIRTILLI*

*RIGHT: MOSTARDA DI CREMONA*

## MIRTILLO / BLUEBERRY

Pollution has made this berry difficult to find growing in the wild and there is little interest in hunting out the few that are left, which means that the only blueberries you can get are the larger commercially cultivated ones. These are available all year round but they lack the flavor of the real thing. In the wild, the blueberry grows through the summer into the autumn in hills and mountains at altitudes over 4,500 feet. The blue-black berries are very small, and a special wooden comb is used to collect them in order to avoid damaging the structure of the plant.

The cultivated blueberry from America is much bigger, with a more distinct bluish tinge to the skin, and paler flesh. They can be eaten on their own or with other wild berries in the fruit salad known as *sottobosco*, or used to fill fruit tarts. They are also used to make a sauce for game and poultry, a jam called *confettura di mirtilli*, a sweet sauce for pâtisserie, and a liqueur.

## MORA DI GELSO / MULBERRY

The mulberry bush, Chinese in origin, is mostly grown for its leaves, which are used to feed silk worms. The berries come in two colors, white and black. Both are made up of a series of tightly bunched pods, but the black berry is longer and has a deep-red juice that is slightly sour, but has a wonderful flavor. The mulberry is mostly grown on the plains of northern Italy and is only used locally, as it is not sold commercially. It can be eaten on its own or as part of a fruit salad, and is used to make syrups and jams.

## MORA DI ROVO / BLACKBERRY

In summer, it is common to see Italians making their way through thorny brambles to collect wild blackberries. Agricultural progress means that it is now possible to buy cultivated blackberries, grown on thornless bushes for easy picking. Although less flavorsome than the wild variety, the cultivated blackberry is still good in fruit salads and as a topping for fruit tarts, as well as making delicious jams, compotes, juices, and syrups for use in the liqueur, pâtisserie, and confectionery industries. It is a very perishable soft fruit and should be eaten as soon as it is picked.

## MOSTARDA DI CREMONA / MUSTARD FRUITS

This specialty of the city of Cremona in Lombardy consists of fruit such as cherries, pears, figs, and apricots, candied for a long time in a heavy sugar syrup flavored with extract of mustard. The result is very piquant fruit used to accompany boiled meat like capon and *bollito misto* (see page 92).

In Veneto there is another version of *mostarda* in which the fruit is minced together, resulting in a paste which is used in the same way.

The *mostarda* made in Piedmont has a totally different use, and is made in a different way (see *cotogna*, page 265).

## NESPOLA COMUNE / MEDLAR

The medlar is a round, walnut-sized, rusty-colored fruit, borne on an ancient plant between the end of October and the beginning of November. The fruit cannot be eaten when it is harvested, but needs to be kept in a well-ventilated area to "rot" for a fairly long period of time, when it matures into a sweet and juicy fruit. It can be used to make a delicious, hard gelatin or cheese like quince (see *cotogna*). The medlar is not commercially grown but, like the pomegranate, it is often planted in Italian gardens for its appearance.

## NESPOLE DEL GIAPPONE / LOQUAT

A popular fruit in Italy, the loquat is available during the spring and summer. The tree has long and distinctive dark-green leaves that make it popular in the gardens of the coastal regions, and there is some commercial cultivation of the fruit in Campania, Calabria, Sicily, Puglia, and Sardinia. The loquat can be oval or round, depending on the variety, and is pale orange, with a very smooth, thick skin that peels easily when the fruit is ripe. Its flesh is extremely juicy and sweet, but with enough acidity to lift the flavor. It is a very pleasant fruit to eat on its own, but can also be used to make jam and sorbet.

## NOCCIOLA, AVELLANA / HAZELNUT

The city of Avellino in Campania takes its name from the product for which it is celebrated, the hazelnut. The hazelnut tree comes from Turkey, but has been successfully adapted to grow in various parts of Italy. More than half of the 110,000 tons produced each year come from Campania. The rest comes from Lazio, Piedmont, and Sicily, where the nuts are particularly good. The variety called Tonda Gentile delle Langhe grows in the same area as the white truffle, and it is said that the truffles that grow beside hazelnut trees are the best. Other varieties include Mortarelle, Gentile Romana, and Nostrale di Sicilia.

Hazelnuts ripen in autumn. The round kernel is encased in a tough wooden husk so it keeps for a long time, although, like all foods that contain fat, it will turn rancid and go bad if it is badly kept. The nuts are very nutritious, containing a balance of fat (600 calories per $3\frac{1}{2}$ ounces), protein, vitamins, and minerals.

In Piedmont, the best hazelnuts are roasted, then ground into an extremely fine paste to make nougat and *gianduiotti* chocolate, while in Campania they are used to make *croccante di nocciole* (see page 280). They are also used in a huge variety of cookies and cakes all over the country.

## NOCE / WALNUT

The best Italian walnuts come from the Sorrento area in Campania, and the best variety is the eponymous Sorrento, a large nut with a thin, easily breakable shell and very tasty meat. Other good varieties include the late-ripening Sorrento Giovanni and a French variety called Franquette.

The nut grows in bunches from large trees that came originally from Asia and are as much sought-after for their wood as their fruit. The nut is formed inside a fleshy green outer skin called *mallo*, which peels open when the nut is ripe, around September or October, allowing the nut, protected by its hard, wrinkled casing, to fall to the ground. Inside, the meat is divided into four sections, called *gherigli*.

Fresh walnuts are delicious, as long as you remove the meat from the bitter yellow skin surrounding it. To enjoy the full flavor of the walnut, however, it is better to wait until it is completely dry, when the meat will have shrunk inside the shell and the yellow skin will have turned brown and papery. The best nuts are those of the last crop, before the oils in the meat turn rancid.

Around Modena in Emilia-Romagna, a specialty called *nocino* is made with unripe walnuts. They are collected when the nut is unformed, usually around 23 June, Saint Giovanni's day. The green walnuts are then quartered, put in a glass container, and covered with pure alcohol flavored with cinnamon, then left to marinate in the sun for 40 days. The resulting liquid, once diluted with water and mellowed with sugar, is dark brown and about 30 to 40% alcohol, and is drunk as a *digestif*. It is available commercially, but it is

LEFT: *NESPOLE COMUNE*

LEFT: HAZELNUTS AND GREEN AND DRY WALNUTS

much more fun producing it yourself.

Walnuts are also used to make cookies, cakes, and confectionery. In Liguria, there is a pasta sauce based on olive oil, ground walnuts, garlic, and Parmesan cheese (see *pansôti al preboggion*, page 167). Walnuts are also served at Christmastime with dried fruits and nuts such as dates, hazelnuts, and apricots. Finally, the oil extracted from the walnut is used to make tasty salad dressings.

## PASTA REALE, SEE MARZAPANE

## PERA / PEAR

The pear originated from the area around the Caspian Sea and was introduced into Europe about 2000 years ago. Today there are around 5,000 varieties, and Italy is one of the biggest producers in the world, cultivating about ten varieties. Nearly two-thirds of all the pears cultivated in Italy come from Emilia-Romagna, with Campania, Veneto, Lazio, Sicily, Lombardy, and Piedmont making up the balance.

Early varieties, maturing around July, include Coscia, Butirra Morettini, and Guyot, all of which have a juicy flesh and yellow skin. In August, the red or yellow Williams pear ripens and is followed by the winter varieties such as the Abate, the orangey-yellow Kaiser, and the large Decana del Comizio, or Comice, and finally the largest and longest-keeping, green-yellow pear, Passa Crassana. While these are all grown commercially, the small and delicious rusty-colored St. Martin pear from Piedmont is worth seeking out. Winter varieties can be

kept for a few months if properly stored, but summer fruit should be eaten when ripe.

Pears are usually eaten on their own or in fruit salads, but they can also be cooked, either in red or white wine with spices, lemon zest, and sugar, or just with sugar and water to make compote, or baked in the oven with wine and sugar. They can be candied or air-dried and used to make jams, syrups, and sweets. They are even distilled to make Williams liqueur and Williams Schnapps, after the German tradition, based on a spirit distilled, naturally, from the Williams pears. The area where this specialty is made is the Trentino Alto-Adige, but these drinks are popular all over Italy as *digestifs*.

Finally as in the old Italian proverb *"Al contadin non far sapere come e' buono il cacio con le pere,"* meaning "don't let the farmer know how good it is to eat fresh pears and cheese," there is a no nicer way to finish a meal.

## PERA COTOGNA, SEE COTOGNA

## PESCA, PESCANOCE / PEACH, NECTARINE

The Mediterranean region, and Italy in particular, seems to be ideal for growing peaches and their cousins, the nectarines. The tree was originally brought to the area from Persia by Alexander the Great, but now Italy produces about 80% of Europe's total consumption, despite the Italians being avid consumers of the fruit themselves. There are two major types of peach, although there are many varieties. The first type is Pesca Comune di Pasta Bianca, the common peach, an apple-sized fruit with a thin downy skin and a white,

juicy, and deliciously scented flesh. The second variety is much like the first but has a yellow flesh and a reddish-yellow skin.

Other types of peach include the Percoca, a peach from the South with a yellowy-green skin and a firm flesh that is widely used by the preserving industry, and the wild Pesche di Vigna that grows alone in the vineyards of Italy. The latter has a very intense flavor and is usually white-fleshed with a green-and-red skin. This lovely peach can be prised in half and popped straight into your mouth because it is so small. Vineyard owners try to keep these peach trees, with their beautifully scented pink flowers, hidden away so that they can enjoy their fruit fresh or preserved in syrup for Christmas.

The nectarine is a not a hybrid, but a true variety of peach. It is very similar to the peach but has a completely smooth and shiny skin. Again, there are two main types, one with white and the other with yellow flesh, and countless varieties have been developed to crop from May to September. In the end, however, the peach has much more flavor.

Peaches and nectarines are mostly eaten on their own or in fruit salads, but peaches are more widely used in the kitchen than nectarines. In Piedmont, peaches are sliced, dipped in red wine, and sprinkled with a little sugar before being eaten. They can also be halved, stuffed with a mixture of beaten egg, crumbled *amaretti*, cocoa powder, and sugar, then baked in the oven. Peaches are pulped to make *succo di pesca*, which is mixed with champagne to make the famous Bellini cocktail. Peaches are also used to make jam and a solid paste rather like *cotognata* called *pasta di frutta*, as well as being dried for long keeping.

### PINOLO / PINE NUT

The pine nut or kernel is the seed of the pine tree. It is held in the familiar pine cone, made up of a series of wooden tongues. The creamy-white kernel is about $^1/_2$ inch long and slightly pointed at one end. The seed can only be gathered from the cones of mature trees at least 70 years of age, which is why the nut is not cultivated on a large scale. The trees themselves are part of the Ombrella family and are typical of the landscape of the coastal regions of Tuscany, Campania, and Sicily. The kernel can only be harvested if the cone is completely open when it is collected, although a short spell in a hot oven will encourage it to open to release the seeds.

Despite its high fat content, the pine nut is very nutritious, with a high proportion of proteins, vitamins, and minerals. Always make sure you buy fresh pine nuts, as their fat can turn rancid, making them inedible. The pine nut has been popular as an ingredient since Biblical times and is often used along with raisins as a flavoring for meat, and to make stuffings for meat and poultry. This is a reminder of Arab influences on southern Italian cooking. In Liguria, pine nuts are an essential ingredient for the famous pesto sauce (see page 228) and it is also used to make pastries and cookies (see the recipe for *panpepato*, page 230), and as decoration for other cakes and sweets.

### PISTACCHIO / PISTACHIO

The pistachio is the fruit of a wonderful little tree that is typical of the southern Mediterranean and in Italy unique to the island of Sicily, the only region with the right climatic conditions for its growth. The nut grows in bundles enclosed within a fleshy red pod that bursts open to reveal the nut bulging out of its woody envelope. Inside, the pistachio is bright green, which makes it ideal for decorating cakes, cookies, and other sweets. It is also used as a stuffing for meat, and even finds its way into the salami *mortadella*. The nut is also ground into a powder and used as the base for a very tasty ice cream and it is also popular eaten salted, as a snack with drinks.

### POMPELMO / GRAPEFRUIT

The largest of the citrus fruits, the grapefruit is full of vitamin C, contains little sugar and no protein or fat, and is extremely juicy. It is mainly cultivated in Sicily, Calabria, and Liguria, where the mildness of the climate favors its growth. The slightly bitter scent and flavor of the yellow Pompelmo Giallo is ideal for marinades and makes a perfect fruit juice. The pink or red varieties are much sweeter than their yellow cousin and are delicious eaten on their own. Choose grapefruit by their weight; the heavier the better. I like to serve pink grapefruit in segments, stripped of their membranes, with orange juice poured over them.

### POPONE, SEE MELONE

### PRUGNA, SUSINA, PRUGNA SECCA / PLUM, PRUNE

In Italian, the words *prugna* and *susina* are both used to refer to plums, while *prugna secca* refers to prunes. The plum originates from Asia but grows very successfully all over Europe, as well as in many other parts of the world. Italy produces about 165,000 tons a year, concentrating on Regina Claudia (my preference), Prugna d'Italia, Precoce die Guignao, Formosa, Dane Aubert, Santarosa Stanley, Blue Gestetter, and California Blue, as well as greengages, with their sweet flesh and green skin. The main regions for plum cultivation are Emilia-Romagna, Campania, Morele, Alto Adige, and Piedmont.

ABOVE: *PRUGNE*

They can be eaten fresh on their own, or can be baked in sweets or simply stewed with sugar or made into jam. The dried version of the fruit, the prune, is used in confectionery and for baking. Prunes are wonderful preserved in brandy, when they can be eaten with ice cream or with creamy desserts, or simply plumped in water as an accompaniment to pork or game dishes. They are also used to make *slivovitz*, a well-known Yugoslavian type of schnapps.

### RIBES / BLACK CURRANTS, RED CURRANTS, WHITE CURRANTS

These soft summer fruits come from a bushy plant that can be found in the wild. The translucent black, red, or white berries grow in small bunches. The black currant is used for making jams and by the beverage industry to make *cassis*, an alcoholic syrup that can be diluted with wine or *spumante* to make kir. In jam-making, because of their high pectin content, *ribes* are often added to low-pectin fruits like strawberries, cherries, and peaches. They are used in pâtisserie, in fruit tarts, and for decorating sweets. Along with other berry fruit, currants are used to make summery fruit salads called *macedonia sottobosco* or *frutti di bosco*.

LEFT: PINE CONES FOR NUTS IN CAMPANIA

**ROVO, SEE MORA DI ROVO**

**SORBO / SORB APPLE**
This little tree, common in the hills all over Italy—especially Sardinia—produces a small applelike fruit that turns from yellow to red, indicating that it is ripe and ready for eating. It is not grown commercially and can only be found in the wild, although it may be found in specialist fruit shops towards the end of the summer.

**SOTTOBOSCO / WILD BERRIES**
This is a fairly recent term used to describe all the wild soft fruit can may find in the woods, such as wild strawberries, wild raspberries, wild blackberries, etc. It is also applied to a salad made of such fruit, or sauces incorporating the fruit for use in cakes and tarts. The term has even found use in the language of wine-tasting, to evoke flavors reminiscent of woodland, like moss and fungus.

ABOVE: *SOTTOBOSCO*

**SULTANINA, SEE UVA**

**SUSINA, SEE PRUGNA**

**TAMARINDO / TAMARIND**
Originally from India, the tamarind tree produces a beautiful brown pod. Although it is not grown in Italy, the tamarind is widely used in Italy to make a soft drink, a syrup, and confectionery.

RIGHT: *UVE DA TAVOLA*

**UVA, UVA DA TAVOLA, UVETTA, SULTANINA / GRAPE, RAISIN, GOLDEN RAISIN**
There is an unbelievable variety of grapes grown in the world; some are cultivated exclusively for wine making, while others are for eating fresh—*uva da tavola*, or table grapes. While it is possible to eat wine grapes at the table, table grapes cannot be used to make wine.

The vine is a climbing plant, introduced to Italy thousands of years ago from the area around the Caspian Sea. The Romans took this vital plant with them everywhere they went, introducing it into France and many other countries as they conquered Europe. Italy is now the biggest producer of grapes in the world, followed by Spain and France. The majority of these grapes are used to make wine—the most common type is the thin-skinned white, pink, or red Vitis Vinifera. The best-known and most successful table grape is the Italia, which—thanks to new techniques for delaying ripening—is available from August to December. It is much appreciated in Italy and Europe, and it is exported in large quantities to Germany and France. Other varieties include the Uva Regina, the Red Cardinal, Primus, and Baresana.

More than half of the grapes grown in Italy come from the fertile region of Puglia, with Sicily, Abruzzi, Lazio, Basilicata, Calabria, and Sardinia making up the difference. Together they produce 544,000 tons of grapes a year, of which 96,000 are exported. In Piedmont, Veneto, and most of the other wine-grape-producing regions, wonderfully ripe grapes like Uva Americana, Fragola (with the scent of strawberries), and the very sweet Moscato are often sold locally. I think the only variety worth eating is the Muscat. Bunches of these are hung on strong string until they turn from golden yellow to a wrinkled golden brown, when they become intensely and deliciously sweet. In Italy its considered good luck to eat grapes on New Year's Eve and, although I am not superstitious, I still do it now (sadly, however, not with the same quality of grapes).

More and more foreign varieties are taking over, including the popular seedless Thompson variety

Table grapes are eaten raw as dessert, or in fruit salads, or to used cover fruit tarts. Some grapes are preserved in alcohol and served in a small bowl with a little of the liquor.

When they are dried, grapes turn into *uvetta*, or raisins, and *sultanina*, or golden raisins, which are often made with seedless grapes. The largest golden raisin is the pale-blonde Malaga, which has a few seeds, and the smallest raisin is the seedless blue-black Corinth, which is imported from the Middle East. Both raisins and golden raisins are used in pâtisserie, featuring in a range of recipes from *panettone* to *panpepato* (see pages 218 and 230), and are used with *ricotta* in sweet fillings for tarts and cakes. In Naples, Sicily, and Liguria they are also mixed with pine nuts as a stuffing for meat and game. They make a delicious snack when soaked in brandy or rum.

Probably the most sought-after raisin to eat by itself is that made from the Zibibbo grape, the fruit of a vine grown in Italy for the making of the famous *moscato di pantelleria*. These raisins are dried still attached to the stalks and sold like this.

**UVA SPINA / GOOSEBERRY**
This spiky bush is related to the red currant. The berries are delicious when golden-yellow and ripe, but are only grown privately in Italy. They can be eaten in pies, cooked with sugar and puréed as a dessert, and used to make gooseberry fool.

**VISCIOLA, SEE AMARENA**

MELECOTOGNE
IN COMPOSTA

# PANFORTE
## TRADITIONAL TUSCAN CAKE

**FOR 10**

1²/₃ CUPS ALMONDS, BLANCHED, SKINNED, AND TOASTED

SCANT 1 CUP WALNUTS OR PECANS

2 OUNCES CANDIED *CEDRO* (CITRON PEEL), CUT INTO SMALL STRIPS

9 OUNCES CANDIED PUMPKIN, CUT INTO SMALL CHUNKS

2 TEASPOONS GROUND CINNAMON

2 TEASPOONS GROUND CORIANDER SEEDS

½ TEASPOON FRESHLY GRATED NUTMEG

1³/₄ CUPS ALL-PURPOSE FLOUR

1¹/₃ CUPS CONFECTIONERS' SUGAR

SCANT ½ CUP HONEY (ACACIA IS BEST)

A FEW SHEETS RICE PAPER

2 TABLESPOONS VANILLA SUGAR

*This Tuscan specialty has been eaten since the Middle Ages, when the first spices were imported from the Mediterranean. Siena is the city that assumed paternity of this "strong bread," now famous all over the world. The recipe includes candied pumpkin, which is easy to find in Italy, but not so easy elsewhere. It can be replaced with candied citrus peel, although the flavor will not be the same. You could try looking for candied pumpkin in Turkish and Middle Eastern food stores.*

Preheat the oven to 325° F. Mix the almonds, walnuts, or pecans, candied peel, pumpkin, and spices together in a bowl. Add the flour and combine very well. Put the confectioners' sugar, honey, and 1 tablespoon water in a heavy-bottomed pan and heat gently until dissolved. Increase the heat so that the mixture bubbles and then stir with a wooden spoon until it forms a thick, pale-brown caramel. Pour it onto the flour and nuts and mix until smooth.

Use the rice paper to line an 8-inch cake pan, 1¹/₂ inches deep. Spread the mixture in it, smoothing the top with a spatula. Bake for about 30 minutes, then remove and leave to cool in the pan. Dust with the vanilla sugar. It can be kept for a long time but I doubt you will be able to!

# CASTAGNACCIO
## CHESTNUT CAKE

**FOR 8 TO 10**

HEAPING 6¹/₂ CUPS FRESH CHESTNUT
    FLOUR
PINCH SALT
6 TABLESPOONS SUPERFINE SUGAR
6 TABLESPOONS VIRGIN OLIVE OIL
3 TO 4 SPRIGS ROSEMARY
²/₃ CUP *ZIBIBBO* RAISINS (SEE *UVA*,
    PAGE 273) OR ORDINARY RAISINS

*There exist various versions of this seasonal dish, which is made with the flour of new autumn chestnuts. Chestnut flour tends to become stale quite quickly, which is why it is best used fresh. This is one of the simplest and tastiest ways of using it.*

Preheat the oven to 350° F. Mix the flour, salt, and sugar with enough cold water to obtain a soft but not too runny mixture. Put the oil in a deep 12- x 16-inch baking dish and spread evenly, then pour in the batter. Sprinkle with the rosemary and raisins and bake for 20 minutes, until golden. Cut into squares to serve. It's best served hot but can also be eaten cold.

# ORZATA
## ALMOND MILK DRINK

**FOR 4**

5¹/₂ OUNCES SWEET ALMOND PASTE
    (SEE PAGE 267)

*This wonderfully refreshing summer drink was originally made with barley, but now a thick, sugared almond paste is more likely to be used. It is also called* latte di mandorle, *or almond milk.*

Put the almond paste and 2¹/₂ cups water in a blender and blend until it forms a white, milky fluid. If it is too strong, dilute with a little more water.

# FRUTTA SCIROPPATA
## FRUIT IN SYRUP

**MAKES ENOUGH TO FILL A
2¹/₂-QUART JAR**

2¹/₄ POUNDS FRUIT (SEE RIGHT)
4¹/₂ CUPS SUPERFINE SUGAR
1 VANILLA BEAN

*This is halfway between a compote and candied fruit. The secret is to achieve a degree of sugar concentration in the liquid that allows it to function as a preservative. The fruit should keep its shape. Ripe peaches, plums, or kumquats are all ideal. It is often served with ice cream or* panna cotta.

If using peaches, blanch them briefly in boiling water, then skin and halve them and remove the pit.

    Put the sugar, 4¹/₂ cups water, and vanilla bean in a large pan and heat gently until the sugar has completely dissolved. Add the fruit and cook gently until just tender—25 minutes for the softest fruit to 40 minutes for harder ones. Remove the fruit with a slotted spoon and set aside. Increase the heat and boil the liquid until reduced in volume by one third. Lower the heat, return the fruit to the pan, and cook over very low heat for 30 minutes more. Transfer to a sterilized jar, seal, and store in a cool place until needed.

# FRUTTA SOTTO SPIRITO

FRUIT IN ALCOHOL

It is best to use very high spirit (95% alcohol) for this, which is readily available in Italy, but not everywhere (see page 310). You should always use ripe fruit no larger than a small tangerine. Grapes, cherries, apricots, and dried fruits such as raisins are ideal. Soft fruits such as berries are not suitable. Pack the fruit tightly into a sterilized preserving jar, then pour in the alcohol and seal the jar. The rest is done by time—let it soak for at least 3 months. Serve the fruit in small glasses either on its own or accompanied by cream or ice cream. It should not be given to children; this is a serious grown-up affair!

# BREADS & BAKING

## PANE E CIBI DA FORNO

The origins of baking, especially that of bread baking, go back to at least 2,000 years before the Common Era, and the Egyptians seem to be the first to have had any expertise in the field. Since then, bread has spread all over the world to become, after rice, the principal element of human nutrition. Every country or race has chosen different ways to produce it, using the most favorable local grains and utensils. Basically, however, it is the same for everybody. Flour of various grains is combined with water, a little salt, and yeast, this dough is left to rise through the action of yeast, and then it is baked for immediate use.

As a small child in Castelnuovo Belbo, my brother Carlo used to head off on his bike with a huge willow basket balanced on the handle bars. This basket was lined with an immaculate linen cloth containing a huge lump of fresh bread dough that my mother had prepared to send to the local bakery to be baked into loaves for the family's needs. She used to knead the dough for a long time before letting it rise and then she placed it gently into the basket and covered it. Carlo then had the task of cycling to the bakery in the village, where the dough was divided into various large portions and baked. The result was stunning! This was bread made with love, and had a fragrance that even impressed

the baker, who always wanted to keep a piece for himself.

The function of a bakery, especially one in a small village, wasn't only the baking of bread. All sorts of things lovingly prepared at home, like roasts, tarts, cookies, and various other things, including loaves of bread cut in slices to be biscuited (see *frisella*, page 293), were brought by the villagers on trays to be baked once the actual bread baking was finished for the day, while the oven was still hot. The fragrance of those dishes, mingled with the wonderful smell of the burnt wood, was something out of this world!

This was at the end of the war, when we were very lucky to have many ingredients that were otherwise hard to find. My father had obtained two big sacks of sea salt, which he bartered for merchandise such as wheat. I will never forget the slice of bread eaten for *merenda*, the Italian equivalent of high tea, topped with *mostarda* jam— also made by my mother.

The way of baking today has changed completely. It is rare to find a bakery still with a wood-burning oven to impart the full flavor to the bread. Everything is industrialised in the name of progress, but, in my opinion, it is really only in the name of commercialization, which does not understand real quality. I really feel sorry for the younger generation in this respect, because with every bakery that closes down a piece of artisan culture is probably gone forever.

A little revival of this art does, however, seem to be underway, thanks to some nostalgic people reviving the old ways of making bread. These artisans prepare all sorts of specialties from the past, like *pane di segala*, dark, hard rye bread as they used to make in the Aosta Valley for long keeping, which is edible only when dipped in water or milk. All sorts of other interesting breads, made using whole meal flour in response to modern dietary demands, as well as bread made with half corn flour and half wheat flour, are on offer to help us rediscover some of the textures and tastes of bygone times.

Industrially produced bread is absolutely diabolical, keeping its freshness and crispness for only a few hours and tasting mostly of cotton wool. Unfortunately, even the Italians—who usually make a big fuss about the quality of food—seem to have accepted this sort of bread for the sake of convenience. The only real use of the wood-fired oven today is usually for making pizzas, which have taken the world by storm. Even in the pizza industry, however, wood-fired ovens are the minority, as commercialization dictates more economical methods.

RIGHT: TUSCAN FIELDS, NEAR MONTALCINO, PREPARED FOR GRAIN

LEFT: A RANGE OF SICILIAN BREADS

# A-Z OF BREADS & BAKING

### AMARETTO / MACAROON COOKIE

There are many varieties of this popular cookie, the best-known being the crispy *amaretto di Saronno*, a pair of small *amaretti* wrapped in paper and served with coffee in almost every Italian restaurant or trattoria. It takes its name from the town of Saronno, where it has been made for the last hundred years by Lazzaroni. *Amaretti* can be found all over Italy, however, ranging in texture from dry and crisp to moist and soft,

## MAKING AMARETTI COOKIES

To make your own moist and soft *amaretti* cookies (see page 279 for a recipe for crisp ones), mix a scant $4^1/_2$ cups peeled and freshly ground almonds with a scant 1 cup ground bitter almonds or *armelline* (ground apricot kernels, see *albicocca*, page 262).

Carefully fold 2 cups superfine sugar into 4 lightly beaten egg whites, then add the ground almonds and the finely grated rind of $^1/_2$ lemon.

Place the mixture in a piping bag and pipe round discs onto a buttered baking tray. Sprinkle with some coarsely crushed sugar, then place in an oven preheated to 375° F and bake until brown.

depending on the recipe and cooking time. The most sought-after are those of Mombaruzzo, a small town in Piedmont. These *amaretti* are soft, and each one is wrapped by hand in characteristic oiled paper.

### ANICINO / ANISE COOKIE

These Umbrian cookies testify to the popularity of aniseed in Italy. The cookies are a specialty of Orvieto, although they are also made in Sardinia, and can be eaten either on their own or dipped in wine like *cantuccini*. In Sardinia they are dipped into the local strong wine, Monica di Sardegna. As a variation, the cookies can be made with olive oil instead of the usual hard fats, making them tastier and healthier.

### BABA / RUM BABA

This typically Neapolitan sweet is said to have been introduced to the area by the French during their invasion, although the exact origin is not known. What is certain, though, is that Neapolitans are very fond of it, especially when it is drenched in rum. The round cake sponges can also be served with cream and fruit, but the original recipe is the best (see page 309).

### BACO DI DAMA / LADY'S KISSES

This Piedmontese cookie gets its name from the fact that the two circles of shortcrust cookie, sandwiched together with plain chocolate, look like a pair of lips. To make them: mix together $1^1/_4$ cups finely ground almonds with $1^1/_4$ cups 00 (*doppio zero*) flour, a heaping $^1/_2$ cup superfine sugar, 10 tablespoons soft butter, a little grated lemon, orange, or lime zest, and 3 egg yolks. Work the mixture until well combined, then form it into little balls, then place them on a buttered baking tray and bake in an oven preheated to 375° F until golden brown. Allow the cookies to cool, then sandwich them together with a little melted chocolate.

## MAKING BIGNOLE

To make *bignole*: combine $2^1/_4$ cups water, a pinch salt, and 14 tablespoons butter in a pan and place over high heat. As soon as it comes to a boil, take the pan off the heat and add a heaping $2^1/_2$ cups all-purpose flour. Mix well, then allow to cool before adding 6 whole eggs and 4 egg yolks, and 3 tablespoons sugar. Mix thoroughly, then place the mixture in a piping bag fitted with a plain nozzle. Pipe cherry-sized dots of dough on a buttered baking tray, and bake for about 20 minutes

in an oven preheated to 400° F. When they are done, remove them from the oven and leave to cool. They should have puffed up to 3 or 4 times their initial size and should be hollow so they can be filled with cream or *zabaglione* (see the recipe on page 65). Dip part of each *bignole* in a lemon-flavored glacé icing, allow to set, then serve.

### BARCHETTA / LITTLE BOAT, BARQUETTE

Little boat-shaped cookies, made from shortcrust pastry, *barchetta* may be filled with fruit, jam, or *crema pasticcera*, and eaten as a dessert. They can also be filled with shrimp, scrambled egg, and caviar, and served as canapés.

### BASTONE / STICK, BAGUETTE

This long stick of white bread is similar to the French *baguette* (see *pane*).

### BIGNÈ, BIGNOLE / PROFITEROLE

*Bignè* refers to any cake made with choux pastry, including profiteroles and eclairs, among others. Piedmont has moved even closer to France, with the creation of *bignole*, little balls of choux pastry filled with

**ABOVE:** *BIGNOLE*

**LEFT:** *AMARETTI*

cream or *zabaglione*, then partially dipped in glacé icing.

### BIOVA, BIOVETTA / PIEDMONTESE BREAD

This Piedmontese bread is now eaten in most of the northern regions of Italy. It is made with *pasta dura*, a hard dough that is worked well to get rid of air bubbles and to make it softer. The crust of the cooked bread is quite crispy, while the center is very dense and white. It is often formed and cut in the most incredible shapes, or it can be bought in loaves, small ones called *biovetta*, and the large called *biova*.

**RIGHT: BRUSCHETTA**

### BISCOTTO / COOKIE

This was originally a slice of bread, twice baked as the name suggests, to achieve dryness. This was a means of conserving bread by drying it, for later reuse by adding moisture again in the form of water or milk (see *frisella*). Today the *biscotto* is more a kind of cookie, which can be made of eggs and flour with the addition of sugar, honey, and yeast, and other ingredients like almonds, chocolate, or a combination of these. *Biscotti* can also be savory, like *taralli* or crackers to take the place of bread. *Biscotti* are made both for immediate use or for long keeping, the best examples of each being fresh and dry *amaretti*. Italians use a great deal of *biscotti* of every kind, but mostly sweet, and mainly to dip into *caffè latte*, the morning breakfast drink.

**BELOW: A RANGE OF COOKIES FROM PFATISH IN TURIN: ALUMETTI, CANNONCINI ALLA CREMA, BACI DI DAMA, BISCOTTINI DA GELATO, BISCOTTINI FROLLINO OVALE, LINGUE DI GATTO AL CIOCOLATTO, BISCOTTO NOVARA**

**BOMBOLONI, SEE KRAPFEN**

### BRUSCHETTA

*Bruschetta* are slices of toasted bread flavored with oil, fats, or garlic, to be eaten on their own as a snack or served with *antipasto*. The most common way of serving *bruschetta* is brushed with a clove of garlic and drizzled with a little extra-virgin olive oil. Another method is to spread the toast with good-quality pork lard or goose fat. In Lazio and

Abruzzi, olive oil is drizzled over and a little chopped tomato and basil is added. In Tuscany, *bruschetta* is called *fettunta* or *panunto*, meaning "greased slice of bread" and it is usually made with an unsalted bread called *pane sciocco* (see *pane*).

### BUCCELLATO LUCCHESE / LUCCHESE CAKE

This simple cake, looking more like a bread than a cake, is a specialty of Lucca in Tuscany; however, a much more complicated version is made in Sicily, based on eggs and including candied peel. Both cakes are eaten in the same way, though, as dessert or for breakfast, dipped in milk. They keep very well if stored in an airtight box.

**BUGIE, SEE CENCI**

### CALZONE / FOLDED PIZZAS

*Calzone*, from the word for "trousers," are made with the same dough as pizza crust, and are folded into pockets around stuffings. The Neapolitans fill theirs with *provolone* cheese, *mozzarella*, hot Neapolitan sausage, or salami, all cut in cubes and mixed with beaten eggs. Other recipes include one from Puglia calling for braised sliced onions, *ricotta forte*, eggs, and Parmesan cheese; or cooked Swiss chard or spinach with eggs, Parmesan, and *pecorino* cheese.

Whatever combination of ingredients is chosen, to make the pocket of dough, roll out the dough, to fit in a 12-inch pizza dish, then sprinkle your mixture of ingredients on top. Fold over one half, seal the edges, and bake for 40 minutes in an oven preheated to 425° F. Smaller envelopes of filled dough can be fried in olive oil and are good eaten either hot or cold.

### CANAPE

Canapés are slices of bread that have been cut in small squares, triangles, or rectangles, then spread with butter or mayonnaise and topped with a range of meat, fish, or

## MAKING BUCCELLATO LUCCHESE

To make *buccellato lucchese*: combine 4 cups all-purpose flour with ¾ cup superfine sugar, 4 tablespoons soft butter, 2 beaten eggs, and 1 cup milk with ¾ ounce fresh brewer's yeast, or the equivalent of dry yeast. Combine all the ingredients until you have a fairly soft dough, then add ¼ cup raisins, 2 teaspoons aniseed, and a pinch of salt. Mix well and leave the dough to rise for about 2 hours. Cut off chunks of dough and form them into log shapes with your hands. Using a knife, cut a few diagonal slashes in the top of each log, then brush with a little beaten egg and leave to rest for an hour. Bake for about 1 hour in an oven preheated to 375° F.

salad combinations. They are usually served as an appetizer with drinks. If warm, they are known as *crostini*, and are particularly popular in Tuscany.

Canapés are served all over Italy at receptions and private parties, but they are never too substantial, as they are usually followed by a full meal. The toppings can be made from a whole range of ingredients, but the most popular are anchovies, smoked salmon, salami, and tomato and *mozzarella*. The bread used is *pane in cassetta*, a square slice of special white bread with a very thin crust.

## CANNOLO / FILLED SWEET PASTRY TUBE

*Cannoli* are probably the best-known Sicilian dessert and get their name from the fact that they are deep-fried around a piece of cane (*canna*). They used only to be made for *carnevale* (carnival) and for the feast day of San Carlo. Now they are eaten all year round, not only after meals, but also as a snack. The special pastry is filled with a mixture of *ricotta*, sugar, candied fruits, and chocolate. See recipe, page 256.

## CANNONCINO / LITTLE CANNON, PUFF PASTRY HORN

A popular pastry in Italy, the pastry horn is made from a rectangular piece of puff pastry about 12 inches in length and $1^1/4$ to $1^1/2$ inches wide. It is rolled very thin, then wound tightly around a metal cone to make the horn shape. The pastry is then brushed with beaten egg and baked. When the horns are cool the metal cone is removed and the pastry is filled with

flavored cream or *zabaglione*.

## CANTUCCI, CANTUCCINI / TUSCAN ALMOND COOKIES

In Tuscany, it is common to finish a meal with these cookies, dipped in a glass of the strong wine, *vin santo*. It is such a pleasurable way of finishing a meal that the custom has spread all over Italy, as well as to other countries. The cookies come from Prato in Tuscany and so they are also known as *cantucci di Prato*.

To make them: beat heaping $1^1/4$ cups superfine sugar with 3 eggs and 3 egg yolks until you have a well-amalgamated foam. Add heaping 4 cups 00 (*doppio zero*) flour, $1^1/4$ cups lightly toasted unpeeled almonds, a pinch of salt, 1 teaspoon orange extract, and 1 teaspoon baking soda or baking powder. Mix gently until you have a soft dough. Divide into 8-inch logs and place on a buttered baking tray, pressing each log until it is flattened to about $3/4$ inch high and $1^1/2$ inches wide. Make sure the dough logs are far enough apart to give them room to expand as they bake. Brush each one with a little beaten egg and bake in an oven preheated to 375° F for 15 minutes. Remove from the oven and cut each piece diagonally into $3/4$-inch-wide strips, separate the pieces, and return to the oven until completely cooked

and dry, about 10 minutes. Remove from the oven and allow to cool before storing in an airtight container until needed.

## CARTA DA MUSICA, PANE CARASAU / FLAT SARDINIAN BREAD

This very thin, flat, crispy bread, which resembles old parchment or music manuscript paper (hence its name), is difficult to make and is usually bought now rather than made at home. It is sold in piles of 10 or 20 slices, which are carefully packaged because of their fragility.

The dough is made with two-thirds durum wheat fine semolina and one-third all-purpose flour, mixed with yeast, water, and a little salt. All the ingredients are mixed together very thoroughly and worked until smooth, the dough is then left to rise for 6 hours, after which time it is knocked back, kneaded, and left to rise for a second time. The dough is then formed into balls and rolled thin to fit a dish that is just $1/12$ inch deep. All the filled dishes are piled up on top of each other, with linen cloth separating them. A weight is placed on top of the pile and the dough is then left to rest for 2 or 3 hours. The dishes are then placed in an oven (traditionally wood-fired), and baked briefly until the dough puffs up.

While it is still warm, each disc of dough is cut into two even thinner discs, placed into even shallower dishes, and piled up as before to keep them flat until completely cool. They are then baked again, one by one, in a hot oven until they are slightly colored and crispy. They keep for about a month, which is why farmers used to go to such lengths to make this bread.

Sardinians eat this bread either

*LEFT: CARTA DA MUSICA*

*LEFT: CANTUCCI AL MIELE*

soaked in water and served with ripe tomatoes and grated *pecorino* cheese or brushed with oil and briefly heated in a hot oven until very crisp. After being softened in water, it can also be layered, like *lasagne*, with a tomato sauce, cheese, and meat *ragù*, sprinkled with Parmesan cheese, and baked.

## CASATIELLO, CASATELLO /
NEAPOLITAN EASTER BREAD
This special savory bread is made in Naples for Easter, usually in batches of two or three, so there are always spare loaves to give as presents to friends.

## CASSATA
*Cassata* gets its name from *qus'at*, the Arab word for the small conical container in which the dessert is traditionally made. It used to be made only by nuns during Holy Week, but is now available all year round. There are two versions of the dish, both of which come from Sicily, where it was created. The first is a cake made with marzipan, *ricotta*, and candied fruit; and the second, a later development, made with ice cream. A smaller version of *cassata*, called *cassatina*, is often sold in Sicilian bars, cafés, and pastry shops.

RIGHT: *CIABATTA*

CASTAGNACCIO, SEE PAGE 282

## CENCI, CHIACCHERE, BUGIE /
PASTRIES
*Cenci*, meaning "rags," are usually made for *carnevale*, but are now available all year round. They are made from a dough of 00 (*doppio zero*) wheat flour with the addition of butter, sugar, eggs, and a little *vin santo*. The pastry is rolled out, then cut in ribbons and deep fried, usually in lard but also sometimes in olive oil. They are dusted with confectioners' sugar when cool.

CHIFEL, SEE CORNETTO

## CIABATTA / BREAD
One of the most popular breads in Italy and around the world, *ciabatta* is made with type 0 wheat flour and is characterized by its softness and moisture, both of which are due to the long rising time of 6 hours, when large air holes are formed. Its soft crust is the result of cooking the bread in ovens where water is allowed to evaporate as the bread cooks (see *pane*).

## CIALDA / WAFER
To make wafers one needs a wafer iron. Wafers are made from a smooth dough called *cialda* or *cialdone*, made with 3 cups all-purpose flour, 1 egg and 2 egg yolks, a scant $^1/_2$ cup sugar, 4 tablespoons butter, and a pinch of salt. Mix all the ingredients together until you have a fairly soft dough, adding a little water if the consistency is not loose enough. Heat the wafer irons until they are very hot, brush with a little oil or fat, and put a tablespoon of the dough on one side of the iron,

press the other side of the iron on top and bake on both sides for a few minutes. Open the iron and peel off the hot wafer. While it is still warm, shape it into a cone or leave it to cool flat, depending on how you want to use it. Fill with cream or ice cream and anything else you like, or eat it plain.

## CIAMBELLA, CIAMBELLONE, CIAMBELLINA / RING-SHAPED CAKE
There is a proverb in Italy, "*Non tutte le ciambelle riescono con il buco*," which translates as "not

every *ciambella* comes with a hole," meaning not everything can be perfect. The *ciambella* is made from a dough that is baked in a ring mold or simply shaped into a ring. It can be either savory or sweet, depending on the ingredients added to the basic dough mixture. *Ciambellone* are the larger cakes and *ciambellina* the smaller.

One of the most the most popular recipes consists of 3 cups 00 (*doppio zero*) flour, a scant 1 cup superfine sugar, 3 eggs, $5^1/_2$ tablespoons soft butter, 3 tablespoons dark rum, the grated zest of a lemon, a pinch salt, 1 sachet yeast, and enough milk to make a soft dough. Mix all the ingredients together thoroughly, then place in a buttered ring mold and bake in an oven preheated to 375° F for 40 to 50 minutes.

## COLOMBA / EASTER DOVE
This cake, made in the shape of a dove, is an Easter offering representing peace. Like *panettone*, it is now eaten all over Italy and sold abroad in specialist shops. It is quite different to *panettone* in that it does not include raisins, has a higher proportion of eggs and butter, and includes candied orange peel. It is covered in a sugar-and-almond icing and is eaten as a dessert, ideally with a glass of *moscato* or any other sparkling dessert wine.

## CORNETTO, CHIFEL / HORN BREAD
*Cornetto* is a bread shaped like the French croissant, made with a 00 (*doppio zero*) flour dough folded to create layers of pastry, much like puff pastry. It is sometimes made with *pane all'olio*, a dough made with oil or butter to make it more crumbly. A similar bread, called *chifel*, is made in Trentino-Alto Adige.

CROSTATA, SEE RECIPE, PAGE 277

## CROSTINI DI PANE / TUSCAN TOASTED BREAD

*Crostini* have recently become very fashionable all over the world. Originally from Tuscany, they are made with slices of unsalted Tuscan bread that is toasted and spread with a pâté of chicken livers, a wild boar *ragù*, or vegetables. Tuscans eat this canapé with aperitifs, but selections with various toppings are now also served as a first course. The finest *crostini* are spread with a pâté and topped with a slice of truffle.

## FARINATA / UNLEAVENED BREAD

The most ancient methods of making bread used just flour and water, with no raising agent. A wide range of flours, including those of wheat, rye, and barley, can be used, but an old and unusual bread, which is still made today in Piedmont and more particularly in Liguria, is based on chickpea flour.

The bread is made as follows: mix 1 part fine chickpea flour with 4 parts lukewarm water and a pinch of salt to make a very thin batter, and leave it to rest for about an hour. Sprinkle a baking tray with some very good extra-virgin olive oil, then pour in the mixture until it is about $^3/_4$ inch deep. Stir the mixture in the tray to distribute the oil evenly and bake in an oven preheated to 450° F until golden brown. *Farinata* has to be eaten hot, cut in small squares and dusted with freshly ground black pepper.

A delicious variation used in Palermo is *panella*, in which fennel seeds and freshly chopped parsley are added to the flour-and-water mixture. When cooked, the soft bread is laid on an oiled surface to cool, then cut in sticks or squares and fried in oil. A similar, but much more complicated method, is used in making *castagnaccio*, a bread made with chestnut flour (see page 282).

## FAVE DEI MORTI / ALMOND COOKIES

On 2 November, Italians celebrate the Day of the Dead. *Fave dei morti*, which literally translates as "fava beans of the dead," is the name given to the cookies eaten during the festival in Piedmont, Lombardy, and many other regions.

They are based on a mixture of $1^3/_4$ cups finely ground almonds, 2 eggs, a heaping 1 cup all-purpose flour, $3^1/_2$ tablespoons softened butter, a scant $^1/_2$ cup sugar and 2 tablespoons good honey, a pinch of salt, $^1/_3$ cup coarsely chopped pine nuts, toasted hazelnuts, or toasted almonds, a pinch of cinnamon powder, and 2 tablespoons grappa. Combine the ingredients thoroughly and make a paste that can be cut in small pieces,

each of which should be shaped like a fava bean. Place each "bean" on a buttered baking tray and bake in an oven preheated to 400° F for 20 minutes. They keep for some time in an airtight jar.

## FOCACCIA / FLAT BREAD

*Focaccia* is also known as *pinza* in Veneto, *pitta* in Calabria, *pizza* in Naples, *pissalandrea* in Genoa, *schiacciata* in Emilia-Romagna, *fitascetta* in Lombardy, *sardenaria* in Liguria, and *stiacciata* in Tuscany. Whatever it is called, however, this bread has the same basic characteristics: it is a flat bread made with a bread dough (see the basic recipe, page 301) mixed with olive oil and salt. A simple version of *focaccia* was eaten by the ancient Romans, and over the centuries has developed until now there is a multitude of varieties, both salted and sweet, depending on taste and the availability of local ingredients.

Before it is cooked, the dough is pressed flat in the pan and little indentations are made with the fingertips so that the olive oil that is drizzled abundantly over the dough collects in the hollows to give the dough a wonderful flavor. Coarse salt is then sprinkled sparingly on top and the dough is baked until golden brown.

*Focaccia* is eaten on its own as a snack and is used to make sandwiches, when it is particularly good filled with *mortadella*. *Focaccia* has given rise to the pizza in Naples (see pages 298 and 303) and the savory and sweet version of pizza, *pinza*, in Veneto and Emilia-Romagna, using cornmeal to make the dough.

There is a huge number of different varieties of *focaccia*, including the *smacafam* from Trentino, a type of *focaccia* made with buckwheat flour. The dough has onions in it and is topped with sausage meat and baked in a larded baking tray. The Calabrian *pitta* is similar to the Middle Eastern bread, except that it is formed into a ring, cut open, and filled, while still hot, with *ciccioli* (pork fat, page 73), oil, and chili or grated *pecorino* cheese. In Lombardy, especially around Como, they make *fitascetta*, a *focaccia* bread topped with a jam of red onions and salt or sugar, while the Tuscans make *stiacciata*, a proved dough that is mixed with sugar, eggs, and spices before being

LEFT: A VARIETY OF *FOCACCIA* FROM CAMOGLI, INCLUDING *FOCACCIA AL FORMAGGIO* AND *FOCACCIA* STUDDED WITH OLIVES

RIGHT; *GRISSINI*

baked in a hot oven. Finally, the Ligurian specialty, known variously as *pizzalandrea* or *pissadella*, and *sardenaria* in Genovese, is related to the French onion tart, *pissaladière*.

Perhaps the tastiest version of them all is the *focaccia al formaggio*, a specialty of Camogli, an enchanting fishing town near Genoa. Two very thin layers of dough made of plain flour, water, oil, and yeast, are worked in a similar way to strudel dough. The layers are filled with plenty of *stracchino* cheese, drizzled with olive oil and baked until the cheese has melted (see the photograph opposite).

### FRISELLA, FRESELLA, FRISEDDA, PAN BISCOTTO / TWICE-BAKED BREAD

*Frisella* was born of the necessity to create a completely dry bread that would not be susceptible to mold. It was widely used by the army and navy because of its keeping qualities. The bread, made mostly with durum wheat flour, is partially baked, then removed from the oven and, while still warm, cut into thick slices or, as with the Campanian and Pugliese *frisella*, which are shaped like a small *ciambella*, cut in two. The sliced bread is then put back in the oven until all its moisture has evaporated and it has become crisp like a cookie. Before it is used, it is held under running water for a few seconds so that it is not too hard to eat. It has its own special flavor and is often served with ripe tomatoes, olive oil, salt, and basil. It was once a favorite snack of farmers but is now enjoyed by everyone.

### FROLLINO / SHORTCRUST COOKIE

Made with shortcrust pastry (see *pasta frolla*), these cookies come in various shapes and sizes and are produced and sold all over Italy. They are often eaten dipped into milk and coffee for breakfast.

### GALLETTE / DRY BISCUIT

This biscuited hard bread is specifically baked for long conservation. It used to be produced for the army and navy, and the only way to eat it was to dip it in water to make it edible.

### GRISSINO / BREADSTICK

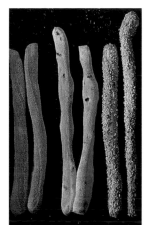

*Grissini*, crisp thin breadsticks made using type 0 flour, water, yeast, and sometimes a little olive oil, originally came from Turin but are now eaten all over the world. The long sticks of bread can be up to 28 inches in length, and are still handmade by stretching a piece of dough until it is round and thin before baking it until crispy and dry.

To achieve an even more crumbly texture, oil or butter is added to the dough. *Grissini* are also commercially made, and those wrapped in plastic wrap can keep for many months. *Grissini* can be eaten with any food, but are mostly served with *antipasti*, or as a substitute for normal bread during a meal. They can also be wrapped in a thin slice of Parma ham to make a delicious snack.

### GUASTEDDE / SICILIAN BREAD

This special bread roll is sold filled with a variety of ingredients, but most famously the local delicacy of fried spleen sold at Vucceria market in Palermo. The bread roll is made with a leavened dough of plain and semolina flour, yeast, and water, and sprinkled with sesame seeds. The roll is cut in half and filled with the spleen, which has been boiled, then thinly cut and fried, along with *ciccioli* (pork fat, page 73), in lard and spices. The whole thing is sprinkled with *pecorino* cheese to make a wonderful and unusual snack.

### KRAPFEN / DOUGHNUT

As the name suggests, this deep-fried sweet is German in origin. An Italian version, called *bomboloni*, is very popular in Emilia-Romagna. It is made of a leavened dough formed into balls, which are deep-fried until brown. *Bomboloni* are usually dusted with sugar, but may also be filled with jam, like apricot or cherry, or with custard.

### LIEVITO / RISING AGENT

There are two types of yeast, one natural and one synthetic. They both have the task, through fermentation, of producing bubbles in the mixture of flour and water, and other ingredients, in order to raise and aerate the mixture and thus create a softness in the baked good. Bread without yeast would be flat, hard, and inedible. The best yeast is a by-product of making beer. The pinky-brown substance is diluted with water and mixed with whatever is to be baked. It is important to allow the fermentation to occur in a warm place, before putting the dough in a hot oven. Synthetic yeast does not need such pre-fermentation.

### MARITOZZO / SWEET ROMAN BREAD

This sweet brioche-type bread is traditionally eaten during Lent in Lazio and Umbria, although today it is available all year round. It is made with a sour dough that requires a long process of rising before ingredients such as eggs, sugar, olive oil, and salt are added. The dough is then left to rise again for about 4 hours, before further kneading and the addition of more ingredients such as flour, raisins, orange peel, more eggs, and a little milk. It can then be divided into small pieces and baked.

### MARTURANA, MARZAPANE, SEE PASTA DI MANDORLE

### MOLLICA DI PANE / BREAD DOUGH, FRESH BREAD CRUMBS

The internal, soft part of the bread, called *mollica*, is used in Italy as an ingredient for stuffing vegetables (see *pepperoni ripieni*, page 126) or meat. See also *pane grattugiato.*

## MOSTACCIOLO, MUSTAZZOLI /
### MUST COOKIES
One of the most common of the Italian cookies, *mostacciolo* (or *mustazzoli* in Sicilian) are made and eaten in many regions, although there are usually slight variations on the basic recipe.

The hard, dry cookies, which were made by the ancient Romans, consist of a mixture of plain flour, cooked grape juices (the product of wine-making called must) or honey, and spices like cinnamon, clove, and nutmeg; but they do not contain yeast or eggs. When the mixture has been worked into a firm dough, it is rolled out to a thickness of $1/2$ inch, cut into lozenge shapes, and baked in a moderate oven for about 25 minutes. When they are removed from the oven they are brushed with a glaze made of 2 parts sugar to 1 part water and left to dry and cool.

They are a specialty of Erice in Sicily, and are eaten after meals, dipped in sweet dessert wines such as Moscato, Passito di Pantelleria, and Marsala. They were probably brought to Italy by the Arabs, and spread through Italy via Sicily and the southern regions.

**PAN BISCOTTO, SEE FRISELLA**

## PAN DE MEI, PAN MEINO /
### SWEET LOMBARDIAN BREAD
A small, sweet bread made with a combination of corn and wheat flour, *pan de mei* is typical of Lombardian cuisine. The simple recipe consists of a scant 1 cup sugar, 14 tablespoons soft butter, a scant $1^1/4$ cups cornmeal, and $1^3/4$ cups wheat flour, all of which is mixed together with 3 eggs and $1^1/4$ ounces brewer's yeast dissolved in a little milk. Once all the ingredients are well combined, allow the dough to rise until about doubled in volume. Then divide it into small chunks and shape these into rounds. Place each roll on a buttered baking tray, brush with beaten egg, bake put in an oven preheated to 400° F for 20 to 25 minutes.

## PAN DI RAMERINO /
### ROSEMARY BREAD
*Pan di ramerino* is a sweet bread made and eaten at Easter in Tuscany. As the name suggests, the dough includes rosemary oil, together with the more usual sweet ingredients of sugar, raisins, and butter. It is shaped into small loaves or rolls.

## PAN DI SAN GIUSEPPE /
### DECORATIVE BREAD
This bread, skilfully modeled into a variety of shapes and symbols, is used to decorate altars before being offered to the Holy Family and given to friends as a good omen on San Giuseppe's day. The bread is a reminder of the legend of the saint, who is celebrated annually with a special meal, *la cena di San Giuseppe* (the supper of St. Joseph) in Salemi, a small village built on top of a high hill near Trapani in Sicily.

The story that inspires this celebration is about a fisherman and his wife who lived in the village. One day, as the fisherman went off on a fishing trip, his wife promised that, should he survive his next fishing trip, she would invite the entire village to dinner. However, the fisherman and his wife were so poor that when he suddenly returned all she had to feed to her guests was flour and water, which she made into bread in the shapes of Christian symbols and the food she dearly would have loved to have served.

## PAN DI SPAGNA, PASTA MARGHERITA, PASTA MADDALENA, PASTA VIENNESE /
### SPONGE CAKE
*Pan di Spagna* is a basic soft, sweet sponge cake, made by beating 6 egg yolks with a heaping 1 cup superfine sugar until you have a foamy mixture. Add to this the beaten whites of the six eggs and a pinch of salt. Slowly add $1^1/4$ cups fine 00 (*doppio zero*) flour and $1^1/4$ cups potato flour, stirring carefully with a wooden spoon. Add a few drops of vanilla extract or the seeds of one vanilla bean, and the finely grated zest of $1/2$ lemon. Pour the mixture into a high-sided baking tray that has been buttered and dusted with flour. Bake for 30 minutes at 350° F, then remove and allow to cool. Cut in half and fill with cream, preserves, custard, or chocolate.

## PANDOLCE / SWEET BREAD
Like *panettone* for the Milanese, *pandolce* is the centerpiece of the Christmas feast for the Genovese. It is a much smaller and heavier cake than

*panettone,* as it contains so much candied fruit, raisins, and nuts, as well as special flavorings like orange water or aniseed. It takes quite a long time to bake because of the amount of time it takes for the dough to rise.

LEFT: *MOSTACCIOLI WITH MARSALA WINE IN ERICE, SICILY*

LEFT: *PAN DI SAN GIUSEPPE*

## MAKING *PANDOLCE*

To make *pandolce*: mix together 1¾ ounces sour-dough (fermented bread dough) with 2¼ cups oo (*doppio zero*) flour and a little warm water, until you have a soft, silky dough. Cover and leave to rise in a warm place for 12 hours. Then mix together a separate dough of 5¾ cups oo flour, scant 1 cup superfine sugar, 10 tablespoons soft butter, 1 small glass of *Moscato* or *vin santo* and 2 tablespoons of orange flower water, until well combined and soft. Mix the two doughs together and knead well, before adding 3 tablespoons finely diced candied citron peel, 3 tablespoons golden raisins, and 1 teaspoon aniseed or fennel seeds. Knead again until all the ingredients are perfectly combined and the dough has a soft and elastic texture. Put the dough in a well-greased and floured high-sided cake pan, making sure that the dough does not come more than one-third of the way up the sides of the pan. Leave to rise again for a further 12 hours, or until the dough has doubled in volume. Bake for 50 to 55 minutes in an oven preheated to 400° F. Allow to cool before removing from the pan.

## PANDORO / VERONESE CHRISTMAS CAKE

RIGHT: *TRAMEZZINI* (SANDWICHES) IN THE CAFFÈ MALISSANO, TURIN

Literally translated, *pandoro* means "golden bread," because of its deep yellow center, due at least in part to the number of free-range eggs included in the cake along with 00 (*doppio zero*) flour, sugar, butter, and yeast. It is an extremely light, moist, and spongy cake, made by the Veronese and Venetians at Christmas. Due to the lengthy method, taking several days and requiring three rising stages, the Veronese no longer make it at home, preferring to buy commercially made versions. This tall cake is traditionally made in an eight-pointed star-shaped mold. It is usually eaten on its own, although I like it buttered and then toasted, so the sugar in it caramelizes slightly.

## PANE / BREAD

Breads is one of the basic elements of the Italian diet. Italians eat a great deal of bread, of all types and shapes, according to the regional resources of grain and the type of food with which it is to be eaten.

The most common flour used for breadmaking in Italy is wheat, which is milled to make a very fine white flour. The flour is graded as 00 (*doppio zero*) and is also used to make, among other things, fresh egg pasta. Slightly less-refined flour is graded 0, and so on down to whole-wheat flour, called *integrale*, which contains the husk of the grain. It is, of course, well known that whole-wheat flour is more nutritious and is a better source of roughage than white flour, but white flour and white bread are still more popular than the brown in Italy. In southern Italy, 00 (*doppio zero*) flour is mixed with durum wheat semolina to give the bread a much more solid consistency than the more delicate bread made in other parts of Italy. There are many other flours used to make bread, each of which gives a special quality to the finished product. Other flours used to make bread in Italy include rye, corn, and cornstarch, which is mixed with white flour for a more develop-ed taste and more digestible bread.

The North prefers very white bread, and mostly in small shapes, Liguria prefers *focaccia*, Emilia-Romagna *pane a pasta dura*, a type of white bread with a hard consistency, and a flat bread called *piadina*. Tuscany has a saltless bread called *pane sciocco*, to accompany its various savory dishes, *salami*, and spicy preserves. Rome loves the *sfilatino*, a short baguette also called *bastone*, or "stick." The entire South is definitely much happier with more substantial bread, like the *pugliese*, which is made of hard durum wheat and keeps fresh for a longer period of time. The round loaves can be gargantuan in size, to satisfy large families.

Special breads are also made using a wide variety of flavoring ingredients, including lard, butter, olive oil, sun-dried tomatoes, herbs, olives, nuts, and a whole range of seeds.

Because it has to be fresh, bread is mostly bought on a daily basis. This is true especially in the North, because white bread rolls do not keep for more than a day. There are, however, various recipes calling for stale bread, which is turned into soups, salads, and other specialties.

## PANE A CASSETTA, PAN CARRÉ / SANDWICH BREAD

This white bread, made from type 0 flour, water, and yeast, is baked in a special mold called a *cassetta*, which keeps the bread compact and dense, limiting the amount it can rise when baked and giving it an even square shape and thin crust. This means that, after the crust has been removed, it can be cut in smaller squares and stamped into circles to make *tartines*, canapés, and

sandwiches, or cut into small cubes and fried to make croutons for salads and soups.

## PANE CARASAU, SEE CARTA DA MUSICA

## PANE CON L'UVA / FRUIT LOAF

The Milanese make this bread with a sweet dough, including butter, sugar, and lots of raisins or currants. It is shaped into small loaves or rolls, which are left to rise for half an hour before being baked. It is usually made as an Easter treat.

## PANE GRATTUGIATO / DRIED BREAD CRUMBS

Leftovers of good-quality bread (never artificially colored or spiced) are further baked in the oven at a low temperature to drive off all the moisture but not long enough to color. The bread crumbs produced from this are called *grattugiato* (meaning "grated") because, before the existence of food processors, the pieces of bread were grated to obtain the crumbs.

Bread crumbs are widely used in Italian cooking; for example *sardine ripiene* (page 31), *arancini* (page 179), *fritto misto alla piemontese* (page 89) are all specialties coated in bread crumbs before being deep-fried. Bread crumbs are also used to thicken stuffings and sauces.

## PANETTERIA, PANETTIERE / BAKER'S SHOP, BAKER

Traditionally the term *panetteria* was used to indicate a bread shop where the bread was baked on the premises. You could discover the location following the irresistible smell of freshly made bread inviting you to buy. Unfortunately many of these shops keep the name, but are only outlets for selling all sorts of baked goods like bread, cakes, etc., made elsewhere.

I have a very fond memory of going to the baker to buy fresh bread in the morning. The bread was sold by the kilo and the hand-made loaves didn't always reach that weight. To make it up, the baker would just cut a piece of bread from another loaf, called *l'aggiunta*, which regularly ended up in my watery mouth before arriving home.

To be a *panettiere* one has to have considerable experience; in fact it is truly a vocation, because in order to have the freshly made bread available to the public in the morning, the baker has to get up at about 2 a.m. and work through the night. It is a highly appreciated artisanal craft, which is unfortunately sadly disappearing with the advent of huge commercial bakeries.

## PANETTONE / MILANESE CHRISTMAS CAKE

The most widely made and eaten of the regional Christmas cakes in Italy, *panettone* or "the big bread" is the tallest and largest cake of all; a result of the lengthy procedure required to make it, including many rising periods. It is a difficult cake to make at home because it involves the mixing of two sets of dough—one made with flour, yeast, butter, and sugar that needs to rise for about 10 hours, and the other a mixture of flour, butter, eggs, sugar, salt, cubes of candied citron and orange peel, and raisins, which has to be mixed with the first dough and the whole thing left to rise for another 4 or 5 hours. It is then baked in precise, temperature-controlled ovens, which allow the cakes to mushroom up and gently cook until they are dark brown but not burned, leaving the insides wonderfully fluffy and moist. Like the other traditional Christmas cakes, *panettoni* are only baked from October to November.

The most important thing to look for when buying your *panettone* is the quality of the fats used in making it, as this will determine the flavor of the cake. It is also worth checking the date, as the freshest are the best. In response to consumer demands, many cakes are now covered or filled with chocolate or sabayon sauce. However, the simple classic cake is still the best.

## PANFORTE / FRUIT AND SPICE CAKE

This typical Tuscan specialty dates from the Middle Ages, when the first spices were imported from the Mediterranean. Siena is the city that assumed paternity of this "strong bread," now famous all over the world. (See recipe, page 281).

PANPEPATO, SEE PAGES 218 AND 230

## PANZANELLA, PAN BAGNATO / SOAKED BREAD

Similar to the specially dried bread, *frisella* (see page 293), *pan bagnato* is simply stale or dry bread that is soaked and eaten in soups, dipped in milk, or softened with the juice of freshly cut tomatoes. In Tuscany, salted bread is used, the custom being to top the water-softened bread with chopped tomatoes, sweet onions, celery leaves, basil, and a little trickle of olive oil.

My mother's *panzanella* was made with leftover bread, which she broke into pieces and put into a bowl with very ripe and juicy tomatoes. This was left to soak for a while, and then she would mix it with her hands until it broke into small pieces. She would then add extra-virgin olive oil, salt, finely chopped sweet onions, capers, and sometimes a little finely chopped garlic, along with a little basil or oregano, like the Neapolitans and Sicilians do. It looked like chicken feed, but it tasted delicious, and I still make it the same way today.

## PARROZZO / ALMOND CAKE

A specialty of Pescara in the Marche region, this simple cake is made with flour, eggs, sugar, and yeast, enriched with ground almonds and covered with chocolate.

ABOVE: SIGNOR GARELLO, THE BAKER IN TURIN'S VIA MADDALENA

LEFT: *PANETTONE TRADIZIONALE*

## PASSATELLI / BREAD CRUMB NOODLES

In addition to all the usual ways of using bread crumbs, Emilia-Romagnans also mix them with beaten egg, Parmesan cheese, salt, and pepper, to make a soft dough, which is then pushed through a special utensil with holes (you can use a colander) over a pot of boiling water or broth to make *pasatelli*, little noodles or dumplings. Boiled in water, they can be used in the same way as pasta, dressed with a simple sauce.

## PASTA DI MANDORLE, PASTA REALE, MARZAPANE, MARTURANA / MARZIPAN

A sweet paste based on ground almonds and sugar, marzipan is used by pastry chefs to make cakes and *petits fours*, and is especially popular in the South and Sicily, where almonds grow in abundance. Another special almond paste called *marturana* was originally made by nuns in a convent at Marturana in Palermo, Sicily. It is used to make figures and various shapes like fruit and animals, which are then colored and used to decorate cakes and other desserts.

*Pasta di mandorle* is very simple to make and tastes much better if homemade. To get the best results, grind the almonds yourself using fresh nuts, as pre-ground almonds tend to dry out quickly and lose their flavor. (See recipe, page 278.)

## PASTA FROLLA / SWEET SHORTCRUST PASTRY

The easiest pastry to make, shortcrust pastry is used in a large number of different sweet dishes. To make 2³/₄ pounds: mix together gently but quickly a heaping 2 cups 00 (*doppio zero*) flour with 5 eggs, 1 cup plus 2 tablespoons soft butter, a heaping 1 cup superfine sugar, a pinch salt, and the grated zest of 1 lemon. Let this dough rest for at least 1 hour in a cool place, before using it to make cookies and other sweets. It can be refrigerated for a few days, if necessary, but before using it make sure the pastry has

RIGHT: TYPICAL MARZIPAN COOKIES IN THE SHOP OF MARIA GRAMMATICO IN ERICE, SICILY

first come back to room temperature. Shortcrust pastry usually needs 30 minutes in a medium to hot oven, and is cooked when it is a light golden brown. *Pasta sable*, a richer sweet shortcrust pastry from the French tradition, contains more butter. It is crumblier than *pasta frolla*, but can be used in much the same way and is especially good in fruit tarts.

## PASTA MARGHERITA, PASTA MADDALENA, SEE PAN DI SPAGNA

## PASTA REALE, SEE PASTA DI MANDORLE

## PASTA SFOGLIA / PUFF PASTRY

Puff pastry is the only pastry one needs to see being made to learn the art and, if you cannot do this, then the easiest way to get puff pastry is to buy it ready-made, especially as the quality is so good nowadays. Puff pastry is made by putting butter, or other fats like lard, between sheets of pastry and rolling and folding it until the pastry is built up into many layers with fat separating each one. The difficulty lies in trying to roll out the pastry with the hard fat beneath it without allowing the fat to break through the pastry. It also takes some time to make, as the pastry has to be left to cool and rest between rollings. The end result, however, is a pastry that puffs up when baked, as each sheet is cooked and separated by the layers of fat. It is used to make both savory and sweet tarts, pies, and cookies, and can be combined with cheese to make tasty snacks.

## PASTA VIENNESE, SEE PAN DI SPAGNA

## PASTICCERIA, PASTICCINI / PASTRY SHOP, PASTRIES

Italians are very fond of *pasticcini*, small cakes like *bignole*, *bigne*, and various tarts, which are eaten with

coffee or tea, or with hot chocolate, or even with a glass of Moscato Spumante. The *pasticceria* is the place where such *pasticcini* are produced, but very often functions also as a café, where you can sit and enjoy *pasticcini* with your coffee. At lunch time, the *pasticceria* may also serve *salatini*, small savory snacks like mini pizzas, small breads filled with truffle butter, anchovy rolls, or small canapés with smoked salmon.

## PASTIERA DI GRANO / WHEAT TART

*Pastiera* is an Easter cake, made with whole-grain wheat and *ricotta* to symbolize wealth; for this reason it is often made in pairs, so there is one left to give to a loved one. The preparation starts long before Easter, as the wheat has to be soaked in water for at least a week to soften it, although it is sometimes possible to buy pre-soaked wheat. (See recipe, page 177.)

## PIADINA, PIADA / ROMAGNAN BREAD

This unleavened bread from Emilia-Romagna is similar to the Arabic pita bread, but tastier. It is usually eaten with the local specialty of Parma ham, *stracchino* cheese, or even sautéed spinach, but may also be served as an accompaniment to other dishes. There are as many recipes as there are families who make this bread, but the basic recipe is to combine a heaping 2 cups 0 flour, 4 tablespoons lard, a pinch salt, and just enough water to produce a soft and elastic dough (some people add yeast). The dough is kneaded briefly and then allowed to rest for 1 hour, before rolling it out to a thickness of ¹/₈ to ¹/₆ inch. It is then cut into discs about 6 inches in diameter.

In Emilia-Romagna there is a special tool for baking the bread, but it can also be cooked in a heavy cast-iron pan on top of the stove. Put the bread in the pan without any fat, and dry-fry the *piadina* for 2 minutes on each side. The little burnt spots add taste to the bread, which should be eaten immediately, topped with whatever you fancy and folded in half.

## PISSALADEIRA / TYPE OF PIZZA

This *focaccia* covered with anchovies and onions is said by the Genovese to come from *pizza alla Andrea*, after Andrea Doria, the famous Ligurian sailor. It is, however, very similar to *pissaladière*, the savory tart of neighboring Provence. See *focaccia*, page 292.

## PIZZA

It is not difficult to prepare an original pizza provided you have the right ingredients, the know-how, and a good oven. This type of *focaccia* has been developed by the Neapolitans, thanks to their imaginative way of using the best local ingredients—the good flour, water, tomatoes, basil, good *mozzarella* cheese, and good olive oil.

There are two periods in the history of pizza: the AP (Ante Pizza) period in which the pizza was considered just a bread to accompany other foods, like the Indian naan); and the PP (Post Pizza) period, when toppings were added, leading to the current idea of the pizza being a bread base for any combination of ingredients.

The optimum way of obtaining a good Neapolitan pizza dough is to produce your own sourdough starter. Mix some flour with water to a soft dough and leave this in a warm place for a day. The natural yeasts will ferment and cause it to rise, making a perfect natural starter for the pizza dough. Alternatively simply use brewer's yeast as follows.

Pizza dough, unlike its predecessor, *focaccia*, is a bread dough made of 00 (*doppio zero*) flour a pinch of salt. Mix 3 1/2 cups 00 flour, 1 1/4 ounces fresh brewer's yeast diluted in 1 cup lukewarm water, with just enough water to make a soft dough. Mix all the ingredients together thoroughly and leave to rest for a while before dividing it into four round balls, each of which will be large enough to fit an 8-inch pizza pan. Cover the balls of dough with a clean cloth and set aside in a warm place to rise for at least 1 hour. After they have doubled in volume, knock them back and knead each dough ball, then roll them out to a thickness of 1/4 inch, leaving a raised edge about 1/2 inch high all the way around the border. Place these in oiled pizza pans or dishes and set on a baking sheet. Add the topping and cook in a preheated, very hot oven, until the topping is melted and the edges are crispy. Pizza should be eaten in quarters with your hands.

*Pizza napoletana* or *Margherita* has a topping based on a pulp of sun-ripened tomatoes or canned tomato pulp, 2 large rounds of *buffalo mozzarella* cut in small chunks, salt, and a drizzle of extra-virgin olive oil sprinkled on top. Just before serving, add a few fresh basil leaves. The *Margherita*, on which the *napoletana* is based, is said to have been invented to please Queen Margherita of Italy. The *marinara* is topped with extra-virgin olive oil, garlic, tomatoes, salt, pepper, and a little oregano. The *romana* has *mozzarella*, tomatoes, anchovy fillets, salt, pepper, oregano, and extra-virgin olive oil.

*Pizza fritta* or *pizzetta*, is the same as a normal pizza, but smaller for easy consumption in bars. An even smaller pizza, called *stuzzichino*, is served at parties with drinks.

*LEFT: PIZZA MARINARA*

## PUGLIESE

This term is used to describe a wide range of items made in Puglia, but perhaps nowadays outside Italy it is mostly used to refer to bread. *Pane pugliese* is a very large round bread, about 16 inches in diameter and 5 to 6 inches high, with a thick, dark crust. It is made using plain wheat flour with the addition of hard durum wheat flour, resulting in a very dense, wholesome, and extremely flavorsome bread, able to last for several days.

## RICCIARELLO / TUSCAN ALMOND COOKIE

This specialty of Siena is a cookie made with almonds and dusted with a large amount of confectioners' sugar. They can be bought ready-made, but the homemade version is much better.

To make them: mix together a heaping 2 1/2 cups freshly ground sweet almonds and 2 1/2 cups sugar, and work thoroughly before adding the grated zest of 1 lemon, 1 teaspoon vanilla sugar or a few drops of vanilla extract, the beaten whites of 2 eggs, and 1 tablespoon honey. Mix again to incorporate all the

*ABOVE: PUGLIESE BREAD NEAR BARI*

*LEFT: NEAPOLITAN STREET CARRIER FOR PIZZA*

RIGHT:
*RICCIARELLI*

ingredients, then roll the dough on a surface dusted with confectioners' sugar to a thickness of 3/4 inch. Using an oval cutter or a knife, cut out lozenges 1 1/2 to 2 inches in length. Place these on a baking tray lined with rice paper which has, in turn, been covered with a 1/8-inch layer of confectioners' sugar. Bake in an oven preheated to 375° F for 20 minutes, but do not let the cookies brown.

## SALATINI / LITTLE SAVORIES

All small savory pastry snacks served with aperitifs are known as *salatini*. They are usually made with puff or shortcrust pastry, topped with cheese, anchovies, capers, olives, or seeds such as poppy and fennel, or simply with ground pepper or salt. You can make these nibbles with frozen puff pastry and the flavoring of your choice, but in Italy they can be bought at the *pasticceria*.

## SAVOIARDO / LADYFINGER

These sponge-cakelike cookies are one of the most important ingredients of the newly popularized Italian dessert *tiramisu*, in which the sponges are dipped in strong coffee or liqueur and layered with *mascarpone*. *Savoiardi* sponges, favored for their light and absorbent qualities, are also used to make other desserts, such as *zuppa inglese*.

RIGHT: *TARALLI* IN PUGLIA

To make the sponges: beat 5 egg yolks until they are white and creamy, then add a scant 1/2 cup superfine sugar, before carefully folding in 1 cup 00 (*doppio zero*) flour, and 1 teaspoon vanilla sugar or a few drops of vanilla extract. Mix well, then carefully fold in the stiffly beaten whites of the eggs and a scant 1/2 cup confectioners' sugar. Butter a baking tray and dust it with flour. Pipe the mixture into 4- to 5-inch-long small sausages of sponge, taking care to leave enough space between them. Sprinkle with a little

of the granulated sugar and bake in an oven preheated to 375° F for 20 to 25 minutes. When cool, store in an airtight jar.

## SFOGLIATELLA / PUFF PASTRY CAKE

In Campania and Naples, *sfogliatella* is sold in bars as a rather wonderful snack. It is usually served warm, but is also very good cold. There are two varieties, one a simple pocket of shortcrust pastry, and the other a much more elaborate affair involving a special puff pastry made with a dough of lard instead of butter. The filling usually consists of cooked semolina with *ricotta*, sugar, eggs, chopped candied peel, and a few drops of vanilla extract.

**STRUFFOLI, SEE RECIPE, PAGE 306**

## TARALLO, TARALLUCCIO, TARALLINO / ROUND SAVORY COOKIE

This round savory cookie was traditionally made in Campania, but from there it spread to Puglia, then Calabria, and finally Sicily. It is beloved for its flavor and crunchiness, as well as for the fact that it is so easy to make and keeps so well in an airtight jar. It can be eaten on its own as a snack or with *antipasto*.

To make the cookie: mix a heaping 4 cups type 0 flour with 1/2 cup lard, 2 ounces brewer's yeast, and spices like pepper, salt, fennel seeds, chili, and anything else you fancy. Add enough water to make a workable dough, then mix again until all the ingredients are well blended. Take small pieces of the dough and shape each one into a small log. Then join all

of them together to form a circle. Sprinkle with oil and place on a baking sheet to rise for an hour or so. Bake for one hour in an oven preheated to about 300° F. Allow the cookies to cool, when they become crumbly and dry.

## TARTELETTA / TARTLET

Although these pastry sheets originate from France, the Italians have adopted them into their own cuisine with enthusiasm. They are used as containers for jams, fruit, nuts, or sauces, and they are eaten for dessert, with tea in the afternoon, or in bars as snacks. Generally made with shortcrust pastry, these mini pastry cases can come in any shape.

## TARTINA / SNACK

Made with *pan carré* or *pane a cassetta* (see page 295), *tartines* are small savory snacks filled with any combination of ingredients, including butter and anchovies, capers, smoked salmon, pâtés, or cheese. They are usually eaten with drinks and are often served in bars.

## ZEPPOLA / CHOUX PASTRIES

This southern specialty, usually produced for the celebration of San Giuseppe's Day, is made with eggs, yeast, 00 (*doppio zero*) flour, and lard. The dough, deep-fried in oil, is usually extruded by a syringe, giving a round shape similar to that of *ciambella*. The cooked pastries are then dusted with confectioners' sugar or filled with cream, or even dipped in honey diluted with water to make them juicy. My mother used to bake a savory version with a piece of anchovy in the middle for an extremely tasty result.

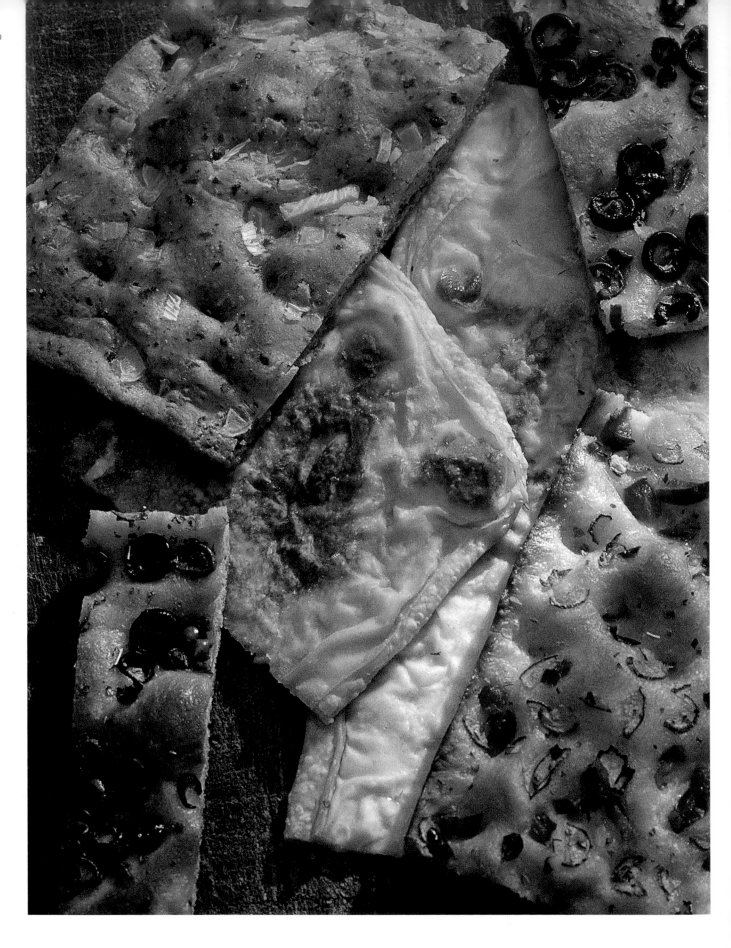

# FOCACCIA

FOR 6 TO 8

1 OUNCE FRESH YEAST
HEAPING 4 CUPS 00 (*DOPPIO ZERO*)
    FLOUR
2 TABLESPOONS OLIVE OIL, PLUS EXTRA
    FOR DRIZZLING
PINCH SALT
1¹/₂ TABLESPOONS COARSE SALT

*A classic of Italian cuisine with ancient Roman origins, this was adopted by the Ligurians first and is now popular everywhere. It is a cross between pizza and bread, with the addition of olive oil and coarse salt. You could include cheese, olives, onions, or even sweet ingredients.*

Dissolve the yeast in ³/₄ cup lukewarm water. Put the flour in a bowl, then add the oil, yeast liquid, and pinch of salt. Mix together, adding more water if necessary to obtain a very soft and smooth dough. Knead for about 10 minutes, until elastic, then place in a bowl; cover and leave to rise in a warm place for 1 hour or until doubled in size.

Preheat the oven to 400° F. Lightly oil a large baking sheet. Punch down the dough, then dip your fingertips in olive oil and gently press out the very elastic dough until it covers the whole tray. It should be about ³/₄ inch thick. Brush with olive oil and then make small indentations here and there in the dough with your fingertips. Sprinkle the coarse salt over the top and bake for 25 to 30 minutes, until a golden-brown crust has formed. As soon as the bread comes out of the oven, drizzle more olive oil on top; this will be absorbed, giving a wonderful flavor.

Allow to cool, then cut in squares and enjoy. It can be eaten plain or, as in Genoa, made into a sandwich with some *mortadella* while still warm!

# TORTA PASQUALINA
## EASTER TART

SERVES 8

4 TABLESPOONS OLIVE OIL, PLUS MORE
    FOR THE TART PAN
2 ONIONS, THINLY SLICED
HEARTS OF 8 VERY YOUNG, FRESH
    ARTICHOKES
1¹/₂ POUNDS SHORTCRUST PASTRY (SEE
    *PASTA FROLLA*, PAGE 297)
6 EGGS
3¹/₂ OUNCES PARMESAN CHEESE
1³/₄ POUNDS SPINACH, BLANCHED, AND
    COARSELY CHOPPED
SALT AND PEPPER

*There are probably as many versions of this savory Ligurian tart, traditionally made at Easter, as there are families who live in the region. It is based on pastry, vegetables, and eggs, and is eaten especially on Easter Monday,* Pasquetta, *when almost everybody goes for a picnic. My mother used to make it quite often, however, regardless of tradition.*

Heat the oil in a heavy-bottomed pan and fry the onions until soft. Add the artichoke hearts with a glass of water, cover and braise very gently until tender.

Preheat the oven to 350° F and oil a 10-inch tart pan. Roll out the pastry and use to line the pan.

In a bowl, lightly beat the eggs. Add the Parmesan cheese, with salt and pepper to taste. Add the spinach, and the artichokes and onions. Mix well. Fill the pastry shell with the artichoke mixture and bake for 40 minutes. Serve hot or cold.

OPPOSITE: A RANGE OF *FOCACCIA* WITH DIFFERENT TOPPINGS, INCLUDING OLIVES, CHEESE, AND ZUCCHINI

# CALZONE CON CICORIA E CARCIOFI
## CALZONE WITH DANDELIONS AND ARTICHOKES

**MAKES 4**

1 POUND WILD DANDELION LEAVES, ROUGHLY CHOPPED

4 TO 6 SMALL YOUNG ARTICHOKES

4 TABLESPOONS OLIVE OIL

1 ONION, FINELY CHOPPED

2 GARLIC CLOVES, FINELY CHOPPED

2 RED CHILI PEPPERS, FINELY CHOPPED

$^1/_4$ CUPS WATER

12 TO 15 PITTED GREEN OLIVES, CHOPPED

2 TEASPOONS SALTED CAPERS, SOAKED IN WATER FOR 10 MINUTES, THEN DRAINED

2 OUNCES *PECORINO* CHEESE, GRATED

FRESHLY GROUND BLACK PEPPER

2 EGGS

OLIVE OIL FOR DEEP-FRYING

**FOR THE DOUGH:**

1 TEASPOON OLIVE OIL

PINCH SEA SALT

$^1/_2$ OUNCE FRESH YEAST

HEAPING 2$^1/_2$ CUPS ALL-PURPOSE FLOUR

*These little turnovers make a delicious, filling snack. Choose young, tender dandelion leaves from plants that haven't yet flowered. If you don't like the bitter taste of dandelions, you could use nettles or spinach instead. However, I find that with the dandelion you get a full country taste.*

To make the dough, put the oil, salt, and yeast in a small bowl, add $^2/_3$ cup lukewarm water, and stir to dissolve the yeast. Mound the flour on a clean work surface and make a well in the center. Gradually pour the yeast mixture into the well, mixing with your hands until all the liquid has been absorbed by the flour. Knead the dough for 8 to 10 minutes, until smooth and elastic, then place in a large bowl and cover with a cloth. Leave in a warm place for at least an hour, until it has risen to three times its original size.

Meanwhile, make the filling. Cook the dandelion leaves in boiling water for 5 minutes (this takes away some of their bitter taste), then drain and squeeze out the excess water. Remove the stalks and outer leaves from the artichokes (see page 105) and cut them into quarters.

Heat the olive oil in a large pan, add the onion, garlic, and chilies and fry for a few minutes, stirring all the time, until the onion has softened. Add the dandelion, artichokes, and $^1/_4$ cup water and stir. Add the olives and capers, mix well, and cook for 15 minutes. By this time, most of the liquid should have evaporated, leaving the cooked vegetables just moist. Remove from the heat and leave to cool. Add the grated *Pecorino* cheese and season with pepper. Beat in 1 egg and mix well.

Punch down the risen dough and divide it into 4 balls. Roll them out into ovals about $^1/_8$ inch thick and divide the filling between them, placing it to one side of each piece of dough. Lightly beat the remaining egg and use to brush the edges of the dough, then fold in half to make turnovers, pressing the edges together with a fork to seal. Leave to rest for 5 minutes.

Heat the olive oil in a large deep pan. Add the *calzone* and deep-fry for about 3 to 4 minutes, until golden brown. Remove from the pan and drain on paper towels. Serve hot or cold.

RIGHT: *CALZONE CON CICORIA E CARCIOFI* (BELOW); *PASTA CON LE SARDE* (PASTA WITH SARDINES, TOP LEFT, SEE PAGE 166); *ASPARAGI SELVATICI* (WILD ASPARAGUS, TOP RIGHT, SEE PAGE 249)

# PIZZETTE MARGHERITA

**MAKES 12 TO 16**

2¼ CUPS TOMATO PULP (SEE PAGE 118)

1 POUND *MOZZARELLA*, THINLY SLICED

SALT AND PEPPER

½ CUP EXTRA-VIRGIN OLIVE OIL

20 BASIL LEAVES

**FOR THE DOUGH:**

¾ OUNCE FRESH YEAST

HEAPING 4 CUPS 00 (*DOPPIO ZERO*) FLOUR

3 TABLESPOONS EXTRA-VIRGIN OLIVE OIL

1 TEASPOON SALT

½ TEASPOON SUGAR

*It is said that this pizza was named after Queen Margherita of Italy in 1889 and was made for her by a Neapolitan pizzaiolo. Whatever its origins, it is the simplest of pizzas and, in my opinion, the best.*

To make the dough, dissolve the yeast in ¾ cup lukewarm water. Pile the flour up on a work surface in a volcano shape; make a well in the center and add the oil, salt, and sugar. Slowly incorporate the yeast mixture, then knead the dough with your fingers and the palm of your hand until it has a silky, soft consistency. Put it in a bowl, dust with flour, then cover and leave to rise for 1 hour or until doubled in size.

Punch down the dough, divide it into 12 to 16 pieces, then knead each piece briefly and reshape it into a ball. Cover and leave to rise for just 15 minutes. Preheat the oven to 425° F.

ABOVE (CLOCKWISE FROM THE BOTTOM LEFT): *PIZZETTE MARGHERITA, RUSTICI* (POTATO, HAM, AND CHEESE CROQUETTES), *ARANCINI DI RISO PALERMITANA* (PAGE 179)

Flatten each ball of dough a little with a rolling pin, then stretch it out with your fingertips until it is about 4 to 5 inches in diameter. The dough should be slightly thicker at the edges. Place on 2 or 4 oiled baking sheets. Spread the tomato pulp over the pizza crusts, then distribute the *mozzarella* evenly over the top. Sprinkle with salt and drizzle with the extra-virgin olive oil. Bake for 8 to 10 minutes, then sprinkle with the basil leaves and some coarsely ground black pepper and serve immediately.

# CASATIELLO

## SAVORY EASTER BREAD

**FOR 8**

1 CUP SOFT LARD (YOU COULD USE BUTTER, BUT LARD GIVES AN AUTHENTIC TASTE)

3¹/₂ OUNCES HARD *PECORINO* CHEESE, GRATED

3¹/₂ OUNCES PARMESAN CHEESE, GRATED

3¹/₂ OUNCES *PROVOLONE* CHEESE, VERY FINELY GRATED

3¹/₂ OUNCES NEAPOLITAN SAUSAGE, CUT INTO VERY SMALL CUBES

1 TABLESPOON COARSELY GROUND BLACK PEPPER

1 TEASPOON SALT

8 EGGS

FOR THE DOUGH:

3¹/₄ CUPS 00 (*DOPPIO ZERO*) FLOUR

4 TABLESPOONS SOFT LARD

1³/₄ OUNCES FRESH YEAST

*Together with* Pastiera di Grano *(see page 177), this is an essential part of Neapolitan Easter celebrations. Every family has its own recipe but the decoration never varies—the Easter symbol of eggs, pushed into the dough before baking. The eggs are shelled after baking and eaten with the bread, which is usually ring-shaped.*

To make the dough, put the flour in a bowl and rub in the lard. Dissolve the yeast in ³/₄ cup lukewarm water, add to the flour, and mix well to form a dough. Knead for 10 to 15 minutes, until it has a soft and silky texture, then put the dough in a bowl, cover with a cloth, and leave for about 2 hours, until doubled in size.

Punch down the risen dough and knead it briefly to eliminate air bubbles. Flatten it into a rectangle about 1¹/₄ inches thick, dot with half the lard, cheeses, and sausage, and sprinkle with half the pepper and salt. Fold up the bottom third of dough, then fold down the top third and knead to distribute the ingredients and work in the lard. Flatten it into a rectangle again and cover with the remaining lard, cheeses, and sausage, then repeat the folding and kneading. Shape the dough into a ring and place it in a greased 10-inch ring mold, or lay it on a greased baking sheet, then cover and leave to rise for another 2 hours.

Preheat the oven to 375° F. Wash the eggs and push them halfway into the dough. Bake for 1 hour, then remove from the oven and leave to cool. It can be kept for a few days.

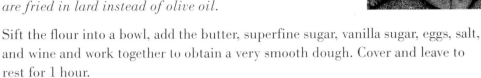

# CENCI
## PASTRY RIBBONS

### FOR 8 TO 10

3 CUPS OO (*DOPPIO ZERO*) FLOUR

3 TABLESPOONS SOFT BUTTER

SCANT 1/4 CUP SUPERFINE SUGAR

2 TABLESPOONS VANILLA SUGAR

2 EGGS

PINCH SALT

3 TABLESPOONS MOSCATO PASSITO OR *VIN SANTO*

1 1/3 CUP CONFECTIONER'S SUGAR

OLIVE OIL FOR DEEP-FRYING

*These addictive pastries are supposed to be eaten during Lent and are associated with* carnevale, *which takes place forty days before Easter.* Cenci *literally means pieces of fabric, and this is what they are called in Tuscany. But with a few variations the same thing can be found in all the regions, under all sorts of names. In the South they are fried in lard instead of olive oil.*

Sift the flour into a bowl, add the butter, superfine sugar, vanilla sugar, eggs, salt, and wine and work together to obtain a very smooth dough. Cover and leave to rest for 1 hour.

Using a rolling pin or a pasta machine, roll out the dough until it is 1/8 inch thick. With a serrated pastry wheel, cut it into strips 6 to 7 inches long and 1 1/4 to 1 1/2 inches wide, then very patiently tie each one in a loose knot. Deep-fry them in olive oil a few at a time, until golden and crisp, then put them on paper towels to drain off excess oil. When cooled, pile them up on a tray and dust them abundantly with the confectioners' sugar. They are irresistible!

# SAVOIARDI
## LADYFINGERS

### MAKES ABOUT 30

6 EGGS, SEPARATED

HEAPING 1/2 CUP SUPERFINE SUGAR

1 1/4 CUPS OO (*DOPPIO ZERO*) FLOUR, SIFTED

SCANT 1/4 CUP CONFECTIONERS' SUGAR

3 TABLESPOONS VANILLA SUGAR

2 TABLESPOONS GRANULATED SUGAR

*You can buy a special baking pan for these super-light and spongy little cookies, which gives a deeper, more regular shape. However, they can also be piped out onto a baking sheet. They are ideal for making* tiramisu, zuppa inglese, *and other desserts in which an extremely absorbent cookie is required.*

Preheat the oven to 350° F. Beat the egg yolks with the superfine sugar until the mixture is very thick and mousselike. Gradually fold in the flour. In a separate bowl, beat the egg whites until stiff, then sift in the confectioners' sugar and carefully but thoroughly fold it in. Fold this into the egg yolk mixture together with the vanilla sugar, being careful not to knock air out of the mixture.

Put it into a piping bag and pipe onto a buttered baking sheet in little rope shapes about 5 inches long and 1 1/4 inches wide, spacing them well apart. Sprinkle with the granulated sugar and bake for about 18 minutes. They should be dry and a wonderful golden color.

Leave to cool on a wire rack, then store them in an airtight container.

# STRUFFOLI NAPOLETANI
## NEAPOLITAN FRIED PASTRIES

**FOR 10**

5 EGGS

3 TABLESPOONS GRANULATED SUGAR

HEAPING 4 CUPS FLOUR

GRATED ZEST OF 1 LEMON AND 1 ORANGE

PINCH SALT

1 TABLESPOON PURE ALCOHOL (IF NOT AVAILABLE, STRONG VODKA WILL DO)

2 OUNCES *CEDRO* (CANDIED CITRON PEEL)

OIL FOR DEEP-FRYING

SILVER DRAGÉES, TO DECORATE

**FOR THE CARAMEL:**

SCANT ¹/₂ CUP SUGAR

GENEROUS ¹/₂ CUP HONEY

In a large bowl, beat the eggs with the sugar, then gradually mix in the flour to make a smooth dough. Add the citrus zest, salt, and alcohol. Knead well for 3 to 4 minutes and roll into a ball. Cover and leave to rest for 2 hours in a cool place.

Taking a little bit of dough at a time, roll it with your hand into rope shapes about ¹/₂ inch in diameter. Cut the rope into small pieces about ¹/₂ inch long. It is quite laborious rolling out these ropes and will take you some time.

In a small pan, pour in oil to a depth of ³/₄ to 1¹/₄ inches and heat until moderately hot. Deep-fry the pieces of dough in the hot oil in batches until lightly browned. Remove and drain on paper towels.

To make the caramel, in a large heavy-bottomed pan, heat the sugar and honey with 2 tablespoons water until the liquid becomes clear. Add the fried dough and the *cedro*. Stir carefully until all the *struffoli* are coated with caramel. Arrange in the form of a crown on a serving plate, decorate with silver dragées (not too many), and leave to cool.

# BUDINO DI ROSA
## ROSA'S PUDDING

**FOR 6**

4¹/₂ CUPS MILK

HEAPING 1¹/₄ CUPS SUGAR

SCANT 1 CUP 00 (*DOPPIO ZERO*) FLOUR

SCANT 1 CUP POWDERED BITTER CHOCOLATE

GRATED ZEST OF 1 LEMON

3 EGG YOLKS

16 *SAVOIARDI* COOKIES (SEE PAGE 305)

5 TABLESPOONS AMARETTO LIQUEUR

*This is not a pudding made from roses, as the title might lead you to expect, but a wonderful creation of Rosa, the pasta queen of the Ristorante Ardenga in Diolo, Emilia-Romagna.*

Put the milk and scant ¹/₂ cup of the sugar in a pan over medium heat, then stir in the flour and chocolate. Stir until smooth and bring to a boil, stirring continuously. Remove from the heat, stir in the lemon zest and egg yolks; mix well.

In a small bowl, combine the liqueur with an equal amount of water. Dip the cookies briefly in the mixture and use them to line a pudding mold. Pour the milk mixture into the lined mold and chill to set.

When the pudding is quite cold and firmly set, in 2 to 3 hours, turn it over and remove it from the mold (dipping it first very briefly in hot water will help).

Dissolve the remaining sugar in 4 tablespoons water and cook until it begins to brown to a caramel. Pour the caramel over the pudding and leave it to set before serving.

BUDINO DI ROSA

# PRUSSIANI

## SWEET PUFF PASTRY COOKIES

**MAKES 24 TO 30**

HEAPING 4 CUPS ALL-PURPOSE FLOUR
PINCH SALT
1 1/4 CUP BLOCK OF HARD BUTTER
10 GENEROUS HANDFULS OF SUGAR

*Puff pastry is one of those recipes that is so difficult that it is seldom made at home; it is more likely to be the ultimate challenge in baking.*

Put the flour and salt in a large bowl with scant 1 cup water and mix well to produce a dough. On a floured surface, roll the dough out to form a square just over twice the size of the block of butter.

Place the butter in the middle of one side of the pastry square. Fold over the other half and press down the edges with a rolling pin to make a sealed package around the butter. Turn the package so the fold is to one side and roll out the package to form a rectangle three times as long as it is wide. Fold the bottom third up and the top third down over that. Again seal the edges by pressing with a rolling pin. Wrap loosely in plastic wrap and chill for at least an hour. Repeat this rolling, folding, and chilling process 4 or 5 times more, each time giving the pastry a quarter turn clockwise before beginning.

Preheat the oven to 400° F.

Sprinkle a handful of sugar over a work surface, place the chilled pastry on it and sprinkle more sugar over the pastry. Roll out into a square, sprinkling more sugar as you roll. Fold in half and then fold this again in half. Roll out again, sprinkling it with more sugar as you go, into a long rectangular shape. Then fold this rectangle in half and repeat the rolling and folding process. Roll once more into a rectangle, then fold this lengthwise to form a sausage shape. Slice into 1/4-inch-thick circles.

Place on a baking sheet well spaced apart. Bake for 12 minutes, then turn the cookies over and bake for 5 minutes more.

RIGHT (CLOCKWISE FROM THE TOP):
*SFOGLIATELLI* (PAGE **299**), TINY *BABA*,
*PRUSSIANS*

# BABA VESUVIO

RUM BABA

**SERVES 10 TO 12**

3/4 OUNCE FRESH YEAST (OR THE
    EQUIVALENT OF DRIED)

1/2 CUP LUKEWARM MILK

HEAPING 2 1/2 CUPS 00 (*DOPPIO ZERO*)
    FLOUR, PLUS MORE FOR DUSTING

PINCH SALT

SCANT 1/2 CUP SUGAR

7 TABLESPOONS MELTED BUTTER, PLUS
    MORE FOR THE MOLD

1 TABLESPOON GRATED LEMON ZEST

5 EGGS

5 TABLESPOONS WARM APRICOT JELLY

FOR THE SYRUP:

HEAPING 1 CUP SUPERFINE SUGAR

GRATED ZEST OF 1 ORANGE

1 1/4 CUPS DARK RUM

*This dessert harkens back to the French occupation of Naples. Finding a mold to make a large baba in the shape of Vesuvius is quite difficult, so this symbol of Naples can also be made using any conical container. Of course, you can make it in any shape ovenproof container you choose. Babas are more traditionally made in ring molds and served filled with fruits in syrup.*

Dissolve the yeast in the lukewarm milk and gradually add to the flour, salt, and sugar in a large bowl. Mix thoroughly. Add the butter and lemon zest. Mix well. Gradually add the eggs, one by one, and work well to obtain a smooth dough. Leave in a warm place, covered with a cloth, until doubled in size, about 2 hours.

Punch down the risen dough and work with your hands to knock out the air built up during rising. Butter the mold and dust it with flour. Put the dough into it (it should only fill it about three-quarters full). Leave to rise again, until the dough reaches the top of the mold.

Preheat the oven to 400° F and bake the baba for 40 minutes.

While the baba is baking, make the syrup. Put the sugar in a pan with 2½ cups water and the orange zest. Bring to a boil, then remove from the heat and stir in the rum.

Remove the baba from the oven and, while it is still warm, pour half of the syrup over it. Leave for a few minutes to let the baba absorb the syrup, then pour the remaining syrup over it. Transfer the baba to a serving platter and brush with the apricot jelly. Chill briefly and serve. It should have a springy texture.

# WINES & LIQUEURS

## VINI, LIQUORI E BEVANDE

**ALCOL** / PURE ALCOHOL In Italy it is possible to buy pure alcohol for cooking purposes, mainly to make liqueurs or to preserve fruit. Usually it is produced from grapes, but it may also be made from other fruit, and is distilled to the highest possible percentage of alcohol, 95%. It is white and tasteless, and quite dangerous to use because it is highly flammable.

**AMARETTO** This is the most typical of Italian liqueurs taken, mostly by ladies, as a digestif. Like the cookies of the same name, it is based on bitter almonds, but the liqueur also contains other fruit extracts and aromatic herbs. With its very distinctive bitter-almond taste, it can also be added to desserts, fruit salads, and cocktails.

**AMARO** / BITTER
From the Italian for "bitter," the word *amaro* signifies a *digestivo*, which is a very popular drink in Italy. These are made from infusions of various herbs with the addition of alcohol and sugar. An *amaro* is drunk in small quantities after dinner to help the digestion, but some types of *amaro* may also be used as an *aperitif* (see *aperitivo*) or mixed with hot water to produce a soothing hot drink. The best

known *amari* are Fernet, Amaro Lucano, Amaro Averna, Amaro Varvelli, and Centerbe ("a hundred herbs"). See also *digestivo*.

**AMARONE DOC** This deep ruby-red wine comes from the Valpantena in Veneto. There are two best-known types, both having as a base the Recioto della Valpolicella (see Valpolicella) made from the Corvina Veronese, Rondinella, and Molinara grapes. One, usually known as Reciota della Valpolicella Amabile, is a very velvety semi-sweet red wine which is quite high in alcohol content because it is made from dried grapes. The other, a dry wine goes very well with roast meat or game and strong cheeses.

**ANISETTA** This liqueur probably originates from Greece, descending from the same source as the ouzo of today. It is very often used in southern Italy where, especially in Naples, it is diluted with water as a drink, or small quantities are added to espresso coffee, as they do in Sicily. Made from an infusion of star anise with alcohol and sugar, it is also used in pâtisserie.

**APERITIVO / APERITIF** This word comes from the Latin *aperire*, meaning "to open," and generally signifies an alcohol-based drink taken before a meal to stimulate the appetite. It is today more generally served as a means of marking the beginning of a celebration or a simple meal among friends.

At midday, *aperitivi* are taken in Italy's numerous bars. In summer, water or soda water is often added to make refreshing drinks as well. Aperitifs are usually based on stimulating herbs, and are sometimes strongly colored, as in Campari. Other well-known aperitifs are Americano, Cordiale, and Cynar (which is based on artichokes). There is also a series of aperitifs based on wine, with the addition of a little alcohol and of herb infusions. Vermouth is the most widely known, of which Cinzano and Martini are the most popular worldwide. These wines, which can be dry, sweet-white, and sweet-red, are served on ice or diluted with soda water, but are also used for mixing cocktails like negronis or martinis.

There is also a range of non-

alcoholic aperitifs which consist only of herb infusions, with added coloring, which are then diluted with soda water. These are generally known as *aperitivi analcolici*. When you want to order one at the bar you simply say "*un analcolico per favore.*"

**AQUA VITE, SEE GRAPPA**

**ARNEIS DOC** This Piedmontese dry white wine is made with the Arneis grape in the area of Roero near Alba. It has a very intense bouquet and is often drunk as an aperitif, but is also served to accompany *antipasto*.

**BARBARESCO DOCG** This is one of the most popular DOCG Piedmontese red wines. This status is given only to a few wines in Italy, and in this case means that the wine can only come from a small area in the South of Piedmont, near Alba in the towns of Barbaresco, Neive, and Treiso. With a minimum alcohol content of 12.5%, the wine has a garnet-red color, with orange reflections, and a pleasant and deep scent. The flavor is well balanced, dry, and velvety. It goes very well with game and all roasted and broiled red meat. Barbaresco can be called *riserva* only if it is aged for at least 4 years.

**BARBERA DOC** This is another classic Piedmontese wine which may only be made in that region. The grape gives the name to the ruby-red wine, which is considered a good table wine, and everybody drinks it in Piedmont. There are three areas that vie for supremacy in making this wine—Asti, Alba, and Monferrato, with some general differences in their product. The Barbera D'Asti is exclusively made with Barbera grapes, while the Alba wine can be made with a small percentage of Nebbiolo, and that of Monferrato can include Freisa, Grignolino, and Dolcetto grapes.

There are various qualities of Barbera: from the normal, which sometimes can be quite rough, to the superior, which has been aged for at least 2 years. It is drunk with all the Piedmontese food, especially with *bagna caôda* and dishes accompanied by *polenta*. There is a dry, sparkling version of it, which is wonderful chilled in summer.

**BARDOLINO DOC** This wine comes from the Veneto, near Lake Garda around Bardolino. It is a light ruby-red wine which, when young, is quite pinkish. Its alcohol content does not exceed 12%, and it is one of the most exported Italian wines, together with Valpolicella. In fact, Bardolino, Valpolicella, and Chianti were the first three Italian wines to be exported successfully.

**BAROLO DOCG** Often called the "King of Italian wines," Barolo is made mostly with Nebbiolo grapes growing in the Piedmontese areas of Barolo, Castiglione Falletto, Serralunga D'Alba, Cherasco, Diano D'Alba, Grinzane Cavour, La Morra, Monforte D'Alba, Novello, Roddi, and Verduno in the province of Cuneo. This wine undergoes serious analysis and judgement before it is put on the market in order to safeguard the very high reputation it has in Italy and abroad as one of Italy's best wines. It is a very strong wine and a very deep red color, with a bouquet of violets and roses. A full, balanced, velvety dry wine, it should be served on grand occasions.

A *riserva* has to be at least 5 years old, while the basic version requires a minimum of 3 years ageing, starting from the January following the harvest. Barolo chinato is an aperitif made with the addition of quinine (see *vino chinato*). A good Barolo goes with all traditional meat dishes. Game, such as venison or pheasant, red meat, and hare always goes well with this wine. In cooking, the most important use is for *brasato al barolo*, a dish of beef cooked for a long time in the wine.

**BRUNELLO DI MONTALCINO DOCG** At an altitude of about 2,000 feet, the town of Montalcino in Tuscany dominates an area of vineyards which all seem to be exposed to the intense sun. Brunello is one of the grand wines of Italy and the Cooperativa dei Coltivatori di Brunello makes sure that all the wines bearing the name are worthy of it. Every year they present the new vintage to the national press and it is remarkable how every producer of Brunello would go to the barricades to defend the reputation of the wine. The Sangiovese Grosso grape used for making Brunello gives a very

aristocratic wine able to age for up to fifty years. Due to the care they take to make it and to its esteemed (and valuable) reputation, the wine is produced only in the best years, omitting a year if the quality of the wine is not good enough. To be saleable the wine has to be at least 4 years old, of which 3 years are spent in wooden barrels. The Brunello aged for 5 years is called *riserva*. This is an ideal and very fine wine to drink with roasted and broiled meat of any kind, especially game—locally, wild boar is abundant.

**CABERNET DI PRAMAGGIORE DOC** This magnificent deep ruby-red wine comes from the provinces of Venice, Treviso, and Pordenone. With a minimum 11.5% alcohol, its dry softness makes it an ideal wine for light meat dishes. Cabernet Sauvignon and Franc are French grape varieties recently introduced to Italy, which now form the backbone of many very good modern Italian wines.

**CAMPARI** This aperitif, known worldwide, is made from an infusion of herbs with alcohol (about 18%), sugar, water, and the typical red coloring. It is drunk chilled, mixed with water or orange juice. It is also used to produce sorbets, like Campari and passion fruit sorbet.

**CANARINO** Literally translating as "canary," this is the simplest drink ever—hot water and lemon peel. Very soothing, it is said to be excellent for the digestion and is often drunk by those who cannot drink tea or coffee.

**CANNONAU DOC** This very well-known full-bodied Sardinian ruby-red wine comes in two versions, dry or semi-sweet. The Cannonau grape may be late-harvested or indeed allowed to dry on mats, and in this case the alcohol content can rise to produce a wine that is dry or *amabile* (semi-sweet), and is mainly used as dessert wine. Otherwise, Cannonau is excellent with broiled meat.

**CAREMA DOC** As is so often the case, the town or village where certain grapes grow also gives its name to the wine made from them. Carema is a very picturesque little

village surrounded by impressive vineyards at the hilly bottom of Piedmont's Aosta Valley. This particular piece of country enjoys the sunshine for a large part of the day, and the Nebbiolo grape, cultivated on arduous terraces, benefits fully from this situation. This wine has been known since the sixteenth century and it is said that Napoleon, who passed by on the way to Piedmont, particularly appreciated this excellent dry garnet-colored wine. With a minimum alcohol content of 12% and an excellent body, it offers a soft and velvety bouquet and is ideal for the local cuisine based on beef, veal, and game.

**CARTIZZE, PROSECCO DOC** This very fashionable white wine from the Veneto is made from the Prosecco grape growing in the area of Conegliano or Valdobbiadene in the province of Treviso. There are two types of wine produced with this grape. The slightly sparkling *tipo frizzante* is obtained by natural fermentation and can be dry or semi-sweet. The straw-yellow *spumante*, especially the Superiore di Cartizze, is also dry or *amabile* (semi-sweet) but pleasantly fruity. Cartizze is usually decanted to get rid of some of the sparkle! One of the most popular drinks made with this wine is the Venetian specialty, the bellini cocktail, in which fresh peach juice is added to the wine to make a delicious summer drink.

**CENTERBE, SEE AMARO**

**CHIANTI DOCG** Next to Barolo, Chianti is probably one of the best-known Italian wines. Tuscany has produced this wine for many centuries—the Frescobaldi and Antinori companies can both count more than 600 years of wine-making tradition. In all this time the wine has been made using Sangiovese and Canaiolo Nero grapes. In the last century Chianti underwent quite a complicated set of government decrees to safeguard the quality and the good name. The era of the red liquid in the traditional raffia-covered *fiasco* is generally gone, although some companies are still bottling the improved modern Chianti in these typical bottles, which used to decorate the walls of Italian restaurants all over the world. The better Chianti is now put in normal

bottles, and they can carry the DOCG status only if they comply with the tough and complicated legislation.

**CINQUE TERRE DOC** Only recently were roads built to the little towns of Monterosso, Vernazza, and Rio Maggiore, where the famous Cinque Terre and Cinque Terre Sciacchetra are made. Indeed some of the vineyards, which are splendidly exposed to the sun in this corner of Liguria extending to La Spezia, may still only be reached by boat. The terraces on which the vines are planted are very steep indeed, and most of the work can be done only by hand, and by climbing. The results are exquisite white wines produced with Bosco, Albarola, and Vermentino grapes. The Cinque Terre, with 11% alcohol, has a straw-yellow color and a dry and pleasantly delicate taste. It is ideal for the fish specialties of the Ligurian coast. The Cinque Terre, Sciacchetra is a dessert wine produced with the same grapes, but the sugar in the grapes is concentrated by a short drying on mats, which gives a higher alcohol content. It is an ideal dessert wine, with a wonderful scent and a rich amber color.

**CINZANO, SEE MARTINI**

**DOC & DOCG** The Italian equivalent of the French *appellation contrôlée*, DOC means *Denominazione di Origine Controllata*, and DOCG means *Denominazione di Origine Controllata e Garantita*. It is only since 1966 that the Italian government has introduced legislation to control the previously chaotic production and classification of all Italian regional wines. Italy is quantitatively the biggest wine producer in the world, but qualitatively Italy has suffered for a long time by being seen as the producer, with a few exceptions, of simple wines. This is despite the fact that Italy perhaps offers the widest differentiation of types of soil, climate, and grapes among all the wine-producing countries. A few far-sighted Italian wine producers, who have looked over the shoulder of their French cousins already advanced in the method of producing exceptional wines, have in the last 30 years or so produced such improvements that Italians can count on perfectly made wines that can compete with the best in the world. The combination of the new legislation and private initiative has given birth to a new breed of wines like Tignanello, Sassicaia, and Solaia.

The DOCG denomination is reserved for wines originating from a very small, defined area, in which only the grapes from that area are used. Of the more than 300 DOC wines in 1994, only 13 had this specification.

Curiously Tignanello, Sassicaia, Solaia, and a few others, although by name and fame the very top of the range of Italian wines, do not have a DOC denomination, but have a simple classification *vino da tavola*, table wine.

### ERBALUCE DOC

From Canavese in the province of Turin, and Vercelli at the estuary of the Aosta Valley in Piedmont, comes this exquisite white wine, of which several versions are made. Erbaluce Caluso is dry, with a straw-yellow color. Its very fine bouquet makes it suitable for all fish and delicate dishes. The Caluso Passito is also made from Erbaluce grapes, but they are dried after harvesting to increase the natural sugar content. This produces a wine that is dark amber, with a 13.5% or 14% alcohol content, making it a wonderful aperitif wine. A third type, Caluso Passito Liquoroso, is fortified with alcohol, making it the perfect dessert wine.

### FERNET, SEE AMARO

### FIANO DI AVELLINO DOC

From the center of Campania, more precisely Avellino and the surrounding province, comes this remarkable white wine which was known even to the ancient Romans. The Fiano grapes produce a straw-yellow wine with a dry taste and a deep characteristic bouquet. The wine is extremely drinkable with all types of dishes, delicate and less so. It is a typically robust white wine from the fertile, volcanic local soil.

### FRANCIACORTA DOC

This name is given to four wines made in the province of Brescia in Lombardy. The Franciacorta Bianco (white) and Franciacorta Spumante (sparkling) are both made with a mixture of Pinot Bianco, Pinot Grigio, Pinot Nero, and Chardonnay grapes. A minimum alcohol content of 11 or 11.5% is required for the production of this soft and delicate wine with an intense bouquet. The Franciacorta Rosato Spumante (sparkling rosé) is made with Pinot Bianco, Chardonnay and Pinot Nero grapes, giving a very fragrant sparkling wine for the summer. Franciacorta Rosso (red) is made from Cabernet Franc, Merlot and Barbera or Nebbiolo grapes. Brilliant red in color, becoming garnet with age, it has a balanced and dry taste, and since it is light (a minimum alcohol content of 11%), it is suitable for local meat and cheese dishes.

### FRASCATI DOC

From the region southeast of Rome, where the town of Frascati is situated, comes this very well-known white wine, traditionally appreciated by Roman clergy and nobility. Produced on the hills around Rome (Castelli Romani), Frascati is the result of the union of Malvasia Bianca and Trebbiano Toscano grapes. The *amabile* (semi-dry) and *dolce* (sweet) types, which the Romans like very much, are made with the addition of concentrated must to increase the sugar content. Straw-yellow in color, with a delicate taste, the Frascati Secco (dry) has a minimum alcohol content of 11% and is considered the wine that best suits most Roman dishes, including *porchetta* (see page 80). For such a rich dish, perhaps the Frascati Superiore, with an alcohol content of 12%, is more suitable.

### GATTINARA DOC

The province of Vercelli in Piedmont is mainly known for rice cultivation, but where the sunny hills of the northern part of the region start to build up to the pre-Alps, there you will find Gattinara, an excellent garnet-red wine made with the Nebbiolo grape, the same used in Barolo. A dry and almost bitter flavor characterizes this fine wine with 12 to 13% alcohol, which is excellent with game dishes, especially hare and wild boar.

### GAVI (CORTESE DI GAVI) DOC

This fine straw-yellow Piedmontese wine is made almost at the border with Liguria. The town of Gavi and the surrounding fertile and sunny hills grow the Cortese grape, which produces a crisp and pleasant white wine that is also suited to sparkling wine. It is a very popular wine, especially with *antipasto* and first courses.

### GENEPY

This specialty of the Aosta Valley is a liqueur made by infusing local herbs, especially *genzium* (gentian), in alcohol, and mixing this with sugar and water. There are clear and green versions of Genepy, which has an alcohol content of 40% and up. It is a wonderful *digestivo* or winter warmer, especially *après ski*.

### GRAPPA, ACQUA VITE

Grappa is for Italians, especially northerners, what whisky is for Scots. It is produced both commercially and privately. The best grappa is made by distilling the leftovers after the grapes have been pressed, including pips, skin, and stalks. The grappas made in this way are very aromatic. There are grappas made with selected grapes, tasting for example of Muscat or Barolo or Chianti. Grappa is served at room temperature as a *digestivo*. Some people add a few drops of grappa to their espresso coffee, to make the coffee corretto (corrected).

### GRECO DI TUFO DOC

From the province of Avellino, from which the Fiano also comes, this wine is made with Greco grapes and is one of the most popular Campanian wines. A golden-yellow wine, it is soft and dry, and suitable for delicate fish dishes and pale meat dishes.

### GUTTURNIO COLLI PIACENTINI DOC

From around Piacenza on the very fertile and sunny hills of Emilia-Romagna comes this excellent dry red wine, made with Barbera and Bonarda grapes. It can be dry or *demi-sec* if all the sugar hasn't turned into alcohol.

### LACRYMA CHRISTI DEL VESUVIO DOC

The area all around Vesuvius has rich volcanic soil on which the Coda di Volpe and Verdeca grapes grow vigorously, giving birth to the Vesuvio Bianco wine. When this has a natural minimum alcohol content of 12%, it can be called Lacryma Christi ("tear of Christ"). Pale yellow in color, and dry with a touch of acidity, this excellent Neapolitan wine is perfect for the light local dishes. The Vesuvio Rosso (deep red) and Rosato (rosé) are made with the Piedi Rosso and Sciascinoso grapes, which also grow locally. Again, if these have a minimum alcohol content of 12% they are also called Lacryma Christi.

### LAMBRUSCO DI SORBARA

For the Emilians, Lambrusco should be so dense it has to be eaten and drunk at the same time. This is the real Lambrusco, locally produced in Emilia-Romagna from the Lambrusco di Sorbara and Lambrusco Salamino grapes, which grow in the province of Modena. Although only 11% alcohol, the intensity of this wine makes it very dense and extremely dark red, almost violet. It is naturally sparkling, which makes it foamy, and it has a very pleasant bouquet and tastes of fruit. It is most suitable for the various pork and duck dishes of the area. There are a few other varieties of Lambrusco made with slightly different grapes, but with the same characteristics; Lambrusco Grasparossa, Lambrusco Reggiano, and Lambrusco Salamino di S. Croce are the best known. This is a wine that does not travel too well, so it is better to drink it locally.

### LOCOROTONDO DOC

From the Trulli region of Alberobello, the Locorotondo is a gentle white wine with a pleasant bouquet and a dry and delicate taste. This typical Pugliese wine is made from the Verdeca and Bianco d'Alessanro grapes. It is a typical summer wine, which goes well with the local fish dishes.

### MALVASIA DOC

There are various wines called Malvasia, usually followed by the name of the area from which they come. The Piedmontese types are red, not very alcoholic, and slightly sparkling, due to the use of grapes like Freisa and Barbera or Grignolino. Malvasia di Casozo, and Malvasia di Castelnuovo don Bosco are the best of this type. The others come from the islands of Sicily and Sardinia and are of a totally different nature. The Malvasia delle Lipari, from the island of that name, is made with golden and yellow aromatic grapes which become amber after being dried. The resulting wine, called *Passito*, has a high alcohol content but is still sweet. The Sardinian wine comes from Cagliari and is of a similar nature, but straw-yellow to golden-yellow in color. Another type, called *liquoroso*, is fortified with alcohol to 17.5%, but retains a lot of sugar, making it a refined but pungent dessert wine, to be served with dry cookies and cakes.

**MARASCHINO** Originally from Dalmatia in Yugoslavia, this liqueur made from Marasca (morello) cherries was adopted by Italians mainly to add to fruit salads or for cocktails or for use in pastrics. It has a sweet, slightly almond taste and is produced mostly in the Veneto region, where it is made by lengthy processing of the cherries, which are crushed, fermented, and distilled.

**MARSALA DOC** Named after the city where most of the cellars are located, Marsala is perhaps the most famous Sicilian wine. It is produced in the province of Trapani from the Catarrato, Pignatello, Nerello, Calabrese, and Grillo grapes. It comes in three different types, according to alcohol and sugar content. Ageing of Marsala in wooden casks also determines the variety, and so does the addition of cooked must before fermentation. The Marsala Fine must have a minimum alcohol content of 17% and has to age for 1 year. Marsala Superiore has a minimum 18% alcohol content, with the Ambra type including 1% cooked must, while for the Oro and Rubino types, aged a minimum of 2 years, no addition is allowed. Marsala Vergine, with 18 % alcohol, a 5 year ageing, and no addition, is one of the finest Marsalas, only topped by the M. Vergine Stravecchio or Riserva with an age of 10 years. The degree of sweetness varies also, based on the added must or alcohol. This wine is widely used in cooking, and for the preparation of the famous *zabaglione* (see page 65). *Scaloppine al Marsala* is another classic of Italian cooking.

Today Marsala in the old, dry

version is enjoying a come-back as an aperitif or after-dinner drink.

**MARTINI** The name of a Piedmontese family who started to produce vermouth wines in 1863. Today, after a merger with Rossi, they are the best-known producers not only of the well-known red, white, and dry vermouths, but also of dry and sweet sparkling wines, aperitifs like China Martini, and more. Martini vermouth is the basis for various cocktails and drinks worldwide, but it is also widely used in cooking as, for example, in the mushroom dish *finferli al liquore* (page 201). The other slightly less famous house sharing the world vermouth market is Cinzano.

**MERLOT DI PRAMAGGIORE DOC** Red-to-garnet in color, this delicious wine is made almost entirely of Merlot grapes in the Veneto, where Pramaggiore is the main area of production. It has a deep bouquet, and a dry well-balanced taste. The alcohol content of 11.5% makes it easy to drink, especially with light game.

**MONICA DI CAGLIARI DOC** This deep ruby red wine, made in Sardinia from grapes of the same name, is a rare red dessert wine most suitable to accompany all the local almond-based sweet pastries. It is aged for at least one year before drinking.

**MONTEPULCIANO D'ABRUZZO DOC** From the provinces of Chieti Aquila, Pescara, and Teramo, comes this excellent red wine which is largely representative of the Abruzzo region. Made of the Montepulciano grape, it has a typical cherry-red color, a vinous and pleasant bouquet, and a dry taste. This very interesting wine should be served young with *antipasti*.

**MOSCADELLO DI MONTALCINO DOC** From the sunny and hilly area of Montalcino comes this highly regarded dessert wine made from the Moscato grape. This straw-yellow wine comes in two versions. The first is a sweetish wine with only 10.5% alcohol content and a wonderful delicate but aromatic flavor. The second, called Liquoroso, is fortified to 19% alcohol. It is ideal as a dessert wine,

with *cantucci* or other baked goods from the area.

**MOSCATO DOC** I can say I grew up with this wine because, as a child, I often drank the freshly pressed must—with dramatic consequences! Especially in Piedmont, where I grew up, there exist at least 10 different types of Moscato, according to the provinces in which it is made. Asti is the main area, followed by Alba and Alessandria. The Moscato grape produces a very flavorsome wine, which is sold as Moscato d'Asti. There is a famous sparkling version, Asti Spumante. The Moscato Naturale d'Asti is not sparkling and has a natural muscat bouquet, which makes it very desirable. This is a dessert wine par excellence and its lightness makes it delightful after a large meal.

**NEBBIOLO D'ALBA DOC** The Nebbiolo grape gets its name from *nebbia*, the word for the fog covering the hills of Piedmont in autumn. It grows on the hills of Alba and Langhe, in the provinces of Cuneo, famous for the white truffle. Although it is the father of such illustrious wines as Barolo, Barbaresco, and Carema, it makes a fine wine in its own right.

**NOCINO** This liqueur, a specialty of Modena, is based on unripe walnuts, traditionally collected around the 24th of June. The nuts are cut in quarters and macerated in a mixture of alcohol, sugar, cinnamon, and cloves for 40 days, until the liquid is dark brown and drinkable as a perfect *digestivo*. Nocino is now made almost everywhere in Italy and is often home-made.

**NURAGUS DI CAGLIARI DOC** A pleasant Sardinian dry white wine made from the grape of the same name in the province of Cagliari, it is pale straw-yellow in color and has a pleasant bouquet, making it suitable for fish dishes.

**ORVIETO DOC** For centuries this ancient wine was regularly served at the table of the Popes. Made in the area of Orvieto, the southern part of Umbria, from grapes like Trebbiano, Verdello, Grechetto, and Malvasia, it can be dry (*secco*) or semi-sweet

(*abboccato*), depending on the proportions of each grape used. Orvieto has a straw-yellow color, a delicate taste, and a pleasant bouquet. It can be served as an aperitif and goes very well with *antipasto* and light first courses.

**PASSITO** This term indicates a wine made with grapes that have been left to dry on the plant, or hung in drying rooms or laid on straw mats, to achieve a better concentration of the natural sugars, resulting in strong wines that are mostly sweet dessert wines.

**PROSECCO, SEE CARTIZZE**

**ROSOLIO** An old-fashioned "ladies'" liqueur, based on sweetened alcohol with flavors from rose petals to strawberries, it is a very pleasant drink that is currently enjoying a revival. It can be served as a mild after-dinner drink.

**SABA, SAPA, VINO COTTO** *Saba* is a preparation obtained by cooling down the freshly pressed must of Sangiovese di Romagna grapes and reducing it by cooking it to a thick dark liquid, 25% of its original volume. This liquid is mainly used for making the celebrated balsamic vinegar, but is also diluted with water to be served as a drink and used as an ingredient in some types of cookie.

Equivalents exist in Puglia, there called *vino cotto* (cooked wine), and in Sardinia, there called *sapa*, but made with a white grape variety. As a boy I remember it being poured on a snowball for an instant sorbet.

**SALICE SALENTINO DOC** From the province of Lecce, deep in Puglia comes this jolly wine in two versions, a red and a rare rosé. As is to be expected in a truly Pugliese wine, the warmth and dryness of the red is accompanied by 12.5% alcohol. The rosé version is milder, and enough power for it to be served on warm sunny days with roasts or broiled fish, as well as with the roasted vegetables of the area.

**SAMBUCA** This typical central Italian liqueur is based on star anise seeds. It is well known in Italian restaurants because of the trick of floating a coffee bean on the surface and lighting the alcohol vapors.

This is more a gimmick than an enhancement of flavor.

### SANGIOVESE DI ROMAGNA DOC

This wine is made from the Sangiovese grape, which is cultivated in a very large area of Emilia-Romagna included in the provinces of Forlì, Ravenna, and Bologna. The ruby-red wine is vinous, dry, and well-balanced, and goes well with *lasagne*. When this wine is aged for at least two years it can be called *riserva*.

### SASSICAIA, SOLAIA, TIGNANELLO (VINI DA TAVOLA)

Sassicaia and a couple of other special wines, Solaia and Tignanello, come from precisely the same area, Tenuta S. Cristina in Val di Pesa in Tuscany. They are the result of the most modern wine-making technologies introduced into Italy a couple of decades ago. By using Cabernet Sauvignon, Sangiovese, and Cabernet Franc grapes, with a different proportion of the grapes in each wine, taking the best care of the vine and using the best method of vinification and ageing in *barriques* (wooden barrels) as they do in France, three of the top Italian wines have been achieved. They don't even belong to the usual DOC classification system. They are, in fact, called Tuscan table wines and still command the highest respect and price. With high alcohol contents (from 12.8 to 13%), these are wonderful smooth wines, ideal for red meat and game dishes.

### SCIACHETRA CINQUE TERRE DOC, SEE CINQUE TERRE

### SLIVOVITZ

A schnapps, or fruit spirit, of Yugoslavian origin, this is made by the distillation of plums. It has been adopted in the border area of Trieste and is used as a spirit.

### SOLAIA TOSCANA, SEE SASSICAIA

### STREGA

This famous herb liqueur from Benevento in Campania is yellow in color. It is drunk as a *digestivo*, but it is also used for flavoring puddings and many southern pastries.

### TAURASI DOC

A proud representative of Campanian red, this full-bodied dry red wine is produced in the province of Avellino and Benevento from Piedirosso, Agliancico, and some Barbera grapes. It has a pleasant and deep bouquet, and is excellent for meat or very spicy dishes.

### TIGNANELLO TOSCANA, SEE SASSICAIA

### TORCOLATO

Although a non-DOC wine, this is still highly appreciated by dessert wine lovers. Made with Tocai, Vespaiolo, and Garganega grapes, it has a sweet fruity taste, so it can also be served with a soft and creamy *Gorgonzola* or *dolcelatte* cheese.

### TORGIANO DOC

An Umbrian wine of character, the Torgiano is produced in the commune of the same name in the province of Perugia, and can be red or white. The red is produced with Sangiovese, Canaiolo, and Trebbiano Toscano grapes. The deep ruby Torgiano red has a delicate bouquet and a dry well-balanced taste, making it excellent with game, pork, and lamb dishes. The Torgiano white is straw-yellow in color and produced with Trebbiano Toscano, Grechetto, and Malvasia Toscana grapes. It has a fruity and pleasant dry taste, so it is served with first courses and pale meat or fish dishes.

### TRAMINER AROMATICO DOC

From the Traminer grape, grown so much in Alsace and Germany, this wine is appreciated for its extremely fruity and aromatic taste. The wine is cultivated in Alto Adige, in the northernmost part of Trentino and Friuli. Its golden green color and its distinctive bouquet make it stand apart from the other white wines of the area. It is served as an aperitif, but also to accompany light first courses.

### TREBBIANO DI ROMAGNA DOC

The Trebbiano grape is cultivated in the provinces of Bologna, Forlì, and Ravenna. The Roman legionaries were responsible for the introduction of this grape to the area. The grape is widely used mixed with many other grapes and in other areas. This very well-known wine is straw-yellow in color and has a pleasant bouquet and dry balanced taste. There is also a sparkling version.

### VALPOLICELLA DOC

This wine has a long history, and was known and appreciated by the ancient Romans, but still today has a worldwide appeal. Together with Chianti, Valpolicella has been popularized by the *trattorie* and other restaurants in Italy and abroad. Having enjoyed early commercialization, Valpolicella is made with Corvina Veronese, Rondinella, and Molinara grapes growing in 19 communes in the province of Verona. Ruby-red in color, with a delicate pleasant scent and almond taste, it has 11% alcohol, and is a very easy-to-drink wine. There is a version, Recioto della Valpolicella, made with partly dried grapes to impart a higher sugar and alcohol content. See *amarone*.

### VERDICCHIO DEI CASTELLI DI JESI DOC

This very popular dry white wine, which is excellent with fish and seafood, is made in the province of Ancona, the capital of Marche, from Verdicchio, Trebbiano Toscano, and Malvasia grapes. With a pale straw color, delicate bouquet, and dry balanced taste, it is bottled in a characteristic amphora-like bottle and is now highly commercialized. It should be served very young because it tends to oxidize with age. A second, similar type of Verdicchio is called Verdicchio di Matelica, and is made in the province of Macerata.

### VERMENTINO DI GALLURA DOC

The Gallura is the northernmost tip of Sardinia, in the provinces of Sassari and Nuoro. This very dry straw-yellow white wine made with Vermentino grapes has a deep and delicate bouquet and a slightly bitter aftertaste, making it ideal for fish, especially crustaceans.

### VERMOUTH, SEE MARTINI

### VERNACCIA DI SAN GIMIGNANO, V. DI ORISTANO DOC

The favorite wine of Pope Paul III comes from around the splendid Etruscan town of San Gimignano in Tuscany. It is made with vernaccia grapes, which came originally from Greece, producing a golden-yellow wine with a deep and fine bouquet. It is a very dry, almost bitter wine, but its fresh balanced taste makes it ideal as an aperitif, or with *antipasto* and fish dishes. Another Vernaccia is no less popular. It is made with the eponymous grape in the province of Cagliari, in Sardinia. It has an amber yellow color, a delicate bouquet, and a slight aftertaste of bitter almonds. This wine is ideal as an aperitif. There is also a Liquoroso (liqueur) version which, is used as a dessert wine.

### VIN SANTO DOC

Some attribute the use of the word *santo* here to the fact that this wine is used sometimes for celebration of the Mass, others because the wine originated from Xantos in Greece. This rich, aromatic Tuscan wine is a delicious dessert wine, traditionally used to dip *cantucci* cookies after a meal. It is produced from Malvasia and Trebbiano grapes which, after harvesting, are put on straw mats to dry to increase the sugar content before making wine. Depending upon the fermentation, the ageing process in wooden casks for at least 3 years produces a wine that may be sweet, semi-sweet, or dry. Vin santo is also used as a flavoring in pastries and creams.

### VINO NOBILE DI MONTEPULCIANO DOCG

A noble wine indeed, this is highly appreciated by connoisseurs. It is said to have been given the name because a few noble families of Montepulciano used to make it for their own use. This is a DOCG wine made with Prugnolo Gentile, Canaiolo, Malvasia del Chianti, and Trebbiano Toscano grapes, all growing at an altitude of 850 to 2,000 feet in the area of Montepulciano. The wine has a deep garnet color, becoming orange with age, and a delicate bouquet with a hint of violets. The taste is dry and it has abundant tannin, so it ages well. This brilliant wine is ideal for game and robust red meat dishes.

### VINO CHINATO

This traditional Piedmontese aperitif is made from Barolo wine with the addition of the rind of *china*, an Asian evergreen plant (*Cinchona succirubra*), as well as many other herbs and spices and is used as a flavoring in other wines and liqueurs. Vino chinato has a dark red-brown color and is served either cold on ice or as punch.

### VINO COTTO, SEE SABA

# INDEX

THE TORTIA FAMILY
WHO RUN THE FINE
RESTAURANT
CANNON D'ORO IN
COCCONATO—
PAOLO AND FRANCA,
MARIA GRAZIA, AND
GUIDO.

# ACKNOWLEDGMENTS

This book could not have been made without the enormous generosity of our friends in Italy, who lent us their homes, their kitchens, their families, their production and their time. THANK YOU.

Eva Agnesi, *Imperia*
All our friends at *Altesino*, Montalcino, Toscana
Adelvio and Bedullia in their garden, Umbria
*Ristorante Ardenga*, Diolo, Emilia-Romagna
Baratti e Milano, Torino
Famiglia Bartolini, especially Ulderico, Umbria
Famiglia Bava, Cocconato
Famiglia Battista, Lago Maggiore
*Valtusciano Battipaglia*
Sig. Bottera, *La Bottera*, Cuneo
*Noé Bovo*, Piemonte
*British Airways*, London
Rosalba Carluccio, Ivrea
Famiglia Carluccio, Ivrea
Cappelli Sergio e Patrizia Ranzo *Arch.*, Napoli
*Dai Fratelli*, Orvieto
Riccardo Dalisi, *Arch.*, Napoli
Da Marco Norcia
Dr Silvano Dametto, Roma
Gianni e Anna Daneri
Daneri (coltivazione di basilico), Liguria
Giuseppe D'Urso, Positano
Sig. Eustachio, *Nettis Impianti*, Puglia
G. Sig. Ferraris, G. Pfatisch, Torino

Guido Ferrero, *Salumificio*, Cocconato
Conca at *Fiorella*, Camogli
*De Fillipi Pasta*, Torino
Bitten Eriksen
Franco Fasano (pottery), Grottaglie
*Ceramiche Fedolfi*, Montalcino
*Fiat Roma* (for the loan of their Ulisse)
Antonio Fiordelisi, Puglia
Luciana Florio of Napoli
*Giuseppe Garello Panificio*, Torino
Antonucci Gianfranco, Foggia
Sig.ri & Sig.ra Giacobazzi, Modena
Maria Grammatico, *La Pasticceria*, Erice, Sicilia
Conte de La Gatinais, Rapitalá, Sicilia
*Instituto ICE*, Roma
*Trattoria Italia*, Castelletto Stura
*Il Pane di San Giuseppe*, Salemi (Giuseppe Lo Castro), Sicilia
Signor Antonio Marella, Puglia
*Bar Marotta*, Palermo
Masseria San Domenico, Puglia
Molisano Caffè, Torino
Carlo Montani, Umbria
Palace Hotel, Palermo
Paola Navone, Milano
*Pinuccia Novara Ristorante* San Giovanni, Casarza Ligure
Signor Pazienza, PAP, Puglia
*Pesce Azzurro*, *Sicilia*
Sig. e Sig.ra Bruno Peyrano, Torino

*Pasticceria Revello*, Camogli, Liguria
Rino, wine-maker, Altesino, Montalcino
Dr Bruno Roncarati
Louisetto Marco, Settimo Vittone, Piemonte
Giovanetto Alberto, Settimo Vittone, Piemonte
*Urbani Tartufi*, Umbria
Hotel Verbano, Isola dei Pescatori
Lella and Giorgio, Pistoni, Ivrea
Collezione di Vetro Antico, *Museo del Vetro*, Villa Banfi, Montalcino, Toscana
Associazione di Categoria Regionali
Quinto & Famiglia Tagliavini, Caseificio Motta, Polesine, Emilia-Romagna


Thank you as well to the team who helped to produce the book:
André Martin for his wonderful photography, Jan Martin and Jean-Christophe Moreau who assisted him, Fabrice Moireau for his beautiful and helpful illustrations, Paul Welti for designing the book, Lewis Esson for editing the text, Jane Middleton for editing the recipes, Liz Przybylski for typing all the many drafts, and—last but by no means least—Gennaro Contaldo for his help in testing recipes.